A GOVERNMENT BY THE PEOPLE

D1603858

A GOVERNMENT BY THE PEOPLE

Direct Democracy in America, 1890–1940

THOMAS GOEBEL

The University of North Carolina Press Chapel Hill & London

© 2002
The University of North Carolina Press
All rights reserved
Manufactured in the United States of America
Set in Carter Cone Galliard
by Keystone Typesetting, Inc.
The paper in this book meets the guidelines for
permanence and durability of the Committee on
Production Guidelines for Book Longevity of the
Council on Library Resources.
Library of Congress
Cataloging-in-Publication Data
Goebel, Thomas, 1964–
A government by the people : direct democracy in
America, 1890–1940 / Thomas Goebel.
    p. cm.
Includes bibliographical references (p.)
and index.
ISBN 0-8078-2694-4 (cloth: alk. paper)
ISBN 0-8078-5361-5 (pbk.: alk. paper)
    1. Referendum — United States — History. I. Title.
JF494 G64 2002
328.273′09′041 — dc21   2001057002

cloth 06 05 04 03 02 5 4 3 2 1
paper 06 05 04 03 02 5 4 3 2 1

FOR JEN-FAN

CONTENTS

ACKNOWLEDGMENTS

Many individuals and institutions contributed to the preparation of this book. The idea to conduct research on the history of the initiative and referendum in America first took shape while I was a postdoctoral fellow at the John F. Kennedy Institute for North American Studies at the Free University of Berlin. I am very grateful to the German Research Society for awarding me the fellowship. Many of the professors at the Kennedy Institute, in particular Willi Paul Adams, Knud Krakau, and Hans Joas, provided valuable aid by helping me conceptualize the scope of the study and getting me started. I also would like to thank other friends and colleagues at the institute — Berit Bretthauer, Thomas Gebhardt, Fabian Hilfrich, Arne Delft, and many others — who offered their help and constructive criticism in the early phases of the project.

A research grant by the German Marshall Fund in the spring of 1996 provided me with an opportunity to spend some time at the University of California at Berkeley. I am very grateful to the staff at the Institute of Governmental Affairs for welcoming me as a visiting scholar and vastly facilitating my research at Berkeley. I also profited from the helpfulness and expertise of the librarians at the Bancroft Library, an indispensable resource for any scholar working on California history.

I finished the research and writing of the book at the German Historical Institute in Washington, D.C. The five years I spent there as a research fellow were very rewarding and enriching. I am grateful to the former director, Detlef Junker, and to the acting director, Christof Mauch, for their expertise and critical judgment and for giving me time to work on this study. Among many friends and colleagues at the institute, I would like to thank Andreas Daum, Eckhardt Fuchs, and David Morris for their willingness to discuss aspects of my work and for making the institute such a collegial place.

I have benefited from the help and cooperation of many other libraries: the Library of Congress, especially the Manuscript Division; the Department of Special Collections at the University of California in Los Angeles; the California State Archives in Sacramento; the Regenstein Library at the University of Chicago; and the library of the John F. Kennedy Institute. In particular, I would like to thank Monika Hein, Luzie Nahr, and Elisabeth Mait at the library of the German Historical Institute for their expert assistance during my five years at the institute.

I have greatly profited from the comments and questions of the many scholars to whom I have had the privilege of introducing parts of my work over the last few years, including John Allswang, Kathleen Conzen, Mary Furner, Gary Gerstle, Sarah Henry, Robert Johnston, Michael Kazin, and Daniel Rodgers. I am also grateful to the audiences at presentations I gave at the conventions of the American Historical Association, the Organization of American Historians, the Social Science History Association, the European Social Science History Association, the Western History Association, and the German Association for American Studies.

I am also indebted to Chuck Grench for supporting the publication of my book by the University of North Carolina Press; to anonymous reviewers who offered many valuable ideas and suggestions; to Paula Wald, the project editor; and to the entire staff of the press, who made the process of revision and publication a smooth and enjoyable one.

I have undoubtedly omitted many individuals who played a role in the preparation of the book. For this I apologize. Although I did not always agree with what they had to say, and even less often heeded their advice, the book is much better because of their willingness to confront the issues of direct democracy that I deal with here.

A GOVERNMENT BY THE PEOPLE

Building a Government by the People

To create a government of the people, by the people, and for the people has been one of the most enduring challenges of American history. The concept of popular sovereignty, so vital to the self-understanding of the nation since the eighteenth century as the ultimate legitimization of all political power and authority, has been a highly contested term in American politics. If the people are the repository of all political authority, how is one to define such an elusive entity? Even under the conditions of universal white male suffrage established in the early nineteenth century, significant groups of Americans remained excluded from participating in the most crucial act of citizenship, voting, a situation that rendered problematic many of the premises of democratic self-rule. If the goal of American government is the pursuit of the common good and the public welfare, how can this goal be defined in a republic split apart by partisan conflict, with a population composed of a multitude of different social and ethnic groups, each with their own set of cultural values and political orientations? The republican language of civic virtue and devotion to the public good that had animated the revolutionary generation would prove fragile under the conditions of a mass democracy in the nineteenth century. And if government rested on the active participation of the citizens, was the mere act of voting for candidates enough to ensure the representation of political interests in legislative debates? Or did other mechanisms have to be found to arrive at a polity that truly involved the citizens in the governing of their own affairs? T. V. Smith, a professor of philosophy at the University of Chicago, stated in 1933: "Government by the people represents the maximum, as government for the people represents the minimum of the democratic process."[1] Two centuries after the nation's founding, these questions remain central to discussions of government and politics in America.

The most problematic of this set of axioms has been the creation of a government by the people. Restrictions on the suffrage have been removed over time. A liberal language of interest-group politics has replaced notions of civic virtue and the common good. But no solution has been found to the quandary concerning how to enable citizens to take an active part in political affairs. That problem has grown more intense over the last decades. Voter turnout rates remain at a historical low in the United States and are noticeably lower than those in most other Western countries. The 1990s were marked by an increase in the political alienation of many Americans. Disillusionment with the political system runs high. The major parties do not seem responsive to the demands of ordinary citizens; instead, they appear to be firmly under the control of the interest groups that contribute to political campaigns. Attempts to reform the system from within, as with the recent debates on campaign finance reform, have failed. Movements such as term-limit reforms are expressions of voter disgust with career politicians interested only in their own reelection.

In the midst of this crisis in American politics, direct democracy has emerged as one way to bypass political parties and enable voters to make their voices heard on policy issues. The 1990s were a decade of unprecedented growth in the number of ballot propositions. In California, for instance, always a bellwether state in matters of direct democracy, at least 50 percent more popular initiatives have been on the ballot in this decade than in any previous decade since the introduction of the reforms in 1911.[2] Other states manifest the same trends. In the western United States, direct democracy has become deeply embedded in the political culture of the region. The notion that citizens should have the right to vote directly on issues of their choice rests on a broad base of popular support. Many observers look to direct democracy as a way to reengage voters with the polity. The rising spread of the Internet has spawned visions of an "electronic democracy," of "wired" citizens casting their ballots from home. Direct democracy is far from uncontroversial, but there are no indications that the increase in ballot propositions will slow down anytime soon.

This remarkable development is a useful reminder of the importance of direct democracy in American history, a topic that has not received much historical attention of late. There are many similarities between political conditions today and those around the turn of the century, when direct democracy, or direct legislation as it was more commonly known around 1900, was first introduced to the United States. Both periods were marked by strong criticism of the entrenched major parties and by a growing distrust of legislative bodies. Different political issues galvanized public debate, but the search for new avenues of political participation and mobilization was common to both. It is thus timely to take another look at the historical origins of direct democracy in America. This book will present the first comprehensive overview of the initiative, referendum, and recall in the United States between 1890 and 1940.[3]

Before outlining the structure of the book, it seems useful to briefly sketch the meaning of the three components of direct democracy. All three elements — the initiative, referendum, and recall — are based on the collection of a sufficient number of signatures on petitions directed at state or local legislative bodies. The initiative gives citizens the power to place a proposition on the ballot subject to popular vote. Some states allow the use of the initiative for both constitutional amendments and statutes; others limit its application to statutes only. The referendum, which is much less frequently used today than the initiative, gives citizens the power to either accept or reject specific legislation that was enacted by a legislature. The recall compels an elected official to face a special election before his or her tenure in office has come to an end. The specifics vary from state to state; there are, for instance, indirect initiatives in place in some states that grant the state legislature some role in the initiative process, but the general outline of the devices used is fairly uniform across the country. Direct democracy must be carefully distinguished from other forms of ballot propositions and referenda. New state constitutions and constitutional amendments are also subject to popular vote, but they originate with state legislatures and not with citizens' petitions. Some other policy issues, such as bond issues or the annexation of new territory by a city, may require mandatory referenda. In addition, local and state representative bodies may call for special referenda on isolated policy issues, but all these forms are not based on the expression of popular interest as is shown in the form of signatures on a petition. Direct democracy, as it is most commonly defined, marks a reversal in the flow of political power that enables citizens to place propositions on the ballot.

The initiative, referendum, and recall were innovations of the Progressive Era in American history. They were first discussed in the 1890s, and about twenty states adopted direct legislation between 1898 and 1918. Another handful of states have followed suit in the decades since the end of World War II. Direct democracy formed part of a broad wave of electoral reforms that transformed American politics from 1890 to 1920. Among the more important reforms were the Australian ballot, the direct primary, the direct election of U.S. senators, corrupt practices acts, nonpartisan ballots, and the form of government for municipalities that provides for a commission and city-manager. Once regarded as innovations to make government both more efficient and more responsive to the popular will, they are more widely interpreted today as an attempt of upper- and middle-class elites to centralize political power in their own hands at the expense of immigrant workers and their political allies.[4] The decline of interest in a political history that takes institutions seriously has also resulted in the neglect of a number of highly salient historical issues. Neither celebrations of direct democracy as an instrument of popular government nor its dismissal as an insignificant alteration in political procedures does justice to a remarkable reform movement that left an important legacy for contemporary American politics. In taking a more nuanced historical look at these issues, this study will offer a type of political history that endeavors to incorporate impulses from other historical fields but still insists on the importance of political institutions and the rules that govern political conduct.

While this study will also analyze the initiative and referendum in relation to fundamental problems of democratic governance, it will offer a novel "economic" interpretation of the origins of the reforms that deal primarily with the implications of centralized economic power for American democracy. Direct democracy has commonly been interpreted as a genuinely political reform movement, as a response to corrupt legislatures and powerful special interests. Yet a closer analysis of the rhetoric of reformers clearly demonstrates a strong economic component. The call for the initiative and referendum in the 1890s, triggered by the example of Switzerland, unfolded within a model of political economy that located the origins of oppressive monopolies, corporations, and trusts in the special privileges bestowed on private parties by dishonest lawmakers and legislative assemblies. This model, labeled "populist republicanism" in this book, had its origins in the eighteenth century and provided inspiration for a number of reform movements throughout the nineteenth century, including that of the Populists of the 1890s. Because specific political acts were blamed for inequalities of wealth and economic misfortunes, direct legislation was seen as a way to provide the means for political and economic emancipation. By enabling the people to remove the power wielded by special interests, and by preventing legislatures from handing out special privileges, the people would be empowered to abolish monopolies and trusts. The vision that inspired many direct democracy reformers was a distinctly economic one, that of a republic of small independent producers freely competing in an unfettered marketplace. The immediate appeal of direct democracy in the 1890s derived from its ability to link a specific set of political reforms to calls for a thorough regeneration of American society. These reforms were not exclusive to the Populists but animated a much larger number of reform communities. The first chapters of this book will trace the evolution of populist republicanism in eighteenth- and nineteenth-century American political thought as well as the rapid dissemination of information about the initiative and referendum in the 1890s.

Direct democracy has overwhelmingly been a phenomenon of the American West. Most of the states west of the Mississippi River have adopted these reforms, but only a few in the East and South have done so. This geographically differentiated pattern can be explained primarily by the specific political opportunity structure in place in the western United States and the stronger presence of antimonopoly sentiments there. The region was marked by weaker political parties, greater shifts in voting behavior, a stronger anti-party spirit, and more effective nonpartisan movements. Reformers, relying on reform organizations that were mostly weak, were underfunded, and had few organizational resources, nevertheless were able to exploit factional divisions inside the major parties and place their programs on the political agenda. Wielding powerful arguments of popular sovereignty and self-government, they overcame whatever resistance the weak parties were able to muster. Conditions in the rest of the country were different, however. In the East, parties were much stronger, rooted in distinct ethnocultural milieus, and much better positioned to deny reformers access to the political arena. Only in situations when the party system was temporarily destabilized, as was the case in relation to constitutional conventions and with the brief rise of the Progressive Party, were direct democracy advocates able to operate effectively. In the South, finally, what doomed reform efforts was the one-party rule of a Democratic Party focused on preserving white supremacy. Calls for direct democracy were labeled as attempts to weaken white domination, a charge that reformers were not able to counter.

The core of the reform movement always remained small and never included more than a few hundred activists nationwide. The success of the reforms cannot be explained solely by looking at the efforts of these few reformers. Their issue-specific movement was linked to a number of larger interest groups, such as labor, farmers, prohibitionists, single taxers, and women suffragists, that endorsed direct democracy as a way to expand their repertoire of political strategies. Their support provided the movement with enough leverage to influence skeptical lawmakers and reach the public. This coalition was a fragile one because the goals of the various interest groups overlapped only intermittently. As soon as the devices were adopted and emerged as political tools available to different contenders, the fault lines would become visible. Direct democracy was both a social movement and a tactical choice, and the interest groups that were aligned behind the reforms often held incompatible visions of what they were supposed to accomplish. In mapping out the terrain on which the struggle for direct democracy unfolded, however, one should keep in mind that the tenets of populist republicanism shared by most in the reform coalition linked groups together even beyond mutual tactical interests.

Direct democracy formed an integral part of the Progressive movement. It embodied many of the most impressive aspects of progressivism — its insistence on popular government, its belief in the perfectibility of political institutions, its trust in the ability of the people to act in an informed and enlightened fashion, its dynamic insistence that the United States was on the verge of an economic and social transformation — as well as the opposing racial and class prejudices and the undemocratic tendencies that marred so many reform proposals. The demand for the initiative and referendum resulted in a widespread debate about the nature of the American political order, about whether the United States was a republic or a democracy. By insisting that the will of the majority should be the only arbiter of political decisions, reformers openly challenged central tenets of American constitutionalism. Yet in their discussions of the role of "the people" in politics, they also displayed many of the prejudices and stereotypes that blinded them to the side effects of their agenda. Many progressives, particularly in the East, only belatedly supported direct democracy. More interested in strengthening state power and making government more efficient and rational, intellectuals such as Herbert Croly shared little of the unbridled enthusiasm for the reforms that one encountered among western Progressives. It was only amid the destabilization of the party system, triggered by the brief rise of the Progressive Party in 1912, that support for direct legislation emerged as a litmus test for progressivism. But in becoming closely attached to a partisan agenda, reformers lost their ability to construct the kind of nonpartisan reform coalitions upon which they had relied previously. With the collapse of progressivism, direct democracy ceased to be a viable political issue.

The appeal of direct democracy also began to wane because the central tenets of populist republicanism became increasingly anachronistic. By the 1910s the corporate transformation of the American economy had reached a point at which demands for the dissolution of monopolies and trusts no longer commanded political credibility. The new economy demanded policies designed to cope with poverty, economic deprivation, unemployment, and a host of other social issues. The initiative and referendum were ill-equipped to furnish these policy initiatives. If antimonopoly formed the glue that had held the reform coalition together from the 1890s to the 1910s, its declining importance signaled that the reform movement had reached an impasse.

In a highly ironic development, however, the same economic interests that direct democracy was originally supposed to rein in and even eliminate became important players in initiative and referendum politics. The second part of the book will turn to the practical experiences with the new devices between 1910 and 1940 and will demonstrate how these devices became useful tools for corporate politics. Some of the states that adopted the reforms, particularly those in the East and South, made scant use of the devices. The situation was strikingly different in the West, however, where they quickly emerged as highly important tools of policy-making. By 1940, voters would cast their ballots on more than 700 ballot propositions. The results of the practical operation of direct legislation were a distinct disappointment. Measured by the expectations of early reformers, it accomplished little.

Corporations and trusts continued to flourish, voter turnout rates did not increase, civic awareness was rarely heightened, American politics were not purified, and interests groups only grew stronger. Little, if any, power was restored to the common people. On the contrary, many abstruse and confusing propositions cluttered state and local ballots, voters usually displayed only limited interest in propositions, interest groups eagerly exploited the initiative and referendum as new tools of pressure politics, and political parties became less able to aggregate voter demands. The widespread use of the initiative was often based less on voter interest in a specific measure than on the ability of its sponsors to secure sufficient funds to retain the services of professional petition circulators to place the petition on the ballot.

Especially troubling for many observers was the close connection between direct legislation and the professionalization of campaign consulting and other modern campaign methods. The first professional campaign-management firm in America, Campaigns, Inc., or Whitaker & Baxter, emerged in California in the mid-1930s and specialized in the handling of initiative campaigns. Individuals who concentrated on the circulation of petitions and the gathering of signatures had emerged as early as the 1910s. Initiative campaigns in California in the 1930s witnessed the first application of scientific public-opinion polling in an individual campaign. Sharply escalating campaign costs, the growing role of some public relations and advertising firms in direct democracy campaigns, and the increasing sophistication of direct mail and other campaign techniques further altered political campaign styles. The initiative was not solely responsible for the application of modern advertising techniques to campaigns, but it played a significant role in the growth of a consultant industry in California that would rapidly spread to other parts of the country after World War II. As special interests became ever more adept and sophisticated in their abilities to harness the initiative for their own purposes, the practical usage of the reforms underlined the growing gap between the theory and the practice of direct democracy. Direct democracy proved unable to create a government that could withstand the influence of wealth and corporate power in America. A reform idea steeped in the tradition of American antimonopoly sentiment created a set of tools highly adaptable to corporate interests and political strategies.

Amid the contemporary discussions regarding the potential of the initiative to reenergize American democracy, it seems timely to bring some historical depth and perspective to this topic. The limits and the accomplishments of direct democracy can be assessed by reconstructing its rise in early twentieth-century America. This study will reveal that very few of the aspects of direct legislation that capture attention today are novel. The reforms were highly flawed and ambiguous achievements from the beginning, holding out the hope for the empowerment of ordinary citizens while being largely employed by strong interest groups. It is this dubious legacy that makes one wonder whether the initiative, referendum, and recall will ever be able to live up to the many hopes that have been connected to direct democracy since it was first introduced to America one century ago.

FROM THE REVOLUTION TO THE POPULISTS

The Antimonopoly Tradition in American Politics

Most scholars have interpreted the introduction of the initiative, referendum, and recall as a typical political reform movement of the Progressive Era. Reformers, mostly of middle-class and Protestant backgrounds, were spurred into action by the sordid spectacle of American politics during the Gilded Age. They developed a number of reform proposals designed to break the power of political machines and urban bosses, eradicate the rampant corruption of legislative bodies, make government more efficient and based on professional expertise, and purify the body politic. Among the most important reform proposals generated by this impulse were the Australian ballot, direct primary, direct election of U.S. senators, direct democracy, commission government for municipalities, and corrupt-practices acts. As the titles of many of these ideas imply, they were framed in the political idiom of popular sovereignty, defined as attempts to return political authority to the people by removing the corrupt influences that thwarted popular rule. In their effects on American politics, however, they often achieved the opposite results. As pointed out by many standard interpretations of this period, these reforms helped reduce voter turnout, disfranchised blacks in the South, and minimized the role of urban immigrant voters. In rewriting the rules governing elections in America, these reformers clearly reallocated political power to their own benefit.[1]

Such an account, however, presents a rather one-sided picture of the genesis of the direct democracy movement. It is one of the central arguments of this book that much of the impetus for the introduction of direct legislation stemmed from a specific mode of economic analysis, from a model of political economy that permeated reform communities in late nineteenth-century America. Surely, political concerns were highly important in the rhetoric of reformers. But a closer reading of their arguments clearly reveals that the initiative, referendum, and recall were primarily intended to abolish oppressive monopolies and artificial trusts in America by removing the legislative basis for their existence. Reformers moved within a powerful antimonopoly tradition in American history, the origins of which reached back to the eighteenth century. In order to fully understand the motivations and discursive strategies of the reform movement, it is crucial to situate the call for direct democracy within larger traditions of American political thought and culture. This chapter will thus outline the importance of antimonopoly sentiments as a force in American politics from the Revolution to the end of the nineteenth century.

The Political Economy of American Populism

During the nineteenth century, no other Western country industrialized as quickly as the United States. For many Americans, their country seemed the virtual embodiment of the material progress and restless spirit of the age. Most foreign observers were likewise impressed by the hustle and bustle of life in America, the boundless energy of its people, and the entrepreneurial spirit that shaped the course of the nation. But there was also a different side to the image of a nation engaged in the never-ending pursuit of material riches: a pervasive fear of the consequences of commercialization, industrialization, and modernization that manifested itself most clearly in an abiding American hostility to monopolies and corporations. Of all the Western nations that witnessed the rise of large industrial firms in the nineteenth century, only the United States also produced a strong, enduring, and politically potent antimonopoly movement. Beginning as early as the American Revolution and extending to the Great Depression, Americans were locked in a contested debate about the political and social consequences of centralized economic power. If, in the final equation, the rise of big business reshaped American society, it triumphed only after a protracted battle. And antimonopoly, more than any other critique of corporate capitalism, proved to be the most tenacious opponent big business interests had to overcome.[2]

The Populist movement of the 1890s, with its heated attacks on corporate charters, special privileges, franchises, and monopolies of all kinds, formed the most powerful eruption of the antimonopoly tradition in American history. Despite the substantial progress made in the study of Populism, we are still confronted with a highly truncated view

of its larger significance in American history.[3] Populism seems to un-
fold in something of a historical vacuum, suddenly emerging in the
1890s to briefly light up the political landscape before rapidly disinte-
grating after 1896. Although some mention is usually made of such intellectual and political precursors to Populism as Jeffersonian and Jacksonian democracy, producerism, Greenbackism, and the Grange, the
precise relationship of Populism to the political culture of nineteenth-
century America has not been systematically explored. Instead, historians have portrayed Populism as "a political culture at odds with the
mainstream of political habits and attitudes."[4] Closer inspection of
Populism, however, reveals that the political concerns and the rhetoric
of American Populism, if not its policy proposals, were strikingly un-
original. In their concern with monopoly and corporations, in their
denunciations of political corruption and governmental favoritism, in
their calls for "equal rights to all, special privileges to none," the Populists stood squarely in an American intellectual and political tradition
that stretched back to the early decades of the nineteenth century and
that would continue to influence politics until well into the twentieth.
They drew on a complex amalgam of ideas, attitudes, rhetorical strategies, and reform demands, here labeled populist republicanism, which
revolved around a distinctive model of economic affairs.

Populist republicanism provided a model of political economy, a
theory of the relationship between the political realm and the economic sphere, that endowed it with the distinctiveness and the focus
needed to provide a coherent explanation of the economic problems of
nineteenth-century America. At the heart of populist republicanism
stood the argument that the abuse of political power caused economic
inequality. By manipulating and exploiting the power of the state,
private interests acquired their wealth and their monopolistic position.
Although this belief informed the perception of the "revolutionary
generation" of the connection between legislative favoritism and the
growth of monopolies, and retained a powerful hold on Americans in
the nineteenth century, modern historians have neglected it.[5] It is a
belief that is diametrically opposed to much of modern economic theory, both in Marxist and liberal versions. Oligopolistic and monopolistic market positions are achieved via the economies of scale and scope,
via the superior efficiency of large corporations. Because of their economic clout, these corporations then also acquire political leverage.

While the role of the state was not a passive one, the state's help was not crucial in the genesis of modern industry.[6]

Convincing as this theory might sound in late twentieth-century America, it would not have swayed large numbers of Americans in the nineteenth century, including the Populists of the 1880s and 90s. In the political culture of antimonopolists, there was little that was efficient about large corporations and monopolies. In their interpretation of the rise of modern industry, financial and political speculation and manipulation took center stage. Special interests, already influential but far from dominant, acquired illicit political power and induced the state to grant them special privileges, charters, franchises, and resources, which then allowed them to exploit and tax the public. The railroads received the power of eminent domain and huge land grants, and they proceeded to fleece the public through high rates. Private banks were allowed to control the money supply, to contract the currency, and to exert pressure on creditors. Corporations used discriminatory practices to undermine their competition, while the tariff taxed their consumers via inflated price levels. In all of these instances, public power was transferred to private interests without mechanisms for public control. The objects of Populist rage might shift from banks to railroads to trusts, but the language of protest proved remarkably resilient. The real strength of Populism did not derive from the way its language and arguments offered a challenge to the American political system, but rather from the manner in which it connected to a long and rich tradition of oppositional politics in American history.[7]

In tracing the various permutations of this model of political economy, it will be argued that populist republicanism formed a remarkably cohesive language of protest acting as the most important source of reformist and radical politics in America. It was republican in its understanding of the relations between politics and the economy, in its model of political economy that seemed to offer a cogent analysis of the encroachment of inequality and monopoly upon American liberty. It was populist, also, in its confidence that the mass of the people could correct the faults in the American polity. Populist republicanism was based on the fusion of republican concerns about corruption and special privileges with the mass democracy of Jacksonian America. For almost a century, it afforded Americans a chance to frame their economic grievances in terms that harked back to the legacy of the American Revolution. Because the political economy of populism focused on the political arena as the fountainhead of special privileges obtained through corruption and bribery, most of the reforms advocated in the name of antimonopoly were of a distinctly political nature. Their common thrust was to place more power into the hands of the only incorruptible agency in the country, the people. Over the course of the nineteenth century, Americans severely weakened state legislatures, adopted the popular ratification of new state constitutions and amendments, and increasingly resorted to popular referenda to decide crucial issues. In the 1890s, some groups embraced the most radical proposal yet to break the power of corrupt lawmakers: direct legislation in the form of the initiative and referendum.

The Legacy of the Revolution

The study of republicanism, built on the pioneering work of Bernard Bailyn and Gordon Wood, has led to a new understanding of the motives and forces behind the American Revolution. No longer seen as just a liberal experiment in self-government, the revolution is now widely viewed as having been driven by a pervasive fear of corruption and the imminent moral decay of American society, and by the desire to counteract the British plot to fully enslave the American colonies.[8] Republicanism continued to be a reservoir of ideas, arguments, and rhetorical choices and conventions throughout the nineteenth century.[9] Most historians concerned with republicanism have probed its implications for political and constitutional issues. Amid the discussions about the chances for a republican form of government, these questions did indeed preoccupy the generation of the Founding Fathers. But already in the 1780s and 1790s, some observers began to argue that the growing commercialization of American society and the involvement of state and the federal governments in economic affairs paved the way for some of the corruption and aristocratic monopolies that had plagued England.[10]

According to James Huston, this argument formed an integral part of republican explanations for social inequality and a rising concentration of wealth. Within this "political economy of aristocracy," the source of oppressive economic conditions could clearly be located in those government policies that bestowed special privileges, charters, and public powers on private individuals and groups, ostensibly to promote economic development. Through the corruption of legislative bodies, elites were scheming to procure for themselves those special privileges and monopolies that would enable them to appropriate the fruits of the labors of common Americans for their own selfish purposes. Corruption, that central fear of the revolutionary generation, emerged as the crucial link in accounting for the willingness of politicians to actively support the creation of artificial monopolies.[11] The American Republic only recapitulated the mistakes that had caused so much misery in Europe.[12]

Soon after the Revolution, it became obvious that the country would be faced with the same problems of economic inequality and political corruption that the revolutionary generation had hoped to leave behind. The rapid economic development of the United States created a host of controversies about political and economic issues, especially the issue of the role of the state in economic affairs. Political scientists have repeatedly remarked on the weakness of the American state in the nineteenth century. It was primarily a state of "courts and parties," as Stephen Skowronek has written, incapable of effective regulation, dominated by the spoils system, and easily accessible to private interests.[13] It is also true, however, that American governments on the state and national level were by no means inactive. They functioned primarily as dispensers of privileges and resources. By giving away vast stretches of public land, by granting the right of eminent domain or the right to build a ferry or to dam a river, and by granting corporate charters, governments sought to promote economic development and to stimulate private industry in the capital-scarce economy of the early nineteenth century.[14] In the process, American governments often blended the boundaries between the public and private spheres, granting public powers to private individuals. It was a system of economic promotion that invited private parties to seek access to the political process in order to partake of government largesse.

One key instrument in the attempts of political elites to stimulate economic development was the granting of corporate charters. The corporation had a long tradition in Anglo-American law as a policy tool of the state. Both in England and in colonial America, a corporation was regarded as a quasi-public association of individuals endowed with public powers for the exercise of a function beneficent to the body politic.[15] By the 1830s, it was becoming obvious that a new legal definition of the relationship between the state and the corporations was emerging. Spurred on by the rapid rise in the number of chartered corporations — Pennsylvania alone granted more than 2,000 until the Civil War — a number of jurists began to dissolve the bond between the state and the corporation. A distinction was made between public and private corporations; while the former, such as a city or township, continued to be under close state supervision, a corporation chartered for purely private (that is, mostly commercial) purposes was emancipated from its dependency upon the state. The business corporation was reinterpreted as just another device to facilitate the transaction of business affairs. The social benefits inherent in economic advancement and the rise of American industry were, in the eyes of the legal scholars and judges who pushed this reinterpretation, reward enough for granting private individuals such rights as limited liability or eminent domain.[16] Yet, even if the distinction between public and private corporations had become well established by 1830s, the notion that a corporation was a creature of the state, operating under a burden of public responsibility and subject to state supervision, remained a crucial argument in "populist republicanism."

Prior to the 1830s, the republican analysis of economic trends had little political impact. Impressed with the rapid progress of their nation, most Americans supported the policies designed to promote private industry. Warnings about the rising levels of inequality and poverty found little popular resonance. By the 1830s, Jacksonian Democracy made a strand of republican economic analysis populist, linking it to popular government, universal suffrage, and egalitarianism. A mode of economic argument was transformed into a powerful political movement. Thoroughly American in its individualism, in its belief in the free market and private property, and in its conviction that a competitive system of private capitalism was most conducive to preserve the freedom and autonomy that formed the birthright of every American, populist republicanism also rendered a constant critique of political and social events in America. Caught up in the drama of the emergence of the first mass democracy the world had ever seen, populist thought and its model of political economy suggested a meaningful explanation of economic and social dislocation and became a potent weapon in the partisan strife that enveloped the American polity.

The Jacksonian Era

The election of Andrew Jackson brought to the forefront the pervasive fears about the effects of rapid commercialization on the political and social fabric of the country. Jackson's decision to attack the Second Bank of the United States was founded on growing public resentment against governmental favoritism, and it transformed a segment of the Democratic Party into a crusader for antimonopoly and placed the role of the state in the promotion of economic affairs at the center of American political debate. In his belief that the "concentration of wealth arising suddenly from financial manipulation and special privilege" was the artificial product of corruption by groups that "require grants of special privilege for economic success," Jackson succinctly expressed the mode of economic analysis at the center of populist republicanism.[17]

The use of state power and the law to concentrate wealth in the hands of the few could result in nothing less than the creation of a new aristocracy. As explained by John Taylor of Caroline, what defined an aristocracy was "an accumulation of wealth by law without industry." Arguing that "the transfer of property by law is aristocracy," the Jacksonians saw the specter of aristocracy raised everywhere as the actions of government on behalf of selected individuals and groups led to a rising concentration of wealth.[18] Nothing could be further from the true functions of government. Americans had not fought a victorious revolution only to reintroduce feudal conditions to the American Republic by allowing vicious laws and class legislation to act as regulators of individual and national prosperity and as devices to shift wealth into the hands of shrewd manipulators. Having learned their lessons about the essence of aristocracy and the economic and political foundations of feudal rule, Jacksonians were determined to not let history repeat itself. Throughout the 1830s and 40s, banking policies continued to be hotly contested in most states, pitting hard-money Democrats against Whigs and soft-money Democrats. The two parties clearly differed in their attitudes toward economic development. With the rise of a mass democracy in the 1830s, populist republicanism emerged as a widely popular political creed, centering on the role of the state in economic affairs.[19]

It is one indication of the powerful reach of populist republicanism that the antebellum labor movement supported its basic tenets and premises. A number of historians, most notably Sean Wilentz, have concentrated on two basic arguments: that antebellum workers shared in the republican language that dominated political discourse in America, but that they also used this language to express a radical critique of the emerging system of capitalism. Slowly, they began to understand more clearly the opposition between them and their employers and developed an economic theory that focused on economic exploitation and the ownership of the means of production.[20] Yet while a segment of the antebellum labor movement did indeed break with populist republicanism, most workers did not. Most historians have chosen to overlook the many connections, both in term of idea and personnel, that united reform and labor circles in this period.[21] Workers and their leaders throughout the antebellum era contended, like other reformers, that the political arena was the main source of corruption and inequality, and that the power of the ballot was the only weapon labor needed to rectify the situation. Charles Douglas, for instance, a labor leader in New England, asserted that it was "by the force of unjust laws, which the people have not made, which they never consented to, and can never comprehend, that property is gradually passing into a few hands, and is made sure to a few rich families while the mass of the people are fleeced, and made to pass their lives in toil." The remedy could only be "a radical reform — and this can only be accomplished at the ballot boxes." Political action against the monopolists and speculators that took advantage of governmental favoritism remained of crucial importance for most antebellum workers.[22] Populist republicanism, the belief that state-sponsored privileges and monopolies led to economic inequality, formed a central part of discussions about economic issues in the antebellum period.[23]

The Rise of the Populist Movement

After the controversy over slavery and the Civil War briefly relegated economic questions to a back burner, the reform politics of the 1870s centered on the twin issues of currency reform and the regulation of railroad rates. Both reform movements were rooted in the economic analysis of populist republicanism. At first view, there seemed to be few analogies between the antibank crusaders of the 1830s and the Greenbackers in the 1870s. The former had adamantly opposed the emission of paper money as a tool of idle speculators to defraud the public. Nothing was anathema to them more than the practice of local and state banks flooding the country with worthless paper notes. Under the deflationary conditions of the 1870s, when the decisions of the federal government to gradually retire the paper money issued to finance the Civil War and to demonetize silver (the famous "crime of '73" in Populist mythology) constricted the availability of money and squeezed debtors, inflationary monetary policies took on a new light. Populist republicanism proved flexible enough to accommodate a new set of economic circumstances and interests while retaining its focus on the state as the source of inequality. The severe economic recession of 1873 dramatically augmented the appeal of paper money. Midwestern farmers began to take note of the arguments for currency reform and for inflationary policies. By 1876, a national Greenback Party had been formed that would garner about one million votes in the congressional election of 1876, albeit in many places through fusion with the Democratic Party. Although the political appeal of Greenbackism declined sharply afterward, it would continue to form a key demand in the arsenal of reform politicians until the call for free silver in the 1890s.[24] Diametrically opposed monetary policies should not obscure the fundamental commonalties in the economic analysis of the Jacksonians and the Greenbackers.[25]

Whereas Greenbackism had formed a continuation of economic controversies with deep roots in the antebellum period, the demand for railroad regulation that erupted in the 1870s, usually associated with the agricultural reform movement called the Grange, represented a new political issue. Although states and communities in the West had at first eagerly embraced the new method of transportation that promised to bring them into closer contact with their markets, discontent over allegedly discriminatory rates soon erupted all across the western states. In the political universe of populist republicanism, organizations of such a monstrous size as the railroad corporations could only be regarded with apprehension and fear. With their dependency on the power of eminent domain and large land grants, they were seen as another example of government-sponsored monopolies.[26]

All across the Midwest, the Grange entered politics, usually under the name "Antimonopoly Party," and scored some significant successes in the early 1870s. Although not able to dislodge the dominant Republicans from power, the antimonopolists, often acting in fusion with the Democrats, forced the GOP to deal with the issue of railroad regulation. A number of Midwestern states, including Illinois and Wisconsin, enacted laws to lower railroad rates via legislative intervention.[27] In its campaign against railroads, the Grange clearly acted in the tradition of antimonopoly sentiment in America. One element of the Granger's Ten Commandments, adopted in 1874, reflected their position within populist thought: "Choke monopolies, break up rings, vote for honest men, fear God, and make money" was the goal of the Grange. Conceiving of themselves as independent producers threatened by the exactions of railroad monopolies and other unscrupulous middlemen, farmers turned to the legislatures for relief.[28] In the end, the agrarian crusade to regulate railroad rates achieved little lasting success as several legal decisions in the 1880s effectively insulated the railroads from legislative interference.[29]

The Populist revolt of the 1890s briefly threatened to reconfigure the American political landscape. Since the collapse of the Second American Party System in the 1850s, no third party had posed such a serious challenge to the major parties. Looking at the ground swell of economic and political discontent mobilized by the Populist movement, many historians have argued that the farmer cooperatives and the People's Party represented a radical alternative to the corporate America that was rapidly emerging in the country. Populists were not old-fashioned agrarian romantics who clung stubbornly to a pastoral past that never actually existed. Instead, they used the traditional images of republicanism, producerism, antimonopoly, and the labor theory of value to fashion a thorough reappraisal of laissez-faire economics and the emergence of a corporate economy. In place of the free market and unrestrained competition, the Populists organized in a variety of cooperative ventures to build a cooperative commonwealth. They also embraced an expansion of power of the federal government, especially in the area of the nationalization of the railroads, as a means to counter the power of big business.[30]

It seems more accurate, however, to view the Populists as the culmination of a long reform tradition and of a specific mode of economic analysis that reached back to the beginnings of the American Republic. At the heart of the Populists' political thinking remained the concept of antimonopoly. Like no other article of Populist faith, the conviction that shaped their demands was that the economic misery of American farmers was due to a system of artificial laws passed in the interest and on the demand of special interests to concentrate wealth and power in the hands of the corporations and trusts. As James Baird Weaver, Populist presidential hopeful, argued in 1892: "The corporations and special interests of every class created during the past twenty-five years by various species of class legislation and favoritism, have grown rich and powerful."[31] Not the workings of industrial capitalism nor the mechanisms of an unfettered market place, but specific actions in the political sphere was causing the growing centralization of economic institutions.

Accordingly, Populists focused their reform efforts on the political arena. While the successes of farmer cooperatives and trade unions might be impressive, only political action could "prevent the growth of a general monopoly of opportunities," as one Populist agitator argued in 1892. The contributions of Populists in the 1890s to the analysis of the political economy of privilege and corruption, and the legislative remedies they proposed, added little that was new to populist republicanism as it had evolved over more than half a century. Their novel proposals — such as the subtreasury plan, the nationalization of the railroads, and direct democracy — were not directed at creating a radically different economy, but were seen as means to restoring the economic and political independence of the American farmer.[32] What set the Populists apart was not so much their political program, shared by antimonopolists in the other parties, but their willingness to organize a third party, their belief that the Democrats and Republicans were too corrupt to be able to redeem the country.[33]

Nowhere was this attitude more pronounced than in the Populist's view of modern industry. In their response to big business and trusts, Populists focused on political corruption and legislative manipulation, with special emphasis on the interplay between legislation, privileges, and corporate power. As Benjamin O. Flower, editor of the most influential reform journal of the 1890s, *The Arena*, argued in 1891: "If you will subtract from our millionaire aristocracy all the wealth that has accrued from class or protective laws, or from special privileges and land monopoly, you will find how great a part the law-making bodies of our government have had in fostering wealth and producing poverty."[34] Change the laws and monopolies would vanish.

Because the railroads and financial interests targeted by the Populists usually acted in corporate form, the legal privileges of corporations emerged as central components of their arguments. In their view, corporations "had absorbed the liberties of the community and usurped the power of the agency that created it."[35] Over and over, Populist speakers reiterated that "monopolies exist by law, are chartered by law, and should be controlled by law."[36] Political corruption, law-sponsored privileges, lack of public regulation of corporations charged with the exercise of public responsibilities, private control over the currency, and corporate charters all ultimately led to the specter that haunted Populists like no other, monopoly. In the final equation, Populists contended, "special legislation builds up special privileges; special privileges build up private fortunes; and private fortunes built up by special legislation are a detriment and an insult to the community."[37]

Many historians have stressed the willingness of the Populists to embrace an enlarged vision of the role of the federal government. Calls for the nationalization of the railroads and the telegraph system did indeed form a remarkable departure from the minimalist government envisioned by Jacksonian Democrats. But the Populists were not advocates of a modern interventionist state. They had little conception of the administrative structures needed to manage a government-owned transportation system. Conspicuously lacking in their writings were discussions of the intricate details involved in nationalizing whole industries. For many Populists, a mere act of Congress appeared to be sufficient to transform the railroads from oppressive monopolies to servants of the public. Unfamiliar with modern management methods, Populists generally had little understanding of the internal operations of modern corporations. Their vision of a more powerful state remained rooted in an eighteenth-century tradition of a government that respected local autonomy and functioned without an intrusive bureaucracy. A social movement that championed the power and independence of local communities, that regarded with distrust impersonal, bureaucratic institutions, and that resented the growing concentration of power in metropolitan centers, was incapable of visualizing a modern interventionist state acting through a bureaucratic apparatus. If the Populists had succeeded in implementing their policy proposals, the federal government, as it existed in the 1890s, would have proved entirely inadequate for the tasks of managing national transportation and communication systems. In all their willingness to call upon the government to help rein in corporations and trusts, the Populists were never state-builders of the kind found in the Progressive Era.

In using old theories of corporate privileges and antimonopoly, the Populists only formed part of a much broader reform spectrum troubled by the new economic conditions. Democrats all across the South used a language similar to the Populists to protest the dominance of northern industrial interests and the exactions of monopolies and corporations. It also seems that the strength of the People's Party in the various states was conditioned by the response of the other parties to the issue of monopoly. Where the two major parties had sizable antimonopoly wings, the People's Parties remained weaker. The spread of the Populist movement was thus strongly shaped by the flexibility of the parties in adapting to a changing political agenda and a new set of political actors. The antimonopoly tradition transcended party lines and was a potent factor in the political upheaval of the 1890s.[38] In seeking better ways to rein in corrupt state legislatures, antimonopolists were constantly interested in new political devices and reforms.[39] When information about the existence of the initiative and referendum in Switzerland slowly filtered to the United States in the late 1880s and early 1890s, American reformers enthusiastically embraced direct legislation as the solution to their problems.

Antimonopoly formed a powerful component of the political culture of nineteenth-century America. Most of the critics of the unchecked expansion of industrial capitalism drew on an amalgam of ideas and concepts that located the source for inequality and poverty squarely in the political realm, in the specific privileges that venal lawmakers bestowed on private parties and that led to the creation of state-supported monopolies and corporations. Although antimonopolists were never able to effectively halt the centralization of economic power, they succeeded in sustaining a critique of corporate capitalism that resonated powerfully with many groups in American society. Antimonopoly appealed to farmers and workers alike, it was able to attract the support of small businessmen and professionals who saw themselves threatened by the rise of national corporations, and it led to the formation of a number of reform movements and third parties throughout the nineteenth century. A specific model of political economy and a language of protest that combined classical republicanism with popular sovereignty, a type of populist republicanism, emerged in the United States and linked reform movements during the entire course of the century. The advocated reforms varied significantly, with a focus on currency reform and transportation. In addition, reformers developed a series of proposals to increase the political power of the people, to transform American government into a "government by the people"—a polity based on the direct expression of the popular will. It was this tradition of popular sovereignty and majority rule that would find its most succinct expression in the development of direct democracy in the 1890s.

2

THE EMERGENCE OF AN ISSUE

Popular Sovereignty and the Rise of the Initiative
and Referendum in the 1890s

In the Populist worldview, politics determined the economic
and social arrangements and the structure of a society. Political conflict, not merely a reflection of more fundamental transformations in
economic structures and social relationships, was the pivotal arena in
which the battles over the future of the republic were played out. The
lines were drawn between the defenders of equality and popular sovereignty and the forces of privilege, corruption, and self-interest, between moral crusaders and venal politicians. This picture dominated
accounts of the political history of the Gilded Age for a long time.
More recently, a new generation of political historians has recast this
image by focusing on, among other things, the ethno-cultural roots of
voting behavior, on the expansion of state governments, and on the
dynamics of party mobilization. These historians have pointed out
that political machines were never as powerful and monolithic as the
clamor of reformers would have one believe, and that the fiscal and
economic policies conducted by machine politicians and upper-class
officials did not often greatly differ. American municipal politics were
never as corrupted as once claimed, and reformers, professional administrators, and technical experts always commanded significant authority and impact on decision-making processes.[1]

This correction had undoubtedly been a salutary one. What needs
to be kept in mind, however, is that for many Americans during this
period, political conflict remained dominated by the fights between
bosses and reformers. The political reform movements that have attracted so much historical attention were central to the political culture
of the period. Not just genteel middle-class reformers, but farmers
and workers as well, positioned themselves in a political universe organized around a bipolar structure of good and evil; morally righteous
reformers strove to preserve the promise of the American Revolu-

tion and scheming, self-serving interests exploited the public and ran roughshod over the principles of democratic rule.

If the political arena was indeed the central arbiter of the distribution of economic and social power, attempts to bring nefarious corporations back under public control likewise had to center on political reform. The solution to the perennial problem of checking the actions of legislative assemblies seemed deceptively simple: deprive legislatures of the authority to enact laws benefiting special interests and restore the power of the people themselves. The axiom that the people would never act against their own interests formed a cornerstone of the convictions of reformers in the nineteenth and early twentieth centuries. The people as a political entity were incorruptible, a force of rectitude and honesty that could be relied upon. Empower the electorate to act directly, so went the argument of many reformers, and the legislative origins of monopolies would vanish. From the early nineteenth century onward, a variety of political reforms were introduced that were designed to restore political power to the people and check the actions of legislative bodies. At first, these innovations remained embedded within a representative system of government, but they familiarized American voters with the use of referenda and acted as precursors of direct legislation. As impatience over the actions of legislatures rose to a fever pitch in the 1890s, reformers discovered the example of the initiative and referendum in Switzerland and quickly appropriated it for their own use. Because these devices could squarely be positioned in American traditions of popular sovereignty, they proved highly popular and led to the formation of a national direct democracy movement.

Restricting the Power of Legislatures

Within the political economy of antimonopoly, state legislatures acted as the main culprits. The promotion of enterprise was largely in the hands of the states in the nineteenth century, and, as pointed out earlier, they acted vigorously as dispensers of various kinds of privileges. For antimonopolists, legislators and lawmakers were notoriously corrupt and venal, always willing to sell themselves to the highest bidder. When Charles Francis Adams wrote around 1870 "that probably no representative bodies were ever more thoroughly venal, more shamelessly corrupt, or more hopelessly beyond the reach of public opinion than are certain of those bodies which legislate for republican America in the latter half of the nineteenth century," he captured a sentiment that was widely shared.[2] If the legislature sessions were indeed an "unavoidable public calamity," reformers throughout the century searched for ways to limit their capacity to harm the public good and the interest of the people.[3] As a result, American reformers experimented with a series of devices that became precursors of direct democracy.

Americans developed a variety of political innovations designed to limit the power of legislative assemblies. The introduction of universal male white suffrage in the 1820s was one reform intended to increase their responsiveness to the popular will. Of even greater consequence for later developments, however, was the submission of new state constitutions to popular ratification by the electorate. Prior to the 1830s, this was only practiced in isolated cases, mostly in New England. But of the new state constitutions drafted between 1830 and 1860, about four out of five were submitted to the voters. Of the new charters enacted between 1860 and 1889, finally, all were ratified in this manner. It emerged as a standard assumption of political thought that legislative assemblies or specially elected constitutional conventions possessed insufficient authority to implement new constitutions without popular approval, an argument that direct democracy advocates would find highly useful later.[4]

The frequent submission to the voting public of amendments to state constitutions likewise familiarized American voters with the idea that certain types of questions should be subject to popular decision. Although both American and European jurists carefully distinguished between constitutional and statutory law, this distinction was constantly eroded by legislative practice in the individual states. The tendency of many states to draft exquisitely detailed constitutions with a wealth of provisions formerly left to legislative discretion had already made that distinction problematic.[5] Many state legislators regarded the submission of constitutional amendments as one of the easiest ways to accomplish their political goals and they resorted to this practice with increasing frequency. In Michigan, for instance, eighty-five propositions, most in the form of constitutional amendments, were subject to popular approval between 1850 and 1908. Massachusetts voters decided on fifty-three amendments between 1821 and 1907.[6]

No wonder that one observer noted in 1908 that the constitutional referendum had "familiarized the American people with the practice of the direct popular ratification of the fundamental law."[7]

This phenomenon continued into the twentieth century. According to the estimate of political scientist Walter Dodd, American state legislatures submitted the staggering number of 472 constitutional amendments to American voters between 1899 and 1908. He estimated that only about sixty of these were of a truly fundamental nature.[8] Interestingly, there seemed to exist a fairly strong correlation between the frequency with which legislatures had submitted amendments to the public and the adoption of direct democracy. Of the ten states with the most amendments between 1899 and 1908, six would also introduce the initiative and referendum. Of the remaining four, three were in the South, where the presence of a large black population and white efforts to disenfranchise them doomed reform efforts. The last state of the ten was New York. Here the political parties were able to successfully hold off calls for direct democracy. When some opponents of direct democracy in the early twentieth century claimed that the referendum and the initiative formed the negation of American traditions of representative government, they chose to overlook that during the course of the nineteenth century the state legislatures had voluntarily delegated much of their authority to the electorate.

One final attempt to deprive legislatures of their ability to harm the interests of the people consisted of the increasing tendency of constitutions to carefully limit legislatures' powers. Many constitutions drafted after the Civil War contained carefully defined lists of the actions legislatures were prohibited to take. These constitutions often prevented the assemblies from enacting certain types of special legislation, limited the length and frequency of legislative sessions, changed the rules of procedure to make lawmaking more difficult, and increased the power of the governor to veto laws. State constitutions became "in effect codes of laws full of restraints, regulations, and prohibitions on the exercise of the legislative will."[9] All these reforms expressed the powerful suspicion of legislation corruption that animated many Americans throughout the nineteenth century.

Beyond the submission of state constitutions and amendments to a popular vote, referenda were also used to decide a number of other policy questions. Many state constitutions called for referenda on decisions to relocate the state capital, levy new taxes, form new bank corporations, spend certain types of public funds, and incur certain types of debts. Over the course of the nineteenth century, the list of issues involved in such referenda grew steadily.[10] Local referenda were employed even more frequently, for instance on such issues as prohibition and municipal bonds. In Chicago between 1880 and 1926, 266 referenda were put before the electorate.[11] Other observers pointed to the New England town meeting as an embodiment of the principles underlying the idea of direct democracy. One could debate whether "the principle of the referendum is an inheritance from our Teutonic ancestors," but there could be no doubt that the New England town meeting formed a type of democratic decision-making process that shared many characteristics with direct democracy.[12] Yet even though referenda had a long tradition in America, none of the previous reforms had lodged the power to initiate new laws directly with the voters. Here, the popular initiative and referendum went beyond the established parameters of American political thought.

Direct Democracy in Switzerland and the American Response

None of the reforms just outlined truly satisfied the critics of state legislatures. Lawmakers could still be corrupted by special interests, legislatures continued to produce a torrent of legislation each year that confused the voters, and the large number of constitutional amendments made it difficult to detect dangerous examples of "class legislation." The perennial problem of making representatives accountable to their constituents and preventing lawmakers from being captured by minority interest had not been successfully resolved. Most Americans had never seriously questioned whether the representative system of government itself, a legacy of the Founding Fathers, was to blame for the actions perpetrated by powerful corporations and their legislative henchmen. Yet the growth of trusts and corporations gave no indication of slowing down by the 1890s. If anything, American society had become more stratified, trusts had become more powerful and oppressive, and legislatures bestowed special privileges on an unprecedented scale. Clearly, new and more radical political reforms were needed. It was amid the upheaval of the 1890s, and under conditions of a growing receptivity to novel ideas, that the initiative and referendum entered the American political imagination.

Switzerland provided the original catalyst for the interest in the initiative and referendum in America. As the country with the most impressive democratic traditions in Europe, Switzerland had fascinated many Americans concerned with the state of the experiment of democracy in all parts of the world. During and after the American Revolution, many observers had looked at America and Switzerland as "sister republics" in a largely monarchical world.[13] The Swiss tradition of placing political decisions directly in the hands of the people originated in the Middle Ages, part of the evolution of local democracy in the "Landsgemeinde," local township, in the country. The referendum became part of the federal constitution in 1848 after the Sonderbund War led to a political reordering of Switzerland. The new charter compelled all cantons to include the popular referendum in their own constitutions. Over the next decades, the initiative also emerged in a number of Swiss cantons, and it became part of the federal constitution in 1891. Although ancient in lineage, the initiative and referendum in Switzerland were innovations of the nineteenth century.[14]

In America, detailed knowledge about the instruments of self-government in Switzerland was scarce. Prior to the late nineteenth century, most American travelers to the country were more attracted by the mountainous scenery than by the domestic political life of the Swiss. Compared to the important changes taking place in such nations as France, England, Germany, and Italy, politics in the Alpine republic seemed sedate, dull. Switzerland was a European backwater, a tiny country of no political significance, unlikely to offer much useful insight for the citizens of a continent-spanning country such as the United States. Yet, by the 1880s, more and more observers in the Anglo-American world became interested in Swiss political institutions. The British author A. V. Dicey published an article on Swiss democracy in *The Nation* in 1886, where he offered some first data on the initiative and referendum.[15] American reformers ventured to Switzerland in the search for inspiration, and there was a slow trickle of articles on conditions there in the periodical press of the early 1890s. Reference to the Swiss model emerged as an almost universal starting point for discussions of the initiative and referendum in America.

It is difficult to recapture today the importance of foreign models for reform movements during the Progressive Era. For a large number of reform proposals ranging from health insurance and workmen's compensation to the Australian ballot and proportional representation, America offered no examples to demonstrate the viability of the various schemes discussed in reform circles. Detailed statistics or scientific investigations of social problems were seldom available. In search of inspiration and convincing proof, reformers increasingly looked to other nations faced with similar social, economic, and political problems. Technological innovations, such as the telephone, and faster means of intercontinental travel enhanced the flow of information among different countries. Many more Americans were able to travel abroad, others developed a dense network of correspondence with like-minded reformers around the world, and a large number of American journals and magazines devoted an often astonishing amount of space to discussions of political conditions in a great variety of nations. Reference to foreign models was an integral part of the political discourse of American progressivism.[16] The initial arrival of the idea of direct democracy to America thus formed a "case of democratic contagion," an example of the ever more rapid spread of political ideas across national boundaries and of the close connections between reformers and political commentators in various countries.[17]

The growing number of American publications about Switzerland in the 1890s set the stage for discussions of the initiative and referendum. But it was the efforts of a somewhat obscure printer, union activist, and occasional writer named James W. Sullivan that provided the spark for the diffusion of direct democracy in America. Sullivan was born in Pennsylvania in 1848 and served an apprenticeship as a printer before moving to New York City in 1882. He worked for a number of newspapers, including the *Times* and the *World*, joined the International Typographical Union, and became a leading figure in union affairs. He was a strong supporter of land reform and the single tax; between 1887 and 1889 he edited the *Standard*, with Henry George, after he had participated in the latter's mayoral campaign in 1886. Later, Sullivan would also serve as a coeditor of the *American Federationist*. In 1888, he visited Switzerland for the first time, investigating local social and economic conditions for close to a year. He initially published a series of letters on the initiative and referendum in the *New York Times* in 1889, and in the following year he wrote a piece for *The Chautauquan*. In 1892, finally, he published *Direct Legislation by the Citizenship through the Initiative and Referendum*, a lengthy account of direct legislation in Switzerland and its possible application to the United States.[18]

Sullivan's close connections to the labor movement played a pivotal role in the early popularization of direct democracy. He was an active member of the typographical union and well acquainted with AFL leader Samuel Gompers. In May of 1892, following the publication of Sullivan's book, Gompers wrote him a complimentary letter. With many trade unions already practicing direct legislation, Gompers contended that "with the growth and development of the trade union movement, much will be done to apply the principles to our political government." A few months later, after the national convention of the AFL had adopted the initiative and referendum as an official plank in its program, the Executive Council of the organization appointed Sullivan as a General Lecturer on the topic of direct legislation.[19] In this capacity, Sullivan traveled around the country and visited local unions to inform them of the practical advantages of the initiative and referendum. His book sold briskly, also especially among union members; by one estimate, 15,000 copies had been sold by the mid-1890s, and Sullivan's writings would come to influence a number of the key figures in the direct legislation movement.

Another American instrumental in spreading more information about the initiative and referendum in Switzerland was William Mc-Crackan. Born in 1864, McCrackan spent much of his childhood in Europe and lived in Switzerland with his parents for a few years. He graduated from Trinity College in Hartford, Connecticut, in 1885. Soon afterwards, he traveled back to Switzerland as a tourist and became fascinated with the history and institutions of the country. He stayed in Switzerland for most of the latter part of the 1880s, collecting material for an exhaustive history of the nation that would be published in 1894. While there, he witnessed a town meeting of the inhabitants of the canton of Uri in 1887 and was deeply impressed with Switzerland's democratic accomplishments. He began to collect more material on the history and the practical application of the initiative and referendum, material that he used to pen a series of articles in the early 1890s extolling the virtues of local democracy in Switzerland. Like many other leaders of the movement, he was a supporter of Henry George's idea of a single tax. McCrackan's role in the popularization of direct legislation did not last long; he rarely participated in reform organizations and soon became a Christian Scientist in Boston. But his many writings on Swiss democracy helped to familiarize American reformers with the tools of popular lawmaking.[20]

After Sullivan's and McCrackan's writings had provided the initial stimulus, the 1890s and 1900s witnessed a virtual outpouring of articles on the political system of Switzerland and the merits of direct legislation.[21] For American observers, conditions in Switzerland appeared as a tranquil counterpoint to the political discord at home. They viewed Switzerland as free from the political strife, rise of large corporations, and rule of political machines that aroused the wrath of reformers in America. The Swiss appeared as a sturdy yeoman people, attached to their land and their old traditions, rooted in a long history of self-government, and proud of their democratic birthright, remarkably similar to the American patriots of the Revolution.[22] In updating methods of direct local government to the needs of an entire country, the Swiss had replaced mass assemblies "by consultations through the instrumentality of the ballot box."[23] Even a usually dispassionate observer such as John R. Commons was full of praise for the Swiss. In 1899 he wrote that "the Swiss people are free from the corrupting extremes of wealth, largely because the referendum headed off the encroachments of boodlers, bribers and monopolists, together with all kinds of special legislation by which so many American fortunes have been created."[24]

A closer reading of their writings on Switzerland, however, suggests that Americans often had little understanding of Swiss conditions and readily interpreted them through an American lens. By the end of the nineteenth century, Switzerland boasted one of the most diversified economies in Europe, with a booming export trade and a number of highly specialized industries that compensated for the lack of natural resources and isolated character of the country. In some rural cantons, the tradition of the Landsgemeinde lived on, but Switzerland was clearly no pastoral idyll far removed from the impact of industrialization and urbanization.[25] In their depictions of the Swiss as "a well-schooled, practical, unimaginative, thrifty and enterprising people, averse to high-flown political speculation, but awake to the possibilities of careful progress," American middle class reformers reflected their unease with conditions at home.[26] In casting Swiss conditions in light of their experiences with American politics, these observers skillfully wove together an idealized portrait of the Alpine Republic that attracted a significant following in the 1890s.

However, Americans did not need to continually refer to the Swiss example as proof of the consequences of direct legislation. The New England town meeting and the long fight for self-government in America could act as indigenous democratic traditions. Some reformers pointed to the role that town meetings still played in some New England towns. Others contended that some early American state constitutions had included provisions similar to the referendum and recall. Many also pointed to the growing use of referenda in the United States throughout the nineteenth century to illustrate the close relationship between direct legislation and the general advancement of popular self-government.[27] These critics argued that the initiative and referendum, in merely reversing the flow of political authority and giving the people the power to decide for themselves when to employ the new devices, formed the culmination of a century-old process of expanding popular sovereignty. Surely, America, long a beacon for self-rule in a hostile world, could not fall behind Switzerland in the role as trailblazer for democracy.

Direct democracy would provide the perfect means to stop the state from granting special privileges, an act that formed the basis for the creation of monopolies and trusts. Because "corporate influence sits serene in the legislative halls of state and nation," legislators had become the servants of various corporate interests.[28] Direct democracy held out the hope of empowering the people to defend their interests on their own, and it attracted the immediate attention of the Populist movement. As a Kansas Populist paper wrote in 1895: "We propose the initiative and referendum as a means of wrestling from a handful of pirates, gamblers and corporation attorneys the power they now exercise without question to determine the policy and conduct of public affairs for purposes of plunder, and of restoring the power to the masses of the people where it rightfully belongs." With the introduction of direct democracy, then, "corporations and monopolies will soon become things of the past" as the people could simply vote them out of existence. The People's Party made the call for the initiative and referendum a central demand in its Omaha platform of 1892, and most People's Parties in the states likewise endorsed the reforms. For a movement primarily concerned about halting the development of state-sanctioned monopolies, direct legislation provided the perfect political solution. From 1892 to the demise of the movement, American Populists were among the most vigorous proponents of the initiative and referendum.[29]

The Formation of a Reform Movement

The growing knowledge of the workings of the initiative and referendum in Switzerland was met with keen interest in American reform circles. In the early stages of the development of the direct democracy movement, which stretched from the early 1890s to the end of the decade, a key role was played by a small number of publicists and activists dedicated to informing the American public about the advantages of direct democracy. Diverse in their backgrounds and political convictions, they agreed that the new devices constituted the pathway to fundamental reforms. In adopting a highly pragmatic, nonpartisan strategy, these individuals could tap into a variety of constituencies and pressure groups to slowly transform the initiative and referendum into a legitimate political issue. By the end of the decade, it was no longer a Populist fad but a proposal that commanded support from wide segments of the public. Beyond this small circle of activists, direct legislation was adopted by a large array of interest groups, such as labor unions, farmer groups, single taxers, and prohibitionists, as a means to directly place their agenda before the electorate. The initiative and referendum expanded the range of political strategies available to political actors. At least until the adoption of the reforms, the interests of the activists and the larger pressure groups intersected, creating the possibility of a potent political coalition able to bring considerable pressure to bear on lawmakers.

James Sullivan, described by Gompers as an "extremely radical individualist," and the Populists were soon joined by a small group of other reformers that functioned as the organizational nucleus of the direct democracy movement. Benjamin O. Flower, a Christian Socialist by orientation, was the editor of the influential reform journal *The Arena*. He opened his journal to a highly diverse group of reform advocates, and almost every issue contained some mention of direct legislation. Antimonopoly constituted the core of Flower's political thinking. "Governmental paternalistic legislation," and not the workings of a capitalist market place, was to blame for economic inequities. By contrast, Populism was "pure republicanism" and promised a return to the virtues preached by the revolutionary generation.[30] His journal, a forerunner of the muckrakers of the 1900s, was the most influential reform journal of the decade. The wide publicity he devoted to the initiative and referendum was essential in disseminating knowledge of these devices among reform circles.[31]

Even more important to the movement was Eltweed Pomeroy, a New Jersey-based reformer who acted as the undisputed leader from the mid-1890s to the mid-1900s. As a "traveler for a manufacturing firm, of which he was the chief partner," Pomeroy was able to tour the country extensively to popularize the cause of direct legislation. He was a partner in a small ink-manufacturing company, Pomeroy Brothers, located in Orange, New Jersey.[32] Politically, Pomeroy was a Nationalist and follower of Edward Bellamy, as well as a supporter of the public ownership of utilities. For him, the main enemy was "the trinity of death — the corporation, the party machine, and the political boss," intertwined in a conspiracy to rob the people of the United States, ready to corrupt lawmakers and legislatures, constantly clamoring for more special privileges. Taking his inspiration from Switzerland, where "a feeling of social solidarity and brotherhood" had emerged as a consequence of direct legislation, Pomeroy's goal was the creation of a "cooperative commonwealth."[33]

Contrary to some of the more moderate reformers who continued to express their belief in the fundamental soundness of representative government, Pomeroy was more radical in his perception of American politics. Contending that "representative government is not democracy; it is a half-way house toward democracy," he believed that "with the Initiative and Referendum we have a government that is in its forms actually democratic."[34] He argued that "representative government is a failure," marked by decades of corporation rule and corrupt politicians. For more than a century, Americans had entrusted their fortunes to a system of government that systematically excluded popular self-government from all the important decisions shaping the life of the nation. The results had been social and economic inequalities and the formation of classes and masses. Now the remedy was at hand: "If we change our Government to a democracy in political affairs, we shall find it alone, without other reforms, will act on our industrial and social conditions to bring equality in them also."[35] As the editor of the main journal of direct democracy reformers up to 1904, Pomeroy was instrumental in organizing state Direct Legislation Leagues (DLLs) across the country; he offered information about the proper drafting of direct legislation statutes, connected the dispersed reformers with one another, and invested a considerable part of his income into the cause.[36] In 1904, a serious illness forced him to leave his position as the editor of the *Direct Legislation Record*. He ultimately retired to Donna, Texas, where he started a fruit ranch, but he continued to publish occasional articles on the issue. In contrast to other reform advocates who propagated the initiative and referendum to advance a specific cause, Pomeroy was highly circumspect about his own political positions, a sound policy for the leader of a movement aiming to attract a diverse constituency. But like many other reformers, he supported, among other things, the single tax, as well as a host of other causes.[37]

Finally, George H. Shibley was a lawyer-turned-reformer and political economist, and a "well-known writer on finance and other politico-economic subjects," who enjoyed close connections to the reform wing of the Democratic Party. Born in Wisconsin in 1861, he studied law at the Union College of Law in Chicago and was admitted to the bar in 1887, although apparently he never practiced. He worked for a publishing firm until 1890 and then tried his hand as an editor and writer of law books. He slowly drifted into Democratic politics; in 1896 and 1900 he wrote laborious campaign treatises for the Democratic Party in which he espoused the causes of silver money and tariff reduction.[38] He served as the main link between direct democracy advocates and the Democratic Party, enjoying particularly close connections with the Democratic U.S. senator from Oklahoma, Robert L. Owen, who emerged as one the most important national champions of direct legislation around 1910. In addition, he "exerted a far-reaching influence through arousing and actively interesting in the people's rule the Grange and the labor unions."[39] Shibley formed the National Federation for Majority Rule, another loose association of proponents of direct legislation, around 1905, after the original *Direct Legislation League* had become defunct following the retirement of Pomeroy.[40]

All these key individuals in the early development of direct democracy had diverse expectations regarding the shape of the reforms to be implemented with the help of the initiative and referendum. In the context of the politically volatile 1890s, when a number of different reform movements flourished, political change seemed just around the corner, and a dense network of contacts linked various reform communities, cooperation was easy. In 1899, a reformer in Nebraska, Laurie J. Quinby, was described as a "Single-Taxer by philosophy, a Socialist by sentiment, a Populist by affiliation, and a philosophical Anarchist by evolution." It was this eclectic mixture of reform impulses and mindsets that acted as a catalyst for the direct democracy movement in the 1890s.[41] Cooperation between the different reform communities was possible because they all drew on populist republicanism in their perception of economic conditions and in their policy ideas. Many individuals supported more than one cause and easily moved between different reform groups. Furthermore, the pragmatic nature of direct legislation allowed them to disregard potential fault lines within the reform coalition. The political landscape of the 1890s was a highly fluid one, including new sets of political actors and new political strategies. Direct legislation added another ingredient to the already volatile mix.

With the publication of Sullivan's book in 1892, the movement for the initiative and referendum entered its formative phase. At first, agitation was concentrated on the Eastern Seaboard, a somewhat surprising development given the lack of success the movement would ultimately encounter there. But Sullivan and most other early leaders resided in the Northeast. In addition, they easily obtained the cooperation of labor unions in such industrial states as New Jersey and Massachusetts. In the latter state, a resolution calling for direct legislation was introduced into the legislature as early as 1891. Several labor bodies, including the Boston Central Labor Union, added the initiative and referendum to their list of demands.[42] Of more consequence for the shape of the movement were events in New Jersey. With the active involvement of Sullivan, a small group of reformers and union activists founded a People's Power League in early 1892. It immediately proceeded to petition the various parties to come out in support of direct democracy. In 1893, the organization was renamed the New Jersey Direct Legislation League. The group drafted a constitutional amendment providing for the initiative and referendum and had a friendly lawmaker introduce it into the legislature. To bring public pressure to bear on the representatives, leaders of the league spoke before chambers of commerce, party conventions, civic groups, and reform associations throughout New Jersey. When a committee of the legislature scheduled a meeting on the amendment, Samuel Gompers traveled down from New York to testify on its behalf. Nevertheless, in 1894, after a heated debate, the House defeated the amendment by a vote of 32 to 27, with Republicans generally opposed to it and Democrats in favor.[43]

The beginnings of the reform movement in Massachusetts and New Jersey illustrate some crucial features of the social and organizational basis of the movement. At least in the 1890s, the role of labor unions in propagating the new devices and sustaining the leagues was crucial. In New Jersey, Sullivan noted: "A most valuable aid to the League has been the action of the labor organizations." The role of labor in Massachusetts has already been noted. From Michigan it was reported in 1894 that "organized labor here has stood squarely on the question of direct legislation in all its conventions during the past two years."[44] On the national level, the American Federation of Labor endorsed the initiative and referendum at its annual convention in Philadelphia in late 1892, arguing "that it finds the principle of direct legislation through the Initiative and the Referendum approved by the experience of Switzerland as a most valuable auxiliary in securing an extension of the opportunities of the wage-earning classes. As a nonpartisan reform of political methods it is our judgment that its adoption by the Commonwealth of America would greatly facilitate the securing of desired legislation in the direction of better social conditions."[45] Sullivan's work as a general lecturer of the AFL on the initiative and referendum symbolized the commitment of the labor movement to the reform effort. Although Sullivan's involvement waned in the late 1890s, his early role was crucial. By converting the AFL to the cause, he provided direct democracy with an instant organizational base and mass support that would prove essential in a number of later state campaigns for the adoption of the initiative and referendum.

The American Federation of Labor appears as an unlikely candidate to support direct legislation because it no longer believed in the tenets of antimonopoly that formed the core of most arguments in favor of the reforms.[46] Samuel Gompers was highly skeptical of the value of independent political action on the part of the labor movement. Believing that partisan strife formed a powerful source of internal dissension among workers, he constantly urged unions to avoid being drawn into party conflicts and advocated a strategy of political voluntarism.

During the campaign of 1892, he rejected calls for an alliance with the People's Party.[47]

Direct legislation, however, formed a proposal that continued to receive the unqualified support of the AFL. Worried that politicians and judges could easily take away the reforms that they had first handed out, the AFL was unwilling to entrust the welfare of its members to political action. But the initiative and referendum were different. They offered labor the opportunity to concentrate on selected economic and social issues while avoiding controversies around candidates. In the form of state constitutional amendments, reforms directly enacted by the people would be safe from judicial interference. At the polls, labor could use its large membership to great advantage. One reformer contended: "The Referendum will give Labor its true weight. Labor's interest in the Referendum is measureless; it is par excellence the workingman's issue."[48] For the middle-class reformers that also clamored for the initiative and referendum, the endorsement by the AFL gave them access to a mass constituency highly useful for pressuring obstinate politicians and disseminating their propaganda.[49]

The cooperation between an organization such as the AFL, which was so careful to avoid partisan political controversies, and other direct democracy advocates, was based on the early decision of the latter to adopt a nonpartisan strategy. In appealing to many different constituencies — Populists, single taxers, prohibitionists, reformist Democrats and Republicans, the leaders of the movement took great pains to distance their cause from any particular group or party and to eschew third-party activities. As Pomeroy explained in 1901: "I have great faith in education and very little faith in the formation of third parties."[50] The rapid demise of the Populist movement after 1896 certainly validated such a strategy. Acutely aware of their need for bipartisan support (since constitutional amendments were necessary to implement direct legislation, the reforms needed a two-thirds majority in state legislatures and could not be pushed through by one party alone), the leaders of the movement positioned themselves as a pressure group, urging all parties and all candidates to endorse the initiative and referendum. They might have been radical in their indictment of American politics, but they were pragmatic enough to adopt highly flexible political strategies.

Beyond the pragmatism of the leaders of the movement and the

specific reasons why individual interest groups endorsed the n
vices, however, antimonopoly formed the common denomir
most of the groups calling for the initiative and referendum.
legislation was not part of any "economic theory or scheme," but it
nevertheless possessed a distinct economic component.[51] For the majority of its supporters, the political reforms were designed to facilitate
economic and social changes. Steeped in the tradition of antimonopoly and firmly believing that political action was to blame for social
inequalities and poverty, these reformers enthusiastically welcomed
the Swiss innovations because they appeared perfectly suited to solve
the problem they had long grappled with: the inability of the American people to control their political representatives.

The close connections between antimonopoly and direct legislation
were evident during the National Anti-Trust Conference, held in Chicago in February 1900 in response to the conference on trusts that
had met a few months earlier. Next to a vigorous enforcement of the
antitrust statutes and a cessation of further special privileges to corporations and trusts, the initiative and referendum emerged as a central demand of the conference. William P. Black, a Chicago lawyer who
had served as the attorney for the defendants in the Haymarket trial,
pointed to the long-standing role of the judiciary as a protector of
corporate interests and argued that the people had to be empowered to
directly deal with economic issues. Under the initiative, "the people
can, by legislation which the courts cannot annul, dominate this whole
question." Another speaker called direct democracy "a single issue
which disposes of all others."[52] In its final report, the conference demanded: "And whereas, The political power of the trust lies in their
frequent representation in and control of the houses of legislation, we
recommend the adoption of the system known as direct legislation; to
make government once more as of right it ought to be, and as it was
conceived alike by Thomas Jefferson and Abraham Lincoln, a government of the people, for the people and by the people."[53] While not all
reformers were primarily concerned with economic issues, and they
engaged in the direct democracy movement for a multitude of other
reasons, the vast majority of committed antimonopolists in the country enlisted in the movement and would shape its agenda for the first
two decades of the century.

In the context of a fledgling movement in the early 1890s, the reform cause needed a national base from which to spread information about the initiative and referendum. Throughout the decade, reformers created an array of organizations designed to foster the reform agenda. The most important national organ was the *Direct Legislation Record*, edited between 1894 and 1904 by Eltweed Pomeroy. When the first issue was published in May 1894, at that time edited by Sullivan, it defined the role of the paper as an aid to reformers in the various states to draft uniform and well-designed bills, to keep the public informed about the true nature of direct democracy, and to coordinate the reform activities across the country.[54] While enthusiasm for the new measures ran high, few individuals were familiar with the intricate details of drafting laws that would be able to pass legislative and judicial scrutiny. The *Record* itself admitted in 1895 that "the laws presented are often crude and would not carry out the designs of the authors."[55] Helping reformers across the country draft uniform state laws and constitutional amendments was critical given the radical and untested nature of the initiative and referendum.

The financial base of the journal remained precarious throughout the decade of its existence. At the height of its prosperity in 1901, only 4,000 copies were printed; around 1500 went to subscribers, some were sent to reform organizations, and the rest were sent to newspapers around the country free of charge in an effort to spread information on direct legislation. Pomeroy claimed that articles in the *Record* were frequently copied and referred to in the regular press, but it remains impossible to ascertain the effectiveness of the journal. Its budget was always small, with receipts never exceeding more than $1,000, and often staying at a far lower level. About 50 percent came from subscriptions, the rest from various donations. In the end, it was Pomeroy's unwavering devotion to the cause that kept the *Record* afloat for a decade. When an illness forced him to resign from his position as editor in 1904, the journal folded.[56]

Pomeroy also functioned as the secretary and president of the National Direct Legislation League, which was founded in 1896 during the national convention of the People's Party. Because so many supporters of direct democracy attended the convention, Pomeroy had issued a call for a meeting to convene on the day before the convention was about to begin. In terms of leadership and finances the league was identical with the *Record*.[57] It was never a properly functioning national body. It operated more as a "letterhead" organization, announcing the support of prominent individuals for the reform on its letterhead, but without the staff and the financial resources to effectively direct the scattered movement across the country. In the words of Pomeroy, the only active officer of the league, it was "little more than a bureau of information, and a clearing-house for Direct Legislation news, carried by its President under his hat." In the *Record*, local correspondents reported on the progress of direct legislation in their home states and communities, model laws for the introduction of the initiative and referendum were discussed, and writers endlessly belabored the benefits of popular self-rule under direct legislation. Yet, in the end "each state must care for itself. If it does the rest are encouraged; if it does not it is its own fault or misfortune."[58] A second national convention of the league was held in June of 1901 in Buffalo in conjunction with the National Social and Political Conference, another national reform meeting. Against his wishes, Pomeroy was reelected to the presidency.[59] As late as 1912, Pomeroy still claimed to be the president of the National Direct Legislation League. The organization never officially dissolved. With the retirement of Pomeroy to Texas, it simply ceased to exist in just the same fashion as the *Record* had expired.[60]

Because few direct democracy advocates seriously contemplated the application of the initiative and referendum to the federal level, a national association such as the National Direct Legislation League occupied a somewhat ill-defined position toward the movement in the states. It could act as an information exchange, but it did not have the organizational and financial resources to render much aid to the different state campaigns. Many of the advocates of the reforms shared in the skepticism toward national authority and national institutions that formed an important part of the Populist worldview. Direct democracy, especially at the local level, was regarded as a means to strengthen local prerogatives undermined by translocal corporations. As one reformer put it in 1894: "Each community passing its own proper laws, government would be decentralized."[61] A decade later, Kansas City single taxers asserted that one advantage of direct democracy was that "lawmaking is localized, not centralized; each city or county (commune) asserts its right to self-government—home rule being a corollary to direct legislation."[62]

In most American states, however, towns and cities were under the control of state legislatures, a situation that stifled local political life. Ideally, the movement toward direct legislation would proceed from the local level, "the natural growth of a democratic movement," but the lack of local self-government might make this impossible, necessitating action at the state and sometimes even the national level.[63] An endorsement of direct legislation by the national conventions of the major parties, the object of much activity during the 1890s, would provide a significant boost for the work at the local and state level by demonstrating the legitimacy of the initiative and referendum. In 1896, Thomas McEwan, a Republican member of Congress and a leader of the New Jersey Direct Legislation League, unsuccessfully pleaded his case before the Republican convention. William Jennings Bryan, in contrast, sympathized with direct legislation, but was unable to convince other Democratic leaders who reasoned that the party platform already contained enough radical planks.[64] After the election, Pomeroy reflected that the people now had no further means to influence national politics until the next presidential election. The situation was different at the local and state levels where "elections come around oftener; the officers elected are closer to the people; they can be more easily influenced; they are more responsive; they are so numerous."[65] Accordingly, the attention once again shifted to the state leagues.

Over the next four years, Democratic parties in about a dozen states endorsed direct legislation. Most were located in the Midwest and West where the Republicans tended to dominate state politics. For a party that was relegated to an opposition role in most states outside the South, support for the devices provided an easy way to attack Republicans as the agents of class rule, as enemies of popular government, and as friends of the trusts. Competition between the parties could be employed to translate the diffuse interest in popular lawmaking into political action. According to one activist, "this can most readily be done by using one of the large political parties as an organizing force and naturally the party out of power is the one most readily available." Consequently, Pomeroy occasionally directed his appeals particularly to members of the Democratic Party.[66] Some Republican state organizations followed the example of the Democrats, but in general they remained more skeptical of the reforms.[67] In 1900, Pomeroy again tried to insinuate direct democracy into the national campaign. In May of that year he issued a circular that called for the promotion of "the extension of Direct Legislation to National Legislation and Federal Affairs by inserting a Direct Legislation into the National Platform" of all parties. While the Democrats heeded the call and finally endorsed the initiative and referendum at the national level, the Republicans continued to hold out.[68]

In the actual campaign, direct democracy played virtually no role. In late October, Pomeroy sent a letter to about one hundred supporters asking them to outline the role played by the measures in the campaign. The responses were not encouraging. The Democrats refused to insert a reference to direct legislation into their national campaign book, and "it was hardly referred to by them during the campaign and certainly not made an issue." A correspondent from Texas reported that "Direct Legislation has played the tail to several kites in this State. The men and women who seem to favor it are prostituting it to party." In Georgia, prospects for reform were bleak unless the Democrats had the courage to submit an amendment to the voters "regarding their pet bugaboo — Negro disfranchisement — a thing they are anxious to do but seemingly afraid to attempt." Mahlon Fulton from Pennsylvania, finally, wrote Pomeroy: "If the system were adopted in one of the States of the East or the Middle West, a State of importance, it seems to me that the work would be made easier. Most people look upon D. L. as merely a pretty theory and when it is shown that the system is practically working in Switzerland and distant parts of our own country it is still unconvincing, for they seem to think the conditions existing here are different."[69] The endorsement of national and state parties only rarely translated into actual work on behalf of the initiative and referendum.

The work of Pomeroy and the National Direct Legislation League had reached an impasse by 1900. On the one hand, the achievements of the direct democracy movement had been impressive. A proposal that was virtually unknown in 1892, and that smacked of Populism and anarchy, had emerged as a serious political issue by 1900, attracting the support of the labor movement and substantial segments of the two major parties. The highly diverse political positions of such key individuals as Sullivan, Flower, Pomeroy, and Shibley illustrate one of the central assets of the movement; its ability to enlist the support of many different groups — Populists, single taxers, prohibitionists, and the progressive wings in the Democratic and Republican parties —

precisely because it left the issue open regarding what final reforms direct democracy would help to achieve.[70] Substantial political differences split this coalition, but all of the reformers "want to curb the trusts, and to accomplish this the voters must clothe themselves with the right to a ballot upon such questions."[71]

On the other hand, up until 1898, when South Dakota became the first state to adopt the initiative and referendum, the movement could show little concrete results. The national organization was weak, always on the brink of bankruptcy, never able to assist state organizations, and had no base at the local level. Ironically, the national organizations were also concentrated in the Northeast, where direct democracy would enjoy little success and where antimonopoly sentiments were weakest. This situation was undoubtedly the result of the dominant role of the Northeast in American publishing and politics. The result was a disjunction between the feeble national organizations and the more effective state bodies. In an ironic twist for a movement dedicated to grass-roots democracy, it never became a truly popular social movement with a solid membership base. Except for the devoted support it received from a few key individuals, interest in direct legislation remained contingent on the self-interest and strategies of pressure groups and parties trying to use it to achieve their own ends. During the heady days of the early 1890s, the introduction of direct democracy seemed imminent. Armed with the argument that the initiative and referendum formed the culmination of the century-old struggle of the American people for self-government and popular sovereignty, most reformers underestimated the resilience of the party system. The early attempts to introduce constitutional amendments in New Jersey and Massachusetts demonstrated that the reformers did not command sufficient resources to overcome the recalcitrance of the major parties.

Despite some early setbacks, however, the demand for the initiative and referendum had become an important topic in American politics. The sudden outburst of interest in new devices for popular self-government had been sparked by the intersection of a longtime distrust of American legislatures, the rising tide of antimonopoly sentiment in the late 1880s and 90s, the availability of the Swiss example, and the dislocations of the party system through the emergence of the Populist movement. At first, direct legislation was advocated by groups on the fringes of the political mainstream, by a People's Party attempting to break the dominance of the major parties and by a labor movement still looking for a solid membership base and for public legitimacy. Yet from the beginning, the reformers displayed their skill in appealing to a diverse set of constituencies and in transforming direct democracy into an issue that transcended party lines. The rise of the reform wing of the Democratic Party under William Jennings Bryan and its support for the reforms was one major factor behind the rapid spread of the new ideas. With the proliferation of state Direct Legislation Leagues across the United States, there existed an organizational nucleus for the state campaigns to follow. As Populism subsided, direct democracy continued to flourish by broadening its support base on the basis of antimonopoly sentiments. With the national movement in place by the late 1890s, but unable to function effectively, attention shifted to the state level where the real contest about the future of the initiative and referendum unfolded.

REPUBLIC OR DEMOCRACY?

Direct Democracy and American Constitutionalism, 1890–1920

The idea that American government is based on the will of the people has been one of the central tenets of American constitutionalism and the political culture of the nation since the beginnings of independence. Few other terms have resonated as powerfully as the concept of popular sovereignty, of a government by the people as the conscious creation of a virtuous citizenry united in the pursuit of the common good. Drawing on the best of what political theory had to offer, the Founding Fathers had fashioned a system of government that managed to combine popular sovereignty with individual liberty, that protected minority and property rights while being able to adapt itself to the rapid economic and social change of the nineteenth century. Different individuals might point to divergent aspects of the American political system as the primary reason for American exceptionalism: the intricate system of checks and balances, the Bill of Rights, the principle of representation. All Americans, however, tended to agree that the American Republic was characterized by the most perfect form of government ever devised by man. At the inception of the American Republic, the political fabric of the country resembled a roof without walls, to use the term of historian John Murrin, with a political superstructure but without the integrative forces of descent, religion, language, or history that marked European nations. Over the course of the nineteenth century, allegiance to the Constitution and pride in American political institutions developed into a kind of "civic religion," uniting Americans of various political persuasions and social conditions.[1]

In stark contrast to the domestic tranquillity enjoyed by Americans, countries in Europe seemed to be convulsed by perennial political upheavals and made slow progress toward democracy. Germany and Italy emerged as modern nations under the guidance of monarchical regimes, France underwent several regime changes throughout the nineteenth century, the despotic Russian Czar governed Eastern Europe, and even in England the franchise was only extended gradually. The connections between a republican form of government and political and economic progress seemed obvious. American accomplishments in constitution-making had clearly demonstrated the ability of a sovereign people to construct a carefully crafted political system superior to other forms of government.

Underneath this general consensus, however, there loomed significant disagreements about the precise character of the American republic, which erupted continually over the course of the nineteenth century. One of the most volatile disagreements surrounded the very issue of popular sovereignty.[2] The idea that the people were the repository of all political authority formed the basis of the legitimacy of political institutions. But the Constitution also provided for a series of devices to limit the rule of the majority, including a bicameral legislature and a Supreme Court vested with the power of judicial review. At the federal level, these devices successfully slowed down the pace of constitutional change. The situation was strikingly different at the state level, an arena of constitutional experimentation that has received little attention from historians and legal scholars. Nineteenth-century state constitutions were constantly revised and redrafted. In the states, discussions about the nature and extent of popular sovereignty clearly revealed diverse opinions about the American experiment in self-government. The constant tensions between popular sovereignty and the protection of minority rights, extending from discussions of the extent of rights to the suffrage to the issue of judicial review, formed a powerful theme of nineteenth-century American political conflict.[3]

One such controversy surrounded the issue of direct democracy between 1890 and 1920. Beginning in the 1890s and without much warning, a motley band of reformers and radicals boldly declared that "representative government is a failure" and began to demand wholesale changes in the existing political institutions.[4] At the heart of the campaign for the initiative and referendum stood the conviction that the republican form of government, based on the principle of representation, one of the key components of American constitutionalism, had failed dismally. Hostility to legislative assemblies and charges of corruption, were, of course, nothing new in the United States. What was new about the direct democracy movement, however, was its contention that representative government itself stood in need of replacement. In leaving the accepted parameters of political discourse, the sudden rise of the direct democracy movement ignited a fundamental discussion about the very nature of the American experiment in self-government, about the meaning of the Constitution, and about the political character of the nation. If the people were directly empowered to make constitutional law, what would happen to the "government of laws" envisioned by the Founding Fathers? Many of the issues that had troubled the revolutionary generation — the precise extent of the power of the people, the relationship between the voters and their representatives, the protection of minority rights and property interests, and the pace and nature of constitutional change — were again brought to the forefront of political debate. Celebrations of the Constitution and of the American political creed, central civic rituals of the nineteenth century, were no longer able to create a discursive space common to all Americans, and new fissures in the body politic emerged.

The Legacy of the Founding Fathers

Any attempt to substantially enlarge the direct role of the voters in American politics was immediately confronted with the fact that the Constitution provided for a republic and guaranteed each state in the Union a republican form of government. In addition, the Founding Fathers had explicitly rejected direct democracy. The drafters of the Constitution, most notably James Madison, had carefully reviewed the existing array of political regimes in their search for a constitutional blueprint for the new polity. They had looked at the pros and cons of direct democracy in the form of the example of ancient Greece and had found it wanting. Madison, in the famous Federalist No. 10, had dismissed "pure democracy," "a society consisting of a small number of citizens, who assemble and administer the government in person," as offering no cure "for the mischiefs of faction." Thus "such democracies have ever been spectacles of turbulence and contention; have ever been found incompatible with personal security or the rights of property; and have been in general as short in their lives as they have been violent in their deaths."[5] Madison's arguments exemplified a significant change in linguistic practice that occurred between the time of the Revolution and the late 1780s. At first, the terms democracy and republic were often used interchangeably, as a form of governance based on the will of the people. Confronted with the social turmoil of the 1780s, a number of Founding Fathers then began to use the term republic to denote a popular government with checks and balances to protect minorities. This latter use was the one stressed by conservatives after 1900, but the proponents of direct legislation could advance a different interpretation with at least some historical validity.[6]

The opponents of direct democracy contended that America had always been a republic, based on the principle of representation, the protection of minority rights, and the carefully controlled exercise of political power. The principle of representation and the intricate set of checks and balances called for in the Constitution were designed to overcome the obstacles that had bewildered previous attempts at self-government, most prominently the unlimited action of capricious and self-interested majorities, the willful disregard of the rights of minorities, and the resulting political instability. The initiative and referendum offered a highly dangerous tool for well-organized minorities to impose their political will on the majority, raising the specter of threats to the values of personal property and personal independence so dear to American conservatives. In the final equation, direct democracy was "the power of popular license against representative government and constitutional security." As expounded by William H. Brown, secretary of the Chicago Civic Federation, in 1905, it "proposes legislation without deliberation, lodges all veto power in the popular ballot, and in its last results transform a constitutional representative government into an unconstitutional irresponsible democracy."[7] Far from being a symbol of political progress, direct democracy meant a misguided attempt at reform "by means of a return to the old, unsuccessful, and discarded method of direct legislation and by rehabilitating one of the most impracticable of Rousseau's theories."[8] Conservatives maintained that "great communities cannot be governed by permanent town meetings."[9]

Throughout the 1900s, opponents tirelessly reiterated that direct democracy was clearly in violation of the federal Constitution that guaranteed each state a republican form of government.[10] The initiative and referendum were "twin institutions of foreign importation, superseding the native product in harmony with representative government."[11] Amidst the political upheaval in turn-of-the-century America, with the legitimate interests of property owners under attack everywhere, any fundamental tinkering with the Constitution could only lead to a social revolution. Far from transforming the United States into a democracy, the events of the nineteenth century had only made more evident the need for constitutional protections against mob rule that only a republican form of government could supply.

The courts did not sustain this formal legal argument, however. The first legal challenge to the initiative and referendum occurred in Oregon where the constitutional amendments, ratified by the voters in 1902, were immediately appealed in court. In 1903, the Oregon Supreme Court rendered a verdict that direct legislation did not violate the guarantee of a republican form of government as contained in the Constitution. It argued: "No particular style of government is designated in the Constitution as republican, nor is its exact form in any way prescribed. A republican form of government is a government administered by representatives chosen or appointed by the people or by their authority. . . . Now the initiative and referendum does not destroy the republican form of government and substitute another in its place. The representative character of the government still remains. The people have simply reserved to themselves a larger share of the legislative power."[12] The California Supreme Court handed down a similar ruling in late 1906 when it sustained a municipal direct legislation ordinance in Los Angeles.[13] Other state courts followed these precedents in the following years and rejected challenges to direct legislation.

The issue was not conclusively settled until the United States Supreme Court became involved. After Oregon voters had used the initiative to impose a 2 percent tax on the gross receipts of telephone and telegraph companies operating in the state in 1906, the Pacific States Telephone and Telegraph Company refused to pay the tax and appealed to the Oregon Supreme Court, which upheld its previous ruling. The company then took the case to the U.S. Supreme Court. Calling the United States a "representative constitutional democracy," their attorneys added that "no republic can safely harbor tyranny. No tyranny is worse than that of an absolute majority." And the drafters of the Constitution had already settled the issue:

In the Federal Convention of 1787 the distinction between a republican and democratic form of government was constantly in the minds of the framers of the Constitution. Steering between the despised absolutism of a highly centralized government or of a monarchy, on the one hand, and the fantastic government and evils of a pure democracy and the rule of the multitude on the other hand, the founders of our Government planted themselves on the principle of legislation by representatives, elected for that purpose, as the foundation of our institutions.

They were well aware of the dangers of democracy, they abhorred such a form of government. The Federalist papers and the debates of the Federal and State Conventions at the time abundantly show that above all else the founders of the Government feared that creation of a government of men rather than a government of laws, and that the people of the nation in the first enjoyment of the powers of self-government would drift to that form which would insure license rather than liberty.[14]

The Supreme Court, however, declined to follow this line of reasoning. It dismissed the case in 1912 by calling the issue of the initiative and referendum a political question outside the purview of the court. It argued that it was up to Congress to decide whether or not the political institutions of a state were republican. Since the Congress had admitted several states with the new devices, Oklahoma in 1907 and Arizona in 1912, this ruling ultimately settled the issue of the constitutionality of direct democracy.[15]

Direct democracy reformers proffered a very different reading of American history. There could be no doubt that America was a democracy, built around the fundamental principle of popular sovereignty. The colonists had not, after all, overthrown British rule only for their descendants to be subjected to another form of arbitrary rule by corrupt lawmakers. Under the conditions of the late eighteenth century, they claimed, with primitive means of communication, an underdeveloped infrastructure, and a population not yet schooled in self-government, direct democracy could not be successfully applied. Things had changed, however. Technological innovations such as the railroad, telegraph, and telephone, and the emergence of newspapers and other print media had vastly enhanced the knowledge of political affairs, intensified political discussions among Americans, and enabled the people to inform themselves quickly about new political questions. U.S. senator Jonathan Bourne of Oregon, one of the most prominent spokesmen of direct legislation, argued in 1912: "Electricity and steam, the telegraph, telephone, railroad, and steamboat have established media of instantaneous intercommunication of ideas and rapid cooperation of action in the individual units of society."[16] Modern life had vastly improved the "means of public and private intercourse," and the conditions for democratic deliberation had been "completely changed by the marvelous mechanical inventions of modern times."[17] A representative form of government was no longer adequate. "With the growth of popular intelligence," one reformist journal contended, "the people have been feeling cramped by the old system of representative government."[18] The whole tendency of American politics since the Revolution had been to extend the role of the people. The initiative, referendum, and recall formed the culmination of a century of progress, the extension of the principles of popular sovereignty and majority rule to empower the people to vote directly on every issue of their choice.

Facing the need to clarify their position toward the constitutional tradition, one segment of the direct democracy movement chose to frontally attack the founding document as an instrument of class rule. The most vocal critic of the Constitution might have been J. Allen Smith, a professor of political science at the University of Washington. Smith had been called to his position in the late 1890s, when the People's Party briefly controlled Washington State. A staunch reformer with Populist sympathies, he offered an analysis of the genesis of the federal Constitution that emphasized its undemocratic attributes. He argued that "the fear of too much democracy, rather than too little, largely determined the form in which our general government was cast in the beginning." The document was primarily shaped by the interests of a small property-holding elite and was full of restrictions on the exercise of the popular will. The many built-in checks and balances were directed at perpetuating unequal social and political relations by frustrating the efforts of the people to liberate themselves from the dominance of particular interests. With the popular initiative and referendum, the means were finally at hand to completely empower the people to take care of their political affairs.[19]

Other direct democracy reformers shared Smith's harsh assessment of American government. Eltweed Pomeroy contended in 1897 that "representative government is not democracy; it is a half-way house toward democracy." Only with direct legislation, he argued, do "we have a government that is in its forms actually democratic."[20] John Sullivan, the typographer and union activist whose initial writings on Switzerland provided an important stimulus for the early development of direct democracy, likewise sharply differentiated between a democracy and prevailing conditions in America: "There is a radical difference between a democracy and a representative government. In a democracy, the citizens themselves make the law and superintend its administration; in a representative government, the citizens empower legislators and executive officers to make the law and carry it out. . . . In other words, democracy is direct rule by the majority, while in a representative government rule is by a succession of quasi-oligarchies, indirectly and remotely responsible to the majority." By breaking the "lawmaking monopoly" of the elites and their political henchmen, a real democracy would emerge in the United States.[21] Conservatives might, in principle, celebrate the popular will, but they remained wedded to a "fundamentally illogical theory of a government by the people in which it was extremely difficult for the people to govern."[22] The goal of the initiative and referendum was to "change this sham democracy into a real democracy" and to "transform this government by elective aristocracy into a government by the people."[23]

Only a minority of direct democracy advocates, however, opted to break decisively with the Constitution by branding it an instrument to block popular sovereignty. This line of reasoning was most influential among the more radical reformers in the West. In their search for allies among Progressives and moderate Democrats and Republicans, many reformers softened their criticism of the Constitution and insisted that they did not reject the principle of representation completely, but only sought to modify it through the initiative and referendum. One wrote in 1913: "Democracy does not wish to divorce itself from representative government, but it does demand the possibility of ultimate popular control of its affairs and its officers."[24] The initiative and referendum would serve as the "gun behind the door," a term coined by Woodrow Wilson, but the bulk of legislative activity would continue to be conducted by legislative assemblies.[25]

Still, direct democracy advocates could not avoid responding to the charge that these innovations violated the American political tradition. They sought to shift the discussion to a different terrain by emphasizing other aspects of the constitutional tradition. Instead of talking about the measures for the protection of minority rights and the limits to the unrestrained exercise of power, they concentrated on the principle of popular sovereignty. Because all Founding Fathers had agreed that the will of the people formed the ultimate basis of American government, how could an innovation that promised to involve the people much more directly in the governing of their own affairs violate the spirit of the Constitution? Instead of regarding the document as permanent and unalterable, they envisioned the Constitution as a living thing, as capable of responding to change and incorporating the progress of the nineteenth century. Thomas Jefferson and Abraham Lincoln, both strong advocates of popular sovereignty, were constantly invoked to legitimize the call for direct democracy and its innovations, which were "in perfect alignment with the theory, ideal, and demands of the founders of our Government."[26]

One prominent direct democracy advocate, Senator Bourne, even developed an ingenious theory, regarding the impact of direct legislation on political behavior, that aimed to update Madison's remarks in the Federalist Paper No. 10. Writing in 1912, Bourne acknowledged that "self-interest is the force controlling every future or postponed action of the individual." But much like Madison, who argued that the conflicts between different political factions in a republic would tend to cancel each other out, Bourne asserted that the clash of individuals motivated by personal interests would result in greater public welfare. Under direct legislation, he proposed, "an infinite number of different forces are set in motion, most of them selfish, each struggling for supremacy, but all different because of the difference in the personal equations of the different individuals constituting the community. Because of their difference, friction is generated — each different selfish interest attacks the others because of its difference. No one selfish interest is powerful enough to overcome all the others; they must wear each other away until general welfare, according to the views of the majority acting, is substituted for the individual selfish interest."[27] Once the individuals realized that they could not realize their selfish desires, they would work toward the greater good of the community because they, as themselves members of that community, also stood to benefit from its improvement.

Defining the Role of "The People"

Nothing illustrated the conflicting perspectives on direct democracy as succinctly as discussions about the role of "the people" in American politics. In theory, the people were the repository of political power and civic virtue in the American Republic. But on a very fundamental level, opponents of direct legislation shared a deep distrust of that "collective personality called 'the people.'" Many were "unable to see how any good, coming to a mass of men, can be felt in any other way than by the individuals who compose it." That entity "the people" that figured so prominently in the arguments for direct legislation was a pure fiction, never to be encountered in practical politics.[28] The reformers, conservatives charged, seemed to believe that the very introduction of direct democracy would somehow produce a magic transformation of the electorate. They talked of an "allwise and beneficent entity, called 'the people'—something different and opposite from individual human beings and free from their limitations and defects." But "human society is not and can never be anything more than the sum totals of the individuals who compose it."[29] As a creature capable of political reasoning and concerted action, the people simply did not exist. The belief that, in the words of James Bryce, "a sort of mystical sanctity not susceptible to delegation dwells in the Whole People," was a dangerously false one.[30] All the initiative and referendum would do, wrote California Republican Thomas Bard in 1912, was to empower "the ignorant, irresponsible, unthinking, prejudiced, and vicious classes" to enact legislation in their own selfish interests.[31] The essence of direct legislation was that "the laws must reflect the *desires* of the greatest number rather than the *judgment* of reason," a proposition unpalatable to American conservatives.[32]

The electorate was also woefully unprepared for the additional burdens imposed on them by the initiative and referendum. Believing that American voters were "better fitted and have greater confidence in their ability to pass upon the qualifications of legislators about whom they know considerable than upon measures about which they know little," conservatives only expected confusion and anarchy as the result of the expansion of popular lawmaking power.[33] A. Lawrence Lowell, one of the most influential conservative thinkers at the beginning of the century, argued similarly when he wrote that "our people are not in the habit of weighing the merits of particular statutes, or for debating the necessity for the various appropriations. Their experience has been confined to passing judgment upon men and upon general lines of policy." In contrast to European countries, where well-organized political parties presented clearly defined political issues to the electorate, elections in America have "less the character of a popular mandate to the successful party to carry out a specific group of policies" than they were an endorsement of personalities.[34] American voters were already "greatly overloaded" and would be "most densely ignorant" on the policy questions contained in ballot propositions.[35] How could they then be expected to make informed and rational decisions when confronted by a bewildering number of choices on issues of a largely technical character?

Finally, American voters did not evince the political interest vital to a functioning of direct democracy. As one observer noted: "In the first place, the people are indifferent, tremendously indifferent, on all except the largest and most important questions of policy."[36] This would not pose a problem if "the actual vote at an election through suitable restrictions were cast by the wiser half of our citizen body."[37] These restrictions did not exist under the American conditions of universal suffrage. It would be the "dangerous" classes that were to function as the arbiters of the destiny of American politics, the great mass of the voters, "a minority of them having at most only ordinary and inadequate ability, and the vast majority practically no ability at all."[38]

In contrast, reformers maintained that the people as a collectivity transcended the abilities of the individuals. "The people is made up of individuals and yet it has qualities that none of the individuals possess." Being able to inform themselves on political issues due to technological innovations, the people would never vote against their own interests, would act wisely in their capacity as lawmakers, and would rise to the challenges of modern life. Not the people but their reactionary enemies were the ones that were truly ignorant of the crisis facing the nation. If the people could not be trusted, what hope was there for self-government? "If faith may not be placed in The People, in The People as a totality, in their solidarity, then government is a farce, a pretense and a fraud, and the sooner we abandon it and join the anarchists the better for our rectitude, our sincerity, and our courage in facing the truth however terrible."[39] Americans had always demonstrated their knack for self-government and had never succumbed to the maladies of democracies in ancient times.

Direct democracy advocates were aware that voter turnout rates for elections involving ballot propositions were significantly lower than for those on the election of candidates, routinely by between 30 and 50 percent.[40] Optimistic predictions that the existence of direct democracy would soon increase civic awareness remained unfulfilled. Other reformers, however, soon realized the potential advantages relating to a limited number of voters. Many of the more middle-class members of the reform movement had always been troubled by political conditions in the urban centers, where corrupt political machines enlisted the support of ignorant immigrants to create nightmarish political conditions. In contrast to Switzerland, where, as one reformer contended as early as 1894, the "dead wood of Society" stayed away from the polls, "the similar element in this country is importuned by friends and bought up by politicians at every presidential election."[41] The key was to ensure that only the more enlightened members of the voting public would participate. In 1900, Frank Parsons, an influential democracy proponent, expected direct democracy to lead to an "automatic disenfranchisement of the unfit — those of least intelligence and public spirit voluntarily refraining, as a rule, from voting upon the measures submitted." He added: "The ignorant voter and the bigoted partisan who constitute the curse of the ballot, sustaining corrupt machines and every political iniquity, are the very ones who ordinarily care least about a referendum vote."[42] While states in the South were enacting special laws to deprive blacks and poor whites of the right to vote, under direct democracy "each citizen should be his own disfranchiser." Not all voters would participate, but "the best people will exercise the right."[43]

Actual experience with initiative and referendum elections soon seemed to confirm these expectations. Alfred Cridge, a labor activist in Portland, Oregon, reported in 1911 that, during the election of 1910, "the disfranchisement automatically of the ignorant or indifferent voter was apparent. In the precincts of Portland where the foreign element predominates is found the heaviest percentage of skipped Initiative measures. Most of them got in a vote for their beer, anyhow, and if they quit at that nobody was harmed."[44] Judson King was also favorably impressed by the elections in Oregon in that year. An initiative adopted by Oregon voters in 1908 prohibited the solicitation of voters within 300 feet of a polling place. Consequently, "there were no excited crowds of party workers to pull, haul or bulldoze. The voters came quietly, marked their ballots, and went their ways in peace."[45] Such a quiet and dignified event was far removed from the wholesale corruption, the shameless electioneering, and the hustle and bustle that usually accompanied elections in the eyes of reformers. Once again, reformers demonstrated their own prejudices in condemning the vibrant forms of political participation that had been so characteristic of nineteenth-century American politics.

As the early grass-roots impetus of the movement waned somewhat after 1910, together with the attempt to win the support of moderate Republicans and Democrats, the reaction of some reformers to the "process of self-disenfranchisement" more and more revealed their own class prejudices. Only "those who have public spirit, knowledge, and convictions" should vote. If the rest excluded themselves, "this is desirable. Voluntary disfranchisement excludes only those confessedly not fit to vote."[46] Throughout the 1890s and 1900s, democracy advocates had stressed their goal to introduce majority rule to America in place of the rule by special interests and corrupt lawmakers. In 1914, by contrast, the tenor had changed: "Intelligent rule, or rule by intelligence, is preferable to majority rule, when the majority fails to exercise their privilege of voting on the proposition. Intelligence in government is preferable to mere numbers."[47] Confronted by the unwillingness of a sizable portion of voters to participate in elections on ballot propositions, an increasing number of reformers aimed to use this fact to alleviate the fears of conservatives about the prospect of mob rule. In addition, many of the middle-class leaders of the democracy movement, usually native-born and Protestant, shared in the general distrust of immigrants and the lower classes that was held by a substantial part of the American middle and upper classes. The leadership of the AFL also had little sympathy with new immigrants and unskilled workers. If direct democracy automatically induced those least fit to vote to stay away from the polls, it could be employed to break the power of bosses and machines that profited from mobilizing the lower classes. In revising their estimates regarding the political ability of the people, however, direct democracy reformers revealed a troubling gap between the theory and practice of direct legislation that was only to widen in the years to come.

The Recall

Prior to 1908, the controversies surrounding direct legislation had centered on the initiative and referendum. The growing diffusion of the recall, especially when applied to the judiciary, soon added another explosive issue. The recall was an American contribution to the arsenal of direct legislation, having first been introduced in the Los Angeles city charter of 1903.[48] The recall was promptly employed in 1904 when six members of the city council voted to award the city's printing contract to the *Los Angeles Times* despite the fact that its bid had been substantially higher than that of other papers. The typographical union in the city, a bitter enemy of the archconservative *Times*, launched a recall campaign to remove one of the six councilmen, J. P. Davenport, from office. Davenport had been targeted because his ward, composed of "artisans, clerks, and people of small means owning their homes," was the home of a large number of union members. Davenport was defeated by a comfortable margin.[49] Over the next few years, voters recalled the mayors in Los Angeles and Seattle, demonstrating that this device enjoyed considerable popularity.[50]

The recall soon spread to the state level. Oregon adopted it in 1908 and California in 1911. Even many Progressives agreed about the radical nature of the recall. One California reformer called it a "desperate remedy for a desperate malady. It ranks next to revolution, an ultimate right possessed by all peoples of all nations, but exercised only with greatest danger." He added that only "a self-restrained and not a volatile or effervescent people" could safely be entrusted with so much power.[51] As the number of signatures required for a recall petition was substantially higher than for an initiative or referendum, usually 20–25 percent compared to 5–10 percent, the proper safeguards were readily available to prevent misuse.

In itself, the recall seemed already a potentially dangerous innovation. Its extension to the bench transformed it into a key issue during the 1912 presidential campaign. Given the intense hostility of many reformers to the state and federal court decisions that seemed to present an almost impenetrable barrier to social and economic progress, the proposal attracted immediate support. The judiciary ranked second only to corrupt legislatures as the object of radical and reformist attack. Progressives of all stripes accused the courts of favoring trusts and corporations, failing to enforce the antitrust laws on the books, blocking progressive legislation, and stubbornly resisting change of any kind. Such infamous decisions as the overturning by the Supreme Court of the federal income tax law in 1895 only reinforced this conviction. Proposals to rein in the power of the judiciary, involving such tactics as depriving them of the right to judicial review, had gone nowhere. The recall now seemed to offer the opportunity to break the domination of corporate interests over the courts by meting out immediate punishment to those judges violating the wishes of the people.

Judges in America exercised powers that were of a distinctly political nature. As one reformer wrote in 1912: "Any important act of any state legislature regulating social or industrial conditions is at the present day often little better than a patent issued by the government in a new art—of doubtful value until it has passed the gauntlet of the courts."[52] In 1912 Charles Beard explained that American judges were "policy-determining officers," and he added: "Whatever the theory, the judges, as long as they continue to exercise this policy-determining function, will be drawn directly into politics; and it must be expected that the same pressure which is brought to bear on other officials to secure more popular control will be brought to bear upon them."[53] Since the judges in about two-thirds of the states were already elected by the people directly, the recall seemed an important and logical step in the expansion of popular sovereignty.[54]

No other element of direct democracy aroused as much strident opposition as the judicial recall. One observer wrote that "the judicial recall is the embodiment in legal form of the principle of mob law when the mob is composed of a majority of the citizens of a community." It struck at the "root of constitutional government" and would be exploited by powerful organizations who would "be in a much better position to initiate the recall than the average man."[55] The judiciary formed the last line of defense against radical groups catering to the whims of the people, bent on overturning the constitutional system in the United States and launching a social revolution. With the introduction of the initiative and referendum, what little protection legislative assemblies had been able to provide in the past seemed to quickly vanish. Only the judiciary remained as the bulwark of law and order in the country, as a staunch defender of industrial interests, as a brake on the tendency of the state to interfere with legitimate business pursuits, and as a guardian of the constitutional order. Extend the principle of the recall—dangerous as it was to the independence of any officeholder—to the judiciary, warned the conservatives, and the United States would be bereft of the final protection of individual liberty and freedom cultivated by the Founding Fathers and would therefore plunge into a social cataclysm.

The issue of the judicial recall soon became a potent factor in the growing factionalism that threatened to tear the Republican Party asunder. The Arizona constitutional convention of 1910, controlled by progressive Democrats and labor leaders, had drafted a charter that included the initiative, referendum, and recall of all elective officers, including judges.[56] The congressional debates concerning the admission of Arizona and New Mexico to the union in 1911 demonstrated the unwillingness of conservative Republicans to condone direct legislation. For observers concerned about the rising diffusion of direct democracy, the Arizona constitutional convention had drafted a "socialistic" document, one that attempted to establish a "democracy" in clear violation of the federal Constitution.[57] Because the admission of both territories depended on Congress passing an enabling act, the topic of direct democracy, its constitutionality, and the judicial recall became topics of a national debate.[58]

True to his announcements during the Arizona convention, President Taft vetoed the enabling act passed by Congress in August 1911. He argued that "no honest, clear-headed man, however great a lover of popular government, can deny that the unbridled expression of the majority of a community converted hastily into law or action would sometimes make a government tyrannical and cruel."[59] In contrast to the legislative and executive branches of government, "the judicial branch of the Government is not representative of a majority of the people." The principles of majority rule and popular sovereignty could thus not be applied to a bench charged with upholding the basic rules of American constitutionalism.[60] Other party leaders, such as Elihu Root, who asserted that "popular will cannot execute itself directly except through a mob," supported Taft's position.[61]

Taft's veto proved highly unpopular among the Republican insurgents and widened the fissures in the party. Even those who remained skeptical of the value of the judicial recall, such as Roosevelt, believed that "it is the negation of popular government to deny the right to establish for themselves what their judicial system shall be."[62] Arizona subsequently dropped the provision from its constitution, was admitted to the union, and then immediately reinstated the judicial recall in the following year. Taft's veto had not only failed to force Arizona to give up the recall; he had transformed the judicial recall into a hotly contested national issue. Debates about the role of the judiciary served to focus on a discrete issue the divergent conceptions of American constitutionalism, representative government, and democracy, which were well-familiar after a decade of contentious debate about direct democracy in general. Especially among western Republicans, anger about Taft's refusal to accept the will of the people of Arizona, as expressed in their constitution, ran deep. For conservative Republicans, by contrast, the episode had highlighted the dangerous radicalism of the West and had strengthened their conviction that no compromises with the advocates of direct democracy were possible. Amidst the widening fissures in the party, the topic of direct democracy acted as another wedge.

Roosevelt's defense of the actions of the Arizona constitutional convention unfolded amid the bid for the Republican presidential nomination that transformed him into an outspoken supporter of the initiative and referendum. He never warmed to the idea of the judicial recall, however, instead offering the novel suggestion that the people themselves should be granted the power to review judicial decisions. He shared in the general dissatisfaction of Progressives with the conservative decisions of the state and federal supreme courts. He argued that these courts should not possess the final authority to decide on the constitutionality of statutes that were of a clearly political character. "It is the people, and not the judges, who are entitled to say what their constitution means, for the constitution is theirs, it belongs to them and to their servants in office — any other theory is incompatible with the foundation principles of our government." On policy issues, such as those involving problems of taxation, social welfare, or the regulation of trusts, a popular vote should ultimately decide whether new laws were valid or not.[63]

But Roosevelt never developed a clear outline of his proposal, leading one reformist journal to remark that "Mr. Roosevelt does not deal in details."[64] His proposal failed to serve as a bridge between Republican insurgents and moderates. Ironically, the proponents of the judicial recall and the proponents of the popular review of judicial decisions often spent as much time criticizing each other as they did uniting their efforts against the conservative opponents.[65] Most of Roosevelt's old allies found the proposal for a popular review of judicial decisions as distasteful and subversive as they did the judicial recall. In the eyes of conservatives, the recall of judicial decisions seemed to be completely at odds with American political and constitutional traditions. Roosevelt's idea was sharply attacked by most jurists in the country and was interpreted by Taft supporters as yet another indication that the ex-president had moved beyond the confines of acceptable political behavior. The sheer notion of entrusting decisions concerning the constitutionality of new laws to popular majorities bordered on heresy; it stood in opposition to every tradition of American constitutional thought and would lead to the same consequences as the recall. Instead of offering a compromise between the warring factions in the GOP, Roosevelt's scheme only divided direct democracy advocates.[66]

In the end, the judicial recall was adopted by only a few states, and the controversies during the years 1910–12 actually hampered the further spread of the device. Of the six states that adopted the recall up until 1912 — Oregon, California, Arizona, Colorado, Nevada, and Washington state — all but the last included the judiciary. Of the six states that introduced the recall between 1912 and 1940, however — Michigan, Kansas, Louisiana, North Dakota, Wisconsin, and Idaho — only North Dakota and Wisconsin included the judiciary. To ensure the further progress of direct legislation, more and more reformers dropped the demand for the judicial recall after realizing that it lacked the political acceptance of the initiative and referendum. Even in the states that had adopted the device, the provision was rarely employed, and judicial autonomy remained virtually unchallenged by the instruments of direct democracy. Roosevelt's proposal for the popular review of judicial decisions left even less of an institutional legacy.[67] For all their willingness to tamper with political institutions, most Americans drew a line when it came to innovations that seemed to eliminate such traditions as the strict separation of the branches of government.

With the rapid decline of the Progressive movement after 1912 and the slowing pace of the diffusion of direct democracy, the debates about the relationship between the new reforms and the American constitutional tradition came to a sudden halt. From the perspective of the 1920s, it was already difficult to see what all the commotion had been about. When one observer warned in 1925 that "the strong trend is away from the indirect to the direct rule of the people; that is, from the republic formed by the Constitution to the very democracy it sought to make impossible," he tried to rekindle a debate whose time was past.[68] The actual experiences with the initiative and referendum illustrated that the widespread fears about their revolutionary impact had been wildly exaggerated. Even with direct democracy installed in almost half of the American states, the system of checks and balances continued to function and the Constitution was not about to be overthrown.

Yet, the contentious history of direct democracy between 1890 and 1920 captured American nationalism and constitutionalism at a moment of profound unease. For more than a century Americans had prided themselves on their form of government. America was a beacon of progress and hope in a world still beset by reactionary forces. The United States had solved the mystery that had confounded political thinkers for so long: how to construct a republican government that rested on the will of the people and furthermore protected property and minority interests. As a result, the American political system, so Americans were convinced, was the envy of the world, a model to be appropriated by other countries, and the foundation for the astounding material progress of the nation.

Direct democracy advocates, however, painted a different picture of the country. Representative government had proven itself to be a failure, popular sovereignty was a sham, special interests ruled the country with the help of corrupt legislatures, and growing inequalities threatened to tear the social fabric apart. Far from serving as a model for other countries, America was in danger of falling behind in the general development of democracy, with a small country like Switzerland boasting of a more democratic form of government. In proffering a set of fundamental political innovations, direct democracy advocates initiated a discussion about the very core of the American constitutional and political order, and, by extension, about the definition of the

American nation itself. In the end, direct democracy did not live up to the expectations of either its opponents or its supporters. It was integrated into the political structures of many American states, with only a moderate effect on policy outcomes. Most importantly, the demise of the direct democracy movement signaled the end of a long democratic tradition in American constitutional thought. Together with the decline of voter turnout rates and the participatory style that had marked the nineteenth-century American political culture, the growing anachronism of terms such as popular sovereignty and "the people" was indicative of larger changes in the ways in which Americans conceptualized the polity.

4

THE KEYSTONE IN THE ARCH

OF POPULAR GOVERNMENT

Direct Democracy in the American West, 1898–1912

In an important recent book, the sociologist Elizabeth Clemens has offered a powerful interpretation of the ways in which the rise of single-issue pressure groups transformed American politics between 1890 and 1920. Made possible by the weakening of the strong party organizations of the nineteenth century, these pressure groups, ranging from well-known groups such as the Anti-Saloon League to obscure citizen's groups at the local level, developed new "organizational repertoires" to influence public policy. They modernized and professionalized their internal organizations, lobbied before legislative bodies, queried politicians about their positions on various issues, cultivated contacts with the press, fashioned ties with state agencies and regulatory commissions, and experimented with new ways to link voters and policy output. In doing so, they radically altered the rules of political behavior and conflict in America, contributing "to the emergence, diffusion, and institutionalization of alternative models of mobilization and representation." In line with the growing importance of managerial hierarchies in business that has been vividly portrayed in the "organizational synthesis" offered by business historians, the growing importance of interest group politics marked one of the most consequential developments of the Progressive Era.[1]

It would seem that the genesis and the political strategies of the direct democracy movement fit in well with the outlines of the model developed by Clemens. Indeed, the "People's Lobby" mentioned in the title of her book was a lobbying group before the California legislature and was financed by the Los Angeles physician and reformer John Randolph Haynes, the main advocate for direct democracy in the Golden State. The state Direct Legislation Leagues were certainly successful. Between 1898, when South Dakota became the first state to acquire direct legislation, and 1918, about twenty American states adopted the reforms. A closer analysis, however, reveals that the organizations created by advocates of the initiative and referendum hardly resembled the professionalized and well-managed interest groups in Clemens's account. Direct Legislation Leagues were small and perennially cash-starved organizations, usually led by a small group of activists or even a single individual, active mostly during the brief sessions of the state legislatures, with no paid staff or means to conduct elaborate publicity campaigns, without formalized ties with legislatures or state agencies, and without much leverage over lawmakers. In this, they were not atypical. Many reform associations during the Progressive Era worked in a similar fashion. That does not mean that direct democracy reformers pursued a fringe agenda or were removed from the mainstream of antimonopoly sentiments. On the contrary, the substantial success that the movement enjoyed, despite its limited organizational resources, can only be explained by its broad appeal within the antimonopoly tradition.

The associations described by Clemens were largely mass-membership organizations active across a range of issues. By contrast, the leagues were small single-issue interest groups with usually no more than a handful of members. Nationwide, the direct democracy movement, if one can apply that label, at no time consisted of more than several hundred widely scattered activists, mostly middle-class reformers. The few nationally known leaders resided mostly in the Northeast, but a far greater number of activists was working in the western states where direct democracy advanced the most. While they generated a large amount of publicity for the initiative and referendum, by themselves they were never able to generate sufficient leverage to force lawmakers into adopting direct legislation. But in the American West, they were able to forge alliances with the mass organizations such as labor unions, farmer groups, and the prohibitionists who have been analyzed by Clemens. For these organizations, direct democracy largely constituted a means to an end, a way to submit their political agendas directly to the people. With their membership base, financial resources, publicity outlets, and ties to lawmakers and political parties, they could bring enough pressure to bear on state legislatures to make possible the rapid spread of the initiative and referendum. By focusing the efforts and the clout of labor unions, farmers' organizations, and middle-class progressive reformers on a discrete proposal, direct democracy advocates were able to create an illusion of strength that proved remarkably effective in their dealings with state legislatures and politicians.

The broad array of interest groups that aligned behind the demand for the initiative and referendum was one factor in the success of the reform movement. Even a cursory look at the geographical distribution of direct democracy, however, reveals the sharply confined diffusion of the reforms. The states that adopted the reforms were overwhelmingly concentrated in the American West; in the East, only Maine, Michigan, Ohio, and Massachusetts followed this path, while only Arkansas, Mississippi, and Oklahoma did the same in the South.[2] Although it was not true, as California reformer Haynes argued in 1916, that "the growth of direct government has moved along the lines of geographical continuity," the West as a region offered structural opportunities for reform absent in other areas.[3] How are we to explain this situation?

The previous chapter has outlined that much of the original impetus for direct democracy can be explained by the strength and endurance of a particular strain of antimonopoly ideology that looked toward the initiative and referendum as the tools to free the political process from the dominance of corporations and bosses. This strain of antimonopoly sentiment carried over into western Progressivism, which was marked by a much greater hostility to corporations and trusts and by a greater emphasis on expanding democracy than its eastern counterpart. In addition, western Progressives confronted a political environment that offered them much greater opportunities to implement their program. Political parties in the western United States were relatively weak, lacked the strong organizations characteristic of parties in the East and South, could not control the political agenda, and were forced to ratify a set of reforms aimed at further crippling their power. In the East, direct democracy advocates faced much more resilient party organizations and were only victorious in special circumstances, most notably in connection with the drafting of new state constitutions. In the South, finally, the conundrum of race relations and white efforts to disenfranchise the black population doomed the reformers from the start. The intersection of the ideology and rhetorical strategies of the reformers with a political opportunity structure in the West, combined with the relations between small direct democracy groups and larger interest groups, shaped the pattern of adoption of the initiative and referendum across the United States.

Structural Opportunities

In the nineteenth century, America had produced the first democratic mass political parties. Often based on fierce ethnic and religious loyalties, the parties dominated the American polity, resulting in a state of "courts and parties," according to political scientist Skowronek, in which these two institutions determined public policies and shaped the political culture.[4] One consequence of this development was the evolution of tight party organizations and machines that controlled the political agenda. Even if the power of the parties began to wane around the turn of the century, which manifested, for instance, in a decline in voter turnout, they remained the most important political institutions in the country.[5] The American West, however, remained an exception to this pattern. Using a variety of indicators, several authors have pointed to the different nature of politics in the region. Voter turnout was lower, more voters supported third parties or split their tickets, fluctuations in party support were higher, and voting behavior was less based on the pervasive ethnic loyalties that prevailed in the East. Parties were weaker, less well-organized and institutionalized, and less able to aggregate voters.[6]

This situation had powerful ramifications for the diffusion of political reforms in the United States. Many reformers in the West opted to act outside of party channels and advocated a variety of measures to further weaken their power. The most powerful tool was the direct primary, first adopted in Wisconsin in 1903, and which had swept the American West by 1910. By depriving the parties of the power to control the nomination of candidates, the single most important source of their authority, the direct primary resulted in important transformations of the political system. In the future, candidates would appeal directly to the electorate, would owe no loyalty to nominating conventions and party leaders, and often campaigned independently of party organizations. The stunning ease with which the Republican insurgents in California took over the GOP in 1910 after the introduction of the direct primary a year earlier provided a vivid testimony to the repercussions of the new measure. In a political culture where parties often appeared as the agents of eastern interests, the anti-party rhetoric of the progressives served as a formidable weapon.[7] The situation was quite similar on the local level where reformers across the West experimented with such innovations as the commission form of government, nonpartisan ballots, and city-wide (as opposed to ward-based) elections in which the city council could fight the power of local party machines. Although these reforms found many supporters in other parts of the country as well, they were most widely implemented in the West.[8]

These factors combined to produce a political system much more open to political outsiders than in other parts of the country. By organizing effective and bipartisan reform associations, direct democracy advocates were able to bypass the established parties. Confronted with an electorate already highly suspicious of the venality of parties and lawmakers, many western politicians were unable to strongly challenge direct democracy. Interest groups looked for alternate ways to inject their demands into the political arena and eagerly welcomed the new opportunities presented by the initiative. The structural features of the political system in the western states — weak parties, strong interest groups, political reforms further crippling party organizations, an electorate imbued with an anti-party spirit, and a more open political agenda — thus conferred opportunities for concerted political action on the direct democracy movement. These opportunities go a long way in explaining the movement's greater success in the western United States.

Organizational Resources and Strategies

Despite the greater opportunities for reform in the American West, the sweeping success of direct democracy remains impressive considering the limited resources at the disposal of reformers. As outlined earlier, the national associations advocating direct legislation were never in a position to render any significant assistance to the state campaigns, beyond some help in drafting constitutional amendments and supplying promotional literature. The state Direct Legislation Leagues themselves were seldom in a better situation. They might boast of the support of labor and farm organizations and carry the names of prominent politicians on their letterhead; for the most part, however, they were cash-starved entities, dependent on the tireless work of a few select individuals, without strong links to other reform organizations, and with limited access to the electorate and limited means to inform the public about their program. It most states one individual was largely responsible for keeping the movement alive. William U'Ren in Oregon, John R. Haynes in California, and Herbert Bigelow in Ohio were among the most prominent men who often used their personal assets to finance the work. In contending with parties and politicians profoundly skeptical of their agenda, they orchestrated campaigns of smoke and mirrors suggesting that the reform movement was much stronger than it really was.

Some reformers in Oklahoma in 1915 tried to found an association in order to change the defective direct legislation provisions in the state constitution; this attempt illustrates some of the organizational obstacles surrounding the formation of reform associations. In the summer and fall of that year, the Oklahoma attorney J. W. Mansell contacted U.S. senator Robert Owen and Judson King, the leading figures in the National Popular Government League. Mansell's goal was to form a new association called the Initiative and Referendum League of Oklahoma. He sent a highly detailed organizational plan to Owen that envisioned organizations at the state, county, and local levels.[9] In response, King contacted Campbell Russell, the president of the People's Power League of Oklahoma, to ascertain whether that organization was still functioning. King preferred to "play the game with the men I know," but Russell had retired from politics and had returned to farming. He cautioned King: "The only way to keep an organization alive (according to my experience) is for some untiring worker (at his own expense) to stay on the job all the time."[10] King proceeded to write to Mansell, warning him against his overly ambitious plans: "Too much organization is cumbrous. Men do things, and not programs." He added in another letter: "My suggestion to all men proposing such a state organization is that they make it a compact, central organization, holding membership throughout the state direct to the central organization, and with no attempt to organize 'locals.' I have seen a score of such proposals, which looked very fine on paper, but which remained there." Finally, King cautioned: "When it comes to getting money, you will have to depend again on a few men for the main part."[11] Mansell's proposal apparently never got off the ground. This example underlines the difficulties encountered by reformers in creating and sustaining effective organizations. Ultimately, whether a diffuse interest in direct democracy was transformed into a potent campaign rested on the efforts of one or a handful of men in each state. Here, they employed a variety of strategies and devices.

One of the most effective weapons wielded by reformers was the questioning of political candidates. As early as 1894, just after the formation of the first Direct Legislation League in New Jersey, the leaders there vowed to query candidates for the New Jersey legislature regarding to their position on the initiative and referendum and to advise them to vote accordingly.[12] In 1899, Davis Inglis, president of the Michigan State Direct Legislation League, outlined a similar strategy. In contrast to other reformers who focused on holding public meetings and writing to newspapers, he proposed concentrating the attention on lobbying the state legislature. He wrote: "Our plan is now this. We intend to make a map of the State, locating all legislators who failed to vote for us. We will not attempt districts in which the Representatives or Senator were elected by large majorities, but shall choose districts in which the election was close, and at the next (intermediate) election, hold mass meetings, send speakers and literature, etc., to down any present legislator who attempts to run for any office. . . . We are feared already; we propose to be more feared."[13] Sometimes, as was the case in Oregon and California, reformers could even finance the work of a lobbyist at the state capitol. In Oregon, U'Ren functioned as the legislative agent of the Knights of Labor, the Grange, and the Oregon Farmers' Alliance, and he focused his attention on direct legislation.[14]

Whether this strategy ever warranted the optimism of some reformers remains open to debate. They were always quick to attribute shifts in political sentiment to the growing importance of direct democracy in shaping the voting behavior of many voters. It seems doubtful that this issue ever reached that importance. It only formed part of a broader progressive agenda, but hardly had enough salience to sway an entire election. And even though many activists wielded an anti-party rhetoric that accused them of being the nefarious instruments of greedy corporations, they ultimately needed them to implement their agenda. The small and issue-driven direct democracy associations needed to align themselves with mass-membership associations in order to achieve their goals. Political parties formed the most logical first choice. Yet reformers quickly realized the limited enthusiasm of most party politicians for devices that threatened to render them superfluous.

Throughout the 1890s, reformers continued to introduce bills and constitutional amendments in various state legislatures only to see them die in committee or be voted down in the legislatures. In 1897, it was reported that "every State legislature west of the Mississippi, save perhaps Arkansas and Louisiana, had a Direct Legislation measure before it, and so did Wisconsin, Michigan, Indiana, New Jersey, Massachusetts, and some other states." None of the measures met with success, but "Direct Legislation is getting known by being beaten, and its advocates are urged to introduce more and more laws and amendments and push to a vote."[15] The introduction of legislative measures, even if it aroused the fervent opposition of many powerful politicians, was one of the easiest ways to center public attention on an issue that was still largely unknown to many voters. Even so, the leagues were never able to wage drawn-out campaigns. Without a permanent, paid staff, activities peaked during the short legislative sessions when there was an actual chance of getting a bill passed. Given the biannual schedule of most state legislatures, agitation for direct democracy often lay dormant for many months.[16]

The Constituencies of the Reform Movement

Besides the opportunity structure present in the Western states, the most important factor in the success of reformers was their ability to enlist the help of a wide variety of interest groups and constituencies. Maybe no other progressive reform assembled such a diverse political coalition behind it, a feat made possible by the fact that the initiative and referendum could be used to advance a multitude of political agendas. One of the most important groups of middle-class reformers supporting direct democracy in America were the single taxers. It is difficult today to recapture the prominence of an economic theory, first developed by Henry George in the 1870s and 80s, that has so completely disappeared. But in the late nineteenth and early twentieth centuries, the single tax—the argument that the monopoly on land was the single most important source of inequality and poverty, and that a tax system based solely on taxes on land values would break up that monopoly—had a substantial following in America, both among the middle class and organized labor. In five states in which middle-class reformers were particularly important for the campaign for the initiative and referendum — Oregon, Michigan, Missouri, Ohio, and Colorado — single taxers led the movement.[17] Many of them were professionals; they were lawyers, physicians, and journalists who had expertise in getting their views before the public, who were respected in their communities, who often had ties to the labor movement, and who had their own single tax publications that could also be used to advance direct legislation. Their interest in the initiative was purely instrumental as a means of bypassing legislatures and politicians and directly placing their agenda before the electorate. But in adopting the cause of direct democracy, single taxers proved to be a uniquely persistent and unwavering reform group.

Their work received a significant boost from the monetary resources provided by the Fels Fund. In 1909, the wealthy British soap manufacturer Joseph Fels established the Fund: $25,000 per year over a period of five years, for the promotion of the single tax cause in the United States. A committee of five, including Lincoln Steffens, Frederick Howe, the Washington-based lawyer Jackson Ralston, and the Cincinnati attorney Daniel Kiefer directed the activities of the Fund. Over the next few years, the Fund contributed to direct democracy campaigns in a number of states, including Colorado, Ohio, New Mexico, and Arizona.[18]

Next to single taxers and other middle-class progressive reformers, organized labor formed the single most important constituency of the direct democracy movement. It has already been demonstrated that the support of the AFL, and of Samuel Gompers in particular, were key catalysts of the acceptance of the reforms in America in the early 1890s. For almost three decades, the AFL never wavered in its support of direct legislation, as it remained a part of its official platform. More important for the shape of the campaigns in the states, however, were the activities of State Federations of Labor and local union bodies. In virtually every state where the reforms were introduced, these associations were part of the state Direct Legislation Leagues, were represented among their officers, and actively campaigned on this issue. The labor organizations urged workers to distribute information material, sometimes donated money, lobbied before legislative assemblies, questioned candidates, and urged their members to vote accordingly. According to one scholar, labor's role was either the determining factor in the success of direct legislation overall, or was at least highly responsible for its success in a number of states: Arizona, Montana, Massachusetts, Washington, Maine, and Ohio. Only in the largely agricultural states of Nebraska, North Dakota, and South Dakota did labor unions play a merely marginal role.[19] Like no other interest group, labor supplied the movement with a membership base that could impress lawmakers and an organizational infrastructure that would complement the publicity campaigns waged in newspapers and magazines.

The leaders of the reform organizations in the various states were aware that the support they received from organized labor could emerge as a liability if it scared off more moderate progressives who might have little sympathy for the goals of the AFL. Consequently, reformers often tried to limit the visibility of labor among the officials of reform associations. Writing in the *Referendum News* in 1906, George Shibley urged that Direct Legislation Leagues should be led by a "business or professional man" because "in this way it can be clearly shown that the campaign is for the sovereignty of the entire people. Furthermore, the business and professional people will follow such leadership. This is human and should be recognized." A few months later, he added that middle-class supporters of direct democracy were often "too class-conscious," too concerned about only working with respectable organizations and individuals, "whereas the laboring man, being educated to the value of the initiative and referendum, will work with whoever takes it up."[20] By carefully balancing the representation of various groups among the leadership rosters of reform associations, the nonpartisan and respectable nature of the reform movement could be maintained.

The prohibition movement formed another key ally of direct democracy advocates. The alcohol issue was one of the politically most divisive issues of the Progressive Era, one reason why the support given by the prohibitionists to the initiative and referendum was kept rather quiet by many reformers. In such states as California, Washington, Ohio, and Michigan, the two sides cooperated closely. Prohibitionists had long supported referenda as a means to fight the liquor interests. The principle of local option had been one of their most effective weapons. As early as the 1880s, they embraced the principle of statewide prohibition referenda and lobbied, with some success, the state legislatures to place them before the electorate. After 1900, this strategy became even more important. Many southern states went dry after the popular ratification of statutes first passed by state legislatures. In other regions of the country, where lawmakers were less accommodating, prohibitionists hoped to secure the initiative as a way to directly place their agenda before the electorate.[21] The principles of the initiative and referendum fit in perfectly with the ideology and the strategies of the American prohibition movement.[22] Even though referenda could also be used against the dry forces, as happened with increasing frequency in Ohio after 1912 when previously dry counties voted to become wet again, most prohibitionists firmly regarded direct legislation as an important asset to their cause.

For direct democracy reformers, the cooperation of the prohibition movement, even if it sometimes had to be kept secret, offered one crucial advantage: the grass-roots organization of the drys enabled them to distribute information to and mobilize large numbers of voters. The Anti-Saloon League was closely associated with Protestant churches all across the country. Prohibitionists were able to channel information regarding the initiative and referendum through a network of hundreds of churches into communities all across a state. Pastors could explain the importance of the issue to their congregations; they could raise much-needed funds, and urge voters to support candidates willing to vote for direct legislation. Many of the leaders of the movement, including Haynes in California, were themselves supporters of prohibition. Quite often the leadership of state Direct Legislation Leagues consisted of individuals with a Protestant, middle-class background similar in outlook to the leaders of the prohibition crusade. That made cooperation easy and worthwhile for both sides. Overall, of the twenty-two states that adopted some form of direct legislation up until 1920, sixteen passed prohibition laws and ten enacted women's suffrage via the referendum. These three reform movements — prohibition, women's suffrage, and direct legislation — were closely linked.[23] But in order to preserve the fragile reform coalition, the actual involvement of prohibitionists and suffragists was usually understated.

In addition to these constituencies, other groups supported direct democracy as well. Farm groups, in particular state Granges across the country, felt confident that the new devices offered a weapon in the fight against the trusts and monopolies oppressing the farmers. Civic reform groups looked toward direct democracy as a means to get rid of bosses and machines and purify American politics. The shape of the coalition assembled behind the reforms varied from state to state, depending on such factors as the party system, the level of party competition, the structure of the state economy, the ethnic makeup of the population, the level of urbanization, and the skill of the reformers. But in each state that adopted direct democracy in this period, the reform movement featured a broad and diverse coalition of constituencies and interest groups.[24]

Successful State Campaigns in the West

Although the western states shared the experience of weak party organizations, stronger interest groups, and successful nonpartisan reformers, the equally significant differences between them accounted for varied roads to success for direct democracy advocates. Sometimes, as in Oregon, factionalism in the dominant party allowed reformers to implement their program. At other times, as in California, reformers virtually took over a political party. In South Dakota, a temporary alliance between minority parties dislodged the dominant GOP from power, if only briefly, and created a political opening. Or, as in Washington State, the pressure from a well-organized reform movement was sufficient to make the legislature bend. While it remains difficult to arrive at a clear typology of the trajectories of the reform movement, the subsequent analysis of selected state campaigns will make clear the interplay between the opportunity structure in place in the western states and the strategies selected by reformers.

South Dakota was the first state to pass the constitutional amendments providing for the initiative and referendum. Success here was made possible by the brief rise of a People's Party capable of temporarily removing the GOP from power. The agitation for the initiative and referendum had begun as early as 1892, when a Referendum and Initiative League was formed. Henry L. Loucks, a prominent leader of the Dakota Farmers' Alliance and of the People's Party, was one of the pivotal proponents for reform in the state. In a pattern that would become familiar in other states as well, a broad-based reform coalition was assembled that included Populists, labor unions, the Knights of Labor, prohibitionists, single taxers, women suffragists, and some reform Republicans and Democrats. The 1897 session of the South Dakota legislature was controlled by an alliance between Populists and Democrats. As part of the bargain, the Democrats had vowed to support the initiative and referendum. The legislature passed the amendments, which were then ratified by the voters, by a margin of two to one, in 1898. But it was the state of Oregon, where direct democracy was adopted in 1902, that served as the inspiration for the march to success of direct democracy all across the West.[25]

The key figure in the adoption of direct democracy in Oregon was the lawyer and reformer William S. U'Ren. Born in Wisconsin in 1859, he had a checkered career. After spending the 1880s in Colorado practicing law and editing a newspaper, he moved to Oregon around 1890. Here he soon became an important activist in the Populist movement of the state, acting as the secretary of the state executive committee of the People's Party. Legend has it that around 1891 John W. Sullivan's book on direct democracy was read by a local suballiance of the Farmers' Alliance in Clackamas county, with U'Ren present. From that day on, his energies were devoted to achieving direct democracy in the state. He soon realized that the Populists alone would never have enough political clout to secure the passage of the needed constitutional amendments. Never a completely committed Populist, U'Ren included the two major parties in his lobbying efforts, advocated fusion politics to accomplish his goals, and became a master at the sort of legislative horse-trading and cajoling essential to political success.[26]

To the dismay of some of his old Populist allies, U'Ren began to cooperate with some Republicans after he was elected to the Oregon House on the Populist ticket in 1896. Here he functioned as one of the instigators of the infamous "hold-up session" of 1897, when an alliance between the Populists and the silver wing of the GOP, under the leadership of Jonathan Bourne, prevented the election of a gold Republican as U.S. senator. In exchange for his help, U'Ren secured GOP support for the constitutional amendments implementing direct legislation. Direct democracy was finally submitted to the voters in 1902. An overwhelming majority approved it.[27] U'Ren pioneered the campaign methods that would be copied in other states. Usually, the state organizations were run by a small nucleus of leaders, very often by one man alone. They functioned as "letterhead" organizations, with the names of influential politicians and other individuals prominently displayed in the literature of the league even though these people were not involved in the management of the association. Many reformers realized that in order to be successful politically, pragmatic strategies had to be adopted. As one journal put it in 1909: "This is politics; so pull all the political strings in favor of the Initiative and Referendum legislation. Induce Grange and Federation constituents to write to and interview their legislators."[28] In doing their work, the leagues usually had to rely on very limited funds. According to U'Ren, the Oregon league was able to spend only $1,700 between 1898 and 1902 on popularizing the cause of direct democracy.[29] The work of the state Direct Legislation Leagues provided an example of how small, cash-starved associations with few members and run by amateurs could, under the structural conditions of the West, create a broad reform coalition and galvanize enough public support for a reform agenda that most party politicians had plenty of reason to fear.

For his willingness to work with all parties in the interest of furthering his cause, U'Ren, much like Pomeroy and Shibley, sought to accomplish a definite economic and social program. He was an ardent supporter of Henry George's single tax idea. When interviewed by Lincoln Steffens in 1908, U'Ren clearly regarded direct democracy as a device to facilitate the introduction of the single tax, and that the initiative could be used "as a tool, remember; as a means to an end; as a first political step toward changing our economic conditions."[30] Around 1910, U'Ren reflected on his involvement with direct legislation: "I knew I wanted the single tax, and that was about all I did know. . . . I learned what the initiative and referendum is, and then I saw the way to single tax. So I quit talking single tax, not because I was any the less in favor of it, but because I saw that the first job was to get the initiative and referendum, so that the people, independently of the legislature, may get what they want rather than what the legislature will let them have. . . . All the work we have done for direct legislation has been done with the single tax in view, but we have not talked single tax because that was not the question before the house."[31]

With the victory in Oregon, U'Ren became one of the most powerful politicians in the state. A Portland newspaper, the *Oregonian*, remarked in 1906: "In Oregon the state government is divided into four departments — the executive, judicial, legislative and Mr. U'Ren — and it is still an open question which exerts the most power."[32] With the help of the initiative and the People's Power League, U'Ren succeeded in introducing to the state the direct primary, the recall, the direct election of U.S. senators, a corrupt practices act, and a series of other reform measures. Taken together, they became known as the "Oregon Plan," an example of reform that enjoyed great appeal among reformers across the entire United States.[33] Many commentators were favorably impressed with Oregon voters' interest in ballot propositions, their civic awareness, and their moderate voting record. The dire warnings that direct legislation would lead to mob rule had not been borne out by the Oregon experience.[34]

By 1908, U'Ren felt confident that direct democracy had become an established part of the political system in Oregon and that the time was ripe to push for the single tax and other measures. Between 1908 and 1914, some kind of single tax proposal was on the ballot at every Oregon general election. With the exception of 1910, when the voters narrowly approved a referendum that allowed home rule in taxation, these proposals were voted down every time, and with increasing majorities. The voters remained unpersuaded by U'Ren's fervent declarations of the positive effects of the single tax. As in California during the same period, single taxers soon had to realize that, contrary to their hopes, direct legislation did not prepare the ground for their cause. They could bypass obstinate legislatures but the voters proved equally as resistant to the lure of the single tax.[35] In 1914, U'Ren's political role came to an end when he finished a distant third in the gubernatorial election (a bid for the U.S. Senate had been unsuccessful in 1908). But for more than ten years, U'Ren acted as one of the most powerful forces in Oregon politics and played a pivotal role in the rise of direct democracy in America.[36]

Around the same time that direct legislation was adopted in Oregon, the reform movement received a further significant boost from the association between the initiative and referendum and the commission form of government. In reaction to the destruction of Galveston, Texas, by a devastating hurricane in 1901, reformers in the city implemented a plan that radically restructured municipal government. Instead of a city council and a mayor, Galveston was now to be governed by a small number of city commissioners in charge of the various city departments. This commission form of government epitomized many of the most important aspects of Progressive municipal reform: the desire to eliminate the power of bosses and machines, the growing importance of professional experts in city service, the centralization of political authority, the removal of party labels from local elections, and the replacement of a political culture based on city wards by city-wide elections. Many historians have characterized the commission government as evidence of the antidemocratic tendencies of many middle- and upper-class reformers, as symptomatic of their goal to break the power of labor and immigrant voters in city politics by replacing them with a government of experts catering to the interests of business concerns.[37]

The centralization of political power occasioned by the introduction of the commission government, however, was often accompanied by the initiative and referendum. The worries of many workers and other reformers that the reform would eliminate popular participation in city politics forced many proponents of commission government to include direct legislation in the new city charters "to overcome the objection that the new form of city government was undemocratic." Only in this fashion could reformers ensure the ratification of the charters by the voters. "While the initiative, referendum, and recall are not necessary parts of nor accompaniments to the commission form of municipal government, a happy association of this democratic trinity and the commission idea has been formed," wrote one observer in 1912.[38] By 1920, about 500 cities were governed in that way. Even though the instruments of direct legislation contained in the majority of the cities that switched to a commission government were not extensively employed, the very need to counterbalance the centralization of political power with the extension of popular lawmaking powers illustrates the conflicting tendencies of Progressive reform.[39]

With the example of Oregon in hand and with the successful adoption of direct democracy in a growing number of municipalities around the nation, the initiative and referendum swept the West in the decade after 1902. By 1912, Arizona, California, Colorado, Idaho, Missouri, Montana, Nebraska, Nevada, and Washington had all introduced the reforms. North Dakota followed in 1914. The territories of Arizona and New Mexico had for some time prior to 1910 attempted to gain admission to the Union, with little success. In 1910, finally, voters in both territories elected constitutional conventions. But despite their similar political situation, the two territories differed strikingly in their economic and social structures and in their politics. New Mexico was largely agricultural in economic orientation, with a large Hispanic population, and was politically under the control of conservative Republicans. The state constitutional convention was controlled by the GOP and drafted a fairly conservative document that only included a weak form of the referendum.[40] Due to the importance of the mining industry in the territory, Arizona had an active labor movement that strongly supported the call for the initiative and referendum. The Democratic Party in the territory was dominated by Progressives, shared close ties with organized labor, and organized the campaign for the election of convention delegates in 1910 around the theme of direct legislation. The coalition between Democrats and labor controlled the deliberations of the convention and ensured that the new charter included the initiative, referendum, and recall.[41]

In states such as Oregon, Arizona, and California, nonpartisan reformers were able to find allies in the two major parties that helped them implement their agenda. The direct democracy movement in Washington State was unusual insofar as the labor unions and farmer organizations that constituted the backbone of the movement had organized as a remarkably cohesive pressure group presenting the political establishment in the state with a specific agenda. They received only limited support from middle-class reformers and found few allies inside the parties. Representatives of labor and farmer interests dominated the leadership of the Washington State Direct Legislation League.[42] After some initial efforts to persuade the state legislature to pass a constitutional amendment had failed after 1907, the state Federation of Labor, the state Grange, and the Farmer's Union of Washington State formed a Joint Legislative Committee to bring more pressure to bear on lawmakers and parties in Washington. Although U'Ren had acted as lobbyist for a similar farmer-labor organization before the Oregon legislature in the late 1890s, such a level of formal and sustained cooperation was unusual.[43] After a brief period of intense agitation, the legislature passed the amendments in 1912, and they were subsequently ratified by the voters in an election where only about 50 percent of the electorate turned out.[44] The Joint Legislative Committee then proceeded to draft seven constitutional amendments, dubbed the "Seven Sisters," pertaining to labor and welfare issues, and placed them on the 1914 ballot. But the voters only approved two of them, an indication that the farmer-labor coalition was not powerful enough to dictate state policy.

The California Campaign

A more detailed investigation of the reform movement in California can fully flesh out the interactions between structural opportunities, the resilience of the party system, the alignment of various constituencies and interest groups, and the efforts of reformers. California was the most important state to adopt direct legislation up until 1920 and was soon to emerge as a national trendsetter in initiative politics. Direct democracy reformers in California, led for about four decades by the Los Angeles-based physician John Randolph Haynes, wielded similar strategies as reformers elsewhere: lobbying before the state legislature, seeking pledges from political candidates, securing the endorsement of party conventions and interest groups, orchestrating statewide publicity campaigns, and cooperating closely with the labor movement, prohibitionists, and others to effect a grass-roots organization. After almost a decade of sustained effort, their moment came amid the virtual takeover of the Republican Party by a group of progressives who had organized within the Lincoln-Roosevelt League. Reformers, with the active support of the new party leadership, were able to step into the power vacuum left by the collapse of the old party apparatus, to draft the constitutional amendments providing for their agenda, and to have their program enacted by a largely cooperative state legislature.

Antimonopoly sentiments in the Golden State, and indeed much of the politics there, revolved around the Southern Pacific Railroad. From the early 1870s to 1911, when a strengthened Railroad Commission finally began to effectively regulate the corporation, antimonopoly sentiments in the form of hostility to the Southern Pacific played a highly salient role in California state and local politics.[45] Many attempts to restrict the power of the corporation were launched, from changes in the state constitution to ballot reforms, but none seemed successful in putting an end to the corruption of the legislature and the blatant acts of special legislation.[46] Throughout the 1900s, a series of reform organizations dedicated to the cause of "good government" proliferated, particularly in Los Angeles where such reformers as Meyer Lissner, Charles Willard, Edward Dickson, and Haynes implemented a series of reforms, including municipal direct legislation. [47] A simple desire to break the power of the Southern Pacific, however, did not necessarily translate into a positive political program. The success of direct legislation in California was due to the ability of one man, John Randolph Haynes, to graft his program onto the progressive reform agenda in California.

John Randolph Haynes was born in 1853 in Philadelphia, attended and graduated from the University of Pennsylvania medical school, and practiced medicine in Philadelphia until 1887 when he moved with his family to California. In addition to establishing a successful medical practice that included many members of the Los Angeles elite, Haynes also became a successful investor in California real estate, amassing a personal fortune of several million dollars. It is unclear when he first developed an interest in the initiative and referendum. But by the late 1890s, he was coming out publicly in favor of the new devices for popular rule. In 1900, Haynes formed the Los Angeles Direct Legislation League, which played a crucial role in making the initiative, referendum, and recall a part of the new city charter of 1903. A state league was formed two years later. Until the adoption of the reforms in 1911, Haynes orchestrated and largely financed the reform campaign.[48]

Throughout the 1900s, the Direct Legislation League of California largely consisted of Haynes and his secretary. There was never any paid, professional staff, no dues-paying members, and no permanent office.[49] Financially, Haynes continued to act as one of the main supporters of the league, but other reformers also pitched in. From December 1908 to the end of April 1909, the league raised almost $1,500, with $400 coming from Haynes, $200 from the Good Government Fund of Los Angeles, and $100 from Rudolph Spreckels, a wealthy businessman. Most of the money was spent on office rent and supplies and printing costs. From May 1909 to November 1911, the league received donations totaling almost $5,700, with most of the money arriving during 1911. By that time, the number of donors had expanded considerably, with most of them concentrated in Los Angeles. On a more solid financial footing, the league was able to spend more money on its publicity campaigns and it played a crucial role in the ratification campaign for the amendments in 1911. But like other state and national leagues, the one in California was chronically short on funds, making its success all the more impressive.[50]

The key to success for the league lay in securing the support of various interest groups and reform constituencies in California. In the early years of the DLL, Haynes cooperated particularly closely with the labor unions in the state. The California labor movement expanded significantly in the 1890s and 1900s, with San Francisco being one of the strongholds of unionism in the United States.[51] Throughout the 1900s, the California State Federation of Labor repeatedly came out in support of direct legislation. In 1903, a number of local unions, at the request of Haynes, sent petitions to the legislature urging passage of the constitutional amendments.[52] In January 1905, just before the opening of the 1905 legislature, Haynes again sent a letter to 300 union officers across the state asking them to pass resolutions in support of his agenda.[53] Timed to coincide with the deliberations of the legislature, Haynes sought to generate grass-roots support for the initiative and referendum and to bring public pressure to bear on the lawmakers.

Among the more important of other interest groups recruited by Haynes was the Prohibition movement. Haynes personally supported prohibition, as did many other progressive reformers. He cooperated closely with the California Anti-Saloon League (ASL), which was able to give the league access to a network of Protestant churches in the state. The ASL helped Haynes in distributing information material across the state and gathering signatures for petitions asking the legislature to enact direct legislation.[54] Supporters of women's suffrage were a second key group solicited by Haynes, who also hoped for an endorsement of their program by the electorate. As Haynes wrote to the National American Woman's Suffrage Association in June of 1905: "Under the Initiative and Referendum you could at any time secure the submission of your measure, by proper petition, in spite of any opposition from the machine."[55] Single taxers were not as prominent in California as they were in other states, but some, such as William Eggleston, occupied important positions in the DLL. In 1911, shortly before the ratification of the amendments, the well-known single tax lecturer John Z. White toured the state to rally support. Many Socialists also supported direct legislation. By opting for a pragmatic, nonpartisan, and highly focused strategy, Haynes was able to assemble a diverse and broad reform coalition that stretched across most of the political spectrum in California.[56]

In addition to securing the support of various interest groups, Haynes was vitally interested in gaining the endorsement of the political parties for his program. In practical terms, that meant dealing with the dominant Republican Party. Although not interested in partisan politics, Haynes used his position as a member of the Los Angeles civic and economic elite to seek the support of the local Republican organization.[57] Always careful to appeal to all parties, Haynes nevertheless became an integral member of a group of Republican progressives in Los Angeles. Repeated attempts, however, to secure the support of the state Republican Party or of such prominent politicians as newly elected governor George C. Pardee in 1902 and 1903 met with little success.[58]

In soliciting the support of interest groups, parties, and politicians, Haynes's ultimate goal was to create enough support for the initiative and referendum to sway the California legislature to pass the necessary constitutional amendments.[59] As in most other states, a two-thirds majority was needed for amendments in California. Between 1902 and 1910, Haynes repeatedly tried to influence both the election of lawmakers and the deliberations of the assembly. Ordinarily before each election, Haynes sent pledge cards to all candidates to ascertain their position on direct legislation.[60] Most of them endorsed the principles underlying the proposal, declaring themselves to be in support of majority rule and popular sovereignty, while often carefully qualifying their position.[61] Few directly promised to support Haynes's amendments; few stated their opposition. In 1909, the DLL and other reform organizations hired George B. Anderson to serve as their representative before the 1909 legislature. During the months of January through March, Anderson cajoled lawmakers, tried to coordinate the efforts of labor and agricultural groups, testified before committees, and sent information to newspapers across the state. At a cost of about $400 a month, this "People's Lobby," as it was called, represented the most sustained effort to date of the DLL to influence the legislature.[62] But not even this novel approach could overcome the hostility and disinterest within the Republican Party.

By the second half of the 1900s, the reform efforts in various California cities coalesced with the growing strength of reformers in the Republican Party to slowly tilt the balance of power. A number of

Lincoln-Roosevelt Leagues were formed around the state after 1905, leading to the founding of a statewide organization in 1907.[63] By getting the San Francisco lawyer Hiram Johnson, who had acquired political prominence in the San Francisco graft prosecution, to run for the Republican gubernatorial nomination, the Progressive movement in California secured the kind of dynamic leadership needed to fuse the various reform proposals and policy innovations into a coherent platform.[64] Johnson himself at first revealed little interest in direct democracy, but Haynes soon convinced him that support for the initiative and referendum would bolster his electoral chances.[65] After Johnson's victories in both the Republican primary and the general election of October 1910, Haynes shaped the drafting of the two constitutional amendments providing for the initiative and referendum, and for the recall. Meyer Lissner, the new chairman of the state Republican Executive Committee, appointed Haynes and his friends to the Committee on Direct Legislation, which drafted the amendments that were then enacted by a compliant legislature.[66] With the backing of Johnson and the Republican Party apparatus, Haynes and his allies had coopted the GOP and had used the resources of the party to finally have their agenda adopted by the legislature. Amid the disintegration of the old ruling faction in the Republican Party, reformers took over control of the party structures to enact measures that in the long run contributed to the further demise of effective political parties in California.

After the passage of the amendments by the legislature, California voters still had to ratify the amendments in a special election scheduled for October 1911.[67] Haynes mobilized some of his allies, including the political journalist Franklin Hichborn, who started to write press articles and hold meetings. The Prohibition movement in the state also formed a crucial ally during the campaign. The ASL wrote to all ministers in northern California urging them to inform their congregations on the importance of the amendments.[68] The state Direct Legislation League itself organized speaking tours for Hiram Johnson and other prominent politicians through the state. Some local Republican politicians were not particularly happy with the prominent role taken by the league, and Johnson grew worried that he would not be able to campaign on behalf of the other amendments subject to popular approval. But the active role of the league in the ratification campaign, and the virtual absence of the Republican Party, demonstrated the key strategic position briefly occupied by the league.[69] The outcome of the contest completely vindicated the efforts of Haynes, U'Ren, and Johnson. California voters adopted direct legislation and the recall by overwhelming margins of more than 3 to 1.

By 1912, the West had been "won" for direct democracy. Small groups of political activists, fashioning ties with larger interest groups looking to employ the initiative and referendum for their own agenda, had been able to generate sufficient publicity and pressure to compel lawmakers to implement a set of political reforms that promised to further weaken the parties in the region. Within a little more than a decade, direct legislation had emerged from a fringe issue tainted by its close association with populism to become a fixture in western local and state politics. As reformers confronted the other regions in the country, however, it soon became apparent that the success in the West would not easily be replicated.

5

THE NIGGER ISSUE IS SURE TO BE RAISED
Direct Democracy in the South and North, 1908–1918

After 1898, and especially after Oregon adopted the initiative and referendum in 1902, the reforms had made impressive progress all across the American West. The greater electoral volatility in the region combined with stronger antimonopoly sentiments to grant nonpartisan reformers better access to the political system. In the early 1890s, activity on behalf of direct legislation had been concentrated along the eastern seaboard, particularly in New Jersey and Massachusetts. The National Direct Legislation League always had its headquarters in Orange, New Jersey, where Eltweed Pomeroy made his home. The fact that the state Direct Legislation Leagues in the West enjoyed much more success underlines their independence from the national movement and the highly decentralized nature of the reform movement as a whole. Yet the ambitions of direct democracy advocates extended to the entire United States. The Northeast was the center of corporate America. Surely any reform movement dedicated to liberating Americans from corporate domination had to deal with the center of corporate power. And the South, maybe more so than the West, was treated as a plundered province whose future was decided in distant boardrooms. Compared to the success of direct democracy in the West, however, the other regions of the country proved to be much more impervious to the appeal of popular self-rule, a failure that spelled doom for the long-term future of the reform movement.

Defeat in the South

The South, where reformers and progressives of all stripes came face to face with the conundrum of race relations and the drive to disenfranchise black voters, illustrated most starkly the limits of grassroots democracy in turn-of-the-century America. Between 1890 and 1910, all southern states introduced literacy tests, grandfather clauses, poll taxes, and other devices to deny blacks and poor whites the suffrage. Some even broke with the custom that new state constitutions had to be ratified by the voters. Mississippi, South Carolina, and Louisiana adopted new constitutions in the 1890s, designed primarily to disenfranchise black voters, without popular ratification.[1]

Usually, direct democracy advocates pointed to the American traditions of popular sovereignty and majority rule as rationales for the introduction of the new devices. The more that ordinary citizens would be involved in political decision-making, the better for the state of the American Republic. Clearly, such a line of argument would not do in the South, where the ruling elites wanted to preserve the exclusion of blacks and poor whites. Some direct democracy advocates responded to the special conditions in the South by portraying the initiative and referendum as ideal devices to complete the disenfranchisement of the black population. It had already been established that a sizable portion of the electorate, between one-quarter and one-third, would not vote on ballot propositions under normal conditions. Around 1910, more and more reformers actually welcomed the abstinence of many voters as it allowed the more informed and intelligent part of the polity to determine public policies. This reasoning applied with special force to blacks in the South. One article in 1911 summarized this neatly: "The southerners do not object to direct democracy in the choosing of candidates, yet they have not arisen, as a rule, to direct democracy concerning measures. They say that they are 'afraid of the Negro vote.' This is a fear without foundation. Direct voting on measures engages only the competent. The submission of measures to direct vote is the most effective means to disenfranchising the unfit. It works automatically. They do it themselves. And it is done without noise or protest. The incompetent simply fail to arise to the occasion, leaving measures submitted to popular vote to be decided by those who have sufficient interest and intelligence to vote on them. This is ideal self-government — ideal democracy; and it is peculiarly adapted to conditions in the south. Arkansas is demonstrating this fact, and when it is demonstrated all the southern states will adopt the Initiative and Referendum."[2]

This attempt to convince southern leaders that direct democracy would actually help to "restore self-government to the white man" fell on deaf ears, however. By 1910, the Democratic parties across the region had already accomplished the disenfranchising of blacks through a series of other devices and did not have to rely on direct legislation. There was simply no need for an untested device whose impact on the political situation could not be gauged. In 1912, southern delegates even prevented the Democratic national convention from endorsing direct democracy in its campaign platform. Despite the powerful appeal of antimonopoly arguments in the South, the peculiar problems connected to white racism and the large presence of blacks permanently stifled direct democracy in the region.[3] Certainly, there were other factors at work as well that worked against reformers. The South lacked the presence of labor unions, single taxers, and middle-class reform groups that formed such an important part of the reform coalition elsewhere. The lack of effective party competition also deprived reformers of the chance to play off the parties against one another, leading one reformer to complain in 1911 that "the chief trouble in the way [of direct democracy] being that the old South has always been democratic in a party sense."[4] It seems apparent, though, that a fear of black political empowerment stood as the basis of most of the resistance to direct legislation. Despite the willingness of many reformers to compromise their democratic aspirations, direct democracy did not resonate in the Jim Crow South.

There were three exceptions to this pattern, however. Arkansas and Mississippi were the only states of the former Confederacy to adopt direct legislation, even though a decision of the Mississippi Supreme Court invalidated the initiative and referendum law in the latter state in 1922. Oklahoma, a state also controlled by a highly racist Democratic Party, included the initiative and referendum in its 1907 constitution upon achieving statehood. Even in the eyes of many direct democracy advocates, however, the statutes passed in Oklahoma and Arkansas left much to be desired. Lacking the more liberal provisions of states like Oregon and California, and soon further eroded by a series of judicial decisions, the initiative and referendum never acquired a large significance.

When Oklahoma entered the union in 1907, the new state constitution was widely heralded as a highly radical document, full of restrictions on the activities of corporations and driven by a spirit of abject hostility toward monopolies. While many conservatives attacked the charter because of its radical nature and mocked its absurd length and detailed provisions, many Oklahomans celebrated their constitution as a model of progressive reform and antimonopoly. Direct democracy formed an important element in the charter. In the years around 1910, one of the new U.S. Senators from Oklahoma, the Democrat Robert L. Owen, emerged as one of most important spokesmen for direct legislation on the national scene, functioning as a member of the reform wing of the Democratic Party, and tirelessly pointing to the example of his home state as proof of the effects of the new reforms.[5]

Conditions in Oklahoma, however, hardly conformed to Owen's assessment. In addition to careful restrictions on the activities of corporations, the constitution also included the stringent measures to disenfranchise blacks that had become commonplace all across the South. Furthermore in 1910, an initiative was circulated, with the wholehearted support of the Democratic Party in the state, which added a "grandfather" clause to the constitution. The amendment was easily ratified in the election. To ensure a favorable outcome, the ballot had been printed in a fashion that required opponents of the measure to cross out the words "For the Amendment" to indicate their objection. Otherwise, the ballot was counted as a "yes" vote. This example of electoral trickery, not unfamiliar from the South during this period, hardly matched the image of genuine popular self-rule.[6] The Oklahoma legislature further made sure that many of the laws it passed would not be subject to a popular referendum. Of the 3,010 laws enacted between 1907 and 1929, it labeled 1,888 of them as emergency measures, thus putting them beyond the referendum.[7]

In addition, the direct democracy statute contained many details, so-called "jokers" in the eyes of critics, that severely curtailed its usefulness. Ballot propositions had to be approved by a majority of all voters participating in the election, not just those voting on the issue, as in most other states. This had the practical effect of limiting the number of laws enacted via the popular initiative. Between 1907 and 1920, Oklahomans voted on 18 initiatives and 5 popular referenda, but only 5 measures were ratified, a very slight legislative output, leading one observer to argue in 1920 "that the initiative and referendum have accomplished nothing extraordinary."[8] Oklahoma furnished a clear example of how direct legislation in the South was undercut by the powerful drive to restrict the suffrage.

The situation in Arkansas looked hardly more encouraging. The state adopted a fairly liberal direct legislation statute in 1910. In addition to a political culture tinged with antimonopoly, Arkansas was also one of the few southern states with an active labor movement, a key component of the direct democracy forces in the state. In addition, the Democratic governor, the State Democratic Party, and the farmers' associations also supported the reforms.[9] The opponents of the reforms immediately challenged them in court, however, effectively limiting the operation of the referendum and initiative. In a series of decisions, the Arkansas Supreme Court ruled that only three initiatives could be proposed at any one election, and that, as in Oklahoma, constitutional amendments would win adoption only when they carried a majority of all the votes cast at the election.

In response, Judson King, in his capacity as executive secretary of the National Popular Government League, drafted a new statute to replace the old one. It was submitted to the voters in the fall election of 1916. The new law not only stipulated that a majority of the votes cast on a proposition would be sufficient for its ratification; King also included a passage stating that no law could be declared unconstitutional except by a unanimous decision of the state supreme court. To ensure victory at the polls, King traveled to Arkansas in October 1916 to manage the campaign. He found the direct democracy forces "weak in money" and with no "vital leadership."[10] The movement was further hampered by the suspicions of prohibitionists that the labor movement wanted to use the revised statute to overturn prohibition in the state.[11] King's efforts were too feeble and came too late. He arrived in Arkansas barely a month before the vote. Many newspapers in the state published editorials and articles that warned voters of the alleged effects of the statute on prohibition. King's assurances that local option would not be permissible received little publicity. He later complained that "the Federation of Labor did not know how to conduct an effective campaign, and simply drifted along until the last moment." The revised direct democracy statute was defeated by a vote of 73,000 to 70,000.[12] The early decision of a segment of the labor movement to try and circumvent prohibition had turned out to be a costly mistake. It was only after 1925, when the Arkansas Supreme Court liberalized the direct democracy provisions and ruled that a majority of the votes cast on a proposition was sufficient for passage, that Arkansas began to make widespread use of the initiative and referendum.[13]

Few states seemed as unlikely to adopt the initiative and referendum as Mississippi, a state with one of the largest percentages of blacks among the general population of any southern state, tightly controlled by a Democratic Party bent on preserving white supremacy, and with a weak labor movement. Nevertheless, in 1914 the state legislature passed a direct democracy amendment, one that was regarded by reform advocates as among the best in the nation. The reformers in Mississippi were led by Norman Mott, a transplanted northerner who ran an insurance business and published a newspaper in Yahoo City. He was a member of the Farmers Union and the sometime editor of the newspaper of the association. In his agitation, Mott stressed the nonradical nature of the initiative and referendum and attempted to assuage southern fears of black voters. Mott was never able, however, to create a broad-based reform movement.[14] In his efforts, he received the welcome assistance of Judson King. In the early part of 1914, King traveled to the state, founded a local People's Rule League as an affiliate of the National Popular Government League, drafted the amendment, and lobbied before the legislature. The amendment was apparently approved without a large fight, and it was placed on the 1915 ballot.[15] King was keenly aware of the crucial importance of gaining a victory in an "ultra southern state." Shortly after returning from Mississippi, he wrote that "to my mind this victory is very significant as we invade the solid South with a good amendment and in a state where the colored people are in greater proportion to the whites than in any other state." Mississippi was of "great strategic importance," and a victory there "opens the way" for the initiative and referendum across the entire South.[16]

King expected a difficult amendment campaign in 1915: "It will be a hot fight as the nigger issue is sure to be raised."[17] Whenever proponents of the initiative and referendum agitated in the South, they confronted deeply held suspicions that direct legislation would empower blacks and would undermine racist political regimes. As one correspondent from North Carolina asked King in early 1915: "If the Initiative and Referendum should be passed, will the colored people and foreigners control our country?"[18] In Mississippi, the task was made even more difficult by the fact that the constitution required new amendments to be approved by a majority of all voters, not just those voting on the proposition. When the election took place in the summer of 1915, Mississippi voters seemed at first to have ratified the measure. But the secretary of state decided to withhold the votes from several counties and claimed that the "corrected returns" showed that the amendment lost by 800 votes. The ruling was immediately challenged in the legislature, and it was decided that the 1916 legislature, to be elected in August 1915, would make the final decision. King again traveled to Mississippi, to "size up the situation," and to campaign for candidates friendly to direct legislation. The legislature ultimately declared the amendment ratified, a decision upheld by the state supreme court in 1917.[19] But in 1922, the Mississippi Supreme Court reversed its position and declared the statute unconstitutional, without the initiative and referendum ever having been put to use. What might have been one of the most unexpected victories for direct democracy turned into another failure in another southern state.

Progress in other parts of the South proved elusive. Maryland adopted a weak form of the referendum in 1915, yet up until 1933 not a single statewide referendum had been held, even though the device was used somewhat more extensively on the local level. Judson King had warned the local leadership of the direct democracy forces about the possible consequences of settling for a tainted law: "I don't think this good tactics . . . I am, of course, afraid that this bagatelle of a referendum will block getting the initiative for a long time but it may prove otherwise."[20] In Tennessee, King stayed in contact with some local union and farm leaders who favored the initiative and referendum. One of them, C. W. Brooks, the secretary of the Farmers' Educational and Cooperative Union of America in Tennessee, personally favored the reforms but warned that "politics is rotten in Tennessee, and we shrink from any sort of mix-up in it. It seems to me it will be almost impossible for us to take a stand without seeming to endorse one of the parties, and we can't afford to do this."[21] With the Democrats opposed to the reforms, interest groups had much less room to maneuver and a nonpartisan reform strategy was not available.

Reform efforts in other southern states were ephemeral. In Texas, voters narrowly defeated a constitutional amendment in 1914 that contained so many flaws and restrictions as to be opposed by many reform advocates. The signature level was set at the absurdly high threshold of 20 percent, and the legislature would have retained authority to tinker with the details of the statute. Politicians in Texas had been pressured into placing the initiative and referendum on the agenda, but had made sure that it would never be invoked. Both sides welcomed the defeat of the measure.[22] Reformers in Florida confronted a disinterest in direct legislation that manifested itself all across the region. In 1899, a Non-Partisan League had been formed in Orlando, but its secretary, A. J. Walker, reported to the *Direct Legislation Record* that "it is hard to stir up enthusiasm amongst people so far South, except just prior to an election." During the winter, they had a lot of northern visitors that dropped by the reading room of the organization. But over the summer, "things are very quiet. The natives do not read much, nor are they attracted by lectures. They are very indifferent to reform work. They are all for Direct Legislation or anything else, providing the National Democratic Convention adopts it."[23] In 1911, both houses of the Florida legislature unexpectedly passed a direct democracy amendment that had been introduced by a representative, without prior announcement. But the law stipulated that signatures of 20 percent of the voters in the previous gubernatorial election were required to invoke the referendum; 25 percent were needed for a constitutional initiative. These provisions rendered the amendment practically useless. Due to a legal challenge by conservatives, it was never submitted to the electorate.[24]

Overall, then, the South remained impervious to the appeal of direct democracy. At a time when southern whites and the leaders of the Democratic Party were busily engaged in sharply limiting the political rights of blacks and many poor whites, and without the presence of such a key ally as the labor movement, direct democracy advocates had little chance of building up the reform coalitions that were so successful in the West. The nonpartisan strategies that had proved so effective in many states failed to sway southern lawmakers. The threat to switch electoral support to another party failed under the conditions of one-party rule. Antimonopoly sentiments were not sufficient in paving the way to reform. The political system had to be accessible and responsive to the demands of the reformers, a situation that the South did not afford. Ironically, a region that made such frequent use of local option and statewide referenda to decide on prohibition (a powerful wedge issue skillfully exploited by direct democracy advocates in a number of states) still offered few opportunities for reformers to advance their cause.[25]

Limited Success in the Northeast and Midwest

Direct democracy made somewhat better progress in the East. Between 1908 and 1918, four eastern states — Maine, Michigan, Ohio, and Massachusetts — adopted the initiative, referendum, and recall in some form. Even here, however, a set of specific political conditions had to prevail to make the reforms possible. Only one state, Maine, adopted direct democracy through a constitutional amendment; all others did so with the help of a constitutional convention, a setting that offered reformers special opportunities. Voter turnout was usually significantly lower in elections for the delegates to these conventions than for general elections. If reformers were able to mobilize their constituencies, as they did in these three states, they could exert a disproportionate influence over the deliberations of the convention. In Ohio and Massachusetts, the rise of the Progressive Party had temporarily weakened the dominant GOP and increased pressure to accommodate reform groups. Only when the political system had become somewhat destabilized and when competition between the parties was more intense did direct democracy advocates in the East stand a chance to implement their program.

In Maine, direct democracy was introduced in 1908, after a campaign that was largely carried by labor and farmer organizations. A Maine Referendum League, modeled on the example of Oregon's People's Power League, was organized in 1905, and in the following year the GOP also came out in support of the initiative and referendum. With the support of both major parties, the adoption of the constitutional amendments was a mere formality. Both houses unanimously passed the bill in 1907, and the voters ratified it in 1908 by a margin of more than 2 to 1.[26] But despite this seemingly easy victory, direct legislation in Maine came with a number of strings attached. The Democrats, labor, and the Grange had favored a liberal amendment that would include the constitutional initiative. The Republicans, however, insisted that the amendment only provided for a statutory indirect initiative, which gave the state legislature the right to amend or repeal any measure approved by the voters. The prohibitionists in Maine were also opposed to a constitutional initiative, fearing that it would be used to challenge the state Prohibition amendment passed in 1864.[27] Consequently, the reach of direct democracy was severely limited. Maine voters used the initiative to adopt a direct primary law in 1910, but altogether only seven laws were proposed via the popular initiative until 1949. The referendum was used more frequently: twenty-nine times during the same period. In general, however, direct legislation in Maine did not reshape the political system of the state.[28]

A similar scenario unfolded in Michigan. A constitutional convention in 1907–1908 made the initiative and referendum a part of the Michigan constitution. But the signature threshold was set at 20 percent of the votes cast for governor at the last general election, a provision that effectively rendered the devices inoperative. In addition, the statute gave the legislature the right to veto any bill proposed via the popular initiative, another attempt to emasculate the new devices. They were never employed up to 1913. In that year, new amendments to the constitution, approved by the voters, lowered the signature requirements to 10 percent for constitutional initiatives and 8 percent for statutory initiatives. Like Maine, Michigan only provided for an indirect statutory initiative, but, in a strange decision, it did introduce the direct constitutional initiative. The state legislature possessed the authority to remove laws from challenge via the referendum by having them take effect immediately. Between 1909 and 1939, between one-third and one-half of all the laws enacted by the legislature in each session had this provision attached to them. All in all, Michigan voters cast their ballots on 23 constitutional initiatives, 5 statutory initiatives, and 4 referenda between 1909 and 1939. This was a higher usage than in Maine, but nevertheless it remained significantly lower than in such states as California and Oregon, where direct legislation emerged as a central element of the legislative process. In both Maine and Michigan, direct democracy remained bound by restrictive provisions and the continued dominance of the political parties.[29]

The next eastern state to adopt direct legislation was Ohio in 1912. Here reformers were able to strongly influence the election of delegates to a new constitutional convention. The single tax movement played a pivotal role in the campaign for the initiative and referendum. Ohio was one of the centers of single tax agitation in the United States, and many prominent politicians including the reform mayor of Toledo, Samuel Jones, and Frederic Howe were members of the movement. The most prominent spokesman for direct legislation was the Cincinnati minister and reformer Herbert Bigelow. As early as 1899, he had worked for the reforms under the banner of the Union Reform Party. Bigelow was an ardent single taxer who, like U'Ren in Oregon, believed that direct legislation provided the perfect means to enact his proposals. In his propaganda, however, he followed U'Ren's example and kept his economic program in the background, while focusing his argument on putting political power in the hands of the people.[30] His work made little headway during the 1900s, however.

When the Ohio legislature decided to call a constitutional convention for 1911, the prospects for the direct democracy forces brightened considerably. In preparation for the election of convention delegates, Bigelow organized the Progressive Constitutional League to further popularize the cause of direct democracy. In his efforts, Bigelow could rely on funds provided by the Fels Fund. But single taxers were careful in keeping their involvement hidden from the eyes of the public. Kiefer argued in 1909 that the Fund "may also be used to extend help to direct legislation, without having it known what is being done." He continued: "In Ohio, the fight in the legislature and outside is wholly financed by the Fels Fund, but nobody knows about it."[31] Nevertheless, conservatives in Ohio knew full well that single taxers favored direct legislation.

Bigelow did not rely on single tax support alone. He had also cultivated the help of the labor movement in Ohio, which strongly supported the call for the initiative and referendum. The opposition Democrats, the Progressives, and the Socialists likewise supported the reforms. In the election, when only 25 percent of the electorate turned out to vote, these groups were able to elect a majority of the members of the convention. During the deliberations of the assembly, Bigelow acted as president of the convention. He once again played down his economic theories and concentrated on popular self-rule and putting an end to the domination by corporate interests.[32] Bigelow invited William Jennings Bryan and Theodore Roosevelt to address the convention and hammered out a compromise that was accepted by the delegates. To placate some moderates, the amendment provided for only the indirect initiative. The convention also refused to adopt the recall, an indication of the limits of eastern progressivism.[33] In the subsequent ratification campaign, the amendments to the constitution were approved in a 1912 election in which turnout was 50 percent lower than during the presidential election of the same year.[34]

In no other state was the campaign for the introduction of direct legislation quite as protracted as in Massachusetts. For more than two decades, from the 1890s until 1918, the direct democracy movement in the Bay State staged a tireless effort to implement their reform program. The eventual success was made possible by the close cooperation between the labor movement and more middle-class reformers. With the growing popularity of direct legislation around the country in the late nineteenth century, and with the New England town meeting to serve as a local example, the labor movement in Massachusetts began to demand the initiative and referendum as early as 1891–92.[35] The small cadre of middle-class reform activists, denied access to much of the regular press and yet unable to penetrate the major political parties, had to rely on the cooperation of labor unions to reach a mass audience. With union help, they could threaten to punish politicians who did not support direct legislation and work for the election of candidates friendly to their cause.[36]

At first, however, the attempts to pressure the legislature showed little effect as reform bills continued to die in committee or fell short of the required two-thirds majority in the General Court. Around 1907, reformers briefly modified their strategy by advocating passage of a Public Advisory Bill, modeled on an Illinois statute of 1901, which would have made advisory referenda possible. Many leaders of the movement regarded such a law as an "opening wedge" in the campaign for the initiative and referendum, easier to implement since it did not require a constitutional amendment, less likely to arouse as much opposition, and an educational tool to familiarize the voters with the instruments of direct democracy.[37] But the bill was defeated during the 1907 legislative session, despite the support of President Eliot of Harvard, certainly no radical by any stretch of the imagination. The conservative Republican establishment in the state realized only too well the implications and potential dangers of advisory referenda. The firm opposition of many political leaders even to advisory referenda delayed their eventual introduction to Massachusetts until 1913.[38]

The reconfiguration of the political landscape in Massachusetts brought about by the growing reform spirit in the Democratic Party and the split of the GOP, however, soon gave the reformers greater access to the political arena. In 1910, the Democratic Party officially endorsed direct democracy, and the Democrats won the gubernatorial election, ending fifteen years of Republican control of the governor's mansion. The new governor of the state announced his support in 1911, and the reformers gained new hope. Yet, the vote tally in the legislature continued to fall short of the needed majority.[39] The 1914 election dealt another serious blow to the Republican Party, which finished third in the contest behind the Democrats and Progressives. Although the legislature still refused to pass the amendments, it was obvious that the rising reform sentiment in the state posed a serious threat to a Republican Party accustomed to political dominance.[40]

In 1916, finally, the state Republican Party, severely weakened by the Progressive Party, decided to support the call for a new constitutional convention in order to attract reformist support. Their gubernatorial candidate, Samuel McCall, had been a U.S. congressman in 1912 and had been one of the most vocal opponents of direct democracy during the presidential campaign. He had heatedly attacked direct legislation as reactionary, as harking back to an outdated theory of government left behind by the Founding Fathers.[41] Now he supported the new convention, knowing full well that direct democracy would emerge as one of the central issues of the deliberations. McCall won the contest, restoring the GOP to political control. Even though the majority of Republicans in the state persisted in their opposition, the constitutional convention gave the direct democracy movement the opening they needed to implement their program.

During the campaign, the reformers made good use of the Public Opinion Bill that had been introduced in 1913. In thirty-six out of thirty-seven legislative districts where the issue was presented to the voters, they supported direct legislation.[42] The reformers waged an active campaign during the election of delegates, while the conservative opposition hardly mustered a serious effort at all. Aided by a low turnout, the reformers ended up in control of the assembly. During the sessions of the convention, the topic of the initiative and referendum occupied about a third of the delegates' time, even though the eventual outcome of the vote seemed a foregone conclusion.[43] Direct democracy was finally adopted by a vote of 163 to 125 on November 27, 1917 (a two-thirds majority was not needed in this instance). The amendments were ratified by large majorities, making Massachusetts the last state to adopt direct democracy before World War II.[44] The triumph of direct legislation was tainted, however. Similar to Ohio, Massachusetts only provided for an indirect initiative and also imposed the rule that signatures had to come from all over the state. Contrary to the hopes of the reformers, Massachusetts would make little use of the initiative and referendum in the period up until World War II.[45]

The example of the four eastern states that adopted direct legislation prior to 1940 illustrates that constitutional conventions presented direct democracy reformers with opportunities analogous to those that occurred in the western states. In the cases of Ohio and Massachusetts, the established parties briefly lost their ability to control the political agenda, allowing reformers to step in and implement their program. Because they were well organized and had a distinct political agenda, proponents of direct legislation were able to wield a disproportionate influence in the election of candidates to the constitutional conventions. Amid low voter turnout and a lack of popular interest, small groups had a much better chance to influence those assemblies than to pressure political parties and state legislatures. The situation in Maine and Michigan was less clear-cut, but even here it seems that the temporary weakness of the parties was crucial to the victory of the reformers. And yet, direct legislation in the East never achieved the same importance as in the West. With the exception of Michigan, no eastern state included the recall, widely regarded as the most radical of all direct legislation components. Even Michigan excluded judges from the recall. Furthermore, most eastern states provided for the indirect initiative that gave the state legislatures some opportunity to influence the legislative process. Maine did not adopt the constitutional initiative at all. Even in defeat, the major parties and conservative forces in the East ensured that direct democracy would not supplant the established means of lawmaking. The distinctive constellation of political forces in the East, marked by stronger parties, less animosity to corporations and trusts, and a weaker and less radical Progressive movement, created a very different position for direct legislation than in much of the American West.

One might expect Wisconsin to have been among the states east of the Mississippi that also adopted the initiative and referendum. Long an acknowledged leader of Progressivism in the nation, the state set the pace for reform in many policy areas. Although the Progressives under Robert La Follette had been in control of the state since 1900, when La Follette became governor, however, the issue of direct democracy initially generated little interest among reformers in the state. Once in power, La Follette apparently felt little need for innovations that threatened to reduce the role of the Republican Party over which he had recently won control.[46] Nonpartisan reform strategies had little appeal to Progressives able to use party structures to implement their program.

It was only during the rise of the Republican insurgency and the split of the party in 1912 that direct democracy emerged as an issue in Wisconsin politics. As he became a candidate for the presidential nomination of the GOP in 1911, La Follette endorsed the initiative and referendum in order to attract western Republican support, where direct democracy had been transformed into one of the key symbols of political reform. In 1912, the Wisconsin legislature finally passed the required constitutional amendments. As in many other eastern states, Wisconsin lawmakers aimed to avoid eliminating the legislature from the initiative process and provided for an indirect initiative that gave the legislature significant powers to debate and amend initiatives. But when the amendments were submitted to the voters in 1913, they were handily defeated at the polls. The defeat was blamed on a large tax increase enacted by the legislature to finance an ambitious building program for the state university and for highways. The voters were incensed about the tax increase and turned down the whole slate of propositions before them in the 1913 election.[47] With the rapid demise of Progressivism in the East, no second chance would be available for many decades to come.[48]

Direct democracy also failed narrowly in Illinois. The formation of the movement followed the pattern familiar from other states. A small group of reformers called a meeting in Chicago in early 1897 and founded the Sovereign Citizens of America, with William P. Black, the lawyer who had defended the anarchists in the Haymarket trial, as president. Simultaneously, there was some agitation among German and Swiss immigrants in Chicago in favor of the initiative and referendum. A meeting between the two groups was organized; a state Direct Legislation League was finally founded in late 1897.[49] Because the state legislature refused to pass a direct legislation law, reformers in Illinois decided to first push for a public opinion law to increase pressure on the political parties. In 1901, the legislature passed a law allowing for nonbinding petitions on public policy issues to be put on the ballot if

25 percent of voters in a city or county, or 10 percent in the whole state, signed a petition. A new Referendum League of Illinois was founded in 1902, and, with the help of the state Federation of Labor and Illinois Teachers' Federation that provided the resources to gather the needed signatures, it succeeded in putting three petitions on the Chicago ballot in 1902. These petitions addressed the ownership of street railways, the ownership of gas and electric utilities, and the direct primary. On the state level, voters in the same election cast their ballots on the issues of direct democracy, local direct democracy, and the direct election of U.S. senators. The Illinois electorate overwhelmingly supported these reforms, and voters in Chicago endorsed public ownership of street railways and public utilities. But even though the legislature passed a law for the direct election of U.S. senators in 1904, it still refused to act on the issue of the initiative and referendum, leading one observer to conclude that "these expressions of public opinions have not been very effective in securing the legislation desired."[50]

One of the most important allies of the reform movement in Illinois was the Prohibition movement. The influential Anti-Saloon League of Illinois endorsed the referendum as a main weapon in the fight against alcohol. In 1907, after an intensive lobbying campaign, the legislature passed a local option law that provided for binding local referenda on the liquor issue.[51] The rise of reformers within the Republican Party in Illinois around 1910 further brightened prospects for reformers. Governor Deneen inserted a plank in the Republican platform in 1910 that called for the initiative and referendum, but it failed to pass during the 1911 legislative session. During the deliberations of the legislature, the Chicago Civic Federation called a meeting at the LaSalle Hotel in Chicago to warn against the dangers of direct legislation. Henry M. Byllesby, president of the association, contended that "we foresee the 'boss-controlled' minorities of our great urban centers holding the balance of power in legislative matters."[52] In 1912, both the Democratic and the progressive parties in the state endorsed the measure, and the election of the Democrat Edward Dunne, a former mayor of Chicago and a long-time supporter of direct democracy, briefly ended the dominance of the GOP. Although the Illinois House passed the constitutional amendments, however, they failed in the senate by a single vote.[53] Dunne continued to agitate for direct legislation but failed to win reelection in 1916, and the return of the GOP to power effectively ended any chance for the initiative and referendum in Illinois.

In New York State, finally, not even a constitutional convention could save the direct democracy movement. Compared to other states, a reform movement was slow to form in the Empire State. It was 1907 before an Initiative and Referendum League was organized. When it introduced a draft for a constitutional amendment providing for the initiative and the referendum in the New York State legislature in the following year, the organization was painfully aware that it lacked sufficient votes to carry the proposal.[54] A year later, one observer complained that the legislature treated the introduction of the same bill "as a joke. It was referred to committee and we find no other allusion to it."[55] While reformers blamed their lack of progress on the power of special interests and corrupt machines, the real obstacle to the introduction of the initiative and referendum in New York consisted of the continued existence of powerful political parties that denied direct democracy a place on the political agenda. Even though the state, especially from 1906–10 under the leadership of Republican reform governor Charles Evans Hughes, had adopted a number of progressive reforms, the dominant Republican Party stubbornly resisted any reform that seemed to endanger its control of the political arena. Direct democracy reformers, without the rural support so crucial in many western states, with a rather disinterested labor movement, and with a Democratic Party that looked at their proposal with as much disdain as had the Republicans, stood little chance of effectively pressuring the parties.[56]

Not even a constitutional convention provided reformers with the leverage they needed. A convention was to be elected in the state in 1915, but the prospects for direct democracy did not look much brighter. The platform of the state GOP explicitly rejected direct legislation, and even the Democratic Party was opposed to the judicial recall.[57] In 1914 Judson King was contacted by a group of reformers in New York State to get his assistance in pushing for the initiative and referendum, but in a letter to William U'Ren in Oregon he expressed his doubts: "I have always held that it was not good tactics for us to spend money on the East or at least states like Pennsylvania and New York but that the way to win the East was to first establish the I and R in the West and when the conservative East found out that the grass still grew, it would be more inclined to take hold."[58] A draft for a model constitution, submitted to the convention by the Referendum League of Erie County, which provided for a unicameral legislature and direct legislation, was soundly dismissed.[59] When the convention gathered in 1915, conservative Republicans tightly controlled the deliberations and prevented any serious discussion of direct democracy. King was able to present his case to a committee of the convention, but to no avail. Not even the labor movement displayed any real interest in the issue.[60] The resounding failure of direct democracy in New York illustrated the importance of the intersection of antimonopoly sentiments, weak party organizations, and the ability of reformers to create broad-based coalitions for the diffusion of the initiative, referendum, and recall.

By 1920, the state-by-state diffusion of direct democracy came to an end. It was to remain a phenomenon of the American West. Even during the heyday of the Progressive movement, success in the East and South had been hard to come by. After 1917, under the rapidly changing political conditions in the United States, further success proved impossible. Even in those eastern states that had adopted direct democracy, its actual operation was often hampered by regulations designed to raise the thresholds to invoke the initiative and referendum. Many reformers complained of "jokers" — a high number of signatures, the prohibition of paid petition circulators, no constitutional initiative, no referendum against appropriation bills, a specified geographical distribution of the signatures, the requirement that all the voters participating in an election needed to approve a ballot proposition, etc. — that hindered the use of the new reforms. All too often, the support of moderate Republicans and Democrats could only be secured by installing those "safeguards" against excessive democracy.[61]

Without wanting to oversimplify the differences between the various regions in the United States, it seems apparent that the respective party structures form the key variable explaining the success and the pattern of geographical diffusion of direct legislation. In the West, the political system was marked by greater electoral volatility, weaker parties, and interest groups willing to explore more innovative forms of furthering their agenda. Here reformers could create tactical coalitions between diverse groups willing to suppress dividing issues until the desired reforms had been enacted. In the one-party South, such conditions were not available. Factional infighting was common within the state Democratic parties, but while this made for lively politics, it also tended to insulate the political system from meaningful discussions about policies. The one-party system suppressed policy initiatives, protected the interests of the while ruling elite, and devalued electoral participation among broad segments of the southern population. Combined with socioeconomic conditions that prevented the formation of strong labor unions and middle-class reform groups and the presence of a substantial black population, the southern party system effectively shut out direct democracy opponents. In the eastern states, largely dominated by the GOP, the party system was equally strong and able to deny reformers access to the political arena. Sometimes, usually in connection with constitutional conventions, reformers were able to briefly destabilize established routines and introduce their agenda. Almost always, however, the strings attached to the direct democracy statutes ensured that the new devices would never become important elements of state politics. At the end of almost three decades of agitation for direct democracy, all the talk about popular sovereignty and more democracy had not been sufficient to pave the way for the nationwide adoption of the new devices.

6

THE TRINITY OF DEMOCRACY
Direct Democracy, Antimonopoly, and the Progressive Movement

In 1915, Benjamin DeWitt undertook the audacious attempt to define the essence of the Progressive movement that seemed on the verge of transforming the United States. Starting from the observation that after the Civil War large corporations had preempted central functions of the state for their own benefit and enrichment, DeWitt isolated three central elements of the Progressive creed. First, the leaders of all of the reform parties agreed that the influence of special and corrupt influences on all levels of government had to be removed. Second, in line with the New Nationalism of Theodore Roosevelt, DeWitt referred to "the rapidly growing conviction that the functions of government at present are too restricted and that they must be increased and extended to relieve social and economic distress." And, finally, Progressive reformers proposed a series of political innovations, including the direct primary, the direct election of U.S. senators, and direct legislation, so that "the structure or machinery of government, which has hitherto been admirably adapted to control by the few, be so changed and modified that it will be more difficult for the few, and easier for the many, to control." While socialism concentrated on economic issues, Progressivism was mainly a political reform movement aimed at bringing American government back in line with the demands of the people.[1] The initiative, referendum, and recall occupied a central position in the Progressive reform agenda. They formed the "trinity of democracy," as one direct legislation advocate phrased it in 1913, able to combine honesty and efficiency in government with responsiveness to the popular will.[2]

While early commentators on the Progressive movement stressed the link between democracy and efficiency and argued that direct legislation was able to achieve both ends, most recent historical work on the Progressive Era has given only slight attention to direct democracy.

In Robert Wiebe's book on the evolution of democracy in America, to take only one of the latest examples, the emphasis is on the precipitous decline in voter turnout that marked the early twentieth century. Mostly interested in limiting the power of political machines and the lower classes, Progressive reformers, usually of a middle-class background, implemented a series of reforms that made the polity less democratic and broad-based when compared to the vigorous public life of the nineteenth century. Such innovations as the Australian ballot, the direct primary, nonpartisan elections, the commission form of government, and the rising importance of experts on all levels of government reduced voter turnout, weakened the power of the political parties catering to the needs of ethnic and lower-class communities, and benefited the very business interests that progressive reformers often claimed to campaign against.[3] Wiebe's assessment is the product of a historical reinterpretation of the Progressive Era that has marked the last decades. The growing lack of interest among historians in direct democracy over the last three decades has coincided with an altered view of Progressivism that has stressed the bureaucratic and illiberal aspects of the reform agenda.

More nuanced analyses have highlighted the regional variations and the different political traditions of the Progressive impulse. Confronted with the bewildering variety of individuals, groups, issues, political goals, and outcomes, historians have long been frustrated in their quest to find some kind of underlying unity that would link these phenomena. Daniel Rodgers has cogently argued that antimonopoly, the concept of social bonds, and the idiom of social efficiency formed the core of Progressivism.[4] These three "languages" often coexisted uneasily alongside each other as different groups and individuals emphasized different elements of Progressive social and political thought. In the case of direct democracy, antimonopoly formed a central component of the movement in the 1890s. It continued to be relevant as many reformers struggled to come to terms with the corporate revolution without abandoning long-established notions of republican liberty and personal autonomy. In addition, the direct democracy movement underlines the differences between eastern and western Progressivism. Reformers in the West were, in general, closer to the Populist movement of the 1890s, with its heated attack on monopolies and its interest in grass-roots democracy. They picked up many of the central legislative demands of Populism, including direct legislation. Eastern Progressives were much more reluctant to endorse the initiative and referendum. Only the split of the Republican Party in 1912 moved them closer to their western counterparts.

Combining these insights into the geographically differentiated nature of the Progressive movement and into the various languages of reform employed enables us to better situate direct legislation within the broader contours of American Progressivism. Up until the 1910s, antimonopoly remained an important element in the economic thinking of many Progressives. Much like in the 1890s, the initiative, referendum, and recall were still regarded as weapons to dissolve monopolies and trusts, as a political reform capable of economic transformation. They needed to be supplemented by the direct regulatory control of corporations made possible by such laws as the Interstate Commerce Act. Political and economic reforms had to work hand in hand to tame rampant corruption and special privileges. But the slow erosion of the political economy of "populist republicanism" revealed growing uncertainties about the outlook for reform. It became more and more difficult to visualize the dissolution of the giant economic institutions that dominated the economic landscape. Heated denunciations of greedy corporations still worked effectively on the campaign trail but rarely translated into concrete and workable policy initiatives. In those regions that had never fully shared the antimonopoly fervor of the West, the linkages between political and economic reform grew more tenuous as reformers focused more and more on measures to make corporations more accountable and transparent, and not on abolishing them altogether.

But if direct democracy would not be able to abolish trusts and corporations, what would their impact be on the principles of administrative efficiency and executive responsibility so important among eastern progressives such as Herbert Croly, who subordinated popular rule to efforts at state-building? The reluctance with which many eastern reformers supported direct democracy was partially based on fears that too much popular rule would weaken the new interventionist state. All these different perspectives on direct democracy converged in the presidential campaign of 1912 when the new devices became important aspects of national politics. The emergence of Theodore Roosevelt as a crusader for direct legislation demonstrated its significance as a wedge issue delineating the boundaries between reformers and reactionaries. But the ensuing national debate concerning direct legislation could not obscure the fact that the reform movement had peaked. The outlook for progress in the Northeast and South was dim, reforms in those states that had adopted the devices had so far not lived up to original expectations, and the intellectual credibility of populist republicanism was fading fast. If anything, the employment of direct legislation as a partisan issue in 1912 hastened the decline of the organized reform movement by depriving it of its nonpartisan basis.

Antimonopoly in the Progressive Era

There is widespread agreement among historians that antimonopoly formed one of the most pervasive languages of social protest in the nineteenth century. Much more controversial is its fate after 1900. A number of authors have argued that antimonopoly ceased to be an effective political force amid the corporate reorganization of the American economy in the last decades of the nineteenth century. James Huston, for instance, contends that by 1890, economic developments had eroded traditional arguments that specific political acts created monopolies. As the corporations demonstrated their superior efficiency, a new interpretation of the developments of trusts and corporations emerged that stressed the economies of scope and scale.[5] Mary Furner has argued that the late nineteenth century witnessed the emergence of a new mode of economic analysis that she calls "new liberalism." A group of economists and social scientists broke with the laissez-faire thinking that had dominated the previous half century. Divided between democratic statists, who envisioned an enlarged role of the state in managing economic affairs, and corporate liberals, who favored cooperative and voluntary agreements among business interests, the new liberals jettisoned the old "grant theory" of corporations and arrived at modern conceptions of corporations.[6]

But these arguments exaggerate the demise of the antimonopoly tradition around 1900. The precise relation between the corporation and American democracy remained a highly problematic political topic, and antimonopoly an integral part of Progressive rhetoric. No other issue set the United States as clearly apart from other Western countries as the deep-running apprehensions about the impact of trusts. James Bryce noted in 1905 that among economic questions, "the one which is most discussed in America is the one least discussed in Europe; I mean the propriety of restricting industrial or mercantile combinations of capitalists."[7] In a comparative perspective, the United States clearly had the strongest antitrust movement of all Western industrial nations.[8]

The Chicago Conference on Trusts, held in 1899 under the auspices of the Chicago Civic Federation, exemplified some of the divergent interpretations of the nature and consequences of the trusts. Bringing together a varied assortment of politicians, reformers, businessmen, and academic scholars, the conference attempted to create a dialogue between the parties interested in the trust issue. More often, however, the speeches and discussion only served to demonstrate the diametrically opposed positions of antimonopolists and the defenders of the trusts. For the latter, the economic efficiency and lower prices resulting from economic consolidation were beyond serious questioning. Others, however, continued to cling to the theory that the corporation was a creature of the state and thus subject to public control.[9] For dedicated antimonopolists, the desired policy toward the trust was evident. Jefferson Davis, attorney general of Arkansas, left no doubt that the "only remedy, in my judgment, for its extermination — because exterminate it we must — the only remedy for its extermination is to bring upon it the strong hand of the law."[10]

While many attendants at the conference maintained their allegiance to populist republicanism, other observers groped for a different explanation for the emergence of the trusts, one that would gain greater prominence in the years to come. George R. Gaither, the attorney general of Maryland, asserted that in contrast to old monopolies based on exclusive state privileges, "modern monopolies or trusts claim no protection from the law, — on the contrary they simply ask that they shall not be interfered with, relying upon the crushing power of the exclusive privileges, which their control of great aggregations of capital has obtained, for their flourishing existence. The old monopoly was a creature of the law, the modern trust seeks to establish itself without legislative assistance, and in many instances in defiance of express enactments." Here one can find the beginnings of a significant shift in the explication of trusts in the early twentieth century. Reformers would continue to rail against the domination of large corporations, but the old belief that changes in legislation would provide an easy way to eradicate monopoly began to wane. This also meant that the argumentative coherence of populist republicanism was increasingly being challenged by economic change.[11]

Many reformers, however, refused to acknowledge that the changing role of corporations, both in their economic functions and in their legal standing, invalidated their economic theories. For them, corruption still served as the avenue corporations used to obtain much-desired privileges and to exert control over the bodies responsible for safeguarding the public interest.[12] As the primary gatekeepers of the political system, political parties and machines mediated the relations between business and politics, earning the wrath of all reformers.[13] Throughout the entire Progressive Era, reformers, including particularly the leaders of the direct democracy movement, railed against the corruption of the machines, attacking the control they exerted over the electorate, especially in the bigger cities with their concentration of workers and immigrants, and endlessly belaboring the venal interactions between economic interests and party organizations.[14] For advocates of the initiative and referendum, in particular, the readily available proof of legislative corruption stood as the vivid testimony to the urgent need for tools that would emancipate the people from the control of venal bosses.[15] Believing that "political reform is a sufficient avenue to the necessary economic reforms," reformers regarded the initiative and referendum as the key to any real reform strategy.[16]

It became more difficult, however, to argue that the new devices would have a meaningful effect on corporations as the nationalization of the economy, the beginnings of federal regulation with the Sherman Act and the Interstate Commerce Commission, and the interstate character of the business transactions of trusts rendered state attempts to bring them under greater public control useless. Many state legislatures still produced large numbers of regulatory laws; the federal arena, however, more and more superseded state efforts.[17] Many of the discussions at the federal level still revolved around the issue of the legal privileges of corporations. Like their counterparts earlier, reformers did not accept that incorporation was just a mere formality for facilitating business transactions without any further public obligations.[18] The various proposals throughout the Progressive Era for a federal law to incorporate business interests operating on an interstate basis were likewise influenced by the concept that such a corporate charter would give the government greater control over the corporation.[19] Such calls for greater public control often coexisted peacefully with arguments for direct democracy, but there can be no doubt that the goal of regulation slowly replaced political reforms as the focus of anticorporate crusaders.

Not all Progressives continued to embrace antimonopoly wholeheartedly. The impact of Populist theories of the detrimental effect of privileges was especially noticeable in the thinking of the western Progressives within the Republican Party that would form the nucleus of the Progressive Party in 1912. Arguing that "the paramount issue in the United States is represented by the legal phrase Special Interests vs. Public Welfare," the so-called insurgents developed a political reform program that included direct democracy, the direct election of U.S. senators, and direct primaries. While its opponents in the GOP believed in "government for the special interests," the insurgents blamed governmental favoritism for the rise of large corporations and trusts.[20]

Others, such as Theodore Roosevelt, shifted their positions among the increased factionalism within the GOP. Roosevelt's role in the chain of events that split the Republican Party needs no further treatment here.[21] During his presidency, he had been identified with a program of trust regulation that stressed the need for federal control of corporations and the need for regulatory commissions staffed by experts to handle the issue. As explained by Herbert K. Smith, the commissioner of corporations in 1912, the results of antitrust actions throughout the presidencies of Roosevelt and Taft had been achieved "by administrative action, by efficient publicity, through a trained force of specialists, whose permanent and continuous work is the handling of business facts and business problems." Roosevelt had never exhibited any serious interest in the initiative and referendum and certainly never believed that they would dissolve trusts and corporations. But while he maintained the conviction that only expert commissions would be able to differentiate between "good" and "bad" trusts, his rhetoric became much more critical between 1910 and 1912.[22]

In March 1911, Roosevelt argued that "in this country at the moment our chief concern must be to deprive the special interests of the power to which they are not entitled and which they use for the corruption of our institutions and to our economic and social undoing."

Defining a special interest as one "which has been given by law certain improper advantages as compared with the mass of our people, or which enjoys such advantages owing to the absence of needed laws," he vowed that "true democracy . . . must set its face like steel against privilege and all the beneficiaries of privilege."[23] At other times, however, Roosevelt seemed to blame unrestrained economic freedom and not special privileges for the emergence of trusts. "Nevertheless, we as Americans must now face the fact that the great freedom which the individual property-owner has enjoyed in the past has produced evils which were inevitable from its unrestrained exercise." He continued: "It is this very freedom — the absence of State and National restraint — that has tended to create a small class of enormously wealthy and economically powerful men whose chief object is to hold and increase their power." One can sense how Roosevelt struggled for an understanding of the nature of trusts that incorporated old understandings of the crucial role of the state while also taking note of the economic underpinnings of corporations. In the end, Roosevelt endorsed a position also taken by many other antimonopolists. "The corporation is the creature of government, and the people have the right to handle it as they desire."[24] His movement toward a stronger critique of corporations illustrates the changes in the political alignments that increased interest in the initiative and referendum.

Much of the same uncertainty about the policy to be adopted toward industrial combinations haunted the Democratic Party. But by 1912, the policy differences between Democrats and Republican insurgents had narrowed considerably.[25] The pivotal figure in shaping Wilson's trust policy, both in terms of content and rhetoric, was Louis Brandeis. At the center of his economic thinking stood the conviction that industrial size did not translate into economic efficiency. He constantly railed against the "curse of bigness," arguing that "privilege, preference, discrimination in favor of very large and powerful interests in the transportation field have been the main causes of the overweening growth of a few concerns as compared with the more struggling growth of many others."[26] During his campaign, Wilson articulated Brandeis' idea that the trusts actually retarded efficiency and innovation.[27] In his willingness to look toward federal regulation of corporations and trusts, Wilson modernized the position of the Democrats toward industrial concentrations. Compared with the attitude of the GOP under Taft, Democrats and Progressives shared important aspects of their antitrust policies in 1912.

Given the continued relevance of antimonopoly elements in Progressive ideas, the economic implications of the initiative and referendum were evident. One observer argued in 1912 that there had always been a "constant relation existing between the movement in favor of direct popular legislation and that in favor of radical social and economic reform."[28] Indeed, experience at the state level seemed to suggest that the introduction of direct democracy was followed by increased attempts at economic reform. Many observers pointed to Oregon, the first state to make extensive use of direct legislation, as an example of the transformation wrought by the introduction of the new devices. The initiative and referendum had liberated the state from the dominance of corporations, had led to the passage of a series of progressive laws, most notably the direct primary, had increased the taxation of corporations, and had uplifted public morality in the state.[29] Even though the denunciations of monopoly and special privileges found among Progressives were less strident than among the Populists in the 1890s, and often tempered by more uncertainty about the relationship between size and efficiency, antimonopoly continued to be an important factor in the spread of direct democracy.

Yet the continued usage of such phrases as "special privileges," "government favoritism," and "class legislation" often masked an important revision of populist conceptions of the rise of trusts. When Roosevelt argued that the absence of restraints had allowed corporations to grow and when Brandeis referred to the ability of aggregations of capital to crush their competitors, they demonstrated the rise of an economic theory of trusts that no longer looked primarily for political explanations. Populists in the nineteenth century had focused their attacks on direct state help to corporations in the form of charters, subsidies, land grants, protective tariffs, and legal privileges. By the early twentieth century, critics of the trusts were more concerned with the ability of large corporations, by their sheer size, to force the railroads to grant them rebates, to buy out competitors, to manipulate their stock, and to stamp out competition. Disagreeing with the defenders about the impact of trusts on efficiency, these critics nevertheless located the source of monopolies in the economic sphere. As argued by Richard T. Ely in 1900: "At the present time, however, monopolies proceed from the nature of industrial society, and are of far greater significance in our economic and political life than ever before. The really serious monopolies of our day are far more subtle, and have for the most part grown up outside of the law, and even in spite of the law. It implies a failure to recognize the most obvious social facts to limit the term monopoly to exclusive privileges expressly granted by the legislative branch of government."[30]

Even economists who asserted that the trust was "essentially artificial" no longer invoked specific acts of legislation as the culprit. Rather, they focused on the ability of trusts to control prices and to deny entry to competitors as the means to create a monopoly. Corporations might often use illicit means in their quest for monopolistic control over a particular industry; they rarely, however, had to resort to those direct subsidies that had so troubled nineteenth-century antimonopolists. The economies of scale and scope enabled large corporations to create monopoly-like conditions in virtually every industry. It was the "possession of a very large capital and the unified control" that invested companies with the leverage to become monopolies.[31]

The impact of this revised understanding of trusts on the political thought of the Progressive Era was visible in such individuals as Wilson and Roosevelt. More and more, the attacks on special privilege that continued to abound among reformers were no longer embedded in a coherent theory of political economy. What seemed more and more important was not the eradication of monopoly, but the control of trusts by regulatory agencies to ensure fair treatment of consumers. In 1916, the Public Utilities Commission of California, for instance, "announced the policy that all existing utilities will be protected against competition in their present fields of operation as long as they accord to the public a complete, adequate, and satisfactory service at rates as low as could reasonably be offered by any prospective competitor." The concerns about large economic organizations shifted from what they did to Americans as citizens to what they did to them as consumers. This shift entailed a host of changes in the ways in which the role of corporations in American society was conceptualized. From suppression to regulation was a momentous shift in the handling of monopolies and trusts, a move that deprived direct democracy of much of its original impetus.[32] Antimonopoly as a political sentiment did not suddenly vanish after 1910, as demonstrated by the success of some antimonopoly rhetoric during the Great Depression and New Deal. But few people continued to seriously believe that corporations could be abolished. From then on, antimonopoly took on the form of a vague resentment against trusts and corporations but lost its character as a coherent reform ideology. In terms of public policy, corporate regulation replaced trust-busting, This change had begun slowly in the late nineteenth century, picked up momentum after 1900, and was largely complete by 1920.

Direct Democracy, Eastern Progressives, and the 1912 Campaign

During the state and local campaigns for the adoption of direct legislation from the late 1890s to 1910, reformers had carefully avoid being drawn into partisan contests. They had perfected the organization of single-issue reform associations that could enlist the help of larger interest groups in their quest to pressure lawmakers and parties. In all the states where the fight had been successful, direct legislation had become a truly nonpartisan issue. As the rising tide of Progressive sentiment threatened to engulf the national parties, however, particularly in the GOP, it was almost inevitable that the issue of direct legislation would be used as a weapon in factional infighting. For such presidential contenders as Theodore Roosevelt and Woodrow Wilson, support for the new devices could serve to shore up their Progressive credentials. Factionalism and hardening lines of intraparty conflicts emerged around 1910 as Progressives in both parties jockeyed for position and competed for control with conservative elements. But involvement in national politics did little to further the reform cause. With direct democracy rapidly becoming a litmus test of Progressive political sentiments, the prospects for nonpartisan cooperation in the name of direct legislation dimmed. Helpless to avoid entanglement in national campaigns, democracy reformers were forced to abandon their prior strategies and they soon saw their movement coopted by such individuals as Roosevelt and Wilson, who looked to the reforms for tactical political gains.

Prior to the events of 1910–12, direct democracy had only rarely entered the national political arena. Advocates of the reforms never doubted their value for local and state politics; few seriously contemplated their extension to the national level. In 1906, George Shibley, the head of the recently founded National Federation for People's Rule, with the help of the AFL, sent out a questionnaire to all congressional candidates in the fall election requesting their position vis-à-vis a national advisory initiative on selected policy issues and a national advisory referendum on all laws passed by Congress. After the election Shibley claimed that 107 members of Congress, seventy-two Democrats and thirty-five Republicans, supported a national initiative and referendum in advisory form.[33] Two years later, another memorial was introduced in the Senate by the Democratic Senator Owen of Oklahoma, which, without binding the members of Congress, called for a national advisory referendum to ascertain the public will on certain policy subjects.[34] Yet proposals for a national system of direct legislation were never seriously discussed in Congress. A California journal noted in 1910: "But the larger the political unit, the less simple the referendum is, and the more rarely it can be used. . . . In a state it can only be used for large and simple issues, and for only a few of these, scattered far enough to make it possible to sustain interest in a campaign of education. In a nation at large, the referendum could scarcely be invoked twice in a generation."[35] For a distended country such as the United States, a national system of direct democracy made little sense.

Furthermore, many eastern Progressives feared the possible consequences of direct legislation for the cherished goals of political and administrative efficiency and rationality, two of the key terms in the Progressive vocabulary. They often looked on corporate models as inspiration for a restructuring of the American polity. For those Progressives who placed a greater emphasis on the capacity for reforms to strengthen centralized responsibility and increased efficiency in public administration on the state and the federal level, direct democracy remained of decidedly less interest. Herbert Croly, widely regarded as the most influential theorist of the Progressive movement, can be used to illustrate this tendency. In his 1909 work, *The Promise of American Life*, Croly, instead of putting the blame for the failure of state governments on legislative corruption, argued that it "is to be imputed chiefly to their lack of centralized responsible organization" and contended that "efficient law-making is as much a matter of well-organized and well-tempered detail as it is of an excellent general principle." The very restrictions of the lawmaking power of legislative assemblies that had been the result of protests against corruption and governmental favoritism had turned into primary reasons for the inability of legislatures to deal effectively with modern problems. Direct democracy offered little to improve administrative efficiency and held little appeal for Croly around 1909–10.[36] He concluded: "The progressive democracy is bound to be as much interested in efficient administration as it is in reconstructive legislation. . . . Its future as the expression of a permanent public interest is tied absolutely to an increase of executive authority and responsibility."[37]

Many other important Progressives shared Croly's skeptical assessment of direct democracy. Walter Weyl feared that direct democracy "tends to transform these legislators from representatives, possessed of personal, individual opinions . . . into mere delegates; into mere mechanical forecasters and repeaters of popular deliverances; into parrotlike political phonographs."[38] In California, Chester Rowell warned not to overestimate the importance of direct legislation since "it is impossible administratively and impractical legislatively" to replace the legislature. For him, the initiative and referendum were only part of the needed restructuring of state government. "The short ballot, the short constitution, direct legislation, executive initiative, a judicial judiciary, expert advice, legislative responsibility — these are the essential goals of the reorganizations of state governments."[39] Many observers, then, argued that direct legislation "tends to undermine the strength of the legislature, which must be the hope of our democracy, if we are to develop a scientific system of laws that will keep pace with the vital demands of a strenuous and complex age."[40] An abiding skepticism in the competence of voters to make enlightened decisions combined with a belief in bureaucratic and administrative solutions kept one wing of the Progressive movement from fully embracing direct democracy.[41]

Others believers in the need for administrative efficiency hoped that the initiative and referendum could be so designed as to enhance or complement much-needed reforms of state governments.[42] The most interesting experiment to combine the principle of majority rule with administrative efficiency was conducted in Oregon. Here, William S. U'Ren, together with U.S. Senator Jonathan Bourne, repeatedly argued that the introduction of the reforms would increase the efficiency of public service and would give the taxpayers better results from their taxes, the aim being the "highest possible efficiency in the public service." Around 1910, U'Ren and the Oregon People's Power League presented a highly ambitious plan for the complete restructuring of the state government. The plan called for a higher degree of executive power, with the governor in control of all boards and commissions, with the power to introduce all appropriation bills, and with authority over the state business manager in charge of state finances. To compensate for this concentration of power, the governor would be limited to one term and would not possess any veto power. The legislature would be elected via proportional representation and would serve one six-year term. Later versions of the plan also included the abolition of the state senate. Finally, U'Ren called for a board of "People's Inspectors of Government," modeled after the Board of Censors of the radical Pennsylvania constitution of 1776, that would continually scrutinize the work of the state government. Even though U'Ren's plan was rejected by Oregon voters several times between 1908 and 1914, it presented a highly ambitious proposal to combine direct legislation with administrative efficiency and centralized political leadership.[43]

The plan framed by U'Ren and his allies won the approval of Herbert Croly. By 1915, when he published *Progressive Democracy*, Croly had somewhat abandoned his earlier disdain of direct legislation. He discussed the Oregon plan at length and praised many of its unique features. Croly warned that "political mechanics" could not replace purposeful action or social reform. All too often, direct democracy advocates seemed to believe that the mere introduction of the reforms would immediately result in instigating other far-reaching reforms. For Croly, only "the organization of executive leadership provides popular opinion with an able and indispensable instrument of formulation and of collective action." Such was not readily available under the conditions of direct democracy. In addition, the recall, when applied to administrative experts, threatened to erode the only recently made advances in extending the role of experts. Croly concluded: "Democracy is not government by peculiarly qualified people or by a peculiarly qualified part of the people. It is or should be government in which the largest possible proportion of the adult citizenship of the country effectively participate. The fact that in this instance the failure of the majority to participate is its own fault makes no essential difference. A democracy should not be organized so that the alert and vigorous minority can easily make its will prevail over the less vigorous fellow-citizens. . . . Such agencies of minority rule as the initiative and referendum in their ordinary form fail absolutely to contribute to the accomplishment of this necessary democratic purpose."[44]

The evolution of Croly's thinking on the issue of direct democracy between 1909 and 1915 revealed how some of the earlier resistance to the reforms had diminished among those Progressives putting a premium on efficiency, but that the combination of direct democracy with executive responsibility remained a difficult balancing act that pointed to the conflicted nature of American Progressivism. Curiously, Croly had argued against one of the features of the reforms that might make them attractive to Progressives who cared more for efficiency than for grass-roots democracy: the ability of direct democracy to restructure the electorate, to eliminate those uninterested in policy issues, those unfit to exercise the privilege of the franchise in the first place. The discussions relating to direct legislation and efficiency in government demonstrated the limits of democratic engagement on the part of those middle-class intellectuals that formed the leadership of the reform movement.

The difficulties of many eastern Progressives to combine their interest in efficiency and expertise in government with support for majority rule had slowed the spread of direct legislation in the East throughout the 1900s. As the presidential bid of Theodore Roosevelt unfolded between 1910 and 1912, this resistance softened somewhat, and direct democracy emerged as a national political issue. The story of the rapid disenchantment of Roosevelt with the administration of his successor, William Howard Taft, after his return from Africa in 1910 is well known.[45] In order to challenge the hold of the President over the GOP, Roosevelt needed to attract the support of the Republican insurgents, a group of mostly western reformers who were increasingly chafing under the control of the party by conservatives.[46] The victory of Hiram Johnson in the California gubernatorial election of 1910, and the growing number of insurgent senators and representatives in Congress, led to the formation of the National Progressive Republican League in early 1911. Among its leaders were Johnson, U.S. senator Borah of Idaho, and Robert La Follette of Wisconsin. The league endorsed a list of five reforms: direct primaries, direct democracy, the popular election of United States senators, the popular election of delegates to the GOP national convention, and effective corrupt-practices acts.[47] As the insurgents began to organize inside the GOP and to challenge Taft and his supporters, they embraced a number of issues to delineate their policy differences. With its connotations of grass-roots democracy and popular sovereignty, direct legislation served this purpose well.

Roosevelt shifted his position in relation to the initiative and referendum in order to stave off the presidential bid of La Follette and to enlist the support of the insurgents. Many of them were not thrilled by the prospect of another Roosevelt campaign. Never impressed with his Progressive credentials, many insurgents viewed him as a political opportunist out for personal power. His significant policy shifts in 1911–12 certainly seemed to indicate his willingness to reposition himself in line with the changing power structure in the GOP. After remaining largely silent on the issue of direct democracy during his presidency, he still showed little interest in January 1911, writing to Senator Bourne of Oregon, an ardent proponent of direct legislation: "Don't forget that the direct primary, the referendum, the direct nominations of Senators, are all merely means to ends."[48] His support of the initiative and referendum grew significantly stronger over the next year. In addressing the Ohio constitutional convention in 1912, he declared: "I believe in pure democracy." He added: "In short, I believe that the initiative and referendum should be used, not as a substitute for representative government, but as methods of making such government really representative."[49] Careful to emphasize that he did not favor the introduction of direct legislation in every state but only in those where local conditions warranted it, Roosevelt nevertheless made it clear during his campaign that he had come to realize the essential usefulness of the initiative and referendum.

Many regular Republicans were shocked by the sudden move of Roosevelt into the insurgent camp. Charles Betts, a Republican newspaper editor from upstate New York and staunch supporter of Roosevelt during his terms in office, engaged in an exchange of letters with the former president in which he laid out the regular Republican position. For Betts, "the three requisites of good government are order, stability and progress. These essentials of good government can only be maintained by constitutions, law, order, and a fearless judiciary." Direct democracy endangered these essentials on every level. Given the rising complexity of modern life and the growing need for expertise in public life, direct legislation formed "a species of political atavism. It is a reversion to the diseases, disorders and deformities of the primitive political state." Rousseau's methods of government, Betts maintained, were not designed to cope with conditions in the twentieth century. While advocates of the reforms stressed their trust in the people to make informed decisions and to act in a wise and restrained manner while using their newfound power, Betts had far less trust in human nature. He wrote Roosevelt: "I know something about the history of the world as it is written in rocks and books. I know that man is an animal who has become polished, refined and rendered kind, generous and attractive by the veneer of civilization, and that under this veneer, liable to be fanned into activity at any time, lies dormant all of the brutal instincts bequeathed to him by a savage ancestry. I am familiar with the outbursts of human temper, the hurricanes of human passion, and the whirlwinds of human brutality, as they are recorded in the pages of history."[50] With his endorsement of the initiative and referendum, and with his proposal for a popular review of judicial decisions that has been discussed in a previous chapter, Roosevelt affronted many of his former allies. It remained to be seen whether he would be able to attract enough insurgent support to gain the Republican nomination.

At the same time that Roosevelt altered many of his previous positions, a similar chain of events unfolded in the Democratic Party where Woodrow Wilson was engaged in a similar task of creating a power base. Trained as a political scientist, Wilson had a strong interest in new reforms such as direct legislation and in their possible consequences for the political system. In his work *The State*, published in the 1890s, he had rejected the increasing use of referenda. They tended to lower the responsibility of elected representatives and assumed, falsely, that voters possessed the ability to pass judgment on issues of public policy.[51] Writing in 1908, he was again sharply critical, calling the initiative and referendum "the virtual abandonment of the representative principle." While many claimed that direct legislation was superior to representatives in arriving at the state of public opinion, Wilson was afraid of the rash judgments made by an electorate confronted with important policy decisions. By 1908, Wilson was not ready to sacrifice his belief in the need for sustained and enlightened legislative deliberation for the principle of majority rule and popular sovereignty.[52]

The rising reform tide within the Democratic Party increased the number of Democrats endorsing direct democracy. The most prominent Democrat pushing the issue was Senator Robert Owen of Oklahoma, a state that had incorporated the reforms in its 1907 constitution. Calling machine rule the "Gibraltar of monopoly," Owen contended that "the people's rule will provide a substantial and just control of monopoly and of every evil of government." With his close connections to several leaders of the direct democracy movement, in particular George Shibley and Judson King, Owen used the Senate floor to call attention to the reforms and organize Democratic support.[53] With progressives clamoring for more power in both parties, direct democracy emerged as one of the defining issues.

By late 1910, Wilson had emerged as a possible Progressive Democratic candidate for the presidential nomination. Such individuals as Senator Owen and the Cincinnati single taxer Daniel Kiefer inquired about Wilson's position on the initiative and referendum.[54] Wilson himself had been in contact with such leaders of the direct democracy movement as William U'Ren of Oregon, who had impressed him with information as to the practical operation of the new reforms. In early 1911, Wilson, to the surprise of many of his friends, reversed his previous opposition to direct democracy and endorsed the initiative, referendum, and recall of administrative officials. On a tour of western states in the spring of 1911, he received a very cordial reception in Oregon where U'Ren, the one-time Populist and Republican, welcomed him as a standard-bearer of Progressive principles. In a newspaper interview, Wilson argued that "it is only a question of time until it [direct legislation] will be extended to the Nation." He even went so far as to assert that the civic education of the electorate in the states through the initiative and referendum would soon allow them "to pass intelligently upon National measures." While Wilson took exception to the recall of judges, calling it an unwarranted intrusion upon the independence of the bench, he had firmly planted himself in the progressive camp.[55]

Wilson's sudden change of position disheartened many of his friends and supporters, particularly in his home state of Virginia and other southern states, a predicament he was only too aware of. In 1911, Wilson wrote to California single taxer William Eggleston that "while it is true that the initiative and referendum are among the 'accepted' means of recovering representative government in some parts of the country, in other parts, as for example the South, the statement would by no means be accepted as true." Most southern Democrats had little sympathy for an issue that smacked of giving more power to the same people that they had just successfully disenfranchised.[56] To appeal to the various factions in the Democratic Party, Wilson attempted to find a position that respected local conditions and interests. In a newspaper interview in Seattle in May 1911, he had already outlined that the need for the initiative and referendum depended on local conditions. In a state with "a large preponderance of prejudiced vote," direct legislation could be disastrous. Later on in the year he explained that direct democracy "is a special question, so far as the South is concerned. The mixed character of the electorate in respect to the races stand there as a very serious bar to their adoption. I have never regarded them as of universal application."[57] Time and time again, Wilson emphasized that in states where "actual, genuine representative government" existed, as he contended was the case in Virginia and the South in general, direct legislation was superfluous. Combined with his continued opposition to the recall, Wilson hoped that this strategy would appease Southerners concerned about preserving white rule.[58] Nevertheless, southern delegates to the 1912 Democratic national convention successfully insisted that the platform omit any mention of direct legislation.[59]

Wilson's insistence that direct legislation need not be introduced in the South, where, as a direct consequence of actions supported by many progressives, blacks and many poor whites had recently been excluded from the franchise, points to the ambivalent nature of direct democracy. His acceptance of white supremacy in the South, and the growing willingness of reformers to welcome the self-disenfranchisement of ignorant voters, highlighted in the preceding chapter, demonstrate the racial and social prejudices that structured the perceptions of the leaders of the movement. Mostly of middle-class and Protestant backgrounds, they looked with disdain on the immigrant voters in large cities, had no respect for the political aspirations of blacks, and were repelled by the allegedly sordid spectacle of American politics. "The People" they so tirelessly invoked in their rhetoric had nothing in common with lower-class voters unversed in American political traditions. They aimed to give more power to the upstanding, moral, and church-going citizens who had disgustedly turned away from political participation. In their heated denunciations of corruption and venal party politicians, one can discern a strong sense of moral outrage at a political system that catered to the mob while ignoring codes of moral conduct, professional expertise, religious piety, and social standing. If direct legislation reshaped the electorate by removing "ignorant" voters and empowering the "respectable" element in society, this outcome was surely to be welcomed as a step toward the purification of American politics. Whether consciously or unconsciously, direct democracy advocates remained confined within a set of assumptions and bias that constantly undercut their democratic aspirations and rhetoric.

In all other regards, Wilson's carefully qualified assessment of the initiative and referendum closely followed standard progressive arguments. Wilson, much like Roosevelt, never endorsed the judicial recall, which he regarded as too dangerous to the independence of the bench.[60] Nevertheless, two of the three presidential candidates in 1912 endorsed direct legislation, transforming it into a prominent topic of national politics. As outlined in a letter from William Jennings Bryan to Wilson in the summer of 1912, the initiative and referendum "are not in the campaign but they indicate a fundamental bias toward aristocracy or toward Democracy."[61] The prediction of the *California Outlook* of June 1911 that "there are indications that direct legislation may become the national issue of 1912" were thus fulfilled.[62]

These developments confronted the leaders of the direct democracy movement with a serious dilemma. Their success had previously been founded on their ability to create nonpartisan and broad-based coalitions that rallied around the cause. Since most of the western states where direct legislation had been introduced were controlled by the GOP, Republican support had always been crucial for the actual implementation of the devices. Democratic endorsements had been instrumental in pushing Republicans to accede to the demands of reformers. Time and time again, reformers had argued that the issue of direct legislation transcended party lines and that support for the reforms was not tied to any specific political or economic ideology. Eltweed Pomeroy had argued in 1902 that direct legislation was "not an integral part of any economic theory or scheme."[63] In 1913, one reform journal noted that direct legislation "has not even the most distant relation to socialism, anarchy, single-tax, nor any other economic or political question. . . . Its advocates are found in every party, and they hold the most varied and contradictory theories and beliefs regarding taxation, temperance, trusts, and all other economic and political questions."[64]

With the deepening factional infighting in both major parties and the eventual formation of a third party, the issue of direct democracy lost much of its position as a nonpartisan issue. For Progressive Republicans and Democrats, the reforms held appeal primarily as weapons in factional infighting and as useful campaign rhetoric. For them, an endorsement was a matter of tactical considerations. The support of such prominent individuals as Roosevelt and Wilson might magnify the visibility of the issue, but could these politicians really be trusted to subordinate their interests to the progress of direct legislation? In September 1910, William S. U'Ren wrote to Daniel Kiefer that "I question very much the wisdom of putting Roosevelt in the position where he must declare for or against. He is a politician and an office-seeker." He continued: "If we wait until four or five more states have fallen into line, it will be favorable. He will have had more time to study and think about it, and also it will be more clearly evident that it is worthwhile studying and thinking about it. To politicians things are not good politics that are very far ahead of the common people. . . . Therefore, I would advise that we make no further special effort on Roosevelt."[65] During the 1912 campaign, the leaders of the movement urged their followers to "remember this: the advancement of the Initiative and Referendum movement in this country is vastly more important than who will be elected president in November."[66] But they could not avoid that their cause was partially coopted by the Progressive and Democratic parties. In essence, the leaders of the reform movement had lost control over their agenda. Previously, direct democracy had been a progressive idea; now it emerged as a Progressive measure, with damaging consequences for the future of the movement.

Initially, the results of the 1912 presidential election seemed to provide further proof of the growing popularity of the direct democracy movement. With the GOP finishing a distant third behind the Democrats and Progressives, a clear majority of the American electorate had endorsed candidates who supported the initiative and referendum. The hopes that had been raised in many direct democracy advocates during the political upheaval of 1912 did not exist for long, however. Even during the campaign, the endorsement of direct legislation by many eastern Progressives had been lukewarm at best, more the outcome of tactical shifts to define their policy differences to Republicans than of a new-found enthusiasm for the reforms.[67] After gaining the nomination of his party, Wilson rarely spoke of direct legislation during his campaign, not wanting to alienate the southern wing of his party and secure in the knowledge that he was virtually guaranteed a victory. The initiative and referendum were more prominent during the party nomination campaigns in the spring of 1912 than in the fall contest. If the Progressive Party had emerged as a stable force in the political system, it might have helped spread the reforms further, but its rapid decline in the years afterward further weakened the chances of direct democracy east of the Mississippi.[68] Only four more states adopted the initiative and referendum between 1912 and 1920. No more did so before 1940. The American entry into World War I, the demise of the Progressive movement, and the conservative backlash after the war all doomed the direct democracy movement.

The year 1912 certainly did not mark the end of the organized direct democracy movement, which actually received a significant boost with the formation of the National Popular Government League in late 1913. Up to 1917, the league, founded in late 1913 by the AFL and some progressive reformers, intervened in a number of state campaigns. Its secretary, Judson King, proved as devoted to the cause as Eltweed Pomeroy had been two decades earlier.[69] The outbreak of World War I took the league by surprise and affected it severely. King observed in 1915 that "the war has very seriously crippled our income" and that "all of the reform movements have been hit hard by the war and will have to go slow till it is over."[70] One of King's correspondents from Oregon, Alfred D. Cridge, reported that "the national butchery in Europe is taking the attention of the people to the exclusion of nearly everything, and things are where it looks blue."[71] After the war, the league soon shifted its attention to other issues, most prominently the public ownership of power resources, and practically ceased working on behalf of direct legislation. The history of the league, which officially remained in existence until the death of King in 1958, after 1920 illustrated the changing political concerns of American reformers.

None of the state Direct Legislation Leagues seem to have survived after the war. The journal *Equity*, which had published the *Direct Legislation Record* since 1907, folded in 1919, thus ending twenty-five years of work for the cause. The *American Political Science Review* would, as it was agreed to with Charles Taylor, the publisher of *Equity*, continue to prepare analyses of votes on propositions, but that hardly filled the void. The number of articles appearing in popular magazines that dealt with the initiative and referendum dropped precipitously around 1920, another sign of the waning public interest in the issue.[72] In 1927, Chester I. Long, a former president of the American Bar Association, observed that "some States do not know whether they have it [direct legislation] or not. They have enacted something but fortunately the courts have so limited it in its operation that they are not sure as to what they have." He continued: "Of course, no State would adopt it now. No State that did not get the initiative and referendum eight or ten years ago would think of passing it now because that fashion is in the discard."[73] For all intents and purposes, the initiative and referendum no longer were a viable political issue.[74] Intellectually, and in terms of the strategic and tactical choices available to it, the reform movement, never very strong to begin with, evaporated around 1920. As a result, direct democracy would remain a regionalized phenomenon tied to the specific political cultures of the American West.

7

DIRECT DEMOCRACY IN ACTION
The United States up to 1940

In 1922, Walter Lippmann published *Public Opinion*, one of the most influential books on American politics to appear in the 1920s. Together with *The Phantom Public*, published in 1925, Lippmann set out to destroy the notion that the people could ever act as a political collectivity capable of reasoned judgment and informed behavior. Like most eastern progressive intellectuals before the war, Lippmann had never developed much sympathy with the western fervor for direct democracy. The wartime experiences, when many intellectuals worked for various war agencies and commissions and the government intervened in economic affairs to an unprecedented degree, had only reinforced Lippmann's insistence on expert administration. Surveying the changing political conditions of the 1920s, Lippmann aimed to redefine the role of the people in public and political life, in the process illustrating the rapidly waning fortunes of direct democracy.

Lippmann based his analysis on the argument that modern society had to increasingly rely on experts to manage an evermore complicated economic system. "I argue that representative government, either in which is ordinarily called politics, or in industry, cannot be worked successfully, no matter what the basis of election, unless there is an independent, expert organization for making the unseen facts intelligible to whose who have to make the decisions." The people might be able to cast their ballots in a yes and no fashion on any number of issues, but they were incapable as a group to intelligently debate the issues or to administer the decisions once they were taken.[1] As far as "the people" who had loomed so large in progressive rhetoric were concerned, Lippmann easily dismissed them as political actors: "The ideal of the omnicompetent, sovereign citizen is, in my opinion, such a false ideal. . . . The individual man does not have opinions on all public affairs. He does not know how to direct public affairs. He does not know what is happening, why it is happening, what ought to happen. I cannot imagine how he could know, and there is not the least reason for thinking, as mystical democrats have thought, that the compounding of individual ignorance in masses of people can produce a continuous directing force in public affairs." Living in increasing isolation, exposed to a variety of conflicting impressions and impulses, and without the proper education to deal with political issues, the ability of the people to act as citizens consisted primarily of electing candidates.[2] In intellectually demolishing central tenets of progressive reform, Lippmann reflected, and helped mold, the changing intellectual landscape of the post–World War I era. Gone were the high hopes of far-reaching reforms. Disillusioned by the aftermath of the war, many American intellectuals adopted an elitist political stance full of disdain for "The People."

Lippmann's scathing indictment of popular sovereignty and democratic government formed only part of a broader shift in public and academic opinion. A new generation of political scientists, influenced by the pioneering work in psychology of Sigmund Freud and applying quantitative methods borrowed from the social sciences, joined Lippmann in reevaluating the role of the American voter and the workings of the political system. They attacked many of the assumptions that had sustained progressive reform. The voters were not rational actors capable of learning, but were guided by irrational impulses and unconscious desires. The people as a group were as prone to irrational behavior as individuals. The rise of dictatorships all over Europe in the 1920s and 1930s rendered earlier assumptions about the inevitable historical rise of democracies problematic. A crisis of confidence affected many in the United States who could no longer sustain the sense of optimism and the belief in the perfectibility of political institutions that had marked the Progressive Era. The only available alternative to a government by a people not competent for self-government was an increasing role of experts in government, the creation of an autonomous sphere not subject to popular control, which would allow these experts to exert influence on policy-making.[3]

Yet the introduction of direct democracy in about twenty American states between 1898 and 1917 left an important institutional legacy for American local and state politics. Even if the further diffusion of the new devices halted, they continued to be widely used in a number of state and municipalities across the United States. Only the outbreak of

World War II reduced the number of popular initiated ballot propositions to an insignificant level before the 1970s witnessed a powerful renaissance of direct legislation. This chapter will document the employment of direct democracy at the state and local levels between 1910 and 1940, focusing in particular on the state of California, then already a national trendsetter in initiative and referendum politics.

The Practical Employment of Direct Democracy

While attempts to revive the direct democracy movement failed in the 1930s, American voters continued to go to the polls to cast their ballots on a large number of popularly initiated ballot propositions. According to one estimate, 726 constitutional and statutory initiatives were placed on the ballots in the states with direct democracy between 1900 and 1939.[4] When he collected information for his projected study on the history of direct legislation in America around 1930, Judson King counted 501 popular initiatives on the ballot between 1900 and 1929. He also found 199 popular referenda for the same period.[5] Combining these two counts, one can estimate that roughly 1,000 ballot propositions were placed before American voters at the state level between 1900 and 1940; about 75 percent of these were initiatives, the rest referenda. Not all of the states that had adopted the reforms made extensive use of them. According to King, up to 1929, 157 propositions were on the ballot in Oregon, 87 in California, 73 in Arizona, 68 in Colorado, and 48 in North Dakota; these five states combined laid claim to more than 60 percent of all popular initiatives and referenda voted on between 1900 and 1929. By contrast, Maryland did not have a single proposition on the ballot, Nevada had only 5, Michigan had 11, and Nebraska and Massachusetts each had 10.[6]

It seems that the overall number of ballot propositions depended on the ability of the parties to control the political landscape and the specific legal provisions surrounding direct legislation. In such states as Maine, Michigan, and Massachusetts, the direct democracy movement had exploited strategic opportunities presented to them by a temporary destabilization of the established power structures to introduce the reforms. But the regular party organizations soon recovered and reacquired their dominance over the legislative agenda. They continued to be resourceful enough to deter interest groups from pursuing their goals via initiatives. In these states, a number of ballot propositions might surface in the first years after the adoption of the reforms, but direct legislation never became an accepted part of the political decision-making process, and the number of propositions soon tapered off.[7] Some states, such as Maine and Idaho, had never adopted the constitutional initiative in an effort to restrict direct democracy. Others, including Michigan and Massachusetts, granted the legislatures substantial authority to get involved in the initiative process. In states such as Arkansas, direct legislation became embroiled in legal conflicts that severely weakened its usefulness.[8] Only in a few states, such as California, Oregon, and Arizona, where weak parties coexisted with powerful interest groups, and under liberal provisions for the use of direct democracy, did the new devices emerge as important tools of policy-making. Here a political culture developed that incorporated direct legislation as a powerful symbol of popular sovereignty.

While American voters approved popularly initiated constitutional amendments at a much lower rate than those submitted by state legislatures, voter turnout rates were substantially higher for the former, an indication of their controversial character. Of the ballot propositions voted on between 1924 and 1936, almost 1,500 in all, voter turnout reached a mere 56.7 percent of all voters participating in a given election on amendments sponsored by legislatures, but stood at 74.4 percent for initiated amendments. Voter interest was highest for propositions involving issues of public morality, education, and revenue, with minor constitutional matters and bond issues eliciting the least response.[9] A rate of about 75 percent voter turnout in elections involving popular initiatives would prove to be the average for the decades 1900–1940. The predictions of early reform advocates that the introduction of the initiative and referendum would dramatically raise levels of political participation were not realized.[10]

In terms of the distribution of ballot propositions across various policy fields, the fact that so many measures touched on several fields simultaneously makes it very difficult to establish clear trends in the employment of the initiative for specific purposes. One observer of the 166 propositions on the ballot in the various states in 1922 estimated that about a quarter of them dealt with matters of finance, another quarter with social problems, and 12 percent with economic and industrial concerns. Some proposed laws dealt with important issues, others were of a largely technical nature, leading the observer to argue for a system "whereby technicalities beyond the capacity of the voters can be eliminated, and trivialities can be dispensed with."[11] Analyzing the ballot propositions for the years 1923–24, another political scientist argued that of the total number of 234 measures, 108 were financial, 90 had a political character, 24 economic, and 12 social. Two years later, finally, financial and social measures predominated at the expense of measures dealing with political and economic issues.[12]

The already mentioned research of Judson King can be used to shed more light on the content of about 400 of the initiatives voted on between 1900 and 1929. For the purposes of this analysis, they have been divided into four broad categories. About 150 of them dealt with matters of government organization, in particular the creation of new state offices, agencies or commissions, questions of the suffrage, etc.; roughly 100 dealt with issues of taxation and finance, including the levying of new taxes and bond issues; around 70 propositions concerned matters of social welfare and economic regulation, such as new welfare laws and the regulation of occupations; about 60 propositions focused on the area of public morality, in particular prohibition, but also gambling, horse-racing, and other moral matters. The sponsors of the initiatives varied widely; prohibitionists and their opponents were, of course, primarily involved in the alcohol issue while labor unions focused on questions of social welfare.[13] It is often impossible to determine what array of groups favored or opposed a specific initiative. The broad classifications employed here are of only limited value in identifying trends in the utilization of the initiative. Overall, there were few limits as to the kinds of issues that could be addressed with the help of direct democracy. Some matters, such as prohibition, the public development and ownership of water and power resources, the regulation of occupations such as medicine, and the sale of oleomargarine, constantly appeared before the electorate in the form of new propositions. As frequently, however, initiatives dealt with relatively minor questions relating to the organization of state and local governments, matters that generated little popular interest and which had been safely handled by state legislatures. As long as willing parties could be found to secure a sufficient number of signatures on a petition, the process of direct democracy could be employed for an endless variety of purposes.

In the early years of direct democracy, when practical experiments with the initiative and referendum remained confined to Oregon, volunteers largely gathered the required signatures. Sometimes existing organizations, such as labor unions, farmers' organizations, or the Oregon People's Power League, mobilized their membership; at other times, ad hoc-organizations emerged that focused on one issue and sought the support of other associations. Paid solicitors were occasionally employed, but they remained the exception. By 1914, however, with more and more states adopting direct legislation and increasingly more campaigns waged every year, a new pattern emerged. In that year, Judson King reported to a correspondent in North Carolina that "it has been found practically impossible to get the large petitions necessary without the aid of paid solicitors when the volunteer effort has exhausted itself."[14] At the same time, King informed another correspondent in Ohio: "Occasionally, on a wet or dry campaign you can get a petition by volunteer effort but upon measures which pass by tremendous majorities it is seldom that you can get more than half or two-thirds of the signatures by volunteer effort alone. The rest has to be secured by paid solicitors, especially when the time grows short for filing petitions." No companies had yet been formed that specialized in the collection of signatures, but a powerful trend toward the professionalization of signature solicitation had set in.[15]

Compared to the initiative, the popular referendum never acquired the same importance. In many states, progressives and reformers had introduced direct legislation as part of a general takeover of political power. Once in power, they had little use for the referendum, which was soon utilized by conservatives aiming to block specific acts of legislation enacted by progressive state legislatures. In 1919, North Dakota conservatives used the referendum to challenge seven reform laws, most of them strengthening state administrative commissions and agencies, passed by the Nonpartisan League.[16] In Missouri, the Republican Party won control of both the legislature and the governor's office in 1920 for the first time since 1869. In trying to block their legislative program, the opposition Democrats decided to use the referendum to challenge twelve bills passed by the legislature. All twelve laws were defeated in 1922, an example of when "the referendum was used by the opposition party to nullify a large portion of the legislation enacted by the party in power."[17]

With the diminishing fortunes of the progressive movement, the use of the referendum declined. Regular Democrats and Republicans returned to political power, and the state legislatures were less and less likely to pass legislation hostile to business or other well-heeled interest groups. These groups no longer had to resort to the referendum to invalidate new laws. Reform groups routinely did not have the funds and organizational resources to engage in similar activities. Consequently, the referendum device fell more and more into disuse. In Colorado, for instance, twelve referenda appeared on the ballot between 1912 and 1916. Only one more can be found between 1916 and 1940.[18]

The recall had only been adopted by about a dozen states between 1898 and 1918. In addition, by 1926, about 1,200 American municipalities had added a recall provision to their city charters. But up to that year, not more than one hundred recall elections had actually taken place, with about 50 percent being successful.[19] Most local recall elections involved infighting between rival political factions rather than fundamental policy disputes or outright corruption.[20] At the state level, the recall never acquired any importance. This was primarily due to the difficulties involved in securing the necessary number of signatures to invoke the recall provision. Between 1908, the year when Oregon became the first state to introduce the recall against state officers, and 1940, there were only two recorded instances of the successful ouster of officials elected on a statewide basis. In 1922, two members of the Oregon Public Utility Commission were recalled over a dispute over rates. And in North Dakota, conservatives in the state used the recall to remove Governor Lynn J. Frazier, Attorney General William Lempke, and the commissioner of agriculture, John Hagden. These three officials, elected on the ticket of the Nonpartisan League, constituted the state industrial commission in charge of state-owned enterprises such as the Bank of North Dakota, flour mills, and terminal elevators.[21] These two incidents, however, formed a clear exception. At the state level, the steep signature threshold for the recall — usually 25 percent of the voters participating in the last election for the office whose incumbent was to be removed from his position — made it far more difficult to employ the recall than it was to employ the initiative and referendum.[22]

There are few investigations that examine voting behavior on ballot propositions. As previously mentioned, the labor movement in Washington State put a series of initiatives on the 1914 ballot that represented the legislative program of labor and farmer groups. Nor surprisingly, working-class voters strongly supported the propositions, while voters in rural eastern Washington were more opposed. These measures, however, were clearly identified as labor initiatives and probably polarized the electorate more than in other elections. They can hardly be taken to represent long-term voting behavior on propositions in the state.[23] In 1916, two political scientists examined voting patterns in Oregon on more than one hundred measures that had been placed before the Oregon electorate between 1908 and 1914. They focused on the differences between urban and rural and between lower-, middle-, and upper-class voters. They encountered substantially different voting patterns between urban- and rural- and between upper-class and lower-class voters, while middle-class voters largely cast their ballots like the upper class. These differences were most pronounced on those propositions that could clearly be labeled as radical; on many other important measures, however, the gaps between the various groups were smaller. Overall, the two scholars concluded that "the most impressive feature of these figures of class differences is their small size." Class conflict only partially shaped political conditions in Oregon.[24] In general, voting behavior on ballot propositions varied widely, depending on the issues before the voters, the groups involved in the campaigns, and the general political climate. The initiative, referendum, and recall were neutral devices, which could, and were, utilized by a great variety of groups for diverse issues, resulting in heterogeneous election results.

California's Bastard Triplets:
The Practice of Direct Democracy in California, 1910–1940

In October 1911, after California voters had ratified the twenty-three constitutional amendments that contained the essence of the Progressive legislative program, Francis Heney wrote to Governor Hiram Johnson to congratulate him on his role in "the greatest movement which ever took place in the history of the industrial freedom of the human race."[25] Like many other California Progressives, Heney believed that the state stood on the threshold of a new era. With direct democracy and a strengthened railroad commission to regulate the erstwhile omnipotent Southern Pacific, unprecedented opportunities for economic and social reform suddenly seemed available. The opponents of direct democracy had quite different expectations. In the words of W. P. Butcher, the city attorney of Santa Barbara, the reforms were "California's bastard triplets," part of a "seditious and insane heresy" sweeping the nation. He continued: "They are weapons put into the hands of the ignorant, the discontented, and the irresponsible by which the peace, harmony and good order of the community are disturbed, and business menaced, and kept in continual turmoil."[26]

The hopes of reformers, as well as the dire predictions of conservatives, were soon to be profoundly disappointed by the practical usage of the initiative, referendum, and recall. The amendments ratified in 1911 marked the crowning achievement of California Progressivism; no further laws of equal importance would be enacted in the coming years. The Progressives were too busy consolidating their hold on power and fending off the attacks of conservative Republicans to embark on another round of reform activity.[27] Direct democracy, however, immediately became a widely popular and extensively used part of state government. It was the initiative that attracted the most attention and that had the most far-reaching repercussions for politics in the Golden State. During the 1910s, 30 initiatives qualified for the ballot, 35 during the 1920s, and 36 in the 1930s. After 1940, the number of initiatives dropped sharply, to 20 in the 1940s, 12 in the 1950s, and an all-time low of 9 in the 1960s, before the rise of new social movements launched a sharp rise after 1970.[28] In addition, many more petitions were filed with the attorney general but failed to qualify for the ballot due to a lack of signatures. In 1938, for instance, it was reported that 59 petitions had been filed, leading one observer to conclude that "judging by the number of them, 'there ought to be a law' is a fixation with no small percentage of the populace."[29] Few of the early advocates of direct democracy had anticipated that the devices would be invoked so frequently.

Far from determining fundamental issues of public policy, the range of issues subject to a popular vote seemed to have no limit. Many of the propositions were of a highly technical nature. Because so many initiatives and referenda straddled the boundaries of different policy fields, it is difficult to arrive at a clear picture of the distribution of propositions across various issues. It seems, however, that a significant proportion of initiatives dealt with issues of public morality during the 1910s and the early 1920s, especially in relation to prohibition. Another focus of attention was governmental institutions and processes, as exemplified by the various nonpartisan elections bills that became embroiled in referenda during the 1910s. During the decade of the Great Depression, increasingly more propositions dealt with economic matters such as the regulation of occupations, including labor unions, or matters of taxation. Some shifts in the general distribution of initiated and referred measures across different policy fields are discernible, but direct legislation in California addressed a broad and diverse array of issues, many of which did not elicit a noticeable popular interest.[30] What is most remarkable is the lack of any truly significant laws passed via the popular initiative. The most controversial initiatives, such as various pension schemes in the 1930s and 1940s or an antilabor proposition in 1938, failed.

In addition to direct democracy at the state level, the initiative and referendum were also widely used to decide local policy issues, particularly with regard to matters of public transportation and the development of water and power systems. In San Francisco, voters approved a number of bond issues and referenda from the 1900s to the 1920s to buy up existing streetcar lines, to construct municipal railways, and to build the Hetch Hetchy aqueduct to transport water from the Sierra Nevada to the city.[31] Overall, voters in San Francisco, between 1902 and 1928, voted on the staggering number of 242 charter amendments, 56 bond issues, 4 recalls, 1 ordinance referendum, 12 initiated ordinances, and 33 initiated charter amendments. The electorate in Los Angeles, during the period 1912–28, cast their ballots on 141 charter amendments, 88 bond issues, 1 recall, 8 ordinance referenda, 8 initiated ordinances, and 141 public policy propositions.[32] Not all of these ballot propositions were the result of the presence of local direct legislation, but they all reflected the extension of a plebiscitary democracy. On the local as well as on the state level, California voters were faced with an avalanche of propositions that formed a constant challenge for even the most civic-minded voter.

What is most remarkable in light of the interest groups that had supported the movement for the introduction of direct legislation is how little they were able to make use of it. As will be described in more detail in a later chapter, single-tax initiatives were repeatedly defeated at the polls. The Anti-Saloon League (ASL) in the state enjoyed only mixed success in using the initiative to make California dry. Three times, in 1914, 1916, and 1918, dry initiatives went down to defeat. The margins of defeat declined each time, a development that encouraged prohibition activists, but the fact remains that California went dry only after the legislature ratified the Eighteenth Amendment.[33] After 1920, the wet forces in California employed the referendum to defeat the Harris bill, which would have set up the law-enforcement machinery to complement the prohibition statutes, a defeat that severely crippled enforcement of the Volstead Act in the state. After the repeal of prohibition in 1933, the dry forces twice attempted to use the initiative to provide for a local-option law, but they were resoundingly defeated in 1934 and 1936.[34]

Other original backers of the initiative and referendum hardly fared better. Labor, unlike its counterparts in Washington State and Arizona, never developed a cohesive political program that it tried to implement via the initiative in California. Middle-class progressives had achieved most of their demands by 1911. The ability of their opponents to derail their legislative program now dismayed many progressives. As long as they had been a minority in the Republican Party, the initiative and referendum seemed ideal tools to implement their demands. After 1910, however, they controlled state government and the legislature. Now the referendum took on a new dimension. It became a nuisance, a "refuge" for special interests that had been unable to have their pet proposals enacted by the legislature. With a party committed to the interests of the people in power, reformers claimed, there was little need for direct legislation.[35] For reformers, "the referendum is the weapon of conservatism," easily exploited by the special interests targeted by a progressive administration and state legislature. Twice, in 1915 and 1916, the voters of California defeated nonpartisan ballot laws passed by a Progressive state legislature in a referendum.[36] The new devices could not be harnessed to advance a specific political agenda, nor could their former champions control them. If anything, the opponents of direct democracy and other Progressive causes, better organized and with more financial resources, were usually in a significantly better position to employ them than liberal or reform groups.

Very quickly after the ratification of the amendments, a number of crucial problems of the direct democracy process drew public attention. These problems were remarkably similar to the ones identified by contemporary political scientists and other observers. The powerful role of interest groups in the initiative process, the importance of money in conducting efficient election campaigns, the further weakening of the political parties, the role of a public relations industry, low voter turnout, and confusing ballot titles were among the more important ones. From the beginning, direct democracy manifested itself as a deeply flawed process that did not fulfill any of the hopes reformers had invested in it. In many ways, discussions about the initiative and referendum have centered on these issues ever since.[37]

The rising campaign costs of direct democracy were first revealed in 1922. After the 1922 Water and Power initiative had been defeated at the polls in a campaign marked by unprecedented expenditures on the part of the private utilities who had united to defeat the initiative, the California Senate launched an investigation under the leadership of reform senator Herbert C. Jones. After extensive interviews with a number of witnesses, including the power executives who had directed the campaigns against the initiative, the committees was surprised to uncover "startlingly large expenditures in campaigns on such measures" and "campaign methods and practices that constitute a menace to our electoral system." The committee estimated that more than $1.1 million had been spent on the thirteen popular initiatives and referenda that were on the ballot in 1922. Three of the propositions involved campaigns where more than $100,000 was spent, and $661,000 was spent on the Water and Power Act alone. These sums far surpassed the expectations of the lawmakers. They concluded: "The power of money in influencing public opinion, its ability to carry popular elections through vast expenditures for propaganda, literature, advertising and organized campaign workers was made strikingly manifest in the investigations of your committee." Yet, after amassing a large body of evidence, the committee was not ready to recommend putting a cap on campaign expenditures. Its findings illustrated that many of the present-day dynamics of lavishly financed initiative campaigns were already in place a mere decade after the adoption of the reforms.[38]

Even more remarkable was the rapid development of an industry that specialized in collecting signatures for petitions. In February

1912, Charles Willard, a Los Angeles reformer and journalist, reported on a flagrant misuse of the referendum process that occurred in his hometown under the local direct democracy statute. A petition had been circulated in Los Angeles to refer to a popular vote an ordinance requiring that cows be tested for tuberculin. The petition was drawn up in a way to convey the impression that the signers actually supported the ordinance. Katherine Edson, another reformer, contended that the dairymen who opposed the measure "effected an organization and employed a man who makes a business circulating petitions, and paid him ten cents a name. He hired men and women at two and a half and three cents per name, and within thirty days turned in 23,000 names, of which 14,000 were good." The collectors for the referendum petition had apparently misrepresented themselves and the content of the petition to the public. In theory, direct legislation was designed to ascertain the popular will. Its usage should reflect genuine public interest in specific policies. But if professional circulators were allowed to gather signatures by disguising the true intent of a petition, how could the proper functioning of the new devices be safeguarded?[39]

The professionalization of petition circulation has always been one of the most persistent problems associated with the direct democracy process. As early as June 1914, attention was directed at the "commercialization of the circulation of signatures" by professional solicitors, as direct legislation had immediately spawned a corps of specialists in handling initiative and referendum campaigns. Unlike Washington State, California imposed no restrictions on professional petition circulators.[40] It soon became clear that almost no organization was able to place a petition on the ballot without the help of professionals. Enterprising individuals seized the opportunity and began to offer their services. For a certain fee, usually between five and ten cents per signature, they could virtually guarantee that a petition would qualify for the ballot. Signatures were solicited "in densely populated metropolitan areas by professional circulators, who stand on street corners or in front of buildings and secure signatures from a large number of voters who do not know the real nature of the petitions they sign." While seven states—Arkansas, Missouri, Massachusetts, Montana, Nebraska, Ohio, and Utah—imposed some geographical restrictions on the collection of signatures, often specifying that signatures had to be collected from all the counties in the state, California did not do so, meaning that solicitors were free to concentrate on dense urban areas where they quickly became a common fixture on sidewalks and street corners.[41]

The theory that a popular initiative reflected public interest was undermined by the presence of these professionals. It was their ability to sell the content of a petition to the public that determined its chances. Complaints about their practices were almost universal. E. A. Walcott, the executive secretary of the Commonwealth Club, argued in 1930: "It seems to me that the petition system has pretty thoroughly broken down. Registrar Zemansky [the California registrar of votes] tells me that, so far as his experience goes, all petitions are paid for. We used to think that propositions would be brought forward by enthusiastic citizens who would take the trouble to petition for their submission because of their interest in public affairs. This has not happened, at any rate in this part of the State, with the exception of charter amendments raising the salaries of policemen, firemen and teachers. All petitions filed have been brought together by paid solicitors."[42] Zemansky reported that solicitors worked in factories and firehouses to gather signatures. He believed, but had been unable to prove, that petitions were left "at cigar stands, soft drink parlors, and 'speak easy' places" to be signed by patrons, in clear violation of the statute.[43]

In the same year, Edward Allen, chairman of the Sub-Section on the Initiative, Referendum, and Recall of the Commonwealth Club, also agreed that the circulation of petitions presented the most troublesome problem. In a preliminary report to the Section of a New Constitution in April 1930, he wrote: "One most outstanding phenomenon is the commercialization in circulating petitions. Though volunteers have successfully completed some petitions, yet it seems that for all practical purposes it is necessary to hire professional solicitors at ten cents a name to get enough signatures. In consequence a tidy sum, additional to all the many other expenses of campaigning, is needed by the backers of the proposition, variously estimated at $12,000 up. It seems also that, as a practical matter, it is necessary to contract with one or two bureaus who make a business of that sort of thing, or else give up in despair of a sufficient petition." Allen realized that "the policy of direct legislation has become permanently embedded in our system and there is not the slightest chance that any material change in it will be permitted."[44] There did not seem to be any proposal that attracted enough support for adoption.

Even as the clamor against the practices of petition circulators intensified in the 1920s and '30s, there remained one major obstacle to any reform on the process, the presence of Dr. Haynes. After the ratification of the amendments, Haynes was transformed into a tenacious defender of the rather liberal provisions for employing the initiative and referendum, now part of the California constitution. Until his death in 1937, he regarded most attempts to change the process, even if they originated with individuals well known to be generally supportive of his goals, as attacks on the institution itself. In 1929, for instance, Frank S. Boggs, a state senator from Stockton, introduced legislation that would have prohibited the employment of paid circulators.[45] Haynes remained unconvinced, arguing that "admitting, for the sake of argument, that very large organizations could do it (and, of course, the large corporations could) the fact remains that the initiative is not intended to be used only by large powerful groups of people but is intended for the use of the people at large."[46] Haynes conveniently ignored that "the people at large" did not have the material resources to hire petition circulators. The rapid population growth of California automatically increased the required number, thereby driving up the costs of collecting the signatures. In 1926, the Automobile Club of Southern California spent almost $8,000 to qualify a petition regarding an expansion of state highways.[47] A year later, the Independent Petroleum and Consumers Association spent more than $53,000 just to secure the signatures to stop a law passed by the legislature via the popular referendum.[48] Only a well-financed organization with the ability to retain the services of one of many professional petition circulation companies could hope to use the initiative and referendum process successfully.

Haynes not only defended the rights of petition circulators; he resisted most proposals to alter the direct democracy statutes in California. Because of his long history of involvement with direct legislation, his strong interest in the issue, and his tenacity in defending its provisions, Haynes was uniquely positioned to block any efforts at change. Governors and lawmakers deferred to his opinion in all matters of direct legislation.[49] He was especially concerned about preserving the fairly low signature levels required to qualify initiatives and referenda for the ballot, which was set at 8 percent of the gubernatorial vote in the preceding election for the initiative and 5 percent for the referendum. In reaction to the continued presence of single tax initiatives on the ballot, an organization was formed in 1919 to qualify a petition that proposed raising the signature level to 25 percent for any initiative dealing with matters of taxation. In 1920 and 1922, this petition appeared on the California ballot. Support came largely from the business community, which would have been adversely affected by the implementation of the single tax. In response, Haynes enlisted the support of such groups as organized labor, teachers, the prohibition movement, and progressives, and of such powerful individuals as U.S. senator James Phelan.[50] The proposition was voted down both times.

In the late 1920s, the Commonwealth Club of California, one of the leading civic organizations in the state, with a membership that included much of the state's political elite, launched a massive investigation of direct legislation. This project was largely the brainchild of A. J. Pillsbury, a long-time reformer, now in retirement. Pillsbury volunteered to devote his entire time to the endeavor; a project that would keep him occupied for more than two years, between 1928 and 1930.[51] His eventual report documented many of the troubling aspects of direct democracy in California. In his voluminous study, based on his personal research and dozens of hearings of his committee, Pillsbury compiled a list of all the ballot propositions between 1848 and 1929, including not just those framed under the direct democracy laws, but also constitutional amendments and referenda placed before the voters by the state legislature. Over the course of the eight decades, California voters had cast their ballots on 384 statewide propositions, 306 of them constitutional amendments. Early fears that direct legislation would lead to radical laws had not been confirmed. "The People have shown themselves to be conservative. All radical measures were defeated." But the hopes of many reformers that the devices would increase popular political participation likewise had been dashed. Between 1912 and 1928, on the average, only 45 percent of the voters who went to the polls voted on propositions, a figure that translated to just 30 percent of all registered voters. "And this is government 'by, of, and for' The People. 'For' the People it may be, but 'by' and 'of' it has never been and probably never will be," was Pillsbury's skeptical conclusion.[52]

The low voter turnout, however, did not overly concern Pillsbury. Like other progressive reformers disillusioned by the failure of the people to act as planned, he found positive aspects in a limited electorate. "The state will be the better to have its affairs in the hands of a small group of intelligent and interested citizens than to have them muddled by ignorance and stupidity no matter how good intentioned." Much more threatening was the ability of a fairly small percentage of the electorate to have a deciding voice in matters of legislation: "There is grave danger in such a wide spread indifference to state affairs as we have in California. It is not safe to have the destiny of the state confided to a trifle more than one-fourth of the qualifiable electorate of the state, with a large percentage of that percentage mainly concerned for their own, entirely personal, interests. And that great body of political punk is highly inflammable and, when their passions are stirred by some self-seeking demagogue, to burst into a flame of passion and do exactly the wrong thing with a vengeance."[53] The initiative, especially, afforded well-organized and financed minorities, small groups "willing to bear the cost of petitioning," the opportunity to put their fads before the public, often repeatedly. Instead of leading to popular rule, "the aspiration of the people of California for a direct participation in affairs of government has imposed no inconsiderable burden upon the attention of would-be intelligent voters." Like many reformers, Pillsbury had come a long way since the enthusiasm of the years 1910–11.[54] In the end, Pillsbury offered few concrete reform proposals, and his investigation produced no lasting effects. It only underlined the prevailing unease with the direct legislation process. Outside of Haynes, few public figures or academic observers were overly impressed with the results of the process. Some of the attacks were certainly politically motivated, but even well-meaning liberals found it difficult to defend an institution that had so clearly failed to achieve its original goals.

The Recall

Pillsbury had concentrated his attention on the initiative and referendum, the two most important aspects of direct democracy. The third element, the recall, attracted much less attention even though it was frequently used. As documented by the two political scientists Frederick Bird and Thomas Ryan in 1930, the recall in California, as was the case in other states as well, was mostly a local affair. Not a single statewide elected politician had ever been removed from office. During the years 1913–14, attempts had been made to recall three state senators. One, Grant from San Francisco, was defeated by the vice interests unhappy with this support of an antiprostitution law. Another senator was recalled after a conviction for embezzlement. But the third try, orchestrated by labor unions upset about a senator who had broken his campaign promises, failed.[55] No further attempt to recall an official at the state level qualified for the ballot until World War II. In contrast, recalls were fairly frequent at the municipal level. There had been 74 recall elections in cities with a population under 20,000, 22 in cities with a population between 20,000 and 100,000, and the devices had been employed 17 times in the large cities of Los Angeles, San Francisco, and Oakland. Adding these numbers to the number of recalls in counties and irrigation districts, the two political scientists arrived at a total of 208 recall petitions and 155 elections, 72 of which had been successful. Seldom used to punish important officials, the recall functioned much more often as a weapon in local squabbles between rival factions.[56]

The judicial recall, which had attracted so much attention in 1910–11, had hardly been used at all. The most famous incident occurred in San Francisco in 1913 and once again dealt with a moral issue. Charles Weller, a judge on the Police Court, stood accused of reducing the bond of a man accused of rape, thus allowing the man to flee the city. This was only the latest in a series of decisions in which Weller seemed to favor criminal elements. Women had only recently acquired the right to vote, giving reformers hope that they would now be able to outvote the Tenderloin district. Outraged by Weller's decision, a number of prominent San Francisco women entered into a recall campaign. Although Weller enjoyed the support of the influential building trades, he was defeated in the recall election by a narrow margin.[57] In 1921, reformers were equally successful in recalling another two police judges in the same city. For some years, there had been the suspicion among reformers that the police courts in San Francisco had become hopelessly corrupt. A grand jury assembled in early 1920 found shocking conditions existed, including judicial corruption, and indicted several bail bond brokers and one judge. But because of largely circumstantial evidence, no guilty verdict was obtained. In the spring of

1921, some reform associations including the bar association and the Civic League of Improvement Clubs began to circulate petitions to recall two police judges. They secured two candidates and forced a recall election. Organized labor vigorously opposed the recall since the judges had always been friendly to labor, while, again, women figured prominently on the reform side. The two incumbents were defeated.[58] Besides these two incidents, no judges were recalled in California between 1910 and 1940, demonstrating that the public prestige of the bench proved difficult to overcome.

Assessing the Impact of Direct Democracy

The proponents of direct legislation during the early part of the twentieth century had regarded the initiative, referendum, and recall as among the most far-reaching political innovations of the time. A number of reforms had been proposed and implemented to make the political system more responsive to the popular will, including the Australian ballot, the direct primary, corrupt-practices acts, the direct election of U.S. senators, proportional representation, the short ballot, and commission government. But none of these reforms went as far as direct legislation. By putting the power to initiate new laws directly in the hands of the voters, the American people would finally be able to liberate themselves from the dominance of bosses and corporations. It would put an end to machines and lobbying, to legislative bribery, horse-trading, and pork barrel politics by removing the incentive for legislative corruption. It would heighten civic awareness, increase voter turnout, educate the public on important issues, revitalize the public sphere, and give American politics a new moral dimension. Whatever their expectations as to the shape of the new American polity, all advocates of the new reforms, as well as their conservative opponents and many outside observers, expected the new devices to have a profound impact on American politics.

When political scientists began to analyze the role of direct legislation in local and state politics, they were surprised to find that few major changes could be traced to the introduction of the initiative and referendum. For one thing, the number of ballot propositions deriving from popular initiative were still dwarfed by the number of measures submitted to popular vote by state legislatures, mostly in the form of constitutional amendments. Between 1924 and 1936, for instance,

American voters cast their ballots on the staggering number of 1,493 measures in forty-seven states, with only a small fraction resulting from direct democracy. Of the initiated constitutional amendments, only slightly more than a quarter were ratified by the people, compared to almost 64 percent in the case of amendments submitted by legislatures. The latter were not only much more frequent; they also enjoyed greater public acceptance.[59] State legislatures continued to produce thousands of new laws each year, and direct legislation did not diminish their importance in the least. No wonder, then, that Walter Dodd, a leading scholar of state constitutions, declared in 1928 that the new devices "have proved neither a panacea for all political ills nor a substitute for representative government."[60] Certainly, no early advocates of direct democracy had anticipated that the voters would directly decide on most issues. But they had hoped that the annual flood of legislation produced by legislatures and city councils would diminish, and that the most important laws would by popularly initiated. Neither had become true in the 1920s and 1930s.[61]

Part of the problem, many observers argued, stemmed from the fact that the initiative and referendum only changed the outward form of government without altering the characteristics of the electorate. As explained by James Bryce in 1924: "These schemes of reforms deal rather with the symptoms of the malady than with its roots in the indifference, or subservience to party, of a large part of the voters."[62] Another commentator, looking at the experiences of Oregon with the reforms, concluded much the same: "An electorate that is active, alert, vigilant and interested in good government will to a considerable degree achieve its ends in spite of the absence of these newer governmental institutions. On the other hand, the presence of these institutions, without an interested and intelligent electorate, will avail little or nothing. Devices and organizations constitute the form; interest and vigilance are the essence of democracy."[63] And Charles Beard wrote in 1944 that "the sources of legislation lie deep in the social and economic life of the people, in their ideas and interests, rather than in mere devices of government."[64] Improving the machinery of government did not automatically remake the electorate. Actual experience with the devices showed rather convincingly that the policy decisions arrived at under the initiative and referendum did not differ at all from laws passed by legislative assemblies.

The expectations of many conservatives that the initiative would be employed by radical groups to bring their proposals before the public were borne out in a number of states. The single tax, especially, was repeatedly put to a popular vote in Oregon and California throughout the 1910s. But the voting behavior of the public turned out to be much more conservative and reluctant to endorse radical changes than anticipated by direct-legislation friends and foes alike. William B. Munro, a leading scholar on the initiative and referendum, pronounced in 1932: "But direct legislation has not proved to be revolutionary; on the contrary, it has been at least of equal value as a bulwark of conservatism. Voters in American cities and states have not hesitated to reject proposals for adopting the single tax or undertaking municipal ownership of public utilities, for giving pensions to city employees or imposing progressive income taxes."[65] Another observer of conditions in Ohio remarked that "at any rate, in Ohio, which is a typical state, the electorate is not eager for innovation."[66] Direct democracy hardly functioned as a stepping-stone for further economic and social reforms.

Instead of enabling the people to overcome the resistance of corrupt machines and recalcitrant legislatures, direct democracy quickly emerged as a useful tool in the arsenal of interest group politics. In order to secure the signatures needed to qualify a petition for the ballot and to organize a campaign for a ballot proposition, substantial financial and organizational resources were needed. Interest groups, most of them representing some kind of business or trade group, were among the few groupings ideally positioned to make use of the new devices. Citizens' groups of reform associations found it much more difficult to employ the initiative and referendum. In the words of one observer, direct legislation was only "superficially democratic. Actually, however, it operates to the advantage of permanent well-organized interests and to the disadvantage of those that can least afford to bear the burden of needless expense."[67] This was particularly true in connection to the circulation of petitions and the collection of signatures. It soon proved impossible even for labor unions and reform associations to gather signatures on a voluntary basis. In response to the creation of a new market, professional petition circulators began to offer their services in all direct democracy states, not merely in California. As reported from Ohio in 1925, "there are said to be organizations in some states that made a business of procuring signatures."[68] Since skilled circulators were able to gather signatures regardless of the nature of the proposal, a petition did not so much reflect the public interest in an issue, as originally conceived, as the financial resources of the backers of a petition drive. Yet, only Washington State prohibited the work of paid petition circulators.

While no studies prior to 1940 systematically analyzed the impact of money on voting patterns, it became increasingly clear that direct legislation favored those who were already powerful and affluent. Looking at the California situation, V. O. Key concluded that "initiated propositions involve disputes between conflicting groups of the possessed."[69] They only rarely empowered common people to more effectively pursue their interests. Consequently, direct democracy had little impact on the formation and the work of pressure and interest groups. In the states where the initiative and referendum emerged as important tools of policy-making, they adopted their strategies to the new conditions and skillfully exploited the expanded opportunities to bring their proposals before the public. Traditional forms of lobbying continued to exist, only to be supplemented by initiative and referendum campaigns. LaPalombara and Hagan observed for Oregon: "It appears clear that direct legislation has neither encouraged nor discouraged the formation of pressure or interest groups. They existed prior to its institution and have adjusted to the conditions brought about by its adoption."[70] Given the intense hostility of early advocates of the reforms toward special interests and pressure groups, it was highly ironic that the very same groups were the ones that acquired even further political leverage with the help of the initiative and referendum.

Many political scientists formulated increasingly harsh assessments of direct democracy. The first comprehensive analysis of direct democracy in California, by V. O. Key and Winston Crouch, was published in 1939. For these two political scientists, the push for direct legislation was an example "of the great stock placed on forms and procedures by Americans." But they concluded that the initiative and referendum "have not had a very profound effect on the great body of legislation." Any hopes for a redistribution of political and economic power had been wildly overblown, as "no profound alteration in the composition, methods, or objective of the ruling elite" had occurred under direct legislation.[71] Particularly troubling were the rising costs associated with direct democracy campaigns. Between 1922, when California began to require expenditure reports from the parties involved in such campaigns, and 1934, almost $3 million was spent, most of that on publicity. The majority of campaigns continued to be fought on small budgets, but the number of high-cost campaigns grew exponentially. The founding of a firm such as Campaigns, Inc., specializing in handling initiative campaigns, was a clear indication of things to come. "The establishment of such a concern, operating successfully on a commercial basis, is extremely significant as an indication of the trend away from personal politics of the precinct variety and toward the use of modern propaganda technique."[72] In line with scholars analyzing the functioning of the initiative and referendum in other states, Key and Crouch concluded for California that the adoption of the reforms, widely regarded as among the most momentous political innovations of the early twentieth century, had produced surprisingly little change. Policy outcomes and the array of politically powerful groups had not been altered.

Even analysts who were somewhat more positive in their assessment agreed that direct democracy had had only a slight impact on California politics. Edwin Cotterell argued in 1939 that "the people have understood most of the measures and as a whole have acted wisely in making their decisions. There has not been much hasty or ill-considered legislation to check." But he was forced to conclude that "corruption and extravagance have been little affected by the process. . . . The character of the legislative personnel and procedure have not changed."[73] The political scientist Max Radin admitted that of the 166 propositions, including constitutional amendments and direct legislation measures, on the California ballot between 1936 and 1946, at least 50 percent had been of a technical nature and should never have been subject to a popular vote. In addition, he was increasingly concerned about the large amounts of money expended in initiative and referendum campaigns, and he remarked in 1939 that " 'propaganda' has become a business, involving considerable investments and an elaborate technique." With the escalating costs of direct legislation, the array of groups able to avail themselves of the new political opportunities was narrowing considerably. The people might register sensible votes on the issues, but they were hardly the ones that initiated ballot propositions.[74]

By the late 1930s, dissatisfaction with the endless flood of new initiatives reached a climax, especially when a pension movement known as "Ham and Eggs" managed to twice qualify the same proposition for the ballot in 1938 and 1939. Conservatives and business interests complained about "radical and vicious" legislation put forward by "fanatical minorities." A number of reform proposals were discussed: prohibiting professional signature collection, increasing the number of required signatures, depositing the petitions at a central place, restricting the subject matter of initiatives, and giving the legislature a role in the process.[75] In the words of one critic of the system, initiatives of the kind submitted by the Ham and Eggers constituted a "serious menace to economic welfare," and "too often catchy slogans, or even mere pictures, with little explanation or understanding of the measures, characterize the campaigns to get the votes to one side or the other.[76] However, as with previous attempts, efforts to seriously revise the direct democracy process went nowhere.

The outbreak of World War II rendered many of these arguments moot. The number of initiatives dropped by 50 percent in the 1940s. By the late 1940s, one observer contended that "the public is inclined to view ballot measures, especially initiatives, with misgivings or outright suspicion."[77] Many the same developments transpired in connection with the recall. The number of recall elections diminished sharply after 1940. When a recall attempt was instigated against the mayor of San Francisco in 1946, he was able to easily beat back the challenge by branding the recall a frivolous device used by selfish interests at the expense of the taxpayers.[78] Direct democracy entered a period of steady decline, which defused many of the controversies that had surrounded it between 1910 and 1940. Only in the context of the emergence of new social movements in the late 1960s, which regarded the initiative as an ideal tool for grass-roots mobilization and to influence state politics, did direct democracy reacquire the central position in the political culture of California that it had occupied for the first three decades.

The historical analysis reveals that the initiative, referendum, and recall were deeply problematic institutions from the beginning. None of the early hopes reformers had invested in them held true: political participation did not increase, special interest groups became stronger than ever, civic awareness was not fostered, politics were not purified, and substantial economic and political reforms were not accomplished.

Instead, the initiative, in particular, fostered a kind of single-issue style of interest group politics that further fragmented the political scene in California. Whether any of the reforms debated between 1910 and 1940 would have improved the situation remains speculation. One may admire the tenacious loyalty displayed by Haynes to "his" reforms, but he was also completely blind to the severe defects of a system that did nothing to usher in a period of popular, responsive government. Popular support for direct democracy remained extensive, however, as Californians clung to the notion that the reforms expanded their abilities as citizens to shape policy-making. Maybe most surprising are the historical continuities in the public discussion of direct democracy. Most of the problems that elicit so much criticism now were widely discussed within ten years of the ratification of the amendments. For all the recent talk about the development of an initiative industry, the role of big money, and voter apathy, all these phenomena existed in the early phase of direct legislation in California. The promise of more democracy was tainted from the very beginning, a deeply ingrained feature of the process that no subsequent reforms have been able to remedy.

INVENTING MODERN POLITICS

Ballot Propositions, Election Campaigns, and
Political Consultants in California, 1920–1940

The last presidential elections in the United States have offered many examples of the dominant role of political consultants
in American political campaigns. A variety of election specialists —
consultants, public relations experts, advertising executives, pollsters,
image consultants, and spin doctors — populate the political landscape
and ply their lucrative trades. Over the last three decades, the number
and the influence of these campaign professionals has expanded vastly.
A number of observers blame them for many of the troubling aspects
of American democracy: rising voter apathy, a pervasive distrust of
politicians and institutions, a debasement of political debate, shrink-
ing voter turnout, and a neglect of the real problems confronting the
country.[1]

For many political scientists and other observers, television has
been the main catalyst in the rise of consultants. It has redefined the
rules and the content of political campaigning, substituting, in the eyes
of many, thirty-second television ads and sound bites, carefully crafted
visual images, and elaborately staged pseudo-events for substantive
political debate. Television has clearly become the dominant medium
of American politics.

Such an account, however, presents a historically truncated view of
the rise of consultants and image-makers in American politics. Without denying the pivotal role of TV in their rise to dominance, one can
locate some of the dynamics behind this process in the practice of
direct democracy in California. The state of California was an early
leader in the application of public relations techniques and commercial
advertising methods to political campaigns, spawning, among other
things, the first professional campaign management firm in America.
It was in the context of campaigns for ballot propositions that consultants first acquired prominence. In a series of electoral contests in the

1920s and particularly the 1930s, they pioneered many of the methods that would sweep the nation after World War II. The very existence of direct democracy, resulting in a substantial number of propositions being placed on the ballot in virtually every election year, created a booming market for the kinds of services commercial advertising specialists and public relations experts had to offer. Because the political parties in California played virtually no role in initiative and referendum elections, the sponsors and opponents of ballot propositions were unrestrained in their ability to hire outside experts.

This analysis will concentrate on a number of selected initiative and referendum campaigns from the 1920s and 1930s: the 1922 Water and Power Act, the 1936 chain store tax referendum, the single tax campaigns, the 1938 anti-labor initiative, and the 1938 and 1939 "Ham and Eggs" propositions. No attempt will be made to explore these campaigns in full detail. Rather, special attention will be directed toward several interrelated aspects of the transformation of campaign methods in California up to 1940: the skyrocketing costs of election campaigns, the expanding role of advertising managers and publicity experts, the innovative use of scientific public opinion polls, and the founding of the first professional political campaign management firm in America, Campaigns, Inc., headed by Clem Whitaker and Leone Baxter. Taken together, these developments signaled the arrival of a new style of political campaigning intimately connected to the practice of direct democracy. While not all of the consultants' methods were new — many had been used in previous political campaigns or were borrowed from commercial advertising — they fashioned a campaign style independent of the political parties that would become dominant in the period after World War II.

The 1922 Water and Power Act

Few other political topics have loomed as large across the American West as the development of water and power resources. In a predominantly arid climate, water was pivotal for the development of the region's agriculture and it had to be carefully controlled to provide drinking water for the rapidly expanding urban centers. Furthermore, the construction of dams, canals, and irrigation systems provided the opportunity to produce cheap electrical power for the benefit of western industry and consumers. But because all too often water resources were not positioned in the vicinity of urban agglomerations where they were most desperately needed, and because western states and cities competed for access to them, the development of water and power resources emerged as one of the most hotly contested issues in western politics. This was particularly true in California. Such colorful incidents as the construction of the Owens River Aqueduct, also portrayed as the rape of Owens Valley, illustrate the pivotal role of water and power resources for the economic development of southern California. By the 1920s, a coalition of Progressives had succeeded in creating the nation's largest municipally owned water and power system in Los Angeles.[2]

Many of the former leaders of the Progressive movement were continuing to concentrate more of their attention on this issue. With the California Water and Power Act, the public ownership advocates attempted to translate their success at the local level into a comprehensive plan for the development of water and power in California; this would have authorized the state to expend $500 million to construct a series of dams, canals, and power plants. In 1921, a small group of reformers that included former San Francisco mayor and U.S. senator James Phelan, former congressman William Kent, industrialist and reformer Rudolph Spreckels, and the Los Angeles physician, John R. Haynes, began to draft the California Water and Power Act initiative. These four individuals directed the affairs of the campaign organization and contributed about 80 percent of the funds. In 1922, the contributions to the campaign committee backing the initiative totaled almost $160,000.[3] In September 1921 they entered into contracts with two professional petition circulators, George Sharp for northern California and R. P. Benton for the South, to garner 60,000 signatures.[4]

The backers of the initiative realized that their plan would be met with staunch opposition. To run their campaign, they retained the services of L. C. Davidson, a public relations expert from Los Angeles. In September 1921 he developed an outline for the campaign. He stressed that "the success or failure of the campaign for California's Water and Power Act depends largely upon *finance*." He estimated that for the final six weeks of the campaign alone, a fund of between $300,000–500,000 would be needed to buy newspaper ads and other forms of publicity. With sufficient funds at hand and a proper campaign strategy, the projected resistance of the private utilities could be overcome: "The art and necessary steps for building the structure of CONVICTION and ACTION in the hearts of the voters is as well known to us as is the business of constructing a sky-scraper or a railroad known to the practical contractor."[5] Despite Davidson's confidence in his own methods, he failed as a campaign manager. After a period of a few months in which not much was accomplished, he was replaced by Franklin Hichborn in the spring of 1922.[6]

Alarmed by the prospect of the initiative, the private utilities, led by the Pacific Gas and Electric Company (PG&E), the largest utility in the state, developed their own campaign strategy in late 1921.[7] The executives of the PG&E hired Eustace Cullinan, a former journalist and lawyer with substantial experience in public relations work, to organize their campaign in the northern part of the state. In the south, the Southern California Edison Company retained the services of Herbert L. Cornish, a former real estate agent, in a similar capacity. Both organizers formed campaign committees, dubbed the Greater California League and the People's Economy League, respectively, to carry out the campaign. Even though the campaign committees operated largely independently from each other, they closely resembled each other in setup and strategy. Ostensibly composed of concerned California citizens, they were fully financed and controlled by the private utilities, relied on printed advertisements and the help of a friendly press, and were directed by individuals that, while not public relations professionals, had some prior experience in publicity work and political propaganda.[8]

To finance their campaign, the private utilities amassed a campaign fund unprecedented in California history. According to the estimates of an investigative committee of the California Senate in 1923, they spent more than $500,000 against the 1922 California Water and Power Act. All the money came from the private utilities. Each company in the state was assessed a certain amount on the basis of the gross revenues in 1921, with PG&E and Southern California Edison being by far the dominant sponsors. In addition to the funds given to the campaign committees, the $500,000 also included the more than $100,000 expended by the two companies for campaign work done by their own employees. On election day, hundreds of employees labored as precinct workers, manned phone banks, and drove voters to the polls.[9]

Apart from the efforts of the utilities to mobilize their own employees against the Water and Power Act, the campaigns conducted by the Greater California League and the People's Economy League largely followed traditional lines. The 1922 contest might have been one of the last hotly contested elections in California that was fought without use of the radio. Instead, Cullinan and Cornish relied on printed campaign materials and a speaker's bureau.[10] Cullinan later reported to the investigating committee that "the total pieces of literature sent out was about 6,612,700, including cards handed out on election day."[11] The People's Economy League operated in an almost identical fashion, even if on a somewhat smaller scale. Like Cullinan, Cornish engaged a publicity director to pen newspaper articles and print ads and saw to it that they were placed in a number of publications. The league had about one million pieces of campaign literature printed and distributed.[12] Yet the innovative character of the campaigns conducted by the Greater California League and the People's Economy League is not attributable to the development of any new campaign tactics and mediums of reaching the electorate; nor is it due to extensive employment of advertising executives. Rather, the innovations arose from the lavish financial resources at hand and the creation of ostensibly independent organizations of concerned citizens acting as smoke screens for corporate interests. No direct democracy campaign in the United States had ever witnessed such a liberal application of cash.

Compared with other campaigns, the backers of the initiative were well financed, but their resources were clearly insufficient to counter the massive campaign waged by the utilities. By the spring and summer of 1922, news of the extensive efforts of the power companies was continuing to reach Hichborn and Spreckels. In May, one campaign worker relayed that "the Power Companies have men in almost every city, town and village and in country districts where power and light is sold. All these men, and their families, are out actively in every community against us, giving out reams and tons of literature."[13] Another correspondent reported from Oxnard in October that "the power companies are leaving no stone unturned to defeat the measure. They have speakers everywhere, at County Chambers of Commerce, Women's Clubs, and at every semi-public organization; and are having resolutions passed denouncing the measure as socialistic."[14] Relying largely on the volunteer efforts of the initiative's supporters, Hichborn and

Spreckels were never able to match the abilities of the power companies. On election day, the initiative was defeated by a margin of more than 300,000 votes, an outcome that was to be repeated in 1924 and 1926.

California Single Taxers in the 1930s

All across the United States, single taxers had been among the most consistent supporters of direct democracy. Their hopes of winning the endorsement of American voters were soon dashed, however. Single taxers in Oregon placed a series of initiatives on the ballot between 1908 and 1914, but they were defeated at the polls, with the exception of one very close election in 1910. Still, the California single taxers stayed persistent. Six times between 1912 and 1922 they gathered enough signatures to qualify a single tax initiative for the ballot; six times their work ended in defeat, by increasingly overwhelming margins.[15] After the resounding defeat of 1922, more and more single taxers realized the futility of further attempts. Without the single-minded devotion of Jackson Ralston and his willingness to invest his private funds in the cause, the single tax would not have rematerialized in the 1930s.[16]

Although Ralston had been born in California, he spent most of his life in Washington, D.C., where he built up a successful practice as a lawyer. He acquired some prominence as the longtime attorney for the American Federation of Labor and as the personal lawyer of Samuel Gompers. He had consistently supported the cause of the single tax since the 1880s when he had first come across the writings of Henry George. In 1924, by then in his mid-sixties, Ralston decided to retire to his native state and he settled down in Palo Alto. The onset of the Great Depression and the changes in the political climate in California raised his hopes that the cause could be revived. He decided to link his cause with the repeal of a recently enacted sales tax that was highly unpopular among the labor movement. Ralston formed a Tax Relief Campaign Committee in the fall of 1933 and began to organize his campaign.

The key problem confronting the campaign in the initial stage was the collection of more than 150,000 signatures needed to qualify a constitutional initiative for the ballot. Early on, Ralston indicated his willingness to finance the circulation of petitions out of his own pocket and solicited some estimates for the projected cost. When informed that it might cost up to $15,000 to get enough signatures, he and some of his co-workers were doubtful. Instead of hiring a collection agency, Ralston hoped to enlist the help of the unions in furnishing the manpower needed to circulate the petitions. The Executive Council of the California State Federation of Labor endorsed Ralston's initiative in September 1933, leading one Ralston ally to conclude "that they can and will gladly circulate the petitions among their members and families, half of whom would be more than we need. . . . They could and should get the names without any expense."[17] But few unions distributed his petition and few signatures came in.[18]

By the spring of 1934 it was clear that Ralston would have to hire professional solicitors if he was to have any chance of qualifying his petition. Instead of hiring a firm to take over the whole state, he instructed his local campaign workers to organize the collection of signatures in the various parts of the state. His manager in San Francisco reported in June that he had hired fifty professional circulators and that signatures were coming in at a rate of 8,000 to 10,000 a day. At two cents per name, the cost for this kind of work came to about $200 per day, all paid for by Ralston.[19] In southern California, Ralston entered into a contract with William G. Stennett, another professional circulator, for the collection of 18,000 signatures at four cents a name.[20] In the end, his effort to qualify his initiative for the ballot in 1934 failed. As was the case with all direct democracy campaigns, a number of the signatures first collected were later found to be invalid. The opposition to Ralston challenged them, county clerks and the California Secretary of State threw out many of them, and the state supreme court ruled in the fall that Ralston's measure had failed to qualify for the ballot. Ralston, however, refused to give up and soon began a new series of efforts for the election in 1936.

At this point in time, in order to avoid a repeat of the 1934 fiasco, Ralston concentrated on what had been his unstable financial base. In an attempt to improve the fund-raising abilities of his organization, he turned to the rapidly growing public relations industry in California, in particular the firm of Joseph Robinson. Robinson had acquired a well-deserved reputation as a pioneer in the professionalization of petition circulation and the collection of signatures.[21] But Robinson also offered his expertise for other phases of the campaign. In February

1935, being aware of Ralston's plans, he contacted him about contributing to his campaign. Robinson wrote: "We are specialists in handling campaigns to the voters, and our files include a complete list of voters covering every county in the state. We believe we can assist you as we have other campaign organizations in accomplishing your purpose."[22] Robinson offered to run over thirty days a test campaign, out of his own pocket, to explore the feasibility of raising money for the single tax initiative.[23]

Ralston was clearly intrigued by the offer. But he was also worried about Robinson's loyalties. Robinson had worked in previous campaigns for the same large industrial interests that formed the target of the single tax initiative. In particular, Ralston queried Robinson as to his prior work for the San Francisco Real Estate Board. In a lengthy letter, Robinson outlined his business methods:

> I am the owner of this business and I have no partners or associates of any kind. Let me also state that we have served and are serving organizations and firms of various kinds. We have a definite service to offer and on political campaigns we only handle one side of the issue and do not take both sides of any campaign. Our organization has been in existence for nearly twenty years, and we specialize in raising funds and handling political campaigns to the voters. You have a problem to solve and we endeavor to solve same for you through our plans and methods. In order to place your message before every voter in the state at the proper time to educate to vote for Repeal of Sales Tax, you must send out letters and literature. We operate and maintain a complete direct-mail department for such services and organizations that have no funds to cover this service, we endeavor to work out a plan to raise sufficient funds to cover this work, as we are interested in getting this business. We believe ourselves reliable beyond any question of a doubt.[24]

When Ralston again wrote to Robinson about his connection to the San Francisco Real Estate Board, Robinson assured him that "while we are handling your campaign no one can come in and sway us to handle any campaign in opposition to yours."[25] Ultimately, Ralston decided not to enlist the services of Joe Robinson. But the latter's aggressive initial solicitation of Ralston's business and the details of his offer illustrate the already central role of professional fund-raisers and public relations experts in California initiative politics in the Depression decade.

Robinson was not the only publicity expert with whom Ralston corresponded. He contacted Joseph Lowe, the owner of Lowe Features, an agency that specialized in radio advertising. Lowe claimed to have served as the radio director for California for the Merriam gubernatorial campaign in 1934 and to have extensive experiences in the field.[26] Ralston also got in touch with W. A. Curtin, a partner in an advertising agency located in Oakland.[27] By the winter of 1935–36, Ralston again contemplated hiring a professional agency to raise funds for him. He received a letter from Joseph O'Connor of San Francisco requesting an interview, contending that his "considerable successful experience in campaign work and money-raising as a background" would allow him to contribute to Ralston's campaign. O'Connor claimed to have worked as the publicity director in northern California for the Merriam campaign in 1934.[28] Ralston and O'Connor did indeed meet, and the two sides even developed a formal contract. It provided that O'Connor would arrange the fund-raising for the campaign, contacting voters "in person, by main contacts, wire, 'phone interviews, and other dignified means." The agency would cover the costs and keep 50 percent of the funds collected. Later, the agency would handle all the radio advertising and would be considered for the statewide newspaper advertising.[29] However, the contract was never signed. Ralston would enter the 1936 campaign as he had the 1934 contest, underfunded and without professional assistance. In the end, the Ralston initiative never appeared on the California ballot in 1936. As a result of a legal challenge to the title of the petition, the California Supreme Court removed it from the ballot.[30] Ralston, however, remained undaunted and vowed to undertake yet another campaign in 1938.

Ralston's first need for 1938 was to once again collect the 186,000 signatures to qualify his petition for the ballot. Based on his experiences in the 1934 campaign, he had learned what other observers of the initiative process had already pointed to: the virtual impossibility of securing enough signatures without the services of a professional petition circulator. To organize the collection effort for his petition, Ralston hired William G. Stennett, who had already participated in a limited capacity in the 1934 circulation effort. This time, Ralston and Stennett entered into a contract that gave the latter the responsibility for managing the drive on a statewide basis.[31] The eventual contract between the two parties stipulated that Stennett would procure 190,000 valid signatures at a total cost of $15,500.[32]

Stennett's business primarily consisted of himself and two associates, Peiter M. Flanton and Colonel R. E. Nordstrom. Their plan of operation was quite simple. Whenever they would start work in a new county, that is, "open up" the area, Stennett or one of his associates would rent temporary office space in the most important urban center of the area and would hire circulators, either by placing ads in the local papers or by contacting the local office of the State Employment Service. With high levels of unemployment and frequent direct democracy campaigns, there was never a shortage of experienced solicitors. Because of the small size of Stennett's organization, they would rarely work in more than a couple of counties at the same time. The organizer would direct the work of the circulators, file the petitions with the local county clerk, and then send the petitions to Ralston. Sometimes it was possible to enlist the cooperation of labor unions, but, as in 1934, the formal endorsement of the proposition by the labor movement did not translate into significant material help.[33] The goal was to finish the work as quickly as possible before the opposition had a chance to respond, with a "crew large enough and ready to go to work at one day and clean up a City in one or two days before the opposition has a chance to hammer at us."[34]

As Stennett commenced the solicitation of signatures in the fall of 1937, he soon ran into a well-organized countercampaign, financed by the San Francisco Real Estate Board and organized by the omnipresent Joe Robinson. In a letter to the secretary of the Contra Costa Real Estate Board written by the secretary-manager of the San Francisco Real Estate Board, Leslie R. Burke, Burke reported that the association was making a strenuous effort to prevent the collecting of enough signatures because "it will prevent a long and expensive campaign prior to the November election."[35] Soon the Real Estate Board adopted even more aggressive methods. In a letter to the secretary of the Contra Costa Board, Robinson explained that his organization was running a statewide campaign of "educating the voters not to sign a proposed initiative petition supposedly repealing the Sales Tax and substituting the 'Single Tax.'" Robinson requested the secretary, P. A. Marshall, to check with the various real estate firms in the county about whether Stennett had rented temporary office space. Also, if any ads for petition circulators had been placed in the local papers, Robinson was to be informed at once and "we will send our wrecking crew and move them out of town." Robinson finally asked Marshall to check with the State Employment Office if any requests for solicitors had come in. Robinson was watching every county in the state closely, ready to move in as soon as the Stennett forces would show up.[36] In another letter written four days letter, Robinson implored Marshall to communicate with every notary public in the county to get the names and addresses of any circulators who might call on them to have signatures notarized and to forward the information to Robinson:

> This will enable us to trace every solicitor whom they might employ and we will forward them literature and call on them personally, showing them that this petition is detrimental to their best interests as well as to the best interests of their community. If the solicitors need work badly, we will give them work on our petitions, which will be out next week, as the petitions we handle have no opposition. Moreover, we pay them at a rate where they can earn from five to fifteen dollars per day. This is our program. With the cooperation of the notaries in your county, we will be able to keep the proponents from getting any workers in that county. This is important. We are also writing every notary in your county, asking them to be on the lookout. Some solicitors go the County Clerk's office to have their petitions notarized, so ask them to also be on the lookout. We have full cooperation from every County Clerk where an attempt has been made to secure signatures.[37]

The actions of Robinson and his "wrecking crew" led to a virtual guerrilla war between the two sides. A number of letters from Peiter Flanton to Ralston document the difficulties Stennett's organization encountered. In late April 1938, Flanton was active in Sacramento and reported that the opposition was picketing his office to urge solicitors not to work for Ralston. The opposition was also using radio broadcasts to attack the initiative. Repeatedly, some of his workers were hired away by the opposition.[38] The same pattern was repeated whenever Stennett or his associates moved into a new county. With the help of local real estate organizations, newspapers, notary publics, and county clerks, Robinson and his helpers picketed the offices of Stennett, hired his workers, offered to purchase petitions, intimidated circulators with threats of losing welfare benefits, visited them at home (after obtaining their addresses from compliant county clerks), and orchestrated a skillful campaign of harassment that slowed the collection effort to a crawl.

It soon became apparent that Stennett would face great difficulties living up to his side of the contract. By January, Stennett was in serious trouble. His original cost projections had been much too optimistic, and he was experiencing financial difficulties. He constantly needed ready cash to pay his workers. "We must maintain sufficient cash on hand here at all times to take care of our circulators. The minute we fail to have the money to pay for names as they are brought in — *we are gone, absolutely finished*. We cannot afford to run this risk."[39] Stennett often seemed to disappear for several days at a time, did not respond to Ralston's instructions, did not wire the money to his two associates that they needed to finance their operations, and proved less and less reliable. Harry H. Ferrell, one of Ralston's allies in southern California, wrote to him in January: "I have been informed by some of his [Stennett's] friends that he sometimes loses control of his personal conduct when he has to face a problem which requires steady nerves."[40] By the beginning of July, he finally ceased working for Ralston, after having incurred a heavy financial loss during the campaign.[41]

Despite the undeniable effectiveness of the campaign orchestrated by Robinson and his employers, Ralston managed to get the 186,000 signatures he needed to qualify his initiative for the ballot, at a cost of $20,986.[42] After the drawn-out and expensive struggle to place the initiative on the ballot, the actual fall campaign proved to be anticlimactic. Ralston had exhausted his financial resources in the signature phase and was unable to make any significant financial contribution to the effort to acquaint the voters with the advantages of the single tax. The entire budget for the fall campaign came to only $3,111, wholly inadequate for a statewide campaign.[43] While the labor press contained some positive coverage of the initiative, the attention of labor was focused on defeating the antipicketing initiative put forward by the employers in the state.[44] The single taxers were forced to organize a campaign with little money, no media support, without organized interest groups supporting them, and with an electorate that faced a number of other more pertinent ballot propositions.

The opposition faced no such handicaps. After the failure of Robinson's counter campaign, organized business interests in the state wasted no time in creating a centralized agency to run the fall campaign. The Statewide Council against the Single Tax functioned as the point organization to defeat the initiative.[45] Large business interests contributed lavishly to the war chest of the organization.[46] In addition, every major newspaper in the state opposed the single tax, the opposition ran a series of radio broadcasts, and the entire business community of the state, together with the associations of civil servants and the educational establishment, were united in their rejection of Ralston's proposal.[47] In the final phase of the campaign, the opponents of the single tax turned to Clem Whitaker of the recently formed company Campaigns, Inc. For a hefty "management fee" of $5,000, he served as the campaign manager for the California Association against Single Tax.[48] As the final sequence in a long and competently handled countercampaign, Whitaker made sure that the single tax initiative drowned in a sea of negative publicity.

With the odds stacked so heavily against the single tax, Ralston's initiative went down to a resounding defeat, losing by a margin of 5 to 1. The worst defeat ever for a single tax proposal in California marked the end of an era; never again would a proposal based on the ideas of Henry George be submitted to the voters anywhere in the United States.[49] The campaign illustrated the power of a central and lavishly funded organization such as the Council to overwhelmingly defeat a proposition bereft of any organizational support base. In reflecting on the lessons of the fight, the state chamber of commerce attributed the outcome to "carefully thought-out plans and programs, exhaustive research, tons of educational literature, well directed publicity, cartoons, speeches, radio presentations, personal calls, questionnaires — all under the direction of effective and well-coordinated organizations of public-spirited citizens." It added: "Organization is the keystone of political success, but in so far-slung an empire as the State of California even the best-intentioned organization is only as effective as the statewide strategy behind it."[50] The rapid evolution of a public relations industry catering to direct democracy in California, and the rising importance of campaign spending, made it virtually impossible for such groups as the single taxers to have any chance of success.

The 1936 Chain Store Tax Referendum

Perhaps no other American state experienced as much political turmoil during the 1930s as California. In addition to the widespread misery and social devastation caused by the Great Depression, highlighted by the Dust Bowl migration to the Golden State, California witnessed a series of highly charged and intensely fought political campaigns that riveted national attention. Upton Sinclair's 1934 EPIC campaign for the governorship, the 1936 referendum on a chain store tax, the election of the first Democratic governor in the twentieth century in 1938, the final campaign for the single tax in the same year, and the battle over the initiatives calling for the introduction of a pension plan, known as "Ham and Eggs," in 1938 and 1939 shook the political system of the state to an unprecedented degree. Because the existence of direct democracy offered pressure groups and citizens additional means to shape the political agenda, California voters were directly confronted with options and policy alternatives not present in many other states.

The 1930s saw the emergence of the first professional political consultants. Due to the notoriously weak parties in the state, candidates were increasingly more forced to create their own campaign organizations and raise their own funds. Consequently, they were much more likely to recruit the help of public relations experts. By the 1930s, a small but rapidly growing industry was emerging in California that catered to the needs of political candidates. The gubernatorial election of 1934 was a crucial event. To defeat Socialist-turned-Democrat Upton Sinclair, who campaigned on a platform called EPIC, End Poverty in California, the Republicans recruited advertising executives, public relations experts, and Hollywood to an unprecedented degree. Charles C. Teague, one of the most important agricultural leaders in the state, organized a committee composed of prominent businessmen to campaign against Sinclair. He recruited Don Francisco, head of the Los Angeles office of the ad agency of Lord & Thomas, to serve as the manager of the campaign. Francisco displayed shrewd political and organizational skills during the campaign.[51]

Two years later, the California chain stores, subject to a graduated tax passed by the legislature as part of a nationwide wave of chain store tax laws, enlisted Francisco's help.[52] After the law had been passed in 1935, the chains used the referendum, with signatures procured by Joe Robinson at a price of more than $15,000, to hold up the measure.[53] Francisco was then retained for the 1936 referendum election. He based his analysis of the task ahead on the widespread popular skepticism of big business. "There is deep-rooted resentment against bigness, authority, power, profits." The chain stores had neglected to court public opinion, wrongly assuming that the cheaper prices they offered were sufficient to create a favorable perception, and they had little political clout.[54] In the California case, the main object of the initial phase of the campaign was to create an organization able to change public opinion: "The primary job is organization — an organization that will run like a successful business. It requires a knowledge of politics, ability to organize and run a speakers' bureau and press bureau, skill in advertising and research, an understanding of agricultural relations. If a job of mass selling is to be done, it requires experts to handle the different phases and demands, the utmost in teamwork and coordination among a great number of people. Above all else centralized direction and control are required."[55]

Insisting on centralized control, Francisco organized an efficient campaign organization that used all available media and advertising outlets — newspapers, radio, magazines, billboards, pamphlets, and a speakers' bureau — to familiarize the voters of California with the advantages of the chain stores.[56] To better gauge the sentiments of the public, Francisco employed public opinion surveys, maybe the first usage of this technique, already well familiar in commercial advertising circles, in a political campaign. During the middle of the 1930s, scientific polling, pioneered by George Gallup, Elmo Roper, and others, developed quickly, offering politicians and public relations experts a new means to sound out public opinions.[57]

The details of Francisco's use of polls are sketchy. When California employers pushed for an antipicketing initiative in 1938, they referred to the surveys conducted for the chains:

> The technique of "market analysis" is an accepted commonplace in the advertising profession. Briefly, it consists of interviewing a representative "sample" or cross-section of those whose opinion is

desired. Experience over the past twenty years has developed a remarkable accuracy, and few major advertising or sales campaigns are now undertaken without a preliminary market analysis. Periodic or continuing surveys are often made to check results, measure success, and guide further efforts.

The first direct application to a major political issue was made in California in 1936 in the campaign to defeat the Chain Store Tax. A continuing survey was used throughout this campaign with remarkable results. Expenditures were allocated, results were measured, and activities were guided by a flow of reports, and an accurate picture was always at hand of the changing state of the public mind with reference to the measure under consideration. The survey predicted the final vote two weeks before the election to within one-half of one per cent of the actual figures.[58]

In the final weeks before the election, Francisco used the lavish financial resources of the chain stores to orchestrate a comprehensive statewide public relations campaign. The expenditure statements filed with the secretary of state later revealed that the chain stores spent the exorbitant sum of $1.147 million, largely contributed by the national parent companies of the chains operating in California.[59] A significant portion of the money, close to $390,000, was paid to Lord & Thomas under the direction of Francisco. With such ample funds at his disposal, Francisco placed large ads in many of the state's newspapers and saturated the airwaves with radio spots attacking the tax. Like no other campaign before, the chain store referendum demonstrated that " 'propaganda' has become a business, involving considerable investments and an elaborate technique."[60]

In response, the Anti-Monopoly League of California, the primary organization fighting for passage of the tax law, organized a campaign that could hardly compare to the efforts of the chain stores. Between late August 1936 and the election in early November, it spent about $65,000. In the final two weeks of the contest, the period when Francisco was able to intensify the public relations output of the chains, the league was able to spend only $500 on radio broadcasts.[61] The interest groups that were represented by the Anti-Monopoly League, California retailers and small merchants, could not raise sufficient funds to compete with the powerful chain stores. They were outspent by a factor of about 15 to 1. On election day, the tax law was defeated by a margin of 300,000 votes.

The Antilabor Initiative of 1938

The election of Franklin Delano Roosevelt and the beginnings of the New Deal found the labor movement in California in a precarious position. The days when San Francisco had been a bastion of organized labor and workers had been able to elect a Union Labor Party mayor were long gone. After the end of World War I, employers in the city had waged a very successful open-shop campaign and had severely weakened the labor movement.[62] But the New Deal and the passage of the National Labor Relations Act in 1933 that guaranteed workers the right to organize profoundly altered the labor situation in California. Membership in unions began to rise, once dormant unions revived their efforts to organize workers, and public opinion grew much more supportive of the labor movement.

One increasingly important element in the fight between business and labor was the cultivation of a favorable public image. Instead of simply refusing to deal with labor unions, business leaders in California slowly developed a new strategy that combined repressive measures against strikers and union organizers with concerted efforts to mold public opinion. This strategy included the formation of "third-party" groups, seemingly independent civic associations fighting the labor movement, which were fully financed by organized employer groups. One of these groups was called Southern Californians, Inc., an organization founded in the fall of 1937 by the leaders of the Los Angeles Chamber of Commerce and the Merchants and Manufacturers Association.[63] The central goal of this group was the maintenance of the open shop in California.

Southern Californians, Inc. soon concentrated its attention on the enactment of antipicketing ordinances, a decision that would culminate in the labor initiative of 1938. In the summer of 1938, it spent almost $50,000 on the successful campaign for an initiative in Los Angeles that sharply limited picketing. Similar ordinances were passed in many other California counties and municipalities, even though voters in San Francisco rejected an initiative similar to the one enacted in Los Angeles.[64] The statewide initiative campaign was launched against this general backdrop of intensifying clashes between employers and unions. In March and April of 1938, Byron C. Hanna, then president of Southern Californians, Inc., engaged in a series of meetings with business leaders in San Francisco to discuss the prospects of using the popular initiative to place a proposition on the fall ballot that would extend the provisions of local antipicketing ordinances to the entire state.[65] In its final version, the employer proposal was a highly convoluted and lengthy document, consisting of twenty-six sections full of stuffy language, wordy definitions, and sweeping indictments. Its general thrust was not difficult to discern. Employers maintained that it was aimed to "eliminate war and to promote peace in employment relations," but in reality, the proposition outlawed virtually all of the most effective trade union tactics. Sit-down strikes, which so recently had forced General Motors to capitulate, were prohibited, as well as secondary boycotts and most forms of picketing. After spending $40,000 to gather the necessary signatures, the backers formed the California Committee for Peace in Employment Relations, composed of business leaders from both sections of the state, and set about to orchestrate a comprehensive and skillful public relations campaign.[66]

From the outset, employers were clearly aware that the crucial battle in the upcoming campaign would be for the state of public opinion. Some of their allies, most notably the Associated Farmers and the Neutral Thousands, two other "third-party" groups financed by business interests, had already made considerable investments in public relations. The Neutral Thousands, in particular, had engaged in a series of radio broadcasts in southern California to warn of the effects of union organizing. The broadcasts, first developed by the advertising agency of Lockwood-Shackleford, and then by the agency of Batten, Barton, Durstine & Osborn, were openly hostile to the labor movement. As reported by Richard Prosser, one of the experts in charge of the employer campaign: "The agency which has developed that technique through long experimentation, finds that the best vehicle for this type of political matter over the radio is a weekly program of 30 minutes, of which about 25 minutes is first-rate entertainment and the other 5 is artfully disguised and beautifully-sugarcoated propaganda."[67] These radio programs continued throughout the summer of 1938, laying the groundwork for the more specific appeals later in the campaign.

Prosser, who was employed by the Peace Committee, then turned to the well-known agency of McCann-Erickson, already active on behalf of San Francisco employers during the 1934 general strike, for help. During a luncheon in June 1938, two representatives of the agency, Henry Hawes and Edgar Persons, raised serious doubts as to the outlook of the employer campaign. Early cost estimates by some employers had generally been below $100,000, a sum deemed far too limited by the advertising executives. They recommended a general survey of public opinion in California to ascertain the outlook toward labor legislation.[68]

The leaders of the initiative campaign took the advice of Hawes and Persons in commissioning a public opinion survey to gauge the public mood. In August 1938, employees of some of the leading advertising agencies, hiding under the title California Institute of Public Opinion, conducted a poll of 22,700 voters across the state on a number of questions, including their positions on labor legislation, the single tax, and the Ham and Eggs proposal. The results were heartening for employers. Of the voters questioned, 53.4 percent believed in the need for a law curbing labor union practices, while only 26.3 percent were against it. However, a second question revealed that only 22.4 percent of the voters were familiar with the content of the labor initiative. The pollsters concluded that a campaign of *"mass education"* was needed to extol the benefits of the proposition. California voters were skeptical of union practices, and *"these vague prejudices must be crystallized into effective and affirmative action on the initiative."*[69] The outlook for undertaking a campaign directed by skilled public relations experts and advertising professionals seemed bright: "The campaign can be won if the proper efforts are expended. Politics is no longer the hit-or-miss proposition of a few years ago. It has entered the realm of 'big business,' and as such must of necessity adapt and utilize the machinery and technique of business. Just as this survey is an adaptation of methods found successful in merchandising commodities, so must other methods be adapted to merchandise ideas. Today the old type of 'professional politician' as a campaign manager has been supplanted by men adept in the manipulation of public opinion by modern methods."[70]

Based on the survey, John Miller, Norman Gallison, and Richard Prosser, the three individuals in charge of planning the campaign for the Peace Committee, outlined a detailed budget for the contest. Their estimates of the costs for the campaign totaled $265,920.25. They recommended that the Peace Committee engage the services of a major advertising agency "to brings its trained personnel and facilities to bear" on the details of the campaign.[71] In the fall, the employers were finally able to enlist the help of McCann-Erickson. Because the results of the survey had been more positive than expected and because the employers had agreed to furnish a larger campaign fund than originally anticipated, the agency had revised its assessment of the chances of the initiative and decided to join the effort.[72] The ultimate expenditures of the employers would reach more than $307,000, with almost all of the funds coming from large businesses and corporations.[73]

In response to the offensive of the employers, labor unions across California rallied to organize a countercampaign, in the process temporarily setting aside the differences that divided AFL and CIO unions.[74] In its efforts to defeat the proposition, labor received the help of many liberals and progressives in California.[75] While the employers had hoped to isolate the unions and had portrayed their measure as bringing industrial peace to California, the opposite development materialized. Troubled by the harsh and one-sided nature of the initiative, with its serious implications for civil rights, most of the liberals in the state, together with important church leaders and a number of civic organizations, rallied to support labor. The employers found themselves facing a united and formidable opposition, undercutting their carefully prepared public relations campaign.[76]

Compared with the highly centralized and professionally run campaign of the employers, labor unions and their liberal allies waged a campaign that was only loosely coordinated and that relied on the simultaneous efforts of a large number of labor committees and citizens' organizations. Financially, labor unions shouldered most of the burden. The California State Federation of Labor contributed $42,000; the Labor's Protective Committee of the Los Angeles Central Labor Council, $32,000; the California State Industrial Union Council, $15,000; and the American Federation of Labor Political League, $10,000.[77] Ultimately, the employers would outspend labor and its allies by more than 2 to 1, $307,373.50 versus $156,913.[78] On election day, the initiative was defeated by a vote of 1,476,379 to 1,067,229. It lost in 42 of 58 California counties, including Los Angeles. The employer campaign was well organized, lavishly financed, expertly run, received the endorsement of many leading newspapers, and could draw on the united support of business leaders in California. The experiences of 1938 underscored a point that has since been well established by a large number of other direct democracy campaigns. While large amounts of money spent against a ballot proposition were usually sufficient to defeat a measure, the outcome was often different when the money was expended to back an initiative.

Ham and Eggs

The Retirement Life Payment Association, popularly known as Ham and Eggs, was only the latest in a series of pension movements and plans to hit the Golden State in the 1930s. During a period that produced a series of various policy proposals and schemes to help alleviate the plight of America's senior citizens, California was a center of agitation for retirement plans. Twice in 1938 and 1939, the movement gathered hundreds of thousands of signatures for their initiative proposition and succeeded in placing it on the ballot. Narrowly defeated in 1938, a more substantial majority voted it down in the following year, leading to the fairly rapid disintegration of the movement. The two contests demonstrated the existence of two highly diverse campaign styles: the Ham and Eggers relied on a combination of radio and press appeals and intensive precinct work undertaken by an army of volunteers, while the opponents of the plan utilized professional public relations agencies and mobilized a host of civic and commercial bodies.

There is no need here to fully reconstruct the tangled history of the Ham and Eggs movement. Originally the brainchild of Robert Noble, a veteran of the EPIC and Huey Long movements, who began to espouse his own pension plan in 1937, the movement was soon taken over by Willis Allen, a lawyer, and Lawrence Allen, an advertising executive. Flamboyant and driven, with a shrewd sense for the possibilities of modern advertising, the Allen brothers created a highly successful grass-roots movement that reached into virtually every counter of the state.[79] By 1939, it was estimated that 5 percent of all Californians contributed to the organization financially, which took in about $10,000 a week.[80] With a mass base, the leaders decided to use the direct democracy provisions in the California constitution to implement their plan in the form of a constitutional amendment. Although there were some minor variations between the ballot propositions of 1938 and 1939, they both provided that the state of California would issue thirty one-dollar warrants each week to every unemployed Californian fifty years or older. Like a number of pension schemes that originated during this period, the plan was predicated on the theory that the Great Depression had been caused by overproduction and that the solution consisted of increasing consumption and the more rapid circulation of money. Like most of the plans, the proposal of the Ham and Eggers was also utter nonsense, completely unworkable, and was rejected by every credible economist in California.[81]

In securing the necessary signatures to qualify their petitions for the ballot and to conduct the campaigns, the Ham and Eggers constructed a highly successful machinery that relied on the work of thousands of volunteers. They gathered four times as many signatures as needed for their petition, a sure sign of the grass-roots support their proposal enjoyed.[82] The organization was tightly controlled from the top, could be mobilized into action very quickly, was capable of reaching voters all across the state, and could be run on a comparatively modest budget.[83] In addition to this highly centralized organization, the Ham and Eggers made extensive use of the radio to reach their followers, broadcasting a series of radio programs on a number of stations that blanketed all of California.[84] The Ham and Eggers were able to mobilize monetary and financial resources that matched those of their opponents. In the twelve months between the inception of the movement in October 1937 and the end of 1938, the organization headed by the Allens took in membership dues of more than $242,000.[85]

The rapidly increasing momentum of Ham and Eggs caught the business community and conservatives in California by surprise. They had been lulled into complacency by a series of public opinion polls, including one conducted by the Gallup organization, which predicted that the proposition would be trounced at the polls. The extent of the popular support for the plan also surprised most Republicans and business leaders. As one participant later recalled, it was only through a "last minute loosely-organized, poorly coordinated, expensive but wasteful campaign" that the plan was defeated.[86] The California State Chamber of Commerce largely conducted the opposition campaign. It seems clear that the pension movement was able to outspend their opponents in 1938, one reason for their success at the ballot box. Their proposition lost, but it still received 45 percent of the vote, more than 1.1 million votes, a margin too close for comfort for their opponents.[87]

The following year found the opposition better prepared. Upon the first defeat of their initiative, the Ham and Eggers had immediately started another petition drive and easily qualified their plan for the ballot again. Not being able to mobilize the same number of volunteers, the California State Chamber of Commerce relied on public relations experts, press agents, and professional campaign managers to work against the initiatives.[88] The Chamber even secured the services of the ubiquitous team of Clem Whitaker and Leone Baxter of Campaigns, Inc. Whitaker functioned as the campaign director for the Northern California Citizens against 30-Thursday, with Baxter serving as his assistant.[89]

The opposition employed a public opinion survey to gauge the mood of the electorate. A survey of 4,145 residents of ten southern California counties older than twenty-one, conducted in September 1938, revealed that 47.4 percent were inclined to vote against Ham and Eggs while 34.9 percent planned to support it; 13.5 percent were still undecided. The polls also showed that lower-class voters were more likely to favor the plan, and that rural voters and men also displayed more support. The survey helped the opposition to better target its public relations campaign. What it lacked in numbers and sheer enthusiasm, it had in money and technology.[90]

In contrast to 1938 when the Ham and Eggers were able to outspend their opposition, the 1939 contest found the two sides much more evenly matched financially. The pension movement reported that it had taken in around $457,000 in the eleven months between November 1938 and the end of September 1939.[91] The campaign waged by the business community of California amassed an equally impressive campaign fund. Combined with the funds spent by a number of other business, civic, and other organizations fighting the Ham and Eggers, the California State Chamber of Commerce later reported that the entire campaign had cost $538,376.[92] The intensive countercampaign paid off in November 1939. In an election in which 82.5 percent of the electorate participated, Ham and Eggs was soundly defeated by a vote of 1,993,557 to 993,204.

Whitaker and Baxter

The developments outlined so far paved the way for the emergence of Whitaker & Baxter, the first professional campaign management firm in America. A legend in California politics, the company, also known as Campaigns, Inc., acted as a trailblazer for the rise of consultants after World War II. Professional public relations was certainly nothing new by the 1930s. After 1900, more and more corporations, put on the defensive by the attacks of muckrakers and other progressive reformers, developed elaborate public relations campaigns to improve their reputation.[93] By applying their public relations expertise to the field of political campaigns, Whitaker and Baxter created a new market. They pioneered many of the methods that came to mark the political public relations industry by extending the methods that had been successfully developed in advertising to the field of politics. Their success demonstrated both the economic viability of the kind of services they rendered and the crucial importance of public relations in modern political campaigning.[94]

The son of a Baptist minister, Clem Whitaker had worked as a reporter in the 1910s and 1920s, and he operated the Capital News Bureau in Sacramento between 1921 and 1930, distributing syndicated political news to a large number of newspapers in the state. After selling the company to United Press International, he began to work as a speechwriter and campaign manager in the early 1930s.[95] A tireless organizer, he drew on his long-time experiences as a reporter and on his in-depth knowledge of political affairs in the state to establish a reputation in a largely unknown field. His big break occurred, in typical California fashion, in connection with a direct democracy campaign, the 1933 referendum election on the Central Valley Project. Financed by a $170 million bond issue, the plan called for the construction of a series of dams, canals, and power plants in the Valley.[96] After the act was passed by the legislature, private utilities under the leadership of the PG&E collected enough signatures to force a referendum.[97] To organize the campaign in favor of the referendum, the public ownership forces turned to Clem Whitaker. Operating on a rather modest budget of $40,000, Whitaker organized an automobile caravan that toured the Valley. Organized labor, the Grange, Farm Bureau units, and the League of California Municipalities all endorsed the plan. In addition, most of the chambers of commerce in the Valley cooperated with Whitaker. It was in this context that he met Leone Baxter, his future wife and partner in business, then the secretary-manager of the chamber of commerce in Redding, the first woman to serve in this capacity in California. In the end, the project was approved by a majority of just 30,000 votes out of 900,000 cast.[98]

After the victory, Whitaker and Baxter founded Campaigns, Inc., a firm that exclusively dealt with political campaign managing. In 1934, they conducted a campaign on behalf of the California State Employees' Association for a constitutional initiative providing for a state civil service; they received $2,000 for their services.[99] Afterwards, Whitaker sent a leaflet to a California newspaper outlining the policies of his organization. He declared: "A new age has come to politics! And with the new age has come Campaigns Inc., the product of a newspaper background and a political environment." He added: "We are attempting to conduct political campaigns somewhat after the fashion we would conduct a newspaper, sensibly and rationally, with a fair regard for the public as well as our pocketbooks."

In late 1936, Whitaker & Baxter added the California Feature Service to their arsenal. The Service distributed a free news-sheet to newspapers all over the state. Although the Service proclaimed to "try to make it a readable, interesting service to editors above all else" and to be free from "political propaganda and commercial publicity,"[100] Whitaker skillfully inserted his own interpretation of political events into the news items, which, of course, reflected the positions of the clients he was working for. One editor wrote him: "After every election it is always interesting to see where you will bob up next. The new idea [the feature service] seems one of the best. It is possible to read between the lines of your stuff, but it is very well written and we can use a portion of it if it remains on the same plane."[101] The organizations founded by Whitaker and Baxter, consisting of Campaigns, Inc., an advertising agency, and the California Feature Service, were uniquely equipped to handle the rapidly increasing demand for professional political public relations.

Whitaker was highly aware of his role in creating a new industry. In an address before the Los Angeles Chapter of the Public Relations Society of America in July 1948, he argued: "Political campaign management is a comparatively new field in public relations — *a great game* and *a challenging profession.*"[102] Previously, the management of campaigns had been "a hit-or-miss business, directed by broken-down politicians. It is rapidly emerging from its swaddling clothes to become a mature, well-managed business, *founded on sound public relations principles*, and using every technique of modern-day advertising."[103] Most of their methods were borrowed from the field of advertising, and both partners clearly perceived their work as an extension of the field of commercial advertising to the political arena. The attempt to mold the political attitudes of California voters did not prove to be very different from shaping the buying habits of American consumers.

Whitaker and Baxter's business proved to be a lucrative one. For a single initiative campaign in 1938, they collected a fee of $15,000.[104] Combined with the fees for the advertising they placed through their ad agency, their fees could often amount to between $25,000 and $50,000. Whitaker and Baxter had received their professional start campaigning for the public development of water and power. But in most of their future campaigns, they could be found as an ally of large business interests or well-heeled pressure groups, the only ones able to pay their fees.[105] They did occasionally represent teachers' unions and state employees associations; but as time went by and as their role within the Republican Party expanded, their selection of clientele became more restricted. In the political climate of California, their agency thrived. They claimed in the late 1950s to have won 90 percent, seventy out of seventy-five statewide contests, in which they had been involved. Over time, Whitaker and Baxter became a legend in California politics.[106]

While the specific political conditions in California favored the emergence of independent political operators such as Whitaker and Baxter, the development of professional campaign management prior to World War II reached the national level. Some well-known advertising executives, most notably Albert Lasker, head of the agency of Lord & Taylor, and Bruce Barton, author of the national bestseller *The Man Nobody Knows*, about the life of Jesus Christ, offered informal advice to Republican presidential candidates in the 1920s.[107] A real breakthrough occurred with the formation of a permanent publicity bureau for the national Democratic Party in 1929. In the words of one observer, it marked the transition from "party campaign publicity to party publicity." Headed by veteran reporter Charles Michelson, the bureau organized an effective campaign against the Republicans, who organized their own publicity bureau a few years later.[108]

The willingness of the Republican Party to enlist the help of outside public relations experts and advertising executives can largely be attributed to its close ties to the business community. Many of the individuals and companies supporting Republican candidates had extensive experiences with commercial advertising methods and placed great stock in their ability to mold public opinion. The most noteworthy example took place in 1936 when the Republican National Committee hired Hill Blackett, of the Chicago advertising agency Blackett, Sample and Hummert, to serve as director of public relations for the presidential campaign. The agency specialized in radio work and was the largest agency in that field in the country. Although the party continued to hire veteran newspaper journalists to participate in the campaign, it clearly attempted to borrow the methods pioneered by advertising to sell its candidate. Blackett ran a smooth radio campaign, but the whole effort was doomed by the internal confusion of the campaign organization, by the lack of coordination between the various branches engaged in publicity work, and, of course, by the popularity of the incumbent president.[109] The 1936 attempt to successfully import commercial advertising methods into a presidential campaign failed, but the Republican Party would continue to rely on advertising agencies in the campaigns to come.

It had become evident by the 1930s that "the central problem of political action today is propaganda." The increased spending for public relations expertise by the political parties, whether to advertising agencies or to independent operators like Whitaker and Baxter, demonstrated significant changes in political propaganda. Political parties and their candidates increasingly sold themselves like commercial products. A new style of political campaigning had arrived, one that had first been pioneered in California but that now began to sweep the entire country. California was thus an early leader in the development of the kind of public relations experts, media consultants, image-makers, and pollsters that have become such a ubiquitous feature of American politics. From the rule of the people to "government by Whitaker and Baxter," that has been the ironic legacy of direct democracy in California.

The More Things Change, the More They Stay the Same

The quest for a government by the people, the search to create a truly democratic polity, has been an ongoing part of American history. In the late eighteenth and early nineteenth centuries, the
United States was a democratic trailblazer, creating the first modern
democracy in the world. Despite the exclusion of significant groups
from direct participation in politics, American achievements in self-
government were remarkable. Yet while it was arguable that government in the United States rested on the will of the people, as expressed
in elections for political offices, the demand that government should
also be marked by the extensive direct involvement of the citizens
posed a different problem altogether. In the nineteenth century, the
mass parties and a host of voluntary associations acted as links between
ordinary citizens and political life. But an abiding distrust of legislatures and political representatives and a constant fear of corruption
and special interests motivated many Americans to look for alternate
means to empower the common people. Direct democracy formed an
innovative response to one of the perennial challenges of American
democracy. It involved a deceptively simple rearrangement of political institutions that nevertheless seemed to contain the potential to
transform the economy and society. It expressed the confidence that a
change of political institutions and procedures would unleash the ability of the people to govern themselves and to throw off the rule of
trusts and corporations. In resting on the time-honored principles of
popular sovereignty and majority rule, the initiative, referendum, and
recall were able to recruit support from many political circles dissatis-
fied with the state of American politics and looking for ways to re-
distribute political power. For three decades, from 1890 to 1920, direct
democracy became a widely discussed and hotly contested issue in
American politics. Even after the dissemination of the reforms had

stopped in 1917, they were extensively used in many states in the western part of the country.

With the outbreak of World War II, this first phase of the history of direct legislation in America came to a close. The 1930s had witnessed a very active usage of the initiative, with 246 ballot propositions. Fueled by the economic dislocations of the Great Depression and the political unrest that marked the entire decade, a number of different groups employed the initiative to advance their diverse political agendas. World War II marked the end of an era of remarkable political volatility and turbulence. The war returned economic prosperity to the nation, a development that continued in the post-war period. With the beginning of the Cold War, much political attention was now centered on the international arena. And the new and powerful federal government in Washington, a result of both the New Deal and the challenges of the war, diverted attention away from the state level where direct democracy had flourished. The period of the 1950s and early 1960s was a comparatively tranquil time for domestic American politics, marked by economic growth, political and cultural conservatism, and social conformity. State legislatures were no longer the object of muckraking attacks on corruption and horse-trading, anti-monopoly had completely disappeared as a political issue, and the initiative and referendum seemed to be anachronistic relics of an altogether different era in American politics.

The decline in the employment of direct democracy clearly reflected this trend. The number of initiatives on state ballots dropped by almost 40 percent during the 1940s, to only 146 for the entire decade. This trend continued for the subsequent two decades; in the 1960s, a mere 85 initiatives were placed on ballots, an all-time low since the introduction of direct democracy in the first two decades of the century.[1] Even in states like California, where the initiative continued to possess a modicum of importance for state and local politics, public support for and confidence in the devices waned. One observer of conditions in the Golden State argued in 1949 that "the public is inclined to view ballot measures, especially initiatives, with misgiving and outright suspicion." The many half-baked pension schemes submitted to the California electorate since the late 1930s had severely taxed its patience and had highlighted the abuses of the initiative system. In 1949 alone, the legislature considered thirty bills and constitutional amendments curtailing direct democracy.[2] One proposal, which limited initiatives to a single subject, largely a response to the Ham and Eggs propositions that had included a variety of subjects, was subsequently adopted.[3] Direct democracy still enjoyed sufficient public support to ward off any major changes, but by the 1960s there seemed little doubt that the institution would continue to atrophy in the future.

In the late 1960s and early 1970s, however, interest in the initiative and referendum slowly began to increase. The most important reasons for this development can be located in a more general quest for more direct citizen involvement in politics, and in the flourishing of a host of reform and pressure groups that made increasing use of new forms of political mobilization. In the 1960s and 1970s, a number of reforms were initiated that sought to eliminate previously existing barriers to political action and to make the existing political institutions more democratic. These changes included the various voting-rights acts aimed at guaranteeing the right to vote for African Americans, the lowering of the voting age from twenty-one to eighteen, the expansion and rise of importance of direct primaries in the selection of presidential candidates, and the loss of power of party officials in selecting candidates. Even before the Watergate scandal and the resignation of President Nixon triggered a wave of disenchantment with the political status quo and increased the distrust of many ordinary Americans in their elected representatives, it had become clear that the politically turbulent 1960s had generated a broad-based search for new ways to foster the political involvement of American citizens.

Of equal importance for the gradual rise in the number of ballot propositions after 1970 was the emergence of a number of new social movements that looked toward direct democracy as a means both to inject new topics into the political arena and to mobilize their own followers. Most of the initiatives and referenda on the ballot before 1970, and particularly between 1940 and 1970, had focused on issues of political governance and administration that elicited little public response. There had always been exceptions, such as the issue of prohibition in the 1910s and 1920s and pension proposals in the 1930s. But the initiative had rarely functioned as an agenda-setting device, and the array of interest groups that had made use of it had been largely confined to the political establishment. The new social movements of the 1970s, however, introduced new topics and issues that significantly broadened the scope of initiative politics. They employed direct democracy to demand an end to the war in Vietnam, to fight for more stringent environmental laws, to enact laws limiting future growth and development, to urge a freeze on the production of nuclear arms, to advocate the closing of nuclear power plants, and to push for tax relief. Many of the groups that resorted to the initiative process had found themselves shut out of the established political system and had encountered politicians and parties unwilling to take them seriously. The initiative, steeped in the tradition of American grass-roots democracy, was ideally suited to serve as an alternate platform to publicize their demands.

The purpose of placing a proposition before voters at the local and state levels could often be located more in the mobilization of their supporters and in creating a platform for the discussion of certain issues than in the passage of concrete laws. Certainly, antiwar or antinuclear power activists could have little hope that a successful initiative would lead to a rapid implementation of their program. But direct democracy offered them a new forum to shape the political agenda, to attract newspaper publicity, and to initiate discussions on new issues.[4] If there was ever a time when direct democracy adhered to the model of an informed citizenry making use of instruments of grass-roots democracy to overcome the resistance of a political establishment interested in preserving the status quo, it can be found in the work of a myriad of new social movements and advocacy groups that revitalized direct democracy in the 1970s. Consequently, the number of statewide initiatives rose from 86 in the 1960s to 120 in the next decade. No figures for the number of local referenda is available, but there is little doubt that it underwent a similar rise.

The 1970s not only witnessed a gradual increase in the number of ballot propositions, the number of states that provided for the initiative and referendum also expanded. Wyoming in 1968, Illinois in 1970, and Florida in 1978 became the first states to adopt direct democracy since Massachusetts had done so in 1917 (Alaska had been admitted to the Union in 1959, with the devices already a part of the state constitution). Many other states discussed a similar move. On the national level as well, direct democracy became a viable issue for the first time in more than a half century. In 1977, the U.S. Senate held hearings on a constitutional amendment providing for a national initiative process that had been sponsored by James Abourezk, a Democratic senator from South Dakota. Arguing that such a procedure would "lessen the sense of alienation from Government to which millions of Americans now profess," he was supported by such public figures as Ralph Nader and many other liberals.[5] After attracting a good deal of initial attention, the proposal made little headway once it became evident that substantial support for such a radical reform of the Constitution would not be forthcoming. Yet the discussions surrounding a national initiative demonstrated the hopes many had invested in direct democracy as a means to restore a greater extent of citizen participation to American politics.

The pivotal event that demonstrated the potential of the initiative was the property tax revolt in California that culminated in the successful passage of Proposition 13 in 1978. The rapid rise of real estate values in California had led to a swift increase in property taxes, causing particular concern for many middle-class families living on fixed incomes who found it more and more difficult to meet their tax bills. Long-time discontent climaxed in the formation of a broad-based anti-tax movement, led by Howard Jarvis and Paul Gann, that easily placed a proposition putting a cap on future property tax increases on the California ballot for the 1978 midterm election. The entire political establishment and most of the business interests in the state were solidly aligned against Proposition 13, warning of the disastrous effect of the initiative on state finances. Undaunted, Jarvis and his followers mounted an impressive grass-roots campaign. The initiative was overwhelmingly adopted, revealing to an astonished nation the power of ordinary citizens to use a plebiscite to overcome the opposition of politicians and business leaders alike. The campaign for Proposition 13 made headlines around the nation. Within a few months, similar movements to cut taxes and limit spending were under way in about twenty states, sometimes in the form of initiatives, sometimes in the form of legislative bills. By the end of 1978, nine other initiatives reducing taxes and government spending had been passed in a number of states, and thirty-seven state legislatures enacted laws reducing property taxes. A virtual tax revolt swept the nation. Taxation, always a sore point for many Americans distrustful of the state and reluctant to pay for the upkeep of an allegedly spendthrift government, formed an issue ideally suited to propel increasingly more Americans to look with interest at the provisions of direct democracy that were in place in many states. Proposition 13 made direct democracy a household name in mainstream America and paved the way for an unprecedented explosion in the number of ballot propositions.[6] During the 1980s, 193 statewide propositions qualified for the ballot, a growth of more than 60 percent compared to the 1970s.[7]

Direct democracy traditionally had been claimed as a means of serving to express the will and the interests of ordinary Americans who were excluded from the political arena. Yet Proposition 13 in 1978, and other tax initiatives launched by Jarvis in the years thereafter, illustrated some of the mechanisms at work rendering these claims dubious at best. Proposition 13 had won because it was advertised as a measure that would primarily benefit middle-class and tax-weary Californians who had been hit the hardest by continued property tax increases. In reality, about two-thirds of the tax cut benefited industrial interests and apartment-building owners while only one-third reached the owners of single-family dwellings. And while the contributions and the volunteer work of thousands of California citizens had fueled this proposition, Jarvis's subsequent initiatives relied on sophisticated fund-raising techniques to solicit both signatures for the ballot petition and financial contributions.[8] Even for such an explosive issue as taxation, volunteer efforts soon proved insufficient to gather the signatures required for a petition. The highly sophisticated methods of petition circulators, fund-raising experts, direct mail businesses, and public relations professionals proved indispensable for virtually all successful initiative campaigns, regardless of the issue under consideration.

Proposition 13 further demonstrated another important change in initiative politics, one that intersected with broader trends in the political landscape. Most of the groups that had pioneered the innovative use of direct democracy in the early 1970s had advocated leftist causes: the end of the Vietnam War, nuclear freeze, environmental issues, and so on. Jarvis and his allies, on the other hand, had tapped into middle-class resentments about high taxes, inefficient government service, and an intrusive government, issues skillfully exploited by Ronald Reagan in his political campaigns and in his administration. The conservative tendencies of many American voters in referendum elections had already been demonstrated in the 1960s when most local and state referenda that were held on the issue of fair housing laws had ended in a defeat for the antisegregationist agenda advocated by liberals.[9] During the 1980s and 1990s, the most visible and controversial campaigns fought with the help of initiatives would originate among the conservative elements in American politics. Topics such as homosexuality, illegal immigration, affirmative action, and bilingual education generated the most headlines and the most public controversy.

The initiative and referendum had always been political devices available to all contenders with sufficient resources to employ them. But prior to the late 1970s, they had clearly been associated with liberal and leftist causes, while many conservatives had shied away from using tools that smacked of mob rule and of political instability.[10] Direct democracy had been the product of American populism, and populism had always been a leftist movement. This equation no longer held true by the 1980s. Populism as a mixture of metaphors and strategies had been captured by a resurgent American Right adept at using the initiative to combat the influence of an allegedly liberal press and a liberal political establishment. Even before Proposition 187 in California in 1994, widely perceived as a punitive measure directed against illegal immigrants, attracted nationwide attention, conservatives had used the initiative to enact laws declaring English to be the official language in a few states, including, once again, California, Florida, and Arizona, all states with a sizable Hispanic population.[11] The most intense conflicts are now fought on the terrain of culture and moral values, on questions of life-style and religion, a development that has left many liberals disenchanted with the tools they once championed.

The growing willingness of conservatives to embrace the tools of direct democracy and the continuing dissatisfaction of many Americans with the political system, manifested in declining voter turnout rates, the movement for term limits, and the support given to third-party candidates, had led to a virtual explosion in the number of statewide ballot propositions in the 1990s. In 1996, for instance, a record number of 106 propositions appeared on state ballots, after 67 in 1992 and 76 in 1994; the number in 1998 was still an impressive 61. Many more petitions were circulated, a total of 1,316 between 1992 and 1996 by one estimate, but failed to qualify for the ballot.[12] The total number for the entire decade is probably close to 400, easily surpassing the previous high of 269 reached during the 1910s. While the range of issues subject to popular vote continues to be vast and some issues attract only a limited amount of attention, many initiative campaigns have come to rival the campaigns for the highest state offices in terms of newspaper coverage, money spent, and symbolic importance. It seems that each new election cycle brings another hot-button topic to the surface. California, not only a behemoth in national politics but also the clear trailblazer in matters of direct democracy, has produced some of the most memorable recent campaigns. In 1994, a proposition strongly supported by Governor Wilson was passed; it imposed restrictions on social services and other benefits for illegal immigrants in the state.[13] Two years later, the topic of affirmative action found itself at the center of controversy as California voters put an end to race-based preferences in hiring practices, college and university admission policies, and the handing out of state contracts. And in the summer of 1998, voters in the Golden State endorsed an initiative putting an end to bilingual education. These three initiatives are examples of the culture wars of the 1990s that were fought with the help of direct democracy. All dealt with the role of minorities in California, all invoked charges of racism, and all were passed on the strength of the support of white voters increasingly uneasy with the changing demographical makeup of California.

These highly controversial campaigns produced stories in newspapers around the nation about the growing importance of direct democracy. There can be no doubt that the initiative looms as one of the more important American political institutions of this era. Ironically, despite the growing number of ballot propositions, public confidence in the device seems to be waning. Public opinion surveys in such states as California still reveal majorities in favor of the general principles of direct democracy and show little support for a fundamental reform of the system, but voters and political scientists alike appear troubled by some of the excesses of the system.[14] Among political scientists, the initiative and referendum have never enjoyed a particularly good reputation. As they tend to weaken parties and reduce the power of legislatures and of elected officials to shape public policy "through the frequent substitution of plebiscitary democracy for representative government," they have contributed to the kind of candidate-centered and issue-less politics that plague American politics today. Models of responsible party government and of parties being able to aggregate voter demands and implement a substantive political program stand little chance in states where the most meaningful policy decisions are made as the result of plebiscites.[15] Students of initiative politics have pointed to the many troubling facets of the system including a flood of often difficult-to-understand propositions, an overburdened electorate, big-money interests dominating campaigns, the role of professional petition circulators, and the reliance on TV and consultants to run the campaigns.[16] The voters at large complain about many of the same trends. The institution of direct democracy seems out of control, ideas for reform are advanced by numerous parties, yet the political consensus for a concerted reform effort is lacking. As long as too many interest groups stand to benefit from the system, and as long as the illusion of a grass-roots democracy empowering ordinary citizens continues to flourish, present trends appear destined to continue in the future.[17]

Furthermore, in at least one fundamental aspect, most analyses of direct democracy share one misperception: that the flaws of direct legislation are of fairly recent origin, thus implying that the initiative and referendum have somehow been corrupted by powerful business interests and professional consultants and that it should be possible, if the proper reforms are introduced, to return to an earlier, purer state of direct democracy. Few political scientists have engaged in a serious historical investigation of direct democracy prior to the 1970s. Sensationalist accounts of individual campaigns and a focus on recent developments have created the widespread impression that large campaign expenses, the use of petition circulators, and the employment of political consultants are an invention of the last two to three decades. If one could find ways to somehow level the playing field, the initiative could emerge as an important tool in making American politics more democratic. Yet the historical record of direct democracy offers precious little evidence to support such a claim. If anything, the extensive analysis of the practical usage of the devices prior to 1940 makes evident that virtually none of the problems most discussed today are in any way new. A review of some of the main features of direct democracy can illustrate that it has always existed as a deeply flawed institution.

One of the most talked-about trends in initiative politics concerns the increasingly escalating campaign costs associated with the procurement of signatures and the actual campaigning for and against ballot propositions. For a controversial initiative to have a chance requires substantial spending on television and radio spots, direct mail campaigns, consultants, polling, and the other customary techniques of modern-day electioneering. Campaign expenditures commonly run into the millions for opponents and advocates alike. Behind the headlines generated by individual campaigns lie the stark figures that reveal the truly staggering costs of initiative campaigns. A commission investigating direct democracy in California estimated that $127 million was spent on these campaigns alone in 1988; in 1996 that figure, according to the California secretary of state, had climbed to more than $141 million. Most of the funds are contributed by business interests. Of the eighteen most expensive petition campaigns between 1956 and 1990, 83 percent of the funds came from business, 8 percent was donated by individuals, 3 percent was raised by labor, 2 percent by officeholders, and 1 percent by the political parties. In 1990, 67 percent of all the money raised came in donations of over $100,000, and 37 percent came as the result of contributions of over $1 million. Small contributions of under $1,000 accounted for 78 percent of the total number of contributions but for just 6 percent of the money received. Business interests clearly dominate the initiative process in California and other states.[18]

Again, however, it must be pointed out that this hardly forms a recent development. Business interests have contributed the bulk of expenditures for initiative campaigns ever since California started requiring the publication of campaign spending figures in 1923. The historical study of selected initiative and referendum campaigns in the 1920s and 1930s has shown that large campaign disbursements had already become a routine part of initiative politics before World War II. Adjusted for the rate of inflation, campaigns such as the 1922 Water and Power Act and the 1936 chain store referendum were marked by expenditures of several million dollars. The recent rash of high-priced initiatives should not blind observers to the fact that the employment of the initiative process has always required substantial financial and organizational resources. There is little evidence to suggest that rising costs have reduced the number of interest groups being able to avail themselves of the process. If anything, the growing professionalization of the initiative industry might have made it easier to use the device since one can readily purchase the expertise needed. The problems for small and weakly funded groups to file successful petitions have not changed markedly. They have never been the primary beneficiaries of direct democracy anywhere in the United States. Rising costs in the 1980s and 1990s should not obscure awareness of much longer historical trends.

It is also important to qualify the impact of money on the outcome of initiative campaigns. Campaign funds do not automatically translate into votes on election day. A number of studies of the effects of money on outcomes in such contests have suggested that one-sided spending in favor of a ballot proposition rarely ends in victory. By contrast, money has usually been found to be much more effective in influencing voters to cast their ballots against a specific proposition.[19] In much the same way as California employers failed in 1938 in the quest to have an antilabor proposal endorsed despite outspending the opposition by a factor of two to one, so have many other business and other groups misfired in their attempts to use the initiative. It is apparently much easier to persuade voters to vote against a controversial idea than it is to make them endorse it. This evidence does not mean that money is not a crucial asset in every initiative campaign. A group might qualify a petition for the ballot, but without money for TV spots and other publicity, it would have no chance to succeed. A campaign does not necessarily have to outspend the opposition to ensure victory, however. One needs to emphasize that blank statements about the impact of money in initiative campaigns do not adequately reflect the complexities of voting behavior. Business interests certainly profit the most from direct democracy, but they can hardly use the initiative to impose their agenda on a public seduced by slick commercials and catchy slogans.

The use of professional petition circulators might be the second most talked about feature of direct democracy today. Every visitor to California has probably been confronted by individuals asking them to sign one or more petitions. These people are only rarely volunteers; generally they are employed by one of the approximately half-dozen large signature-gathering firms that dominate the business. By one estimate, more than 90 percent of the petitions that qualify for the ballot rely on these professionals to collect the signatures. In order to qualify a statute for the ballot in California one needs to collect more than 400,000 signatures. For a constitutional initiative, the number stands at close to 700,000. Few organizations have the personnel or the dedication to collect such a number by themselves. They rely on professional firms that can virtually guarantee success, provided enough money is available to pay for the services. It costs between $1 and 2 million to qualify a petition for the ballot in California. While most of the firms have their headquarters in California, clearly the most lucrative market for the services, they operate in virtually every state with direct democracy on its books. Under these circumstances, ballot propositions do not reflect a genuine popular interest in a specific issue, but rather the ability of the backers of an initiative to raise sufficient funds to hire the petition firms.[20]

Most observers believe that the emergence of these firms dates from the 1960s. In reality, as this book has shown, professional petition circulators began to operate in California one year after the adoption of direct democracy in 1911. By the 1920s, Joe Robinson, the true pioneer of the industry, had founded his company and had begun a remarkable run of success that lasted until the 1960s. By the 1930s, several individuals offered services and employed methods that are virtually indistinguishable from those practiced today. They might not have had computerized mailing lists or other sophisticated campaign instruments, but the basic methods of gathering signatures have remained the same: hiring a large number of individuals to stand in busy public places and ask registered voters to sign a petition. Observers of California politics in the 1920s and 1930s were already in agreement that few petitions had a chance to qualify without the help of these professionals. The costs for hiring them might have risen, in line with the growing population of California, but there never existed a golden age when petitions qualified by the tireless efforts of devoted volunteers. Attempts to limit these activities in order to "restore" the original position of direct democracy miss one central point. Initiative politics have always centered on well-heeled interest groups using the process for their purposes and has never been about empowering common citizens.[21]

The employment of consultants and public relations professionals is likewise not a recent phenomenon. Once again, the technological advances of the last few decades, primarily the now-dominant role of television, the widespread use of polling, and the use of computers, have obscured the fact that consultants began to ply their trades well before World War II. Much has been made of late of the prominence of political consultants who sometimes attract more media attention than the candidates they represent.[22] Their origins are usually located in the 1960s when the rise of candidate-centered campaigns and the growing role of television radically changed campaign styles. But the first professional political campaign management firm, Campaigns, Inc., was founded in California in 1933, and it specialized in initiative campaigns. Many of the leading consultants of the period after World War II received their professional start at Campaigns, Inc. The work of Don Francisco in the 1935 chain store referendum was an example of the early use of advertising talent in a campaign. He also commissioned the first scientific opinion poll ever taken for a specific campaign, a practice followed by California employers three years later. Because political conditions in California, with its weak parties, preceded similar conditions on the national level by two or three decades, consultants flourished there first. Direct democracy did not form a precondition for their emergence, but the frequent campaigns for ballot propositions expanded the market for consultants. With the lavish funds raised by the interest groups that retained them, they made use of every public relations and advertising technique at their disposal. If the methods of their contemporary descendants have become more sophisticated, the underlying principles have stayed remarkably similar.[23] Their central role in initiative campaigns today has hardly transformed the process as a whole.

The historical record of direct democracy over the last century makes it clear that virtually none of the contemporary problems that have attracted so much public attention lately are of recent origin. The initiative and referendum have been highly problematic political institutions from the beginning. By invoking images of grass-roots democracy and the empowerment of ordinary citizens, they continue to enjoy the support of wide segments of the American public. Certainly, there is much discomfort about the flood of ballot propositions, the impact of money on campaigns, and the ubiquitous role of petition circulators. Many liberals have watched with dismay as conservatives have skillfully exploited the process to advance their agenda. And many political scientists contend that direct democracy further undermines already weak parties and contributes little to meaningful debates over public policy. Yet with no consensus likely to emerge about needed reforms, there is little indication that direct democracy will undergo any meaningful change in the near future. Other more hopeful observers have pointed to the emergence of new technologies such as the Internet that can provide new means for citizens to become politically active and to make their influence felt. The track record of other new devices, such as cable TV, that were also believed to be useful in connecting voters and their representatives has been less than impressive.[24] And the image of isolated individuals casting their ballots via the Internet is hardly compatible with the goal of mobilizing the American electorate and reconnecting it to the polity. Technological innovations in and of themselves cannot overcome the sense of alienation and powerlessness that many Americans feel.

What then is the historical legacy of direct democracy? Certainly, it has not lived up to the expectations of its advocates one century ago. As a tool to create a government able to withstand the influence of corporate interests, it has been a conspicuous failure. This is not to suggest that the initiative has only been yet another tool for business interests to achieve their goals. Business has found itself on the defensive in many direct democracy campaigns, and the track record of environmental groups in initiative politics is fairly impressive. Direct democracy has been most importantly an addition to the repertoire of collective action enjoyed by an ever-growing array of interest groups. The key requirement for any group interested in using the process is money; money to procure the signatures, money to hire consultants, and money to pay for the TV spots needed to win the election. The initiative has been subject to the same dynamics as regular election campaigns. What it has not done is contribute in any meaningful way to a revival of democracy in America. It has not empowered ordinary citizens, it has not increased political awareness or participation, it has produced few significant public policy achievements, and it has not reduced the power of special interests. The historical record leaves precious little room for optimism that this rather bleak picture will change substantially in the future. At a time when many citizens feel removed from the political spectacle altogether, when political parties inspire more contempt than trust, when candidates appear interchangeable, and when political decision-making powers are located at far-away places, the sense of grass-roots democracy and popular sovereignty that continues to be attached to direct democracy is perhaps not surprising. But the historical analysis of direct democracy since its inception a century ago makes abundantly clear that the initiative and referendum have never served, and probably never will serve, as the means to strengthen democracy in America, to truly build a government by the people.

NOTES

Abbreviations

AFL Letterbooks
    American Federation of Labor Letterbooks, Library of Congress,
    Washington, D.C.
Bartlett Papers
    Louis Bartlett Papers, Bancroft Library, University of California,
    Berkeley, California
Dickson Papers
    Edward A. Dickson Papers, Department of Special Collections,
    University of California, Los Angeles, California
Drew Papers
    J. E. Drew Papers, Bancroft Library, University of California,
    Berkeley, California
Eggleston Papers
    William Eggleston Papers, Bancroft Library, University of
    California, Berkeley, California
Haynes Papers
    John Randolph Haynes Papers, Department of Special Collections,
    University of California, Los Angeles, California
Hichborn Papers
    Franklin Hichborn Papers, Department of Special Collections,
    University of California, Los Angeles, California
Johnson Papers
    Hiram Johnson Papers, Bancroft Library, University of California,
    Berkeley, California
King Papers
    Judson King Papers, Manuscript Division, Library of Congress,
    Washington, D.C.
Lindsey Papers
    Benjamin B. Lindsey Papers, Manuscript Division, Library of
    Congress, Washington, D.C.
Pardee Papers
    George C. Pardee Papers, Bancroft Library, University of California,
    Berkeley, California

Phelan Papers
  James D. Phelan Papers, Bancroft Library, University of California, Berkeley, California
Pillsbury Papers
  Arthur J. Pillsbury Papers, Bancroft Library, University of California, Berkeley, California
Ralston Papers
  Jackson Ralston Papers, Bancroft Library, University of California, Berkeley, California
Rowell Papers
  Chester H. Rowell Papers, Bancroft Library, University of California, Berkeley, California
Whitaker and Baxter Papers
  Whitaker and Baxter International Papers, Bancroft Library, University of California, Berkeley, California

Introduction

1. Smith, "The Voice of the People," 109.

2. "Ballot Initiatives Flourishing." See also Broder, "The Ballot Battle."

3. For works that deal with direct democracy, see Piott, "The Origins of the Initiative and Referendum in America"; Price, "The Initiative"; Farmer, "Democratic Ideologues"; Sponholtz, "The Initiative and Referendum"; Cronin, *Direct Democracy*; and Magleby, *Direct Legislation*.

4. On the nature of Progressive political reform, see Hays, "The Politics of Reform"; and "The Changing Political Structure of the City"; Wiebe, *The Search for Order*; Rice, *Progressive Cities*; Schiesl, *The Politics of Efficiency*; McCormick, *From Realignment to Reform*; and Hammack, *Power and Society*.

Chapter One

1. On Progressive reform, see Hays, "The Politics of Reform in Municipal Government"; Wiebe, *The Search for Order*; and McCormick, *From Realignment to Reform*.

2. Hofstadter, "What Happened to the Antitrust Movement?"; Keller, *Regulating a New Economy* and "Public Policy and Large Enterprise"; McCraw, "Rethinking the Trust Question"; Piott, *The Anti-Monopoly Persuasion*; Berk, *Alternative Tracks*.

3. Among the more important studies of Populism are Hofstadter,

The Age of Reform; Hicks, *The Populist Revolt*; Goodwyn, *Democratic Promise*; Pollack, *The Just Polity*; Hahn, *The Roots of Southern Populism*; and Cherny, *Populism, Progressivism, and the Transformation of Nebraska Politics*.

4. Turner, "Understanding the Populists," 372.

5. One exception is the excellent article, Huston, "The American Revolutionaries."

6. The most influential historical exponent of this idea has been Alfred D. Chandler. See his *The Visible Hand* and *Scale and Scope*. See also Galambos, "The Emerging Organizational Synthesis."

7. Parsons et al., "The Role of Cooperatives," 885.

8. Bailyn, *The Ideological Origins*; Wood, *The Creation of the American Republic*; Bushman, *King and People*; Shalhope, "Towards a Republican Synthesis."

9. McCormick, "Introduction," 4; Rodgers, *Contested Truths* and "Republicanism: The Career of a Concept"; Ross, "The Liberal Tradition Revisited," 120.

10. Crowley, *This Sheba, Self*, 151–53; Banning, *The Jeffersonian Persuasion*, 199; Shalhope, *John Taylor of Caroline*; Riesman, "Money, Credit, and Federalist Political Economy."

11. See Huston, "The American Revolutionaries," 1083–90.

12. McCoy, *The Elusive Republic*, 161; Appleby, *Capitalism and a New Social Order*; Cornell, "Aristocracy Assailed."

13. Skowronek, *Building a New American State*; Bright, "The State in the United States during the Nineteenth Century."

14. McCormick, "The Party Period and Public Policy," 204–5; Hartz, *Economic Policy and Democratic Thought*; Handlin and Handlin, *Commonwealth*; Scheiber, "Government and the Economy"; Pisani, "Promotion and Regulation"; Taylor, *The Transportation Revolution*.

15. Handlin and Handlin, "The Origins of the American Business Corporation," 22.

16. Hartog, *Public Property and Private Power*, 194–95; Horwitz, *The Transformation of American Law, 1780–1860*, 112; Hurst, *The Legitimacy of the Business Corporation*, 136–38; Nelson, *Americanization of the Common Law*, 135–36.

17. Meyers, *The Jacksonian Persuasion*, 23–24. See also Ward, *Andrew Jackson*; Kohl, *The Politics of Individualism*; and Freyer, *Producers versus Capitalists*.

18. Quoted in Ashworth, *"Agrarians" and "Aristocrats,"* 128.

19. Ershkovitz and Shade, "Consensus or Conflict?," 596–99; Cole, *Jacksonian Democracy in New Hampshire*, 199–200; Watson, *Jacksonian*

Politics and Community Conflict; Sharp, *The Jacksonians versus the Banks*; Shade, *Banks or No Banks*.

20. Wilentz, *Chants Democratic* and "Artisan Republican Festivals"; Laurie, *Artisans into Workers*; Ross, *Workers on the Edge*; Rodgers, "Republicanism," 28–29.

21. Hugins, *Jacksonian Democracy and the Working Class*, 149; Byrdsall, *The History of the Loco-Foco or Equal Rights Party*; Degler, "The Loco-Focos."

22. Laurie, *Working People of Philadelphia*, 109, 173; Pessen, *Most Uncommon Jacksonians*, 121, 191; Faler, *Mechanics and Manufacturers*, 215.

23. For the presence of antimonopoly elements in other reform movements, see Zahler, *Eastern Workingmen and National Land Policy*; Goodman, "The Emergence of Homestead Exemption," 470–98; Brooke, *The Heart of the Commonwealth*, 328, 381–82; and Baker, *Ambivalent Americans*.

24. Unger, *The Greenback Era*; Destler, *American Radicalism*, 3–8; Nugent, *Money and American Society*, 210–12; Woodward, *Origins of the New South*, 84–85; Weinstein, *Prelude to Populism*.

25. Labor largely supported the Greenback movement. See Montgomery, "William H. Sylvis," 19, and *Beyond Equality*, 441.

26. Adams, "The Granger Movement," 421–22; Benson, *Merchants, Farmers, and Railroads*, viii; Miller, *Railroads and the Granger Laws*; Treleven, "Railroads, Elevators, and Grain Dealers," 205–22; Woodman, "Chicago Businessmen and the 'Granger' Laws."

27. Buck, *The Granger Movement*, 89, 98–100; Throne, "The Anti-Monopoly Party in Iowa"; Ostler, *Prairie Populism*, 38–39; Clanton, *Populism*, 8–12.

28. Nordin, *Rich Harvest*, 240; Woods, *Knights of the Plow*; Castensen, *Farmer Discontent, 1865–1900*, 30, 83; Norris, *History of the Grange*; Cloud, *Monopolies and the People*.

29. On the railroads and the courts, see Cortner, *The Iron Horse*. On the railroad issue in Midwestern legislatures, see Campbell, *Representative Democracy*, 66.

30. Palmer, *"Man Over Money,"* 219; Goodwyn, *Democratic Promise*; McNall, *The Road to Rebellion*; Pollack, *The Just Polity*; Hahn, *The Roots of Southern Populism*; Argersinger, *Populism and Politics*; Ellis, "Rival Visions of Equality."

31. Weaver, *A Call to Action*, 394.

32. McDonald-Valesh, "The Strength and Weakness," 729; Peffer, *The Farmer's Side*, 169, and *Populism*, 36; Larson, *Populism in the Mountain*

West, 13; Griffiths, *Populism in the Western United States*; McMath, *American Populism*; Nugent, *The Tolerant Populists*.

33. Parsons et al., "The Role of Cooperatives"; Jeffrey Ostler, *Prairie Populism*; Barnes, *Farmers in Rebellion*.

34. Flower, "Is Socialism Desirable?," 753, "The Menace of Plutocracy," 510–11, and "Twenty-five Years of Bribery."

35. Quoted in Hicks, *The Populist Revolt*, 79. On the Populists and the law, see also Hunt, "Populism, Law, and the Corporation," and Westin, "Populism and the Supreme Court."

36. Quoted in Pollack, *Just Polity*, 29, 56–57; Lustig, *Corporate Liberalism*, 69; Watson, "Why the People's Party Should Elect the Next President," 201–4; Thelen, *The New Citizenship*, 2, 208–10.

37. Bryce, "Errors in Prof. Bryce's 'Commonwealth,'" 352.

38. Anderson, "The Populists and Capitalist America," 125; Hart, *Redeemers, Bourbons, and Populists*, 222–23.

39. On antitrust laws at the state level, see Berk, "Constituting Corporations and Markets"; May, "Antitrust in the Formative Era"; Mc-Curdy, "Justice Field and the Jurisprudence of Government-Business Relations"; Sklar, *The Corporate Reconstruction of American Capitalism*, 51–52; and Forrest, "Anti-Monopoly Legislation in the United States."

Chapter Two

1. See Teaford, "Finis for Tweed and Stevens" and *Unheralded Triumph*; McDonald, *The Parameters of Urban Fiscal Policy*; and Brown and Halaby, "Machine Politics in America," 597–99.

2. Adams, "A Chapter of Erie," 48.

3. O'Neal, "Distrust of State Legislatures," 685. On levels of corruption, see Summers, *Plundering Generation* and *Era of Good Stealings*.

4. Cleveland, *Organized Democracy*, 279; Beard and Schultz, *Documents on the State-Wide Initiative, Referendum, and Recall*, 17–18; Garner, "Amendments of State Constitutions," 214.

5. Dodd, "The Function of a State Constitution," 217; Beard, "The Constitution of Oklahoma"; Hart, "Growth of American Theories," 549.

6. Fairlie, "The Referendum and Initiative in Michigan," 147–49; Hartwell, "Referenda in Massachusetts, 1776–1907," 337.

7. Lobingier, "Direct Legislation in the United States," 577.

8. Dodd, *The Revision and Amendment of State Constitutions*, 270, 275.

9. Reed, "Some Late Efforts at Constitutional Reform," 1; Judson, "The Future of Representative Government," 189; Sheppard, "Concern-

ing the Decline"; Binney, "Restrictions upon Legal and Special Legislation," 621; Merwin, "The People in Government"; Munro, *The Initiative, Referendum, and Recall*, 19; Burrows, "Tendencies of American
Legislation."

10. Cleveland, *The Growth of Democracy*, 185–86, 207; Lobingier, *The
People's Law*; Sterne, "Crude Methods of Legislation."

11. Brown, "Direct Legislation"; Gardner, *The Referendum in Chicago*, 9–10; Maynard, "The Operation of the Referendum in Chicago,"
19.

12. Vrooman, "Twentieth Century Democracy," 566; Pomeroy, "Is
Direct Legislation Un-American?," 267–69; Flower, "Brookline," 505–
19.

13. Hutson, *Die Schweiz und die Vereinigten Staaten*.

14. *Report to the Department of State*, 9–12.

15. Dicey, "Democracy in Switzerland."

16. Clemens, *The People's Lobby*, 69–70; Rodgers, *Atlantic Crossings*;
Coleman, *Progressivism and the World of Reform*, 155–61, 178–81; Ell,
"Direct Legislation in New Zealand"; Horwill, "The Referendum in
Great Britain."

17. Rappard, "The Initiative, Referendum, and Recall," 114.

18. Sullivan, "The Referendum in Switzerland" and *Direct Legislation
by the Citizenship*; *Direct Legislation Record* 4, no. 2 (Mar. 1897): 19.
Other early books on direct democracy included Cree, *Direct Legislation
by the People*. But Cree was much more cautious in his assessment of the
potential of the initiative and referendum, insisting that "we have no
unbounded faith in the wisdom and goodness of mere numbers." Because Cree lacked Sullivan's connections to the labor movement, his
book found only a limited audience.

19. Samuel Gompers to James W. Sullivan, May 17, 1892, reel 6, AFL
Letterbooks, Manuscript Division, Library of Congress; Gompers to
Sullivan, May 24, 1893, reel 7, AFL Letterbooks.

20. McCrackan, "The Swiss Referendum," "The Swiss and American Constitutions," "The Initiative in Switzerland," and *Swiss Solutions*;
Flower, *Progressive Men*, 62–64; *Direct Legislation Record* 1, no. 4 (Aug.
1894): 48; Hammer, *Vom Alpenidyll*, 246–72, and "William Denison
McCrackan (1864–1923)."

21. See, for example, Borgeaud, "Practical Results"; Hazeltine, "The
Referendum and Initiative in Switzerland"; O'B., "Open-Air Parliaments in Switzerland"; and Hart, "Vox Populi." For a different perspective, see Lowell, "Referendum in Switzerland and America."

22. Sullivan, *Direct Legislation*, 15.

23. Wuarin, "Recent Political Experiments," 365–66.

24. John R. Commons, "Direct Legislation in Switzerland and America," 727.

25. Hart, "Vox Populi"; Wuarin, "Recent Political Experiments"; O'B, "Open Air Parliaments."

26. Rappard, "The Initiative, Referendum, and Recall," 364.

27. Vrooman, "Twentieth Century Democracy," 566; Pomeroy, "Is Direct Legislation Un-American?," 267–69; Flower, "Brookline: A Model Town under the Referendum," 505–19; Sullivan, "Direct Legislation in Massachusetts," 9, 13; Jackson, "The Ideal Government"; Ramage, "Municipal Referendum."

28. Barker, "The Initiative and the Referendum," 614.

29. Bowne, "The Initiative and Referendum," 554–55; Hurt, "The Farmers' Alliance," 444; Martin, *The People's Party in Texas*, 53–54; Bicha, *Western Populism*, 19; Morris, *Davis H. Waite*, 107.

30. Flower, "Pure Democracy," 268, 262.

31. On Flower, see Filler, *Muckrakers*, 39–41.

32. Pomeroy, "How the Trusts Stifle Initiative."

33. Gompers, "Initiative, Referendum, and Recall," 695; Pomeroy, "A Conversation," 317–19; Pomeroy, "Direct Legislation: Objections Answered" and "Two Arguments"; Galbreath, "Provisions for State-Wide Initiative and Referendum," 83–84.

34. Pomeroy, "The Doorway of Reforms," 715, "Democratic vs. Aristocratic Government," 124, and "The Failure."

35. Pomeroy, *Papers on Direct Legislation*, 40, 50. On another occasion, the *Direct Legislation Record* characterized representative government as an "utter failure. It fails in the leaders it develops; it fails in its mechanism. It is cumbrous, uncertain, confused, irresponsible, undemocratic, often farcical and dishonest, and commonly partisan." *Direct Legislation Record* 1, no. 6 (Oct. 1894): 84.

36. See Pomeroy, "The Nevada Referendum Victory"; and Buchanan, "A Referendum for Reform."

37. Flower, *Progressive Men*, 64–65.

38. Parsons, *The City for the People*, 613; Shibley, *The Money Question*; *Direct Legislation Record* 7, no. 4 (Dec. 1901): 71–72.

39. Owen, "The Restoration of Popular Rule" and *Judicial Recall*.

40. Shibley, "Initiative and Referendum in Practical Operation," 147, "Judges Attack Oregon Amendment," 613, "Referendum and Initiative in Relation to Municipal Ownership," and "The Possibilities in Recent Electoral Reforms." The *Direct Legislation Record* and the *Referendum News*, published by Shibley, were finally absorbed by another reform

journal, *Equity*, in 1907. *Equity*, under the editorship of the Philadelphia physician and reformer Charles F. Taylor, continued to publish information on direct legislation until the end of World War I when the paper folded.

41. *Direct Legislation Record* 6, no. 1 (Mar. 1899): 16.

42. *Direct Legislation Record* 1, no. 3 (July 1894): 35.

43. *Direct Legislation Record* 1, no. 1 (May 1894): 2–3, 12, 14–16.

44. *Direct Legislation Record* 1, no. 1 (May 1894) 3; 1, no. 3 (July 1894): 43.

45. Shibley, *A Brief Review of Organized Labor's Non-Partisan Campaign*, 5.

46. Fink, "The Uses of Political Power" and *Workingmen's Democracy*; Hattam, "Economic Visions and Political Strategies," 90–92; Oestreicher, "Terence V. Powderly"; Voss, *The Making of American Exceptionalism*.

47. Gompers, "Organized Labor," 93; Civic Federation of Chicago, *Chicago Conference on Trusts*, 330; Oestreicher, "Urban Working-Class Political Behavior"; Brody, "On the Failure of U.S. Radical Politics."

48. Frank Parsons, *Direct Legislation*, 119. In 1902, George Shibley also remarked on the close associations between labor and the various Direct Legislation Leagues: "In some States the movement is entirely in the hands of Organized Labor, in others the Direct Legislation Leagues are the centers. . . ." *Direct Legislation Record* 8, no. 2 (June 1902): 29; Shibley, "The Initiative and Referendum in 1909," 122–23. On the political strategies of the AFL, see Hattam, *Labor Visions and State Power*.

49. Labor support also had its downside. In 1894, a reform journal admitted that "direct legislation is being classed as peculiarly a labor and Populist plank," a situation which contributed to the difficulty of enlisting the support of the main parties. *Direct Legislation Record* 1, no. 6 (Oct. 1894): 86.

50. Pomeroy, "A Conversation," 323.

51. Pomeroy, *Papers on Direct Legislation*, 49; Pomeroy, "Needed Political Reforms," 464.

52. *Official Report of the National Anti-Trust Conference*, 53, 202, 78. See also pages 118, 271–72, 281, 334.

53. *Official Report of the National Anti-Trust Conference*, 352.

54. *Direct Legislation Record* 1, no. 1 (May 1894): 1.

55. *Direct Legislation Record* 2, no. 2 (June 1895): 9.

56. *Direct Legislation Record* 3, no. 1 (Jan. 1896): 1–2; 5, no. 1 (Mar. 1898): 5–6; 6, no. 1 (Mar. 1899): 6; 7, no. 1 (Mar. 1900): 10; 7, no. 3 (Sept. 1901): 45.

57. *Direct Legislation Record* 3, no. 4 (Sept. 1896): 25.

58. Pomeroy, "Direct Legislation," 385; "An Appeal to Friends of Popular Government," 449–55.

59. *The Arena* 7, no. 3 (Sept. 1901): 41–44.

60. When Judson King, another direct-democracy reformer, contemplated the formation of a new national association around 1912 — a plan that ended with the founding of the National Popular Government League in 1913 — Pomeroy recommended that the old League be revived. See Eltweed Pomeroy to Judson King, Apr. 14, 1912, box 2, folder General Correspondence, Texas, King Papers. King's attempts to interest reformers in the states in the work of his organization also occasionally revealed the gap separating the two. While John R. Spencer, secretary of the Texas Federation of Labor, was actively campaigning for direct legislation in his home state in 1913, he showed little enthusiasm for participating in national efforts. King reminded him that "the national league is organized to help struggling state organizations," but local activists clearly realized how little assistance national bodies could render. See John R. Spencer to King, Nov. 25, 1913; King to Spencer, Dec. 26, 1913, box 2, folder General Correspondence, Texas, King Papers.

61. *Direct Legislation Record* 1, no. 3 (July 1894): 29.

62. Weikert, "Direct Legislation," 87.

63. *Direct Legislation Record* 3, no. 1 (Jan. 1896): 1.

64. *Direct Legislation Record* 3, no. 4 (Sept. 1896): 28–30. The attempts of McEwan and the Populist Senator Marion Butler to have Congress pass resolutions forming a committee to discuss a national initiative and referendum failed in 1897. See *Direct Legislation Record* 4, no. 2 (Mar. 1897): 5.

65. *Direct Legislation Record* 4, no. 1 (Jan. 1897): 1.

66. *Direct Legislation Record* 7, no. 4 (Dec. 1901): 59.

67. *Direct Legislation Record* 3, no. 3 (June 1896): 20, 23; 5, no. 4 (Sept. 1898): 53–54

68. *Direct Legislation Record* 7, no. 2 (May 1900): 17–18; 7, no. 4 (Sept. 1900): 39–40.

69. *Direct Legislation Record* 7, no. 5 (Dec. 1900): 59, 67, 65, 64.

70. Beyond these individuals, it remains difficult to get a clear picture of the social and political backgrounds of direct-democracy advocates. It seems that most of the state Direct Legislation Leagues were led by middle-class professionals and small businessmen. Even though labor formed a crucial component of the reform coalition, the presence of middle-class individuals gave the movement more respectability. Politically, a number of activists previously had been active on behalf of such

causes as prohibition and the single tax. In the 1890s, the boundaries between different reform crusades remained highly permeable. See *Direct Legislation Record* 4, no. 1 (June 1897): 35; 4, no. 4 (Sept. 1897): 56; and 5, no. 2 (May 1898): 26.

71. Shibley, "The Victorious March," 179, "Guarded Representative Government," and *The People's Sovereignty versus Trustocracy*.

Chapter Three

1. Murrin, *A Roof without Walls*; Anderson, *Imagined Communities*. On the role of the Constitution in American political culture, see Kammen, *A Machine That Would Go of Itself*.

2. On this concept, see Lutz, *Popular Consent and Popular Control*; and Fritz, "Popular Sovereignty, Vigilantism, and the Constitutional Right of Revolution."

3. On the role of state constitutions in the nineteenth century, see Fritz, "The American Constitutional Tradition Revisited" and "Rethinking the American Constitutional Tradition." For a perceptive study of state constitutions, see Johnson, *Founding the Far West*.

4. Pomeroy, *Papers on Direct Legislation*, 40; Sullivan, *Direct Legislation*; McCrackan, "The Initiative in Switzerland," 548–53.

5. Federalist No. 10, *The Federalist Papers*, 81.

6. Hanson, "'Commons' and 'Commonwealth,'" 165–93, and "Democracy," 68–89; Kammen, *Sovereignty and Liberty*, 61–62.

7. Brown, "The Popular Initiative," 749, 714–15.

8. Root, "Experiments in Government," 13.

9. Judson, "The Future of Representative Government," 194–95; Sanborn, "Popular Legislation," 587–603.

10. Hands, "Is the Initiative and Referendum Repugnant?," 244–48; Myrick, "The Initiative and Referendum"; Sherwood, "The Initiative and Referendum under the United States Constitution," 247–51.

11. Bacon and Wyman, *Direct Elections*, 44; Butler, *The Initiative, Referendum, and Recall*.

12. Quoted in LaPalombara and Hagan, "Direct Legislation," 401; Schaffner, "The Initiative, The Referendum, and The Recall," 42; Shibley, "Judges Attack Oregon Amendment."

13. *Equity* 9, no. 1 (Jan. 1907): 8–9; Myrick, "The Initiative and Referendum," 387–90.

14. Pillsbury and Sutro, *Initiative Legislation in the Supreme Court*, 13, 19, 21, 80–81.

15. "Initiative and Referendum," 308–9; Strum, *The Supreme Court*;

"End of a Bug-a-Boo," 4; Berg, "The Guarantee of Republican Government."

16. Bourne, "Initiative, Referendum, and Recall," 131.

17. Guthrie, "The Initiative, Referendum, and Recall," 25; Wilcox, *Government by All the People*, 7.

18. *Equity* 9, no. 2 (Apr. 1907): 20.

19. Smith, "Recent Institutional Legislation," 141, 147, and *The Spirit of American Government*. On Smith, see Clark, *Washington*, 94–97; Goldman, "J. Allen Smith"; and McClintock, "J. Allen Smith."

20. Pomeroy, "The Doorway of Reforms," 715, and "Democratic vs. Aristocratic Government," 124.

21. Sullivan, *Direct Legislation by the Citizenship*, 5, 100.

22. Elliott, *American Government and Majority Rule*, 136.

23. Parsons, *Direct Legislation*, 15.

24. Taylor, "The March of Democracy," 198.

25. *California Outlook* 10, no. 20 (May 13, 1911): 5.

26. Flower, "Organized Labor and Direct Legislation," 533.

27. Bourne, "Initiative, Referendum, and Recall," 122–23.

28. McCall, "Representative as against Direct Government," 456; Foxcroft, "Constitution-mending."

29. Junkin, *Is Our Representative Government Imperiled?*, 6.

30. Bryce, *Modern Democracies*, 142.

31. Quoted in Hutchinson, *Oil, Land, and Politics*, 327.

32. Barnes, "The Popular Initiative and Referendum," 68.

33. Maxey, "The Referendum in America," 51.

34. Lowell, "Referendum in Switzerland and America," 523, and *Public Opinion and Popular Government*, 78.

35. Kales, *Unpopular Government*, 119, 120; O'Neal, *Representative Government and the Common Law*, 6.

36. Hart, "The People vs. the Representative," 731.

37. Dealey, "The Trend of Recent Constitutional Changes," 60.

38. Hollingsworth, "The So-Called Progressive Movement," 45; French, "When History Repeats," 90–97.

39. "The Foundation of Our Faith," 3.

40. Lobingier, "Direct Popular Legislation," 235–37; Lyon, "What Proportion of Voters," 85–92.

41. *Direct Legislation Record* 1, no. 6 (Oct. 1894): 81.

42. Parsons, *Direct Legislation*, 25, 52; "'Real' Popular Government"; *Direct Legislation Record* 4, no. 2 (Mar. 1897): 7.

43. Post, "The Initiative and Referendum," 376; *Memorial of State Referendum League of Maine*, 6.

44. Cridge, "The People as Lawmakers in Oregon," 53.

45. King, "How Oregon 'Stood Pat,'" 116. For King, the 25 percent of the electorate that did not vote on propositions were "the ignorant, careless, illiterate class of voters who can be interested only in *persons*, but not in *principles*; unless, perchance, the principle involves beer, and 10 per cent will not vote on even beer."

46. *Equity* 15, no. 1 (Jan. 1913): 13; 15, no. 4 (Oct. 1913): 210; Haynes, "The Actual Workings," 589; King, *The State-Wide Initiative and Referendum*, 15.

47. *Equity* 16, no. 2 (Apr. 1914): 67.

48. Sitton, *John Randolph Haynes*; *Equity* 11, no. 3 (July 1909): 83; Crouch, "John Randolph Haynes," 436; Starr, *Inventing the Dream*, 211–12; Mowry, *The California Progressives*, 39.

49. Willard, "A Political Experiment," 473; Pomeroy, "The First Discharge of a Public Servant," 69–71; Ruppenthal, "Election Reforms," 428; Davis, "The Recall as a Measure of Control"; Stimson, *Rise of the Labor Movement in Los Angeles*, 282–85.

50. Works, "A City's Struggle," 357; Catlett, "The Working of the Recall in Seattle," 231–33; Hendrick, "The 'Recall' in Seattle"; "The Seattle Recall," 295.

51. *California Outlook* 11, no. 1 (July 1, 1911): 3.

52. Lewis, "A New Method of Constitutional Amendment," 315.

53. Beard and Schultz, *Documents on the State-Wide Initiative*, 55.

54. Clark, "The Election of Federal Judges," 459; Overton, "Democracy and the Recall"; Manahan, *The Recall of Judges*, 7; Owen, *Judicial Recall*; Poindexter, *The Recall of Judges*; Roe, *Our Judicial Oligarchy*; Ford, "Direct Legislation and the Recall."

55. McCay, "Judicial Recall," 17, 16; Brown, "The Judicial Recall"; Fink, "The Recall of Judges."

56. Berman, *Reformers, Corporations*, 77–79; Everett, *Arizona*, 66–71; Fowler, "Constitutions and Conditions Contrasted"; Houghton, "Arizona's Experience"; Hunter, "The Bull Moose Movement."

57. Lewis, "Arizona's Constitution," 170, 174.

58. *Congressional Record*, Senate, 62d Cong., 1st Sess., July 11, 1911, 2796.

59. "The Statehood Veto," 912; Hubbard, "The Arizona Enabling Act"; Anderson, *William Howard Taft*, 231–32.

60. Taft, *Special Message*, 4.

61. Root, "Experiments in Government," 5.

62. Roosevelt, "Arizona and the Recall of the Judiciary," 379.

63. Ransom, *Majority Rule*, 6; Roosevelt, "Progressive Democracy,"

856, and "The Right of the People to Review Judge-Made Law"; Benjamin B. Lindsey to Dickinson S. Miller, Sept. 27, 1912, box 40, Lindsey Papers; Harbaugh, *The Life and Times of Theodore Roosevelt*, 395–400.

64. *Equity* 14, no. 2 (Apr. 1912): 72.

65. Dougherty, "Substitutes for the Recall of Judges," 99–108.

66. Stagner, "The Recall of Judicial Decisions"; Ross, *A Muted Fury*, 152; Hamill, "Constitutional Chaos"; McDonough, "The Recall of Decisions: A Fallacy"; Thayer, *Recall of Judicial Decisions*; Mowry, *Theodore Roosevelt*, 215–19; La Follette, *La Follette's Autobiography*, 209.

67. Illinois Legislative Reference Bureau, *The Initiative*, 119; Colorado Legislative Reference Bureau, *The Initiative and Referendum in Colorado*.

68. Clark, "The Trend to an American Democracy," 27.

Chapter Four

1. Clemens, *The People's Lobby*, 35.

2. Oberholtzer, "Direct Legislation in America," 504; Bailey, "The West and Radical Legislation."

3. Haynes, *Direct Government in California*; Holcombe, *State Government*, 530.

4. Skowronek, *Building a New American State*.

5. McCormick, *From Realignment to Reform*; McGerr, *The Decline of Popular Politics*.

6. Kleppner, "Voters and Parties" and "Politics without Parties"; Rowley, "The West as Laboratory"; Bridges, *Morning Glories*, 54–56; Allen and Austin, "From the Populist Era to the New Deal"; Owens, "Pattern and Structure" and "Government and Politics in the Nineteenth-Century West."

7. Austin Ranney has called the direct primary "the most radical of all the party reforms adopted in the whole course of American history." See Ranney, *Curing the Mischiefs of Faction*, 121; "The Direct Primary"; Key, *American State Politics*, 120; Shefter, "Regional Receptivity to Reform"; and Huckshorn, *Party Leadership*, 259–61.

8. Bridges, "Winning the West to Municipal Reform"; Ethington, "Urban Constituencies."

9. J. W. Mansell to Robert L. Owen, July 24, 1915; Mansell to Judson King, Aug. 16, 1915; King to Mansell, Aug. 12, 1915; all in box 1, folder General Correspondence, Oklahoma, 1912–16, King Papers.

10. King to Campbell Russell, Aug. 26, 1915; Russell to King, Sept. 18, 1915, in ibid.

11. King to Russell, Sept. 24, 1915; King to Mansell, Sept. 17, 1915, in ibid.

12. *Direct Legislation Record* 1, no. 6 (Oct. 1894): 77.

13. *Direct Legislation Record* 6, no. 2 (June 1899): 26.

14. *Direct Legislation Record* 3, no. 5 (Dec. 1896): 38–39; 5, no. 1 (Mar. 1898): 19.

15. *Direct Legislation Record* 4, no. 1 (June 1897): 21–22.

16. *Direct Legislation Record* 3, no. 5 (Dec. 1896): 38–39.

17. Jones, "Organized Labor and the Initiative and Referendum: 1885–1920," 24–25; Stockbridge, "The Single Taxers"; Piott, "Giving Voters a Voice"; Crockett, "The 1912 Single Tax Campaign in Missouri." On the general appeal of the ideas of Henry George, see Ross, "The Culture of Political Economy."

18. Dudden, *Joseph Fels*, 199–203; Young, *The Single Tax Movement*, 165–67; Jackson H. Ralston Autobiography, 35–36, carton 5, Ralston Papers; Ralston to A. C. Pleydell, Aug. 2, 1910, box 2, Eggleston Papers.

19. Jones, "Organized Labor," 116–17.

20. *Referendum News* 1, no. 7 (Mar. 1906): 12; no. 11 (Sept. 1906): 49.

21. Kerr, *Organized for Prohibition*, 51–53, 140–41, 168 and "Organizing for Reform"; Odegard, *Pressure Politics*; Pegram, "Temperance Politics"; Sponholtz, "The Politics of Temperance."

22. For examples of local prohibition referenda, see Baldwin, "When Billy Sunday 'Saved' Colorado"; and Fea, "'The Town That Billy Sunday Could Not Shut Down.'"

23. Folsom, "Tinkerers, Tipplers, and Traitors," 57–58, 74–75; Ryan, "Male Opponents and Supporters"; Daniels, "Building a Winning Coalition"; Cushman, "Recent Experience," 536; Gould, *Progressives and Prohibitionists*.

24. The analysis of voting behavior on referenda in California during this period has demonstrated that there was little correlation between the support base for different reform agendas. Voting on such issues as women's suffrage, direct democracy, and prohibition shows that each derived its support from a different group of voters. See McDonagh, "The 'Welfare Rights State.'"

25. On South Dakota, see Piott, "The Origins of the Initiative and Referendum in South Dakota"; Grant, "Origins of a Progressive Reform"; Argersinger, "Regulating Democracy," 182; Galbreath, "Provisions for State-Wide Initiative and Referendum"; and Clow, "In Search of the People's Voice."

26. Griffiths, *Populism in the Western United States*, 132–41; Hendrick, "The Initiative and Referendum," 246–48; LaPalombara, *The Initiative and Referendum*, 5–7; Teal, "The Practical Workings"; Thatcher, "The Initiative and Referendum in Oregon," 201; McClintock, "Seth Lewelling."

27. Woodward, "William S. U'Ren"; Pomeroy, *The Pacific Slope*, 196–98; Burton, *Democrats of Oregon*, 10–11; Schlup, "Republican Insurgent."

28. *Equity* 11, no. 1 (Jan. 1909): 4.

29. U'Ren, "The Initiative and Referendum in Oregon," 275.

30. Steffens, "U'Ren," 532; U'Ren, "Single Tax."

31. Barnett, *The Operation of the Initiative*, 5; Gilbert, "Single-Tax Movement in Oregon," 25.

32. Quoted in Barnett, *The Operation of the Initiative*, 17.

33. Eaton, *The Oregon System*; Barnett, "The Operation of the Recall in Oregon."

34. Bourne, "The Initiative on Trial"; Paine, "Lincoln's Ideal Carried Out in Oregon"; Hendrick, "Law-Making by the Voters" and "Statement No. I"; Thatcher, "The Initiative, Referendum and Popular Election of Senators in Oregon"; "Direct Legislation in Oregon"; "Popular Government in Oregon." For a different view, see Holman, *Some Instances*.

35. Haynes, "People's Rule on Trial," 19; Woodward, "W. S. U'Ren."

36. Montague, "The Oregon System at Work," 260; Croly, *Progressive Democracy*, 292–302; *Equity* 9, no. 3(Oct. 1907): 3–4; 10, no. 2 (Apr. 1908): 50.

37. Rice, *Progressive Cities*; Schiesl, *The Politics of Efficiency*, 136–38; Bridges, "Creating Cultures of Reform"; Weinstein, "Organized Business."

38. Gardner, "The Initiative and Referendum," 154; Rice, *Progressive Cities*, 72; Ryan, "The Commission Plan of City Government," 44; Paine, "The Referendum and Initiative in American Cities," 10, and "The Initiative, the Referendum, and the Recall."

39. Ryan, *Municipal Freedom*, 20; Bruere, *The New City Government*, 376; Taylor, "Municipal Initiative."

40. See Bakken, *Rocky Mountain Constitution Making*, 47; Berman, "Political Culture."

41. Berman, *Reformers, Corporations, and the Electorate*, 77–79; Everett, *Arizona*, 66–71; Wagoner, *Arizona Territory*.

42. *Equity* 9, no. 3 (Oct. 1907): 1; Direct Legislation League of the

State of Washington, *Direct Legislation*; *Circular of the "Direct Legislation League" of Massachusetts*, 1; Clark, *Washington*, 94–97; Shippee, "Washington's First Experiment."

43. Clemens, *The People's Lobby*, 131–34; Benedict, "Some Aspects," 175, 71–72; Watkins, *Rural Democracy*, 108–10; Clark, *The Dry Years*, 102–3; Johnson, "Muckraking in the Northwest," 479.

44. Clark, "The 'Hell-Soaked Institution'"; Johnson, "The Adoption of the Initiative and Referendum in Washington" and "The Initiative and Referendum in Washington"; Kerr, "The Progressives in Washington."

45. Deverell, *Railroad Crossing*, 29–31; Bean, *California*, 304–6, 308; Griffiths, "Anti-Monopoly Movements in California."

46. Shumsky, *The Evolution of Political Protest*, 162–65, 209–10; Johnson, *Founding the Far West*, 122–25; Moffett, "The Railroad Commission of California," 476; Nash, "The California Railroad Commission, 1876–1911"; McAfee, *California's Railroad Era*, 176–79; Olin, *California Politics*, 41, 44; Petersen, "The Struggle for the Australian Ballot."

47. Schiesl, "Progressive Reform" and "Politicians in Disguise."; Fogelson, *The Fragmented Metropolis*, 211–16; Stimson, *Rise of the Labor Movement in Los Angeles*, 281–82.

48. Sitton, *John Randolph Haynes*, 29–30, 37–42, and "California's Practical Idealist"; Crouch, "John Randolph Haynes," 436.

49. Report of the Secretary of the Direct Legislation League of California, Feb. 5, 1910, box 50, Haynes Papers; Haynes, "The Adoption of the Initiative"; Hichborn, *Story of the Session of the California Legislature of 1911*, 20, 100–101; "Direct Legislation." Haynes invited the Socialist and Prohibition parties in California, the Building Trades Council, and the San Francisco Labor Council to send representatives to the executive committee of the Direct Legislation League (DLL). Isidor Jacob to Haynes, Dec. 9, 1908, box 42, Haynes Papers.

50. Report of the Treasurer of the Direct Legislation League of California from the Date of Organization to the Adjournment of the Legislature of 1909; Report . . . for the Time Apr. 30, 1909 to Nov. 20, 1911, box 50, Haynes Papers.

51. Taft, *Labor Politics American Style*; Kazin, "The Great Exception Revisited" and *Barons of Labor*.

52. Haynes to R. H. Norton, Nov. 9, 1903, box 35, Haynes Papers; Gompers, "Initiative, Referendum, and Recall," 698; Sitton, "John Randolph Haynes and the Left Wing of California Progressivism"; Burki, "The California Progressives," 32.

53. Haynes to Dear Sir, Jan. 28, 1905; see also letters in reply to the

mass mailing in box 34; Haynes to Frank J. Bonnington, Jan. 19, 1905, box 35, Haynes Papers.

54. Haynes to J. H. Scott, Nov. 22, 1902; Feb. 4, 1903, box 50; Scott to Haynes, Feb. 4, 1903, box 41; To the Ministers and Christian People of California, Dec. 20, 1902, box 35; all in ibid.

55. Haynes to National American Woman's Suffrage Association, June 13, 1905, box 50; E. R. Zion to Haynes, Dec. 14, 1907, box 49; both in ibid. But Haynes also stressed that the cause of direct democracy should not be confused with womens suffrage, and that only eligible voters should become members of the DLL. He wanted to get the help of women "in the lines of educational work; for instance, the gathering and distribution of literature," but their role was to be secondary. Haynes to Zion, Dec. 30, 1907, box 41, in ibid.

56. Haynes, however, at all times retained control over the agenda of the Direct Legislation League and made sure that the presence of some labor and socialist groups did not endanger the vital ties to middle-class reformers. See U'Ren to Edward A. Dickson, Dec. 15, 1908, box 42 and Haynes to Abbot Kinney, Dec. 23, 1908, box 41, both in ibid.

57. Walter Lindley to Hervey Lindley, Aug. 23, 1902, box 41, in ibid.

58. Direct Legislation League of California to the State Republican Convention, Aug. 23, 1902, box 35; John R. Haynes to George C. Pardee, Oct. 10, 1902, box 70; Pardee to Haynes, Oct. 16, 1902, box 3; Pardee to Haynes, Dec. 10, 1902, box 4; Haynes to Pardee, Jan. 19, 1903, box 70; Pardee to Haynes, Jan. 24, 1903, box 5; all in Pardee Papers.

59. In addition, Haynes and other reformers were also active at the municipal level. By 1910, Los Angeles, San Francisco, San Diego, Berkeley, and many other municipalities had adopted local direct democracy ordinances. *Direct Legislation Record* 5, no. 1 (Mar. 1898): 7–8; 5, no. 3 (June 1898): 42–43; Kazin, *Barons of Labor*, 42; Lewis, "San Francisco's New Charter"; Paine, "The Referendum and Initiative in American Cities," 13; Dickson, "Self-Government at Los Angeles," 383.

60. Frederick W. Houser to Guy Lathrop, Oct. 21, 1902; Henry E. Carter to Haynes, Oct. 28, 1902; J. Van Rensselaer to Haynes, Jan. 19, 1903; all in box 35; A. A. Caldwell to Haynes, Jan. 27, 1903, box 41; Haynes to Candidates for the 1904 Election, Oct. 4, 1904, box 50; all in Haynes Papers. In 1905, Haynes also sent 10,000 letters to people across the state urging them to write to their representatives meeting in Sacramento in support of the amendments. Haynes to Dear Friend, Jan. 18, 1905, box 34, Haynes Papers.

61. J. B. Curtin to Haynes, Sept. 28, 1904, in ibid.

62. Isidor Jacob to Haynes, Dec. 29, 1908; Jan. 4, 1909; Dickson to

Haynes, Jan. 11, 1909; George B. Anderson to Haynes, Jan. 8, 14, 1909; U'Ren to Haynes, Jan. 21, 25, 1909; Feb. 1, 1909; Anderson to U'Ren, Feb. 23, 1909; all in box 50; U'Ren to Haynes, Jan. 12, 1909; Feb. 18, 24, 1909; Mar. 6, 1909; all in box 42; U'Ren to Rudolph Spreckels, Jan. 26, 1909, box 124; all in Hichborn Papers.

63. Hichborn, *Story of the Session of the California Legislature of 1911*, Olin, *California's Prodigal Sons*; Mowry, *The California Progressives* and "The California Progressive and His Rationale"; Miller, "The Origins."

64. On Johnson, see Lower, *A Bloc of One*; Olin, *California's Prodigal Sons* and "Hiram Johnson"; McKee, "The Background."

65. Haynes to Hiram Johnson, Mar. 31, 1910, Part I, box 7; Johnson to Haynes, Apr. 21, 1910, Part I, box 1; Haynes to Johnson, May 4, 1910, Part I, box 7; all in Johnson Papers.

66. Meyer Lissner to Johnson, Nov. 23, 1910, Part I, box 8, Letters to Johnson LF-N; Lissner to Johnson, Nov. 25, 1910, Part II, box 20, Letters to Johnson from Meyer Lissner, 1910–14; Lissner to Johnson, Feb. 14, 1911; all in Johnson Papers; U'Ren to Haynes, Nov. 22, 1910, Haynes Papers, box 41.

67. Milton T. U'Ren to Meyer Lissner, May 20, 1911, Part II, box 34, Letters to Johnson, UI–VZ; Lissner to Johnson, June 10, 1911; all in Johnson Papers; U'Ren to Haynes, May 26, 1911; U'Ren to Haynes, June 23, 1911; both in box 42; Lissner to Johnson, Feb. 14, 1911; U'Ren to Haynes, Nov. 22, 1910, both in box 41; all in Haynes Papers.

68. Clark, *Deliver Us from Evil*, 103,107–8; Timberlake, *Prohibition and the Progressive Movement*, 166–67; Blocker, *Retreat from Reform*, 215–16, 236–38; Hichborn to Johnson, June 28, 1911; July 29, 1911; Johnson Papers; Ostrander, *The Prohibition Movement in California, 1848–1933*, 104.

69. Rowell to Johnson, Aug. 26, 1911, box 1, folder 1911, July to December, Rowell Papers; Johnson to Edward Dickson, Sept. 11, 1911; U'Ren to Johnson, Sept. 7, 1911; Johnson to U'Ren, Sept. 11, 1911; all in Johnson Papers; Johnson to Haynes, Sept. 11, 1911, box 41, Haynes Papers; Johnson to Dickson, Sept. 11, 1911; U'Ren to Dickson, Sept. 29, 1911; both in box 2, folder 4, Dickson Papers; Johnson to U'Ren, Sept. 12, 14, 1911; Johnson to George W. Cartwright, Sept. 13, 1911; Johnson to W. F. Chandler, Sept. 13, 1911; Johnson to E. O. Larkin, Sept. 13, 1911; all in Johnson Papers.

Chapter Five

1. Lobingier, *The People's Law*, 301; Bacon and Wyman, *Direct Elections and Law-Making by Popular Vote*, 11; Dodd, *The Revision and Amend-*

ment, 67–68; Kousser, *The Shaping of Southern Politics*; Haynes, "Educational Qualifications"; "Alabama's New Constitution," 751.

2. *Equity* 14, no. 1 (Jan. 1912): 23.

3. *Memorial Relative*, 42–43; *Equity* 14, no. 4 (Oct. 1912): 130–31; 15, no. 1 (Jan. 1913): 13. One indication of the lack of progress in the South was the relative absence of reports about state campaigns to introduce direct democracy in the pages of *Equity*. Whereas the journal carefully documented events in other parts of the country, there was evidently little to relay from the South.

4. *Equity* 13, no. 4 (Oct. 1911): 161.

5. Owen, "The Restoration of Popular Rule," *Judicial Recall*, and "The Initiative and Referendum."

6. Abbott, "The Initiative and Referendum in Oklahoma"; Lewallen, "'Let the People Rule,'" 290–95; Cronin, *Direct Democracy*, 93; "Technical Note," box 74, folder, Oklahoma, 1912–18, King Papers. This was not the sole example of direct legislation used for racist purposes. The first popular vote taken in 1915 under the new city charter of St. Louis, which included the devices, resulted in the overwhelming adoption of an ordinance calling for race segregation. For six years, small property owners and real estate dealers had called for such a measure, but the city council refused to pass an ordinance. The advocates of segregation were among the most vocal supporters of direct democracy. See "Race Segregation in St. Louis," 315.

7. "Enacted Laws and Resolutions, Use of Emergency, 1907–1929," box 74, folder, Oklahoma, 1912–28, King Papers.

8. Bass, "The Initiative and Referendum in Oklahoma," 129, 144–46.

9. Thomas, "Direct Legislation in Arkansas"; Ledbetter, "Adoption of Initiative and Referendum in Arkansas" and "The Constitutional Convention of 1917–1918"; Farmer, "Direct Democracy in Arkansas"; Grantham, *Southern Progressivism*, 91.

10. Judson King to John D. Fackler, Oct. 6, 1916, box 1, folder General Correspondence, Ohio (Cleveland), King Papers.

11. "Technical Note for Chapter on Campaign Methods," box 74, folder, Arkansas, 1912–16; King to Reverend Charles G. Elliott, Nov. 2, 1916; King to Genevieve Draughon, Oct. 28, 1916; L. H. Moore to King, Oct. 11, 1916, box 1, folder General Correspondence, Arkansas; King to Wayne B. Wheeler, Oct. 13, 1916, box 1, folder General Correspondence, Ohio, all in King Papers.

12. King to William S. U'Ren, Nov. 25, 1916, box 2, folder General Correspondence, Oregon; King to Mr. Burge, Nov. 16, 1916, box 1, folder General Correspondence, Ohio (Cleveland); both in King Papers.

13. Thomas, "The Initiative and Referendum in Arkansas Come of Age."

14. Henry, "Democracy and Disfranchisement," 18–23.

15. Judson King to R. M. Wanamaker, Mar. 27, 1914, box 1, folder General Correspondence, Ohio, King Papers; Henry, "Progressivism and Democracy."

16. King to John D. Fackler, Apr. 2, 1914; King to Thomas C. Fitzsimmons, Apr. 3, 1914; both in box 1, folder General Correspondence, Ohio; King to William S. U'Ren, May 25, 1915, box 2, folder General Correspondence, Oregon, King Papers.

17. King to Fackler, Apr. 2, 1914, box 1, King Papers.

18. Lilian Small to King, Mar. 17, 1915, box 1, folder General Correspondence, North Carolina, in ibid.

19. King to Gifford Pinchot, July 19, 1915, box 1, folder General Correspondence, Pennsylvania; *Popular Government* No. 1, May 1917, 16, in box 73B; both in King Papers; People's Rule League of Mississippi to Candidates for the Legislature, July 25, 1915, box 44, Haynes Papers.

20. Winslow, "The Referendum in Maryland"; King to U'Ren, Apr. 1, 1914, box 2, folder General Correspondence, Oregon, King Papers.

21. C. W. Brooks to King, Aug. 11, 1915; King to Brooks, Aug. 13, 1915; King to Brooks, Sept. 23, 1915; all in box 1, folder General Correspondence, Tennessee, King Papers.

22. King to Rev. A. R. Holton, Nov. 15, 1913; King to John R. Spencer, Nov. 25, 1913; King to C. S. Roberts, Feb. 5, 1915; B. F. Loohey to King, Feb. 18, 1915; all in box 2, folder General Correspondence, Texas, King Papers.

23. *Direct Legislation Record* 6, no. 4 (Sept. 1899): 72; 9, no. 2 (June 1903): 30.

24. Kerber, "The Initiative and Referendum in Florida," 304–7.

25. *Direct Legislation Record* 9, no. 3 (Sept. 1903): 48–49.

26. Black, "Maine's Experiences," 178; Nichols, "Present Status"; Piper, "The Victorious Campaign"; *Memorial of State Referendum League of Maine*; Farmer, "The Maine Campaign for Direct Democracy"; "The Referendum in Maine."

27. "Maine General Constitutional Initiative," box 74, folder General Correspondence, Maine 1912–18, King Papers.

28. Pelletier, *The Initiative and Referendum in Maine.*

29. Pollock, *The Initiative and Referendum in Michigan*; Fairlie, "The Referendum and Initiative in Michigan."

30. Warner, *Progressivism in Ohio*, 193–94; *Referendum News* 1, no. 2 (Dec. 1905): 5.

31. Daniel Kiefer to William Eggleston, Feb. 17, 1909, box 1, Eggleston Papers.

32. Bigelow, *Initiative and Referendum*, 7–8; Keller, "The Politics of State Constitutional Revision," 78–79.

33. Warner, *Progressivism in Ohio*, 295–300; Bryan, *The People's Law.*

34. Cushman, "Voting Organic Laws"; Barber, *Proportional Representation*, 42; Ryan, "The Influence of Socialism," 667, 669; Boyle, *The Initiative and Referendum.*

35. Sullivan, "Direct Legislation in Massachusetts," 9; "How The Referendum Would Work"; "The Referendum."

36. *Equity* 8, no. 3 (July 1906): 26–27; 9, no. 1 (Jan. 1907): 14; Paine, "Direct Legislation in Massachusetts"; *Circular of the "Direct Legislation League."*

37. *The Code of the People's Rule*, 113.

38. Lodge, *Speech of Hon. H. C. Lodge*, 10, 15; Luce, *The Public Opinion Bill*; Haynes, "Massachusetts Public Opinion Bills."

39. *Equity* 13, no. 1 (Jan. 1911): 26–27; 13, no. 2 (Apr. 1911): 76; 13, no. 4 (Oct. 1911): 177; 14, no. 3 (July 1912): 107; 15, no. 3 (July 1913): 188; 16, no. 3 (July 1914): 136–37.

40. *Equity* 16, no. 1 (Jan. 1914): 34–35; 16, no. 2 (Apr. 1914): 90–91; 17, no. 2 (Apr. 1915): 117.

41. McCall, "Representative as against Direct Government."

42. "The Public Opinion Law of Massachusetts," 290–92.

43. "The Initiative and Referendum," 186.

44. *Equity* 19, no. 4 (Oct. 1917): 199–201; 20, no. 1 (Jan. 1918): 47; Haynes, "How Massachusetts Adopted the Initiative and Referendum"; Hague, "The Massachusetts Constitutional Convention"; Loring, "A Short Account"; Keller, "The Politics of State Constitutional Revision," 79–81.

45. Powers, *"I & R" Ballot Questions*, 1, 4. Much like other states in the East, with the exception of Michigan in 1913, Massachusetts did not include the recall in its constitution. See "The Recall of Officers."

46. Doan, *The La Follettes*; McCarthy, *The Wisconsin Idea*; Margulies, *The Decline of the Progressive Movement*; Thelen, *The New Citizenship*; Steffens, "Sending A State to School"; Wyman, "Middle-Class Voters."

47. King to C. S. Roberts, Feb. 5, 1915, box 2, folder General Correspondence, Texas, King Papers.

48. *Equity* 17, no. 1 (Jan. 1915): 60–61; Margulies, *The Decline of the Progressive Movement*; Reed, *Government for the People*, 156–57; Reinsch, "The Initiative and Referendum."

49. *Direct Legislation Record* 4, no. 5 (Dec. 1897): 59.

50. Cruice, "Direct Legislation in Illinois"; Schaffner, "The Initiative," 38.

51. Pegram, "The Dry Machine," 185–86.

52. Civic Federation of Chicago, *Dangers of the Initiative and Referendum*, 4.

53. Pegram, *Partisans and Progressives*, 177–78; Morton, "Edward F. Dunne," 225–26.

54. *Equity* 9, no. 3 (Oct. 1907): 5; Flower, "The Direct-Legislation Campaign in the Empire State"; Leubuscher, "The Proposed Direct-Legislation Constitutional Amendment for New York."

55. *Equity* 11, no. 3 (July 1909): 92; 12, no. 4 (Oct. 1910): 155; 13, no. 1 (Jan. 1911): 31; 13, no. 3 (July 1912): 109.

56. On Hughes's attempt to introduce the direct primary in 1909–10, see McCormick, *From Realignment to Reform*, 243–47; *Equity* 11, no. 2 (Apr. 1909): 40–41; and Hendrick, "Governor Hughes and the Albany Gang," 510–12.

57. *Equity* 16. no. 4 (Oct. 1914): 186.

58. King to U'Ren, May 25, 1914; Aug. 17, 1914; both in box 2, folder General Correspondence, Oregon, King Papers.

59. *A Short Form of State Constitution*. On Pennsylvania, see *Report of the Special Committee*.

60. *Equity* 18, no. 4 (Oct. 1915): 215–16; Yellowitz, *Labor and the Progressive Movement*, 240–41; Wesser, *A Response to Progressivism*, 168–69.

61. American Federation of Labor, *Initiative, Referendum, and Recall*. Judson King estimated in 1912 that 50 percent of the states with direct democracy statutes restricted the operation of the initiative and referendum in some fashion. See King, "Demand a Workable Initiative and Referendum."

Chapter Six

1. DeWitt, *The Progressive Movement*, 4–5.

2. Taylor, "The March of Democracy in Municipalities," 196.

3. Wiebe, *Self-Rule*, 137.

4. Rodgers, "In Search of Progressivism," 123–24.

5. Huston, "The American Revolutionaries," 1102–5; McCormick, "The Discovery that Business Corrupts Politics," 321–22.

6. Furner, "Social Scientists and the State."

7. Bryce, "America Revisited," 848–49.

8. See Keller, "Public Policy and Large Enterprise," 523, 531. For a

different perspective, see Weinstein, *The Corporate Ideal*; and Kolko, *Railroads and Regulation*.

9. Civic Federation of Chicago, *Chicago Conference on Trusts*.

10. Civic Federation of Chicago, *Chicago Conference on Trusts*, 418–19, 111, 466, 274. Davis, who was elected governor of Arkansas in 1900, was indeed a tireless crusader against corporations and trusts in his home state, launching prosecutions against a variety of trusts. See Grantham, *Southern Progressivism*, 91.

11. *Chicago Conference on Trusts*, 286.

12. Berge, *The Free Pass Bribery System*, 2, 121; Kenny, "The Legislature That Elected Mr. Hanna." To eliminate corruption, many states enacted corrupt-practices acts in the 1890s and 1900s that prohibited corporate campaign contributions. See Belmont, "Publicity of Election Expenditures"; Sherman, *A Brief Review*.

13. Ostrogorski, *Democracy and the Organization of Political Parties*, 101.

14. On the importance of the theme of corruption in Progressive politics, see, for example, Hendrick, "Governor Hughes and the Albany Gang"; and Phillips, "The Treason of the Senate."

15. Shibley, "Referendum and Initiative in Relation to Municipal Ownership."

16. Chester Rowell, "Progressivism," clipping from the *Fresno Republican*, Jan. 10, 1911, carton 2, Rowell Papers; "A Primer of Direct-Legislation," 511.

17. Between 1902 and 1907, state legislatures passed about 800 railroad laws. See Keller, *Regulating a New Economy*, 47.

18. Perkins, "Corporations in Modern Business," 394; Adams, "State Control of Trusts," 463; Conant, "The New Corporation Tax," 235; Knauth, *The Policy of the United States*; Smith, "Effect of State Regulation," 86, 93.

19. Auerbach, "President Roosevelt and 'The Trusts'"; Johnson, "Antitrust Policy in Transition"; Urofsky, "Proposed Federal Incorporation"; Grosscup, "Is There Common Ground?"

20. "The Paramount Issue," 134; "The Insurgent League"; "The Progressive League Platform"; White, "The Insurgence of Insurgency"; Fillebrown, "The Taxation of Privilege."

21. See, for example, Gable, *The Bull Moose Years*.

22. Smith, "Corporate Regulation," 287.

23. Roosevelt, "Nationalism and Democracy," 622–23, and "Nationalism and Special Privilege."

24. Roosevelt, "The Progressives, Past and Present," 24, 27.

25. Croly, "Democratic Factions," 627, and *Progressive Democracy*, 106; Newlands, "Review and Criticism of Anti-Trust Legislation."

26. Brandeis, *The Curse of Bigness*, 138, 105, and *Other People's Money*, 111, 128; Meade, "The Fallacy of 'Big Business.'" On Brandeis, see also Strum, *Louis D. Brandeis* and *Brandeis*; Urofsky, *A Mind of One Piece*; and McCraw, *Prophets of Regulation*.

27. Wilson, *The New Freedom*, 180; Urofsky, "Wilson, Brandeis, and the Trust Issue, 1912–1914."

28. Rappard, "The Initiative and the Referendum in Switzerland," 357; "Progressive Principles."

29. Bourne, "The Initiative on Trial"; Paine, "Lincoln's Ideal Carried Out in Oregon"; Hendrick, "Law-Making by the Voters."

30. Ely, *Monopolies and Trusts*, 28–29. A few direct democracy advocates agreed with this assessment. Frank Parsons, a lecturer at Boston University Law School, wrote in 1901 that "monopoly we are bound to have; it is an economic necessity; the only question is, shall the people own the monopolies, or shall the monopolies own the people." Parsons, *The City for the People*, 16.

31. Jenks, "Capitalist Monopolies," 486–87; Commons, *The Distribution of Wealth*, 103–6; Durand, *The Trust Problem*; Adams, "Legal Monopoly"; Kleberg, "State Control of Trusts"; Davis, "The Nature of Corporations"; Grosscup, "How to Save the Corporation"; Wyman, "Unfair Competition."

32. Sinsheimer, "Commission Government," 32. Antimonopoly feelings lingered longer in the American West, one factor that explains the greater importance of the initiative and referendum there. See Sanders, "Farmers and the State," 190–94, and "Industrial Concentration."

33. *Equity* 8, no. 4 (Oct. 1906): 17; 9, no. 1 (Jan. 1907): 12; Cronin, *Direct Democracy*.

34. *Memorial Relative to a National Initiative*, 34, 31, 42–43; *Supplemental Memorial*.

35. "Direct or Simple," 122.

36. Croly, *The Promise of American Life*, 324, 328. On Croly, see Forcey, *The Crossroads of Liberalism*.

37. Croly, "State Political Reorganization," 132.

38. Weyl, *The New Democracy*, 307, 310.

39. Rowell, "Remarks on Mr. Herbert Croly's Paper," 151, and "The State"; Rowell to Prof. Charles G. Haines, Mar. 3, 1913, box 1, folder 1913, Jan.–Apr., Rowell Papers; Rowell to Prof. Leonard S. Rowe, Mar. 2, 1912, box 1, folder 1912, Jan.–June, Rowell Papers.

40. Hall, *Popular Government*, 142.

41. One observer in 1916 noted the different perceptions of the value of direct legislation even among its supporters. While some saw it mainly as a "check on representative government," to be employed sparingly and mostly as a device to keep potentially duplicitous legislatures under control, others regarded it as a device "to educate the electorate in self-government to the fullest possible intent." In this argument, the referendum and initiative should be used as often as possible as a tool for improving the character of the voters themselves. See Schnader, "Proper Safeguards," 516.

42. Garner, "Primary vs. Representative Government," 173.

43. U'Ren, "State and County Government," 273, and "Remarks on Mr. Herbert Croly's Paper"; Bourne, "Functions of the Initiative"; Coker, "The Interworkings."

44. Croly, *Progressive Democracy*, 308, 269–325. See also Stettner, *Shaping Modern Liberalism*, 62–64, 101–2.

45. See, for example, Gable, *The Bull Moose Years*; and Milkis and Tichenor, "'Direct Democracy' and Social Justice."

46. Lowitt, *George W. Norris: The Making of a Progressive*.

47. "The Insurgent League," 256; "The Progressive League Platform," 346.

48. Theodore Roosevelt quoted in Sklar, *The Corporate Reconstruction of American Capitalism*, 361. On progressivism in the major parties, see Reiter, "The Bases of Progressivism."

49. Roosevelt, "A Charter of Democracy," 390, 397. Many reformers remained skeptical of Roosevelt's democratic credentials and continued to prefer La Follette. A Colorado reformer wrote in late 1910 that the movement needed a standard-bearer "who not only sees the needs of democracy, but being himself of democracy has an overwhelming sense of its needs." E. W. Scripps to Benjamin B. Lindsey, Nov. 24, 1910, box 123, Lindsey Papers.

50. Betts, *The Betts-Roosevelt Letters*, 8, 5, 25.

51. Wilson, *The State*, 475–76.

52. Wilson, *Constitutional Government in the United States*, 188, 104–5.

53. Owen, "The Restoration of Popular Rule" and "The Initiative and Referendum in its Relation."

54. Robert L. Owen to Woodrow Wilson, Dec. 16, 1910, 245; Daniel L. Kiefer to Wilson, Dec. 24, 1910, 258; Kiefer to Wilson, Apr. 21, 1911, 578; "An Address to the Democratic Club of Philadelphia, Feb. 21, 1911," 448–49; Wilson to Samuel H. Thompson, Mar. 27, 1911, 521; all in *Papers of Woodrow Wilson*, vol. 22.

55. Article in *Portland Morning Oregonian*, May 18, 1911, 61–62, and May 20, 1911, 71; both in *Papers of Woodrow Wilson*, vol. 23; Heckscher, *Woodrow Wilson*, 234–35; Walworth, *Woodrow Wilson*, 182, 206–7; Link, *Wilson: The Road to the White House*, 319, 339–41.

56. Woodrow Wilson to William E. Eggleston, Sept. 5, 1911, box 1, Eggleston Papers. On Democratic disagreements on the issue, see Ellis, "Tilting at the Piazza."

57. *Seattle Daily Times*, May 20, 1911, 77; Wilson to Robert Garrett, Sept. 5, 1911, 302; both in *Papers of Woodrow Wilson*, vol. 23.

58. Wilson to Richard H. Dabney, Nov. 16, 1911, 551; Wilson to Richard J. Montague, Sept. 27, 1911, 361–62; both in ibid.

59. *Equity* 14, no. 4 (Oct. 1912): 130–31. In his draft of a platform, Wilson had argued that it was not a national question, but that the initiative and referendum were consistent with American political traditions. "Planks for a Democratic Platform," June 16, 1916, *Papers of Woodrow Wilson*, vol. 24, 480–81. During much of the campaign, Wilson's support for direct legislation remained muted. After his election, his interest in the matter ceased. In 1917, he sent a friendly telegram to reformers in Colorado trying to prevent the state legislature from passing a law weakening the initiative and referendum in the state. Judson King would later assert that "incidentally, this was the only support or mention given to the I. and R. by Woodrow Wilson after his nomination campaign of 1912." See Judson King, "Colorado 1917 Memo-Attempts at Restriction and Repeal," box 74, folder Colorado, 1912–28, King Papers.

60. Wilson, *The New Freedom*, 25, 77, 109.

61. William Jennings Bryan to Wilson, July 22, 1912, *Papers of Woodrow Wilson*, vol. 24, 565.

62. *California Outlook* 10, no. 23 (June 3, 1911): 5.

63. Pomeroy, "Needed Political Reforms," 464.

64. *Equity* 15, no. 1 (Jan. 1913): 11.

65. William S. U'Ren to Daniel Kiefer, Sept. 26, 1910, box 1, Eggleston Papers; *Equity* 14, no. 1 (Jan. 1912): 8.

66. *Equity* 13, no. 3 (July 1912): 91.

67. Braeman, *Albert J. Beveridge*, 225; Wright, *The Progressive Yankees*, 128, 228.

68. Tobin, *Organize or Perish*.

69. King, *The First Year and a Look Ahead*, 2–3, 4–5

70. King to Gifford Pinchot, July 19, 1915; King to C. G. Hoag, May 13, 1915; both in box 1, folder General Correspondence, Pennsylvania, King Papers.

71. Alfred D. Cridge to King, Aug. 30, 1914, box 1, folder General Correspondence, Oregon, King Papers.

72. Rice, *Quantitative Methods in Politics*, 248–49.

73. Long, *The Return of Representative Government*, 6.

74. An attempt to introduce the constitutional initiative in New York State failed in the late 1930s; this may have been the only example of a state seriously considering adopting direct democracy during the interwar period. Hallett, "The Constitutional Initiative Starts a New Advance" and *The Constitutional Initiative*, 1–2, 8.

Chapter Seven

1. Lippmann, *Public Opinion*, 31, 233, 312; Key, *Public Opinion and American Democracy* 5.

2. Lippmann, *The Phantom Public*, 39, 147.

3. Purcell, *The Crisis of Democratic Theory*, 99–113; Ricci, *The Tragedy of Political Science*, 78–90; Seidelman, *Disenchanted Realists*. As early as 1918, two political scientists had argued that "the theory that every man has a natural right to vote no longer commands the support of students of political science." Seymour and Frary, *How the World Votes*, 12–13.

4. Graham, *A Compilation of Statewide Initiative Proposals*; Magleby, "Taking the Initiative," 603.

5. "Total Number of Measures of all Kinds Submitted at General State-Wide Elections of all Kinds in 18 Initiative and Referendum States, 1900–29," box 76, King Papers.

6. Ibid. The pattern has persisted to this day. Until 1979, Oregon, California, Arizona, Colorado, and North Dakota still accounted for 60 percent of all the propositions ever voted on. See Magleby, *Direct Legislation*, 71.

7. Pollock, *The Initiative and Referendum in Michigan*, 17–18; Powers, "I & R" Ballot Questions, 1, 4; Pelletier, *The Initiative and Referendum in Maine*, 14–15; Schwartz, "Initiative Held in Reserve," 145; Winslow, "The Referendum in Maryland."

8. One observer noted in Arkansas in 1914 that "within three years after the adoption of the initiative and referendum, the Supreme Court has handed down seven different decisions involving eleven different cases." See Thomas, "Direct Legislation in Arkansas," 109.

9. Gosnell and Schmidt, *Popular Law Making*, 319–23.

10. Haynes, "The Education of Voters," 494; Schumacher, "Thirty Years of the People's Rule in Oregon," 244; Shippee, "Washington's First

Experiment," 249; Dodds, "The Initiative and Referendum and the Elections of 1920," 238–39.

11. Wallace, "The Initiative and Referendum and the Elections of 1922," 192, 199.

12. Boots, "The Initiative and the Referendum in 1923 and 1924," 46, and "The Initiative and the Referendum in 1925 and 1926," 642, 644.

13. King Papers, box 74.

14. Judson King to G. D. Curtin, Feb. 10, 1914, box 1, folder General Correspondence, North Carolina, King Papers.

15. King to W. W. Durbin, Jan. 2, 1914, box 1, folder General Correspondence, Ohio, in ibid.

16. Russell, *The Story of the Nonpartisan League*, 282–90; Ramsey, "Initiative, Referendum, and Recall Votes of 1919," 146–47; Gaston, *The Nonpartisan League*, 277–78; Saloutos and Hicks, *Twentieth Century Populism*, 166, 546; Valelly, *Radicalism in the States*, 18, 31.

17. Houghton, "The Initiative and Referendum in Missouri," 288; Barclay, "Proposed Changes in the Initiative and Referendum in Missouri."

18. *The Initiative and Referendum in Colorado*, 5; Shockley, *The Initiative Process in Colorado Politics*. Much the same pattern can be observed for Washington State. See Johnson, "The Initiative and Referendum in Washington," 40–41.

19. Garber, "The Use of the Recall in American Cities."

20. Geiges, "Wildwood's Recall Election"; Budenz, "The St. Louis Recall Efforts," 412.

21. Carroll, "The Recall in North Dakota."

22. Bird, "Recall"; Allen, "Remedies against Dishonest or Inefficient Public Servants," 179–80.

23. Rice, *Quantitative Methods*, 158–65.

24. Ogburn and Peterson, "Political Thought of Social Classes," 313. In 1928, to offer a final example, voters in Arkansas approved an initiative that prohibited teaching evolution in publicly funded schools, a result of the Scopes trial. Somewhat surprisingly, support for the measure was not highest in areas with a strong Baptist population, a high rate of illiteracy, or strong support for Herbert Hoover in the presidential contest. See Gray, "Anti-Evolution Sentiment and Behavior: The Case of Arkansas," 352–66.

25. Francis J. Heney to Hiram Johnson, Oct. 11, 1911, Part II, box 16, folder Letters to Johnson, H–HE, Johnson Papers.

26. W. P. Butcher to John Randolph Haynes, June 3, 1912, box 36, Haynes Papers.

27. On California progressivism after 1920, see Posner, "The Progressive Voters League, 1923–1926"; Melcher, "The Challenge to Normalcy"; Putnam, "The Persistence of Progressivism."

28. For a comprehensive list of California ballot propositions, see Allswang, *California Initiatives and Referendums*; Eu, *A History of the California Initiative Process*.

29. Blythe, " 'There Ought to Be a Law,' " 7; Bell and Price, *California Government Today*, 118.

30. Allswang, *California Initiatives and Referendums*, 13; Lee, "California," 96; Connors, "Constitutional Amendments and Referred Measures," 106–7.

31. Issel and Cherny, *San Francisco*, 173–74, 182–84; Segal, "James Rolph, Jr.," 4, 13, 17.

32. "Direct Legislation," 458–67.

33. Franklin Hichborn to Anna M. De Yo, Jan. 11, 1926, box 43, Haynes Papers.

34. Ostrander, *The Prohibition Movement in California*, 124–25, 127–33, 154, 160, 203; Wasserman, "Status Politics and Economic Class Interests."

35. "Initiatives"; "Fighting Initiative"; "Direct Anger Right."

36. "Non-Partisan Ballot Acts," 463; Rowell, "Non-Partisanship," "The Referendum on Non-Partisanship," and "The Measures on the Ballot"; *California Outlook* 20, no. 7, Oct. 1916, 156; Pitchell, "The Electoral System and Voting Behavior," 459–61.

37. Lee, "Representative Government," 227–53; Ainsworth, "Initiative Wars"; Bell and Price, "Lawmakers and Initiatives," 380–84; Fitzgerald, "Oil-Tax Initiative Campaign"; Price and Waste, "Initiatives"; Price, "Experts Explain the Business" and "Initiative Campaigns."

38. "Report of the Special Committee on Election Expenditures," 1782–83, 1785–87.

39. "Misuse of Referendum."

40. *California Outlook* 16, no. 24 (June 13, 1914): 22; "Direct Legislation to be Protected."

41. California State Chamber of Commerce, *Initiative Legislation in California*, 1, 9, 5.

42. E. A. Walcott to Haynes, Feb. 19, 1930, box 42, Haynes Papers.

43. J. H. Zemansky, "The Petition System for the Initiative," MS, box 42, Haynes Papers.

44. Edward O. Allen, Chairman, Sub-Section on the Initiative, Referendum and Recall, Preliminary Report to the Chairman of the Section on a New Constitution of the Commonwealth Club of California, Apr.

29, 1930, 4–5, folder "Commonwealth Club Initiative, Referendum and Recall," carton 10, Bartlett Papers.

45. Frank S. Boggs to Haynes, Apr. 30, 1929, box 39, Haynes Papers.

46. Haynes to Boggs, May 2, 1929, ibid. His support was well known among petition circulators. In 1926, John P. Steele, one of the earliest professional solicitors in the state, active since the 1910s, complained to Haynes that 24,000 of the 40,000 signatures he had collected in Los Angeles to amend a dance regulation ordinance had been invalidated by the city clerk. He argued that "this petition was secured in the same manner that I have secured others for the past fifteen years" and asked for Haynes's help. See Steele to Haynes, Jan. 18, 1926, box 39, Haynes Papers.

47. Final Report of the Automobile Club of Southern California for the Purpose of Influencing Electors for Proposition No. 8, Nov. 18, 1926, California State Archives.

48. Recapitulation of Receipts and Expenses of the Independent Petroleum and Consumers Association Shown on First and Second Statements Filed and Third Statement Herein, Dec. 5, 1939, California State Archives.

49. See, for example, the correspondence between Haynes and Governor C. C. Young relating to a proposal to prohibit paid petition-circulators. Haynes to Young, Feb. 17, 1927, Nov. 30, 1928; Dec. 7, 14, 1928; Young to Haynes, Nov. 27, 1928; all in box 43, Haynes Papers; Louis Bartlett to C. C. Young, May 27, 1929; Young to Bartlett, May 29, 1929, folder Commonwealth Club Direct Legislation; both in Bartlett Papers.

50. "Restriction of Initiative on Taxation," 250; Haynes to James D. Phelan, Sept. 1, 13, 15, 1920, box 59, Phelan Papers; Phelan to Haynes, Sept. 16, 1920, box 14; Haynes to Governor William D. Stephens, Apr. 9, 1919, box 36; both in Haynes Papers; League to Protect the Initiative, *Vote "No" on Proposition 27*; Haynes, "California Sticks to the I. and R."; Haynes to Chester H. Rowell, Dec. 28, 1918; June 18, 1920, folder Dr. John R. Haynes, Chester H. Rowell Papers.

51. Hichborn to Haynes, Apr. 11, 1928, box 39, Haynes Papers.

52. Pillsbury, "A Study of Direct Legislation," 310, 315, 320.

53. Pillsbury, "A Study of Direct Legislation," 322–23. Even among the voters who cast their ballots on propositions, there was a significant proportion — estimated by Pillsbury to be about 25–30 percent — who voted "no" on all propositions, regardless of their content. See "Legislative Information and the Public," 109.

54. Newspaper clipping from the *Stockton Herald*, Aug. 8, 1934; Pills-

bury, "Propositions, Amendments and Proposed Laws," clipping from the *Berkeley Daily Gazette*, Oct. 12, 1936, Pillsbury Papers.

55. Hichborn, *Story of the California Legislature of 1915*, 66–67, 75, 86, 218; "Insult Themselves"; "San Francisco Disgraced Itself."

56. Bird and Ryan, *The Recall of Public Officers*, 344, 342; Perry and Perry, *A History of the Los Angeles Labor Movement*, 436–38; Viehe, "The Recall of Mayor Frank L. Shaw," 290, 302; Sitton, "Another Generation of Urban Reformers."

57. *California Outlook* 14, no. 5 (Jan. 25, 1913): 3; 14, no. 12 (Mar. 15, 1913): 14; 14, no. 18 (May 3, 1913): 11; Walcott, "The Initiative, Referendum, and Recall in San Francisco."

58. Eliel, "Corrupt Judges Recalled in San Francisco."

59. Gosnell and Schmidt, *Popular Law Making in the United States*, 314, 319.

60. Dodd, *State Government*, 551; Kimball, *State and Municipal Government*, 123–25. See also Finer, *Theory and Practice of Modern Government*, 562–63; Gosnell and Holland, *State and Local Government in the United States*, 230; Graves, *American State Government*, 136–37; Bromage, *State Government and Administration in the United States*, 97; and Mathews, *American State Government*, 198.

61. Hall, *Popular Government*, 142.

62. Bryce, *Modern Democracies*, 153.

63. Schumacher, "Thirty Years of the People's Rule in Oregon," 258.

64. Beard, *American Government and Politics*, 551.

65. Munro, "Initiative and Referendum," 52.

66. Arneson, "Do Representatives Represent?," 753–54.

67. Holcombe, *State Government in the United States*, 547.

68. Arneson, "Improving the Petition," 138.

69. Key, "Publicity of Campaign Expenditures on Issues in California," 722.

70. LaPalombara and Hagan, "Direct Legislation," 417.

71. Key and Crouch, *The Initiative and Referendum in California*, 575, 572. See also Crouch, "The Constitutional Initiative in Operation" and "The Initiative and Referendum in Cities."

72. Key, "Publicity of Campaign Expenditures on Issues in California," 719, 722.

73. Cottrell, "Twenty-five Years of Direct Legislation in California," 38.

74. Radin, "Popular Legislation in California," 583, and "Popular Legislation in California: 1936–1946," 190; Radabaugh, "Tendencies of California Direct Legislation."

75. Ehrman, "Proposals for Revising the Initiative," 5, 41.

76. Initiative Defense League, *Amend the Initiative*.

77. Smith, "Can We Afford the Initiative?," 437; Woods, *Proposals for Changes*, 1–2.

78. Selig, "San Francisco Upholds Mayor."

Chapter Eight

1. The literature on contemporary campaign methods is vast. See, for example, Agranoff, *The Management of Election Campaigns*; Sabato, *The Rise of Political Consultants*; Westbrook, "Politics as Consumption"; Felknor, *Political Mischief*; Chagall, *The New Kingmakers*; Swanson and Mancini, *Politics, Media, and Modern Democracy*; Jamieson, *Packaging the Presidency*; and Luntz, *Candidates, Consultants, and Campaigns*.

2. Erie, "How the Urban West Was Won," 519–22. See also Bridges, "Winning the West to Municipal Reform"; Ostrom, *Water and Politics*, 44–48; Hoffman, *Vision or Villainy*; and Kahrl, *Water and Power*.

3. *Utility Corporations, Letter from the Chairman of the Federal Trade Commission in Response to Senate Resolutions Nos. 83 and 112, Exhibits 4048–4489*, S. Doc. 92, Parts 10–16, 70th Cong., 1st Sess. (Washington, D.C., 1930), Testimony of Rudolph Spreckels, 455.

4. Agreement between State Campaign Committee and George Sharp, Sept. 1921; Agreement between State Campaign Committee and R. P. Benton, Sept. 1921; Status Power Bill Petition Dec. 13, 1921; E. H. Harris to L. C. Davidson, Dec. 18, 1921; Additional Statistical Data for Special Senate Committee Investigating Campaign Expenditures, Summary Receipts and Disbursements, California's Water and Power Act, box 84, Hichborn Papers.

5. L. C. Davidson to Executive Board, State Campaign Committee, Sept. 16, 1921, box 140, Hichborn Papers.

6. Hichborn, *California Politics 1891–1939*, TS, vol. 3, 1982–86, box 181, Hichborn Papers.

7. On private utilities in California, see Coleman, *P. G. and E. of California*; Myers, *Iron Men and Copper Wires*; Davis, " 'You Are the Company.' "

8. *Utility Corporations*, Testimony of Herbert L. Cornish, 433–35.

9. Ibid., Testimony of Herbert L. Cornish, 435. The utilities also employed an ingenious device to cement the ties to the banks in California. The corporation had deposits at 230 banks totaling over $1.5 million. As a special bonus for the bankers, the utility required no interest on these deposits. The managers of the Pacific Gas and Electric made it a

policy to stay in friendly communication with the presidents as well as the directors of the banks, "usually influential business and professional men," and with the entire bank personnel. Ibid., "Letter from A. F. Hockenbeamer," 664, and Hichborn, "Political Activities of the Power Trust in California," 12–13.

10. Ibid., Testimony of Eustace Cullinan, 429.

11. Ibid., Testimony of Cullinan, 430. For some of the pamphlets, see People's Economy League, *"Power At Cost"*; Greater California League, *The ABC of the Water and Power Act*; *Shall California Be Sovietized?*; *Text Book of California Water and Power Act*; *Haven't We Got Taxes Enough?*; and *Do You Want More Taxes? If Not, Get the Truth About the Water and Power Act*, folder Savage 52, Water Resources Center Archives, University of California at Berkeley.

12. *Utility Corporations*, Testimony of Cornish, 433–34, and Luther C. Brown to Herbert L. Cornish, Feb. 14, 1923, 459.

13. Horace Porter to Davidson, May 16, 1922; Hichborn to Porter, June 7, 1922; both in box 144; Davidson to Hichborn, Aug. 1, 1922; Hichborn to Davidson, Aug. 21, 1922; both in box 140, Hichborn Papers.

14. J. H. Canning to William Kent, Oct. 18, 1922; Hichborn to J. C. Dahl, Nov. 3, 1922; Davidson to Hichborn, Oct. 3, 1922; all in box 140, in ibid.

15. *California Outlook* 20, no. 8 (Nov. 1916): 176–77; Seavey, "The Single-Tax Amendment"; William Eggleston to Louis F. Post, Nov. 17, 1922, box 2, Eggleston Papers; Single Tax League of California, *Program of the Single Tax League*.

16. Ralston's efforts to bring the single tax to California have previously been treated in Echols, "Jackson Ralston and the Last Single Tax Campaign."

17. George W. Patterson to Ralston, Sept. 22, 1933; Dec. 6, 1933; both in carton 3, Ralston Papers.

18. J. W. Buzell to Local Unions, Mar. 15, 1934, carton 4; Patterson to Ralston, Apr. 3, 1934; June 29, 1934; S. Edward Williams to Ralston, Apr. 28, 1934; June 4, 1934; Waldo J. Wernicke to Ralston, July 13, 1934; all in carton 3; Jesse M. Southwick to Ralston, Aug. 11, 1934; July 30, 1934; both in carton 3, in ibid.

19. E. Backus to Ralston, June 4, 8, 11, 1934, carton 1, in ibid.

20. Patterson to Ralston, June 24, 29, 1934. See also Patterson to Ralston, June 28, 1934; July 8, 11, 13, 28; and Aug. 4, 11, 15, 1934; all in ibid.

21. Price, "Experts Explain the Business of Buying Signatures"; Price,

"The Mercenaries Who Gather Signatures for Ballot Measures"; California Commission on Campaign Financing, *Democracy by Initiative*, 2:142.

22. Robinson to Ralston, Feb. 14, 1935, Ralston Papers.

23. Robinson to Ralston, Feb, 21, 23, 1935, in ibid.

24. Ralston to Robinson, Feb. 24, 1935; Robinson to Ralston, Feb. 25, 1935, in ibid.

25. Ralston to Robinson, Feb. 27, 1935; Robinson to Ralston, Feb. 28, 1935, in ibid.

26. Joseph Lowe to Ralston, Mar. 2, 1935, carton 2, in ibid.

27. W. A. Curtin to Ralston, Feb. 28, 1935; Ralston to Curtin, Mar. 3, 1935; Curtin to Ralston, Mar. 13, 1935, carton 1, in ibid.

28. Joseph O'Connor to Ralston, Feb. 26, 1936, carton 2, in ibid.

29. O'Connor to Ralston, n.d.; Apr. 3, 1936; O'Connor to Sales Tax Repeal Association, May 7, 1936. There are actually two different contracts in the Ralston papers. The second, dated May 15, contains somewhat different conditions by setting an overall limit of the money (at $200 per week) O'Connor was permitted to keep. See Agreement between Joseph O'Connor and Sales Tax Repeal Association, May 15, 1936.

30. Ralston to Edward D. Vandeleur, Secretary, State Federation of Labor, Sept. 1, 1936, carton 4; Ralston to George A. Briggs, Aug. 6, 1936, carton 1; both in Ralston Papers.

31. Harry H. Ferrell to Ralston, Oct. 3. 1937; George A. Briggs to Ralston, Oct. 1, 1937; Ralston to Briggs, Oct. 2, 1937; all in carton 2. Ralston had contacts with some other professional petition circulators prior to hiring Stennett. See H. B. Learned to Ralston, Aug. 31, 1937; John P. Steele to Ralston, Oct. 16, 1937; all in ibid.

32. Agreement between William G. Stennett and Jackson H. Ralston, Oct. 7, 1937, carton 5, in ibid.

33. See, for example, the letters between R. E. Nordstrom and Ralston, Apr. 28, 1938; May ?, 19, 30, 1938, in ibid.

34. Stennett to Ralston, Jan. 14, 1938, in ibid.

35. Leslie R. Burke to the Contra Costa Real Estate Board, Feb. 25, 1938, carton 4, in ibid.

36. Robinson to P. A. Marshall, Mar. 25, 1938, in ibid.

37. Robinson to Marshall, Mar. 29, 1938, in ibid.

38. Peiter M. Flanton to Ralston, Apr. 21, 1938; May 5, 11, 1938; June 13, 1938, Ralston Papers.

39. Stennett to Ralston, Jan. 14, 16, 1938, in ibid.

40. Ferrell to Ralston, Jan. 12, 1938, in ibid.

41. Stennett to Ralston, May 1, 18, 29, 1938; July 1, 1938, in ibid.

42. Report to the Secretary of State of Advances by Jackson H. Ralston on Account of Proposition No. 20, Sept. 26, 1938, California State Archives; Stennett to Ralston, July 5, 1938; Ralston to Harold S. Buttenheim, Sept. 2, 1938, Ralston Papers.

43. Report to the Secretary of State of Contributions to and Disbursements of the Tax Relief Association of California on Account of Proposition No. 20, Sept. 28, 1938, Oct. 26, 1938, Dec. 8, 1938, California State Archives; Ralston Autobiography, 48–49, Ralston Papers.

44. H. Stuyvelaar to Ralston, Oct. 14, 1938, in ibid.

45. Statewide Council against Single Tax, *Research Reference Manual*, 21.

46. The money was also to be used for the campaign against Ham and Eggs and for the antipicketing initiative. See A. D. McDonald to Guy V. Shoup, Sept. 28, 1938, 27738, Exhibit 14386; Shoup to McDonald, Oct 3, 1938, 27738–27739, Exhibit 14387, *Hearings before a Subcommittee of the Committee on Education and Labor*.

47. See Crouch, *Organized Civil Servants*, 134–36.

48. Report to the Secretary of State of Receipts and Expenditures of the California Association against Single Tax, Oct. 29, 1938, Nov. 10, 1938, California State Archives; Report to the Secretary of State of the Independent Dealers and Property Owners Tax League, Inc., Oct. 31, 1938; Report of the California State Employees' Association, Nov. 1, 1938, Dec. 6, 1938, California State Archives.

49. Alper to Ralston, Nov. 11, 1938; Dec. 14, 1938; both in Ralston Papers.

50. "How the Fight Was Won," 5.

51. Taylor, "Advertising Man," 20–21, 30. On Teague, see Lillard, "Agricultural Statesman"; and Teague, *Fifty Years a Rancher*.

52. The California law was part of a nationwide wave of chain-store tax laws passed in the 1930s. See Bean, *Beyond the Broker State*, 29–30; Monod, *Store Wars*, 335–38; Ryant, "The South and the Movement against Chain Stores"; Horowitz, "The Crusade against Chain Stores"; and Tedlow, *Keeping the Corporate Image*, 91–97.

53. Verified Statement of Campaign Contributions and Expenditures, California Chain Stores Association, Sept. 23, 1936, California State Archives.

54. Francisco, "How Business Can Make Friends," 9. On his conception of advertising, see also Francisco, "Keying Advertising Strategy to 1933 Conditions," 8–9, 26, and "Advertising: An Essential Ingredient of Democracy." See in addition Folger, "Advertising Shoulders Today's Job."

55. Francisco, "How Business Can Make Friends," 39.

56. Francisco, "Inside Story of California Chain Tax War"; Walker and Sklar, "Business Finds Its Voice"; Statement of Safeway Stores, Inc., as to Expenditures Made in Connection with Referendum Campaign, Sept. 24, 1936, California State Archives.

57. Albig, *Public Opinion*, 228–29, and *Modern Public Opinion*, 181–85; Robinson, "Recent Developments"; Bogardus, *The Making of Public Opinion*, 185–203; Key, *Politics, Parties, and Pressure Groups*, 571–72; Lears, *Fables of Abundance*, 243–45; Converse, *Survey Research*.

58. U.S. Senate, *Hearings before a Subcommittee of the Committee on Education and Labor*, Part 75, Exhibit 14381, 27725.

59. Key and Crouch, *The Initiative and the Referendum in California*, 513; Verified Statement of Campaign Contributions and Expenditures, California Chain Stores Association, Sept. 23, 1936, Oct. 26, 1936, Dec. 7, 1936, California State Archives.

60. Radin, "Popular Legislation in California," 583. See also Smith, *Public Opinion in a Democracy*, 376.

61. Anti-Monopoly League of California, Inc., Statement of Receipts and Expenses Aug. 28, 1935 To and Including Oct. 22, 1936; Anti-Monopoly League of California, Inc., Statement of Receipts and Expenses Aug. 28, 1935 To and Including Nov. 24, 1936.

62. U.S. Senate, *Violation of Free Speech, Part II, Organized Anti-Unionism in California Industry prior to the Passage of the National Labor Relations Act*, 112; Auerbach, *Labor and Liberty*.

63. U.S. Senate, *Violations of Free Speech, Part VI, A Study of Labor Policies of Employers' Associations in the Los Angeles Area, 1935–1939*, 844; Report of the Program Committee of Southern Californians, Inc., Jan. 24, 1938, Exhibit 9065, *Hearings before a Subcommittee of the Committee on Education and Labor*, Part 56, 20763–64; *Violations of Free Speech, Part VI, A Study of Labor Policies of Employers' Associations in the Los Angeles Area, 1935–1939*, 863; Exhibit 9057, Southern Californians, Inc., Receipts and Disbursements for Period Nov. 1, 1937 to Nov. 22, 1939, *Hearings before a Subcommittee of the Committee on Education and Labor*, 20748; Exhibit 9058, Contributors to Southern Californians, Inc., 20749.

64. Exhibit 9061, Report of Program Committee of Southern Californians, Inc., Nov. 29, 1937, 20760, in U.S. Senate, *Hearings before a Subcommittee of the Committee on Education and Labor*; *Violation of Free Speech, Part VI*, 880.

65. Exhibit 9541, Excerpt from Minutes of Committee of 43, Apr. 19, 1938, U.S. Senate, *Hearings before a Subcommittee of the Committee on*

Education and Labor, 22423; Exhibit 9542, Excerpt from Executive Committee Meeting, Committee of 43, Apr. 25, 1938, 22423–24; Exhibit 9544, R. D. Lapham to Byron C. Hanna, Apr. 27, 1938, 22424; Exhibit 14372, Byron C. Hanna to Atholl McBean, Mar. 14, 1938, 27717–18; Exhibit 14373, Hanna to Members of the Executive Committee of Southern Californians, Inc., Apr. 8, 1938, 27718–19; Exhibit 14375, Hanna to John J. Miller, June 9, 1938, 27720–21; *Violation of Free Speech, Part V*, 771.

66. Exhibit 9557, Synopsis of Meeting Called by Mr. Wallace M. Alexander for Wednesday Morning, June 29, 1938, 22455, in U.S. Senate, *Hearings before a Subcommittee of the Committee on Education and Labor*.

67. Exhibit 14411, Remarks by Mr. Prosser at Meeting Aug. 25, 1938, 27759, in ibid.; *Violation of Free Speech, Part VI*, 941–46.

68. Exhibit 14410, Memorandum on Conference between Messrs. Hawes, Persons, Miller and Prosser, June 22, 1938, U.S. Senate, *Hearings before a Subcommittee of the Committee on Education and Labor*, 27757.

69. Exhibit 14381, Survey of Opinion and General Plan of Operation of the Campaign, Aug. 16, 1938, 27728, 27725–27728, in ibid.

70. Exhibit 14381, 27728, in ibid.

71. Exhibit 14381, 27733, 27728–27732, in ibid.

72. Richard Prosser to John J. Miller, Sept. 12, 1938; Miller to Frank Partridge, Sept. 15, 1938, Exhibit 14415, 27766–27767; both in ibid.

73. Exhibit 9550, Total Receipts of Southern Californians, Inc. in connection with the Support of Proposition No. 1 at the General Election Nov. 8, 1938, as Reported to the California Secretary of State, 22436–22440, in ibid.

74. *People's Daily World*, Sept. 9, 17, 20, 22, 26, Oct. 24, 27, 1938; *CIO Labor Herald*, Aug. 18, Sept. 2, Oct. 6, 27, 1938.

75. *People's Daily World*, Oct. 6, 10, 1938; Rubens, "The Labor Initiative of 1938," 135–38; Taft, *Labor Politics American Style*, 106–8.

76. *People's Daily World*, Oct. 29, 1938.

77. Statement of Cash Receipts and Disbursements of the Campaign Fund of the California State Federation of Labor, Nov. 9, 1938; Verified Statement of the Labor's Protective Committee of the Los Angeles Central Labor Council, Dec. 7, 1938; Summary of Receipts and Expenditures, Campaign against Prop. No. 1 by the California State Industrial Union Council, Dec. 8, 1938; Statement of the International Longshoremen's and Warehousemen's Union, Dec. 6, 1938; Financial Report of American Federation of Labor Political League; all in California State Archives.

78. California State Chamber of Commerce, *Initiative Legislation in California*, table 8; Minar, "Voting Behavior," 28.

79. For details on the Ham and Eggers as well as other pension movements in California, see Putnam, *Old-Age Politics in California*; Burke, *Olson's New Deal*; Hill, *Dancing Bear*, 87–88; Boone, "Who Is Roy G. Owens?," 13; Moore and Moore, *Out of the Frying Pan*.

80. Ormsby, "Our Neighbors 'The Ham and Eggers,'" 14; McWilliams, *Southern California Country*, 304–7.

81. *Ham and Eggs for Californians*; *Proposed Amendments to Constitution, Propositions and Proposed Laws to be Submitted to the Electors of the State of California to be Held Tuesday, Nov. 8, 1938*, 47–48, Appendix, 56–63; *Proposed Amendments to Constitution, Propositions and Proposed Laws to be Submitted to the Electors of the State of California to be Held Tuesday, Nov. 7, 1939*, 4–5, Appendix, 2–14; Canterbury, "'Ham and Eggs' in California," 408–10; "$30 Every Thursday"; "$30 a Week for Life"; "Ham and Eggs"; Lundberg, "California Republic, 1940 Model."

82. Hamilton, "$30 a Week for Life," 26.

83. Zimmerman, "'Ham and Eggs' Everybody!," 88; Putnam, *Old-Age Politics*, 102.

84. Transcript of a Radio Broadcast by Lawrence E. Allen, Nov. 10, 1938, Drew Papers.

85. Statement of the California State Pension Plan Showing Receipts and Disbursements for the Period From Date of Inception Oct. 4, 1937 to Sept. 30, 1938, California State Archives.

86. "Summary of Campaign Procedure, Ham and Eggs Special Election: 1939," n.d., Drew Papers; Rogers, *The Pollsters*, 188–89. According to a national survey conducted by Gallup in October 1938, 68 percent of the voters rejected Ham and Eggs. For California, Gallup reported that 67 percent of the electorate rejected the initiative. But at the election two weeks later, only 59 percent of the voters cast their ballots against Ham and Eggs. See "American Institute of Public Opinion Surveys, 1938–1939," 593; Gosnell, "The Polls and Other Mechanisms of Democracy," 227.

87. Report to the Secretary of State of the Citizen's Federation to Vote No on 25, Northern Division, Oct. 26, 1938, Dec. 5, 1938; Report to the Secretary of State of the Citizen's Federation to Vote No on 25, Southern Division, Sept. 26, 1938, Oct. 28, 1938, Dec. 7, 1938; Statement of Receipts and Expenditures of the Employees' Association of the Department of Water and Power of the City of Los Angeles, Sept. 28, 1938, Oct. 31, 1938, Dec. 2, 1938; all in California State Archives.

88. G. V. Shoup to A. D. MacDonald, Oct. 3, 1938, U.S. Senate,

Hearings before a Subcommittee of the Committee on Education and Labor, Part 75, Exhibit 14387, 27738–27739.

89. Richard Prosser to Dear Editor, Sept. 30, 1939, Drew Papers; *Tide of Advertising and Marketing*, Nov. 1, 1939, clipping in folder "Clem Whitaker Fan Stuff," carton 91, Whitaker and Baxter Papers.

90. "Survey of Public Opinion regarding California Retirement Life Payments Act," Sept. 1939, Drew Papers.

91. Statement of the Retirement Life Payments Association Showing Receipts and Expenditures for the Period From Nov. 10, 1938 to Sept. 30, 1939, California State Archives.

92. Third Statement of Receipts and Expenses of Southern California Citizens against 30 Thursday; Statement of Receipts and Expenses of Southern California Citizens against 30 Thursday, Dec. 7, 1939, California State Archives; California State Chamber of Commerce, *Initiative Legislation in California*, table 8.

93. Tedlow, *Keeping the Corporate Image*, 18–19, 103–5; Raucher, *Public Relations and Business*; Bernays, *Crystallizing Public Opinion*; Hiebert, *Courtier to the Crowd*.

94. McWilliams, "Government by Whitaker and Baxter," 346, 420; Bean, *California*, 470–72; California Commission on Campaign Financing, *Democracy by Initiative*, 199.

95. Pitchell, "The Influence of Professional Campaign Management Firms," 287.

96. Casey, "Legislative History of the Central Valley Project, 1933–1949"; Roos, *The Thirsty Land*; Montgomery and Clawson, *History of Legislation*.

97. Louis Bartlett to Judson King, Jan. 15, 1934, carton 10, Bartlett Papers; Bartlett, *Memoirs*, 185; Coate, *Water, Power, and Politics*, 25; A. F. Hockenbeamer to Stockholders and Bondholders of Pacific Gas and Electric Company, Dec. 12, 1933, Louis Bartlett folder; Clem Whitaker, Memorandum, Dec. 13, 1933, Bartlett folder, Water Resources Center Archives, University of California, Berkeley, Calif.

98. Coate, *Water, Power and Politics*, 27–29; "The Lord of Press Agents and His Brilliant Lady," clipping from the *San Francisco Chronicle*, Aug. 19, 1956, Women's World Section, carton 45, Whitaker and Baxter Papers.

99. Clem Whitaker to Frank C. Jordan, Nov. 24, 1934, California State Archives.

100. Whitaker to Harry C. Harper, Feb. 11, 1937, carton 91, folder "Leone Baxter Fan Stuff"; Whitaker to Larry J. Smith, Nov. 25, 1936, Whitaker and Baxter Papers.

101. William E. Gould to Whitaker, Dec. 4, 1936; Harry C. Harper to Whitaker, Feb. 6, 1937; Whitaker to Percy M. Whiteside, Dec. 17, 1936; Franklin Anderson to Whitaker, Dec. 24, 1936; Carl Anderson to Whitaker, Jan. 20, 1937, all in ibid.

102. Whitaker, "A New Field of Public Relations: Political Campaign Management," 1, carton 45, in ibid.

103. Whitaker, "The Public Relations of Election Campaigns," 8. See also Whitaker and Baxter, "Election Year Coming Up," 11–12, 98–102, copy in carton 45, Whitaker and Baxter Papers.

104. Clem Whitaker to Frank M. Jordan, Nov. 10, 1938, California State Archives. For other expenditure statements for campaigns managed by Campaigns, Inc., see Clem Whitaker to Jordan, Nov. 11, 1944; Sept. 21, 1946; and Sept. 18, 1948; all in Whitaker and Baxter Papers.

105. Whitaker to Stanley Kelley, Dec. 9, 1955, Carton 9. See also Kelley, *Professional Public Relations*.

106. Ross, "The Supersalesmen of California Politics"; Rosenbloom, *The Election Men*, 61–62.

107. Hynes, "Media Manipulation"; Troy, *See How They Ran*.

108. Barclay, "The Publicity Division of the Democratic Party"; Black, *Democratic Party Publicity*, 25–26; Farley, *Behind the Ballots*; Michelson, *The Ghost Talks*; Jensen, "Armies, Admen, and Crusaders". For an example of the management of an earlier presidential campaign, see Wellman, "The Management of the Taft Campaign."

109. Casey, "Republican Propaganda in the 1936 Campaign," 32. See also Fox, *The Mirror Makers*; Meyers, *The Image Makers*; and Dinkin, *Campaigning in America*.

Conclusion

1. Magleby, "Taking the Initiative," 603; Hamilton, "Direct Legislation," 125.

2. Smith, "Can We Afford the Initiative?," 437.

3. Lowenstein, "California Initiative and the Single-Subject Rule."

4. Hahn, "Correlates of Public Sentiments about War."

5. Quoted in Magleby, *Direct Legislation*, 77.

6. Lo, *Small Property versus Big Government*; Raymond, *Surviving Proposition Thirteen*.

7. See McGuigan, *The Politics of Direct Democracy*; Magleby, "Taking the Initiative"; Zimmermann, *Participatory Democracy*.

8. Magleby, *Direct Legislation*, 64.

9. Hahn, "Northern Referenda"; Zanden, "Votes on Segregationist Referenda."

10. Nisbet, "Public Opinion versus Popular Opinion" and "The Dilemma of Conservatives in a Populist Society."

11. Tatalovich, *Nativism Reborn*; Arington, "English-Only Laws and Direct Legislation"; Mackaye, "California Proposition 63."

12. "Affirmative Action Ban Leading in Washington"; Broder, "Collecting Signatures for a Price." The appeal of direct democracy is not only an American phenomenon. One can discern a renewed interest in plebiscitary forms of democracy in other countries as well. See Butler and Ranney, *Referendums around the World*; Ranney, *The Referendum Device*.

13. Wilson's active involvement in this and other initiative campaigns points to an important recent development. Prior to 1970, state officials and lawmakers in California rarely used the initiative process and worked within the legislative system to achieve their goals. Since then, they have become important participants in the process, having fielded about 15 percent of all initiatives between 1970 and 1988. See Bell and Price, "Lawmakers and Initiative."

14. In 1998, seven out of ten voters in California favored spending limits in initiative campaigns, and a majority wanted to require a two-thirds majority for approval of an initiative. But 70 percent opposed the idea of granting the legislature the right to amend a proposition, and two-thirds supported an initiative at the national level. Such conflicting attitudes make reform efforts difficult. See *New York Times* Mar. 31, 1998. See also Cronin, "Public Opinion and Direct Democracy."

15. See, for example, Lee, "Representative Government and the Initiative Process," 227, and "The Initiative and Referendum."

16. Price, "Initiative Campaigns"; Ainsworth, "Initiative Wars"; Thomas, "Has Business 'Captured the California Initiative Agenda?'"

17. Broder, *Democracy Derailed*; Zimmerman, *The Initiative*; Gerber, *Populist Paradox*.

18. California Commission on Campaign Financing, *Democracy by Initiative*, 16–17; Broder, "Collecting Signatures for a Price."

19. See, for example, Lowenstein, "Campaign Spending and Ballot Propositions"; Zisk, *Money, Media, and the Grass Roots*; Owens and Wade, "Campaign Spending on California Propositions"; Owens and Olson, "Campaign Spending and the Electoral Process"; Jones, "Financing State Elections"; Lydenberg, *Bankrolling Ballots*; and Thomas, "Corporate Political Strategy."

20. Price, "The Mercenaries Who Gather Signatures" and "Experts Explain the Business"; Broder, "Collecting Signatures for a Price."

21. In January 1999, the United States Supreme Court struck down a Colorado statute designed to rein in petition circulators. The law had required them to wear identification badges and to be registered voters in the state, and it made them subject to requirements on how much they were paid for the signatures. The court ruled that the law violated the free speech rights of the circulators. In addition to Colorado, fourteen other states have similar laws. See "High Court Rejects Curbs on Ballot Initiatives."

22. See, for example, Agranoff, *The Management of Election Campaigns*; Sabato, *The Rise of Political Consultants*; and Westbrook, "Politics as Consumption."

23. For a description of a typical initiative marketing campaign, see King, "Political TV."

24. See Wachtel, *The Electronic Congress*; Atherton, "Political Participation and 'Teledemocracy'"; Abramson, Atherton, and Orren, *The Electronic Commonwealth*; and Grossman, *The Electronic Republic*.

BIBLIOGRAPHY

Manuscript Collections

Berkeley, California
    University of California
        Bancroft Library
            Anti-Monopoly League Scrapbook
            Louis Bartlett Papers
            Jack T. Casey Papers
            William Denman Papers
            J. E. Drew Papers
            William Eggleston Papers
            Francis J. Heney Papers
            Hiram Johnson Papers
            Fremont Older Papers
            George C. Pardee Papers
            James D. Phelan Papers
            Arthur J. Pillsbury Papers
            Jackson Ralston Papers
            Chester H. Rowell Papers
            Whitaker and Baxter International Papers
            Oral History Interview with Clement Sherman Whitaker Jr.,
                conducted 1989 by Gabrielle Morris, Regional Oral
                History Office, University of California at Berkeley, for the
                California State Archives State Government Oral History
                Program
            John D. Works Papers
          Water Resources Center Archives
            Frank Adams Folder
            Louis Bartlett Folder
            J. D. Galloway Folders
            Savage Folders
Los Angeles, California
    University of California, Department of Special Collections
        Edward A. Dickson Papers

Franklin Hichborn Papers
John Randolph Haynes Papers
Sacramento, California
California State Archives
Statements of Campaign Contributions and Expenditures, 1922–
1940
Washington, D.C.
Library of Congress, Manuscript Division
American Federation of Labor Letterbooks
Judson King Papers
Benjamin B. Lindsey Papers

Newspapers and Journals

American Political Science Review, 1906–40
Annals, 1890–1920
The Arena, 1889–1909
California Outlook, 1911–18
California Weekly, 1908–10
CIO Labor Herald, 1938
Direct Legislation Record, 1894–1904
Equity, 1907–19
National Municipal Review, 1912–40
North American Review, 1890–1920
The Outlook, 1893–1920
People's Daily World, 1938
Political Science Quarterly, 1890–1920
Referendum News, 1905–6

Books, Articles, Theses, and Papers

Abbott, L. J. "The Initiative and Referendum in Oklahoma." *Twentieth Century Magazine* 5 (Nov. 1911): 38–40.
Abramson, Jeffrey B., Christopher Atherton, and Gary R. Orren. *The Electronic Commonwealth*. New York: Basic Books, 1988.
Adams, Alton. "Legal Monopoly." *Political Science Quarterly* 19 (June 1904): 173–92.
———. "State Control of Trusts." *Political Science Quarterly* 18 (Sept. 1903): 462–79.
Adams, Charles Francis, Jr. "A Chapter of Erie." In Charles Francis

Adams Jr. and Henry Adams, *Chapters of Erie and Other Essays*, 1–99. Boston: Osgood, 1871.

———. "The Granger Movement." *North American Review* 120 (Apr. 1875): 394–424.

"Affirmative Action Ban Leading in Washington." *Washington Post*, Nov. 4, 1998.

Agranoff, Robert. *The Management of Election Campaigns*. Boston: Holbrook, 1976.

Ainsworth, Bill. "Initiative Wars: If You Can't Beat 'Em, Swamp 'Em." *California Journal* 21 (Mar. 1990): 147–49.

"Alabama's New Constitution." *The Outlook* 69 (Nov. 23, 1901): 751.

Albig, William. *Modern Public Opinion*. New York: McGraw-Hill, 1956.

———. *Public Opinion*. New York: McGraw-Hill, 1939.

Allen, Florence E. "Remedies against Dishonest or Inefficient Public Servants." *Annals* 169 (Sept. 1933): 172–83.

Allen, Howard W., and Erik W. Austin. "From the Populist Era to the New Deal: A Study of Partisan Realignment in Washington State, 1889–1950." *Social Science History* 3 (Winter 1977): 115–43.

Allswang, John M. *California Initiatives and Referendums, 1912–1990: A Survey and Guide to Research*. Los Angeles: University of California Press, 1991.

———. "The Origins of Direct Democracy in Los Angeles and California: The Development of an Issue and Its Relationship to Progressivism." *Southern California Quarterly* 78 (Summer 1996): 175–98.

American Federation of Labor. *Initiative, Referendum, and Recall: Warnings Concerning "Restrictions," "Safeguards," and "Jokers"— Proposed Amendments to State Constitutions*. Report of the Executive Council of the AFL to the Seattle, Washington, Convention, 1913. Washington, D.C., 1913.

"American Institute of Public Opinion Surveys, 1938–1939," *Public Opinion Quarterly* 3 (Oct. 1939): 581–607.

Anderson, Benedict. *Imagined Communities: Reflections on the Origin and Spread of Nationalism*. 2d ed. New York: Verso, 1991.

Anderson, Donald F. *William Howard Taft: A Conservative's Conception of the Presidency*. Ithaca: Cornell University Press, 1973.

Anderson, Eric. "The Populists and Capitalist America: The Case of Edgecombe County, North Carolina." In *Race, Class, and Politics in Southern History*, edited by Jeffrey J. Crow, Paul D. Escott, and

Charles L. Flynn Jr., 106–25. Baton Rouge: Louisiana State University Press, 1989.

"An Appeal to Friends of Popular Government." *The Arena* 39 (Apr. 1908): 449–55.

Appleby, Joyce. *Capitalism and a New Social Order: The Republican Vision of the 1790s*. New York: New York University Press, 1984.

Argersinger, Peter H. *Populism and Politics: William Alfred Peffer and the People's Party*. Lexington: University of Kentucky Press, 1974.

———. "Regulating Democracy: Election Laws and Dakota Politics, 1889–1902." In *Structure, Process, and Party: Essays in American Political History*, edited by Peter H. Argersinger, 172–90. Armonk, N.Y.: Sharpe, 1992.

Arington, Michele. "English-Only Laws and Direct Legislation: The Battle in the States over Language Minority Rights." *Journal of Law and Politics* 7 (Winter 1991–92): 325–52.

Arneson, Ben A. "Do Representatives Represent?" *National Municipal Review* 16 (Dec. 1927): 751–54.

———. "Improving the Petition." *National Municipal Review* 14 (Mar. 1925): 137–39.

Ashworth, Jon. *"Agrarians" and "Aristocrats": Party Political Ideology in the United States, 1837–1846*. Cambridge: Cambridge University Press, 1983.

Atherton, F. Christopher. "Political Participation and 'Teledemocracy.'" *Political Science and Politics* 21 (Summer 1984): 620–27.

Auerbach, Jerold S. *Labor and Liberty: The La Follette Committee and the New Deal*. Indianapolis: Bobbs-Merrill, 1966.

———. "President Roosevelt and 'The Trusts.'" *North American Review* 175 (Dec. 1902): 877–94.

Bacon, Edwin M., and Merrill Wyman. *Direct Elections and Law-Making by Popular Vote: The Initiative, the Referendum, the Recall, Commission Government for Cities, Preferential Voting*. Boston: Houghton Mifflin, 1912.

Bailey, Thomas. "The West and Radical Legislation, 1890–1930." *American Journal of Sociology* 38 (Jan. 1933): 603–11.

Bailyn, Bernard. *The Ideological Origins of the American Revolution*. Cambridge: Harvard University Press, 1967.

Baker, Fred A. *The Initiative and Referendum and Recall of Judges Criticized and Condemned*. Detroit, 1911.

Baker, Jean H. *Ambivalent Americans: The Know-Nothing Party in Maryland*. Baltimore: Johns Hopkins University Press, 1977.

Bakken, Gordon M. *Rocky Mountain Constitution Making, 1850–1912.* Westport, Conn.: Greenwood Press, 1987.

Baldwin, David A. "When Billy Sunday 'Saved' Colorado: That Old-Time Religion and the 1914 Prohibition Amendment." *Colorado Heritage* 2 (1990): 34–44.

"Ballot Initiatives Flourishing as Way to Bypass Politicians." *New York Times*, Mar. 31, 1998.

Banning, Lance. *The Jeffersonian Persuasion: Evolution of a Party Ideology.* Ithaca: Cornell University Press, 1978.

Barber, Kathleen L. *Proportional Representation and Electoral Reform in Ohio.* Columbus: Ohio State University Press, 1995.

Barclay, Thomas S. "Proposed Changes in the Initiative and Referendum in Missouri." *National Municipal Review* 13 (Apr. 1924): 194–97.

———. "The Publicity Division of the Democratic Party." *American Political Science Review* 25 (1931): 68–72.

Barker, Elihu F. "The Initiative and the Referendum." *The Arena* 18 (Nov. 1897): 613–27.

Barnes, Donna. *Farmers in Rebellion: The Rise and Fall of the Southern Farmers' Alliance and People's Party in Texas.* Austin: University of Texas Press, 1984.

Barnes, O. M. "The Popular Initiative and Referendum." *Publications of the Michigan Political Science Association* 3 (1898–1900): 57–80.

Barnett, James D. *The Operation of the Initiative, Referendum, and Recall in Oregon.* New York: Macmillan, 1915.

———. "The Operation of the Recall in Oregon." *American Political Science Review* 6 (Feb. 1912): 41–53.

Bartlett, Louis. *Memoirs.* Interviewed by Corinne L. Gilb. Berkeley: University of California Press, 1957.

Bass, John H. "The Initiative and Referendum in Oklahoma." *Southwestern Political Science Quarterly* 1 (Sept. 1920): 125–46.

Bean, Jonathan J. *Beyond the Broker State: Federal Policies toward Small Business, 1936–1961.* Chapel Hill: University of North Carolina Press, 1996.

Bean, Walton. *California: An Interpretive History.* New York: McGraw-Hill, 1968.

Beard, Charles A. *American Government and Politics.* 9th ed. New York: Macmillan, 1944.

———. "The Constitution of Oklahoma." *Political Science Quarterly* 24 (Mar. 1909): 95–114.

Beard, Charles A., and Birl E. Schultz, *Documents on the State-Wide Initiative, Referendum, and Recall*. New York: Macmillan, 1912.

Bell, Charles G., and Charles M. Price. *California Government Today: Politics of Reform*. Homewood, Ill: Dorsey, 1980.

———. "Lawmakers and Initiatives: Are Ballot Measures the Magic Ride to Success?" *California Journal* 19 (Sept. 1988): 380–84.

Belmont, Perry. "Publicity of Election Expenditures." *North American Review* 180 (Feb. 1905): 166–85.

Benedict, Robert C. "Some Aspects of the Direct Legislation Process in Washington State: Theory and Practice, 1914–1973." Ph.D. diss., University of Washington, 1982.

Benson, Lee. *Merchants, Farmers, and Railroads: Railroad Regulation and New York Politics, 1850–1887*. Cambridge: Harvard University Press, 1955.

Berg, Thomas C. "The Guarantee of Republican Government: Proposals for Judicial Review." *University of Chicago Law Review* 54 (Winter 1987–88): 208–42.

Berge, George W. *The Free Pass Bribery System: Showing How the Railroads, through the Free Pass Bribery System, Procure the Government away from the People*. Lincoln, Nebr.: 1905.

Berk, Gerald. *Alternative Tracks: The Constitution of the American Industrial Order, 1865–1917*. Baltimore: Johns Hopkins University Press, 1994.

———. "Constituting Corporations and Markets: Railroads in Gilded Age Politics." *Studies in American Political Development* 4 (1990): 130–68.

Berman, David R. "Political Culture, Issues, and the Electorate: Evidence from the Progressive Era." *Western Political Quarterly* 41 (Mar. 1988): 169–80.

———. *Reformers, Corporations, and the Electorate: An Analysis of Arizona's Age of Reform*. Niwat: University Press of Colorado, 1992.

Bernays, Edward L. *Crystallizing Public Opinion*. New York: Boni and Liveright, 1923.

Betts, Charles H. *The Betts-Roosevelt Letters*. New York: Lyons Republican, 1912.

Bicha, Karel. *Western Populism: Studies in an Ambivalent Conservatism*. Lawrence, Kans.: Coronado Press, 1976.

Bigelow, Herbert S. *Initiative and Referendum: A Speech in the Ohio Constitutional Convention, March 27, 1912*. 62d Cong., 2d sess., 1912. S. Doc.

Binney, Charles C. "Restrictions upon Legal and Special Legislation in the United States," *American Law Register and Review* 41 (July–Dec. 1893): 613–32, 721–95, 816–57, 922–43, 1019–33, 1109–61.

Bird, Frederick L. "Recall." In *Encyclopedia of the Social Sciences*, edited by E. R. A. Seligman and Alvin Johnson, 13:147–49. New York: Macmillan, 1932.

Bird, Frederick L., and Thomas M. Ryan. *The Recall of Public Officers: A Study of the Operation of the Recall in California*. New York: Macmillan, 1930.

Black, J. William. "Maine's Experiences with the Initiative and Referendum." *Annals of the American Academy of Political and Social Science* 43 (Sept. 1912): 159–78.

Black, Theodore M. *Democratic Party Publicity in the 1940 Campaign*. New York: Plymouth, 1941.

Blocker, Jack S., Jr. *Retreat from Reform: The Prohibition Movement in the United States, 1890–1913*. Westport, Conn.: Greenwood Press, 1976.

Blythe, Stuart O. "'There Ought to Be a Law — Or Should There': Fifty-Nine Initiative Titles Have Been Proposed for the November Ballot." *California — Magazine of the Pacific* 28 (July 1938): 7–8, 25–28.

Bogardus, Emory S. *The Making of Public Opinion*. New York: Association Press, 1951.

Boone, Andrew R. "Who Is Roy G. Owens? The Story of the Man behind Thirty-Thursday." *California — Magazine of the Pacific* 28 (Sept. 1938): 13, 30–31.

Boots, Ralph S. "The Initiative and the Referendum in 1923 and 1924." *National Municipal Review* 15 (Jan. 1926): 42–65.

———. "The Initiative and the Referendum in 1925 and 1926." *National Municipal Review* 16 (Oct. 1927): 642–61.

Borgeaud, Charles. "Practical Results Which Have Attended the Introduction of the Referendum in Switzerland." *The Arena* 33 (May 1905): 482–86.

Bourne, Jonathan. "Functions of the Initiative, Referendum, and Recall." *Annals* 43 (Sept. 1912): 3–16.

———. "Initiative, Referendum, and Recall." *Atlantic Monthly* 109 (Jan. 1912): 122–31.

———. "The Initiative on Trial." *The Outlook* (Aug. 24, 1907): 844–45.

Bowne, Charles W. "The Initiative and Referendum." *The Arena* 16 (Sept. 1896): 553–57.

Boyle, James. *The Initiative and Referendum: Its Folly, Fallacies, and Failure*. Columbus, Ohio: Smythe, 1912.

Braeman, John. *Albert J. Beveridge: American Nationalist*. Chicago: University of Chicago Press, 1971.

Brandeis, Louis. *The Curse of Bigness: Miscellaneous Papers of Louis Brandeis*. Edited by Osmond K. Fraenkel. Port Washington, N.Y.: Kennikat Press, 1965.

———. *Other People's Money and How the Bankers Use It*. New York: Harper & Row, 1967.

Bridges, Amy. "Creating Cultures of Reform." *Studies in American Political Development* 8 (Spring 1994): 1–23.

———. *Morning Glories: Municipal Reform in the Southwest*. Princeton: Princeton University Press, 1997.

———. "Winning the West to Municipal Reform." *Urban Affairs Quarterly* 27 (June 1992): 494–518.

Bright, Charles C. "The State in the United States during the Nineteenth Century," in *Statemaking and Social Movements: Essays in History and Theory*, edited by Charles C. Bright and Susan Harding, 121–58. Ann Arbor: University of Michigan Press, 1984.

Broder, David S. "The Ballot Battle: Collecting Signatures for a Price." *Washington Post*, Apr. 12, 1998.

———. *Democracy Derailed: Initiative Campaigns and the Power of Money*. New York: Harcourt Brace, 2000.

Brody, David. "On the Failure of U.S. Radical Politics: A Farmer-Labor Analysis." *Industrial Relations* 22 (Spring 1983): 141–63.

Bromage, Arthur W. *State Government and Administration in the United States*. New York: Harper & Bros., 1936.

Brooke, John L. *The Heart of the Commonwealth: Society and Political Culture in Worcester County, Massachusetts, 1713–1861*. Cambridge: Cambridge University Press, 1989.

Brown, A. A. "Direct Legislation: Now in Operation," *The Arena* 22 (July 1899): 97–100.

Brown, M. Craig, and Charles N. Halaby. "Machine Politics in America." *Journal of Interdisciplinary History* 17 (Winter 1987–88): 581–603

Brown, Rome G. "The Judicial Recall — A Fallacy Repugnant to Constitutional Government." *Annals* 43 (Sept. 1912): 239–77.

Brown, William H. "The Popular Initiative as a Method of Legislation and Political Control." *American Journal of Sociology* 10 (May 1905): 713–49.

Bruere, Henry. *The New City Government: A Discussion of Municipal Administration based on a Survey of Ten Commission-Governed Cities*. New York: Appleton, 1913.

Bryan, William Jennings. *The People's Law*. 63rd Cong., 2d sess., 1914. S. Doc. 523.

Bryce, James. "America Revisited: The Changes of a Quarter-Century,"
  The Outlook 79 (Apr. 1, 1905): 846–55.
———. *Modern Democracies*. Vol. 1. New York: Macmillan, 1924.
Bryce, Lloyd S. "Errors in Prof. Bryce's 'Commonwealth.'" *North
  American Review* 148 (Mar. 1889): 344–54.
Buchanan, Joseph R. "A Referendum for Reform." *The Arena* 22 (Oct.
  1899): 457–58.
Buck, Solon J. *The Granger Movement: A Story of Agricultural
  Organization and Its Political, Economic, and Social Manifestations,
  1870–1880*. Cambridge: Harvard University Press, 1913.
Budenz, Louis F. "The St. Louis Recall Efforts and Its Aftermath."
  National Municipal Review 8 (Aug. 1919): 412–16.
Burke, Robert E. *Olson's New Deal for California*. Berkeley: University of
  California Press, 1953.
Burki, Mary Ann M. "The California Progressives: Labor's Point of
  View." *Labor History* 17 (Winter 1976), 24–37.
Burrows, Samuel J. "Tendencies of American Legislation." *North
  American Review* 175 (Nov. 1902): 642–51.
Burton, Robert E. *Democrats of Oregon: The Pattern of Minority Politics,
  1900–1956*. Eugene: University of Oregon Press, 1970.
Bushman, Richard L. *King and People in Provincial Massachusetts*. Chapel
  Hill: University of North Carolina Press, 1985.
Butler, David, and Austin Ranney, eds. *Referendums around the World:
  The Growing Use of Direct Democracy*. Washington, D.C.: AEI, 1994.
Butler, W. J. *The Initiative, Referendum, and Recall or the Rule of Illusion,
  Rebellion, and Ruin*. Springfield, Ill: 1914.
Byrdsall, Fitzwilliam. *The History of the Loco-Foco or Equal Rights Party:
  Its Movements, Conventions and Proceedings, with Short Characteristic
  Speeches of Its Prominent Men*. New York: Clement & Packard, 1842.
California Commission on Campaign Financing. *Democracy by
  Initiative: Shaping California's Fourth Branch of Government*.
  2 volumes. Los Angeles, 1992.
California State Chamber of Commerce, Research Department.
  *Initiative Legislation in California. History of the Use of the Initiative
  and Summary of Various Proposals for Amendment of the Initiative
  Process*. San Francisco, 1939.
Campbell, Ballard C. *Representative Democracy: Public Policy and
  Midwestern Legislators in the Late Nineteenth Century*. Cambridge:
  Harvard University Press, 1980.
Canterbury, John B. "'Ham and Eggs' in California." *The Nation* 147
  (Oct. 22, 1938): 408–10.

Carroll, Dorr H. "The Recall in North Dakota." *National Municipal Review* 11 (Jan. 1922): 3–5.

Carstensen, Vernon, ed. *Farmer Discontent, 1865–1900*. New York: Wiley & Sons, 1974.

Casey, Jack T. "Legislative History of the Central Valley Project, 1933–1949." Ph.D. diss., University of California, Berkeley, 1949.

Casey, Ralph D. "Republican Propaganda in the 1936 Campaign." *Public Relations Quarterly* 1 (Apr. 1937): 27–44.

Catlett, Fred W. "The Working of the Recall in Seattle." *Annals of the American Academy of Political and Social Science* 43 (Sept. 1912): 227–36.

Chagall, David. *The New Kingmakers*. New York: Harcourt Brace, 1981.

Chandler, Alfred D. *Scale and Scope: The Dynamics of Industrial Capitalism*. Cambridge: Harvard University Press, 1990.

——— . *The Visible Hand: The Managerial Revolution in American Business*. Cambridge: Harvard University Press, 1977.

Cherny, Robert W. *Populism, Progressivism, and the Transformation of Nebraska Politics, 1885–1915*. Lincoln: University of Nebraska Press, 1981.

Circular of the "Direct Legislation League" of Massachusetts and the State of Washington Relative to "Representative Government" or Initiative, Referendum, and Recall. 61st Cong., 2d Sess., 1910. S. Doc. 624.

Civic Federation of Chicago. *Chicago Conference on Trusts*. Chicago, 1900.

——— . *Dangers of the Initiative and Referendum*. Chicago, 1911.

Clanton, Gene. *Populism: The Humane Preference in America, 1890–1900*. Boston: Twayne, 1991.

Clark, John B. "The Trend to an American Democracy." *North American Review* 222 (Sept. 1925): 22–28.

Clark, Norman H. *Deliver Us From Evil: An Interpretation of American Prohibition*. New York: W. W. Norton, 1976.

——— . *The Dry Years: Prohibition and Social Change in Washington*. Seattle: University of Washington Press, 1965.

——— . "The 'Hell-Soaked Institution' and the Washington Prohibition Initiative of 1914." *Pacific Northwest Quarterly* 56 (Jan. 1965): 1–16.

——— . *Washington: A Bicentennial History*. New York: W. W. Norton, 1976.

Clark, Walter. "The Election of Federal Judges by the People." *The Arena* 32 (Nov. 1904): 457–60.

Clemens, Elisabeth S. *The People's Lobby: Organizational Innovation and*

the Rise of Interest Group Politics in the United States, 1890–1925.
Chicago: University of Chicago Press, 1997.

Cleveland, Frederick A. *The Growth of Democracy in the United States, or, the Evolution of Popular Co-operation in Government and its Results.* Chicago: Quadrangle, 1898.

——. *Organized Democracy: An Introduction to the Study of American Politics.* New York: Longmans, 1913.

Cloud, D. C. *Monopolies and the People.* Davenport: Egbert & Fidler, 1873.

Clow, Richard L. "In Search of the People's Voice: Richard Olsen Richards and Progressive Reform." *South Dakota History* 10 (Winter 1979–80): 39–58.

Coate, Charles E. *Water, Power, and Politics in the Central Valley Project, 1933–1967.* Berkeley: University of California Press, 1969.

The Code of the People's Rule. Compilation of Various Statutes, etc. Relating to the People's Rule System of Government and for Terminating the Abuses of Machine Politics. 61st Cong., 2d Sess., 1910. S. Doc. 603.

Coker, F. W. "The Interworkings of State Administration and Direct Legislation." *Annals* 64 (Mar. 1916): 122–33.

——. "Safeguarding the Petition in the Initiative and Referendum." *American Political Science Review* 10 (Aug. 1916): 540–45.

Cole, Donald B. *Jacksonian Democracy in New Hampshire, 1800–1851.* Cambridge: Harvard University Press, 1970.

Coleman, Charles M. *P.G. and E. of California: The Centennial Story of Pacific Gas and Electric Company, 1852–1952.* New York: McGraw-Hill, 1952.

Coleman, Peter J. *Progressivism and the World of Reform: New Zealand and the Origins of the American Welfare State.* Lawrence: University of Kansas Press, 1987.

Colorado. Legislative Reference Bureau. *The Initiative and Referendum in Colorado.* Denver, 1939.

Commons, John R. "Direct Legislation in Switzerland and America." *The Arena* 22 (Dec. 1899): 725–39.

——. *The Distribution of Wealth.* New York: Macmillan, 1905.

Conant, Charles A. "The New Corporation Tax." *North American Review* 190 (Aug. 1909): 231–40.

Connors, Arthur. "Constitutional Amendments and Referred Measures." *American Political Science Review* 10 (Feb. 1916): 104–9.

Converse, Jean M. *Survey Research in the United States: Roots and Emergence, 1890–1960.* Berkeley: University of California Press, 1987.

Cornell, Saul. "Aristocracy Assailed: The Ideology of Backcountry Anti-Federalism." *Journal of American History* 76 (Mar. 1990): 1148–72.

Cortner, Richard C. *The Iron Horse and the Constitution: The Railroads and the Transformation of the Fourteenth Amendment*. Westport, Conn.: Greenwood Press, 1993.

Cottrell, Edwin A. "Twenty-five Years of Direct Legislation in California." *Public Opinion Quarterly* 3 (Jan. 1939): 30–45.

Cree, Nathan. *Direct Legislation by the People*. Chicago: McClure, 1892.

Cridge, Alfred D. "The People as Lawmakers in Oregon." *American Federationist* 18 (Jan. 1911): 52–54.

Crockett, Norman L. "The 1912 Single Tax Campaign in Missouri." *Missouri Historical Review* 56 (Oct. 1961): 40–52.

Croly, Herbert S. "Democratic Factions and Insurgent Republicans." *North American Review* 191 (May 1910): 626–35.

——. *Progressive Democracy*. New York: Macmillan, 1915.

——. *The Promise of American Life*. New York: Macmillan, 1909.

——. "State Political Reorganization." *Proceedings of the APSA* 8 (1911): 122–35.

Cronin, Thomas E. *Direct Democracy: The Politics of Initiative, Referendum, and Recall*. Cambridge: Harvard University Press, 1989.

——. "Public Opinion and Direct Democracy." *Political Science and Politics* 21 (Summer 1988): 612–19.

Crouch, Winston W. "The Constitutional Initiative in Operation." *American Political Science Review* 33 (Aug. 1939): 634–45.

——. "The Initiative and Referendum in Cities." *American Political Science Review* 37 (June 1943): 491–504.

——. "John Randolph Haynes and His Work for Direct Government." *National Municipal Review* 27 (Sept. 1938): 434–40.

——. *Organized Civil Servants: Public Employer-Employee Relations in California*. Berkeley: University of California Press, 1978.

Crowley, J. E. *This Sheba, Self: The Conceptualization of Economic Life in Eighteenth-Century America*. Baltimore: Johns Hopkins University Press, 1974.

Cruice, Daniel L. "Direct Legislation in Illinois: A Story of Triumph for Popular Government." *The Arena* 31 (June 1904): 561–68.

Cushman, Robert E. "Recent Experience with the Initiative and Referendum." *American Political Science Review* 10 (Aug. 1916): 532–39.

——. "Voting Organic Laws: The Action of the Ohio Electorate in the Revision of the State Constitution in 1912." *Political Science Quarterly* 26 (June 1913): 207–29.

Daniels, Doris. "Building a Winning Coalition: The Suffrage Fight in New York State." *New York History* 60 (Jan. 1979): 59–80.

Davis, Clark. " 'You Are The Company': The Demands of Employment in the Emerging Corporate Culture, Los Angeles, 1900–1930." *Business History Review* 70 (Autumn 1996): 328–62.

Davis, John P. "The Nature of Corporations." *Political Science Quarterly* 12 (June 1897): 273–94.

Davis, Thomas A. "The Recall as a Measure of Control by the People." *Proceedings of the National Municipal League* (1906): 382–87.

Dealey, J. Q. "The Trend of Recent Constitutional Changes." *Proceedings of the American Political Science Association* 8 (1911): 53–60.

Degler, Carl N. "The Loco-Focos: Urban 'Agrarians.' " *Journal of Economic History* 16 (Sept. 1956): 322–33.

Denman, William. *The Recall of the Judiciary in California: A Summary of Reasons against Recalling Judges at Popular Elections, Delivered before the Commonwealth Club, June 14, 1911*. San Francisco, 1911.

De Roos, Robert. *The Thirsty Land: The Story of the Central Valley Project*. 1948. Reprint, New York: Greenwood, 1968.

Destler, Chester M. *American Radicalism, 1865–1901: Essays and Documents*. Chicago: Octagon, 1946.

Deverell, William. *Railroad Crossing: Californians and the Railroads, 1850–1910*. Berkeley: University of California Press, 1994.

DeWitt, Benjamin P. *The Progressive Movement: A Non-Partisan, Comprehensive Discussion of Current Tendencies in American Politics*. New York: Macmillan, 1915.

Dicey, A. V. "Democracy in Switzerland." *The Nation* 43 (Nov. 18, 1886): 412–14; 43 (Dec. 16, 1886): 410–12, 494–96.

Dickson, E. A. "Self-Government at Los Angeles." *California Weekly* (May 7, 1909): 383.

Dinkin, Robert J. *Campaigning in America: A History of Election Practices*. Westport, Conn.: Greenwood Press, 1989.

"Direct Anger Right." *California Outlook* 17 (Sept. 26, 1914): 4.

"Direct Legislation." *Transactions of the Commonwealth Club of California* 6 (Sept. 1911): 281–341.

"Direct Legislation." *Transactions of the Commonwealth Club of California* 25 (Mar. 3, 1931): 409–590.

"Direct Legislation in America." *The Arena* 24 (Nov. 1900): 493–505.

"Direct Legislation in Oregon and the Misrepresentations of the Reactionary Press." *The Arena* 38 (July 1907): 80–85.

Direct Legislation League of the State of Washington. *Direct Legislation or the Initiative, Referendum, and Recall*. Seattle, 1910.

"Direct Legislation to Be Protected." *California Outlook* 17 (Oct. 13, 1914): 10.

"Direct or Simple." *California Weekly* (Jan. 28, 1910): 122–23.

"The Direct Primary: Success or Failure." *Transactions of the Commonwealth Club of California* 10 (Dec. 1924): 553–64.

Doan, Edward N. *The La Follettes and the Wisconsin Idea*. New York: Rinehart, 1947.

Dodd, Walter F. "The Function of a State Constitution." *Political Science Quarterly* 30 (June 1915): 201–21.

———. *The Revision and Amendment of State Constitutions*. Baltimore: Johns Hopkins University Press, 1910.

———. *State Government*. 2d ed. New York: Century, 1928.

Dodds, H. W. "The Initiative and Referendum and the Elections of 1920." *National Municipal Review* 10 (Apr. 1921): 232–39.

Dougherty, J. Hampden. "Substitutes for the Recall of Judges." *Proceedings of the Academy of Political Science* 3 (Jan. 1913): 99–108.

Dudden, Arthur P. *Joseph Fels and the Single-Tax Movement*. Philadelphia: Temple University Press, 1971.

Durand, Edward D. *The Trust Problem*. Cambridge: Harvard University Press, 1914.

Eaton, Allen H. *The Oregon System: The Story of Direct Legislation in Oregon*. Chicago: McClurg, 1912.

Echols, James P. "Jackson Ralston and the Last Single Tax Campaign." *California History* 58 (Fall 1979): 256–63.

Ehrman, Sidney M. "Proposals for Revising the Initiative." *California — Magazine of the Pacific* 29 (Dec. 1939): 5, 41.

Eliel, Paul. "Corrupt Judges Recalled in San Francisco." *National Municipal Review* 10 (June 1921): 316–17.

Ell, H. G. "Direct Legislation in New Zealand." *The Arena* 30 (Sept. 1903): 268–72.

Elliott, Edward. *American Government and Majority Rule: A Study in American Political Development*. Princeton: Princeton University Press, 1916.

Ellis, Mary L. "Tilting at the Piazza: Emmet O'Neal's Encounter with Woodrow Wilson, September 1911." *Alabama Review* 39 (Apr. 1986): 83–95.

Ellis, Richard J. "Rival Visions of Equality in American Political Culture." *Review of Politics* 54 (Spring 1992): 253–80.

Ely, Richard T. *Monopolies and Trusts*. New York: Macmillan, 1900.

"End of a Bug-a-Boo." *California Outlook* 12 (Feb. 24, 1912): 4.

Erie, Steven P. "How the Urban West Was Won: The Local State and

Economic Growth in Los Angeles, 1880–1932." *Urban Affairs Quarterly* 27 (June 1992): 519–54.

Ershkovitz, Herbert, and William G. Shade. "Consensus or Conflict? Political Behavior in the State Legislatures during the Jacksonian Era." *Journal of American History* 58 (Dec. 1971): 591–621.

Ethington, Philip J. "Urban Constituencies, Regimes, and Policy Innovation in the Progressive Era: An Analysis of Boston, Chicago, New York City, and San Francisco." *Studies in American Political Development* 7 (Fall 1993): 275–315.

Eu, March Fong. *A History of the California Initiative Process*. Sacramento: State of California, 1993.

Everett, Ray. *Arizona: History and Government*. Tempe: Arizona State University Press, 1977.

Fairlie, John A. "The Referendum and Initiative in Michigan." *Annals of the American Academy of Political and Social Science* 43 (Sept. 1912): 146–58.

Faler, Paul G. *Mechanics and Manufacturers in the Early Industrializing Revolution: Lynn, Massachusetts, 1780–1860*. Albany: SUNY Press, 1981.

Farley, James A. *Behind the Ballots: The Personal History of a Politician*. New York: Harcourt Brace, 1938.

Farmer, Rod. "Democratic Ideologues: The Direct-Legislation Movement and the Ideal of Direct Democracy, 1882–1918." *New England Journal of History* 48 (Winter 1991–92): 33–53.

———. "Direct Democracy in Arkansas, 1910–1918." *Arkansas Historical Quarterly* 40 (Summer 1981): 99–118.

———. "The Maine Campaign for Direct Democracy." *Maine Historical Society Quarterly* 23 (Summer 1983): 13–27.

Fea, Chris. " 'The Town That Billy Sunday Could Not Shut Down': Prohibition and Sunday's Chicago Crusade of 1918." *Illinois Historical Quarterly* 87 (Winter 1994–95): 242–58.

The Federalist Papers. Edited by Clinton Rossiter. New York: New American Library, 1961.

Felknor, Bruce L. *Political Mischief: Smear, Sabotage, and Reform in U.S. Elections*. New York: Praeger, 1992.

"Fighting Initiative." *California Outlook* 17 (Aug. 22, 1914): 4.

Fillebrown, C. B. "The Taxation of Privilege." *The Outlook* (Feb. 5, 1910): 311–13.

Filler, Louis. *Muckrakers: Crusaders for American Liberalism*. Chicago: Gateway, 1968.

Finer, Herman. *Theory and Practice of Modern Government*. New York: Henry Hold, 1949.

Fink, Albert. "The Recall of Judges." *North American Review* 193 (May 1911): 672–90.

Fink, Leon. "The Uses of Political Power: Toward a Theory of the Labor Movement in the Era of the Knights of Labor." In *Working-Class America*, edited by Michael H. Frisch and Daniel J. Walkowitz, 104–22. Urbana: University of Illinois Press, 1983.

———. *Workingmen's Democracy: The Knights of Labor and American Politics*. Urbana: University of Illinois Press, 1983.

Fitzgerald, Maureen. "Oil-Tax Initiative Campaign: Most Expensive in State's History." *California Outlook* 11 (Apr. 1980): 167–68.

Flower, Benjamin O. "Brookline: A Model Town under the Referendum." *The Arena* 19 (Apr. 1898): 505–19.

———. "The Direct-Legislation Campaign in the Empire State." *The Arena* 39 (June 1908): 650–61.

———. "Is Socialism Desirable?" *The Arena* 3 (May 1891): 753–64.

———. "The Menace of Plutocracy." *The Arena* 6 (Sept. 1892): 508–16.

———. "Organized Labor and Direct Legislation." *The Arena* 25 (May 1902): 533–38.

———. *Progressive Men, Women, and Movements of the Past Twenty-five Years*. Boston: The New Arena, 1914.

———. "Pure Democracy versus Vicious Governmental Favoritism," *The Arena*. 8 (July 1893): 260–72.

———. "Twenty-five Years of Bribery and Corrupt Practices, or the Railroads, the Lawmakers, the People." *The Arena* 31 (Jan. 1904): 12–49.

Fogelson, Robert M. *The Fragmented Metropolis: Los Angeles, 1850–1930*. Cambridge: Harvard University Press, 1967.

Folger, Walter A. "Advertising Shoulders Today's Job." *California Journal of Development* 23 (May 1933): 6, 28–29.

Folsom, Burton W. "Tinkerers, Tipplers, and Traitors: Ethnicity and Democratic Reform in Nebraska during the Progressive Era." *Pacific Historical Review* 50 (Feb. 1981): 53–75.

Forcey, Charles *The Crossroads of Liberalism: Croly, Weyl, Lippmann, and the Progressive Era, 1900–1925*. New York: Oxford University Press, 1961.

Ford, Henry J. "Direct Legislation and the Recall." *Annals* 43 (Sept. 1912): 65–77.

Forrest, J. D. "Anti-Monopoly Legislation in the United States." *American Journal of Sociology* 1 (Jan. 1896): 411–25.

"The Foundation of Our Faith." *California Outlook* 11 (Sept. 9, 1911): 3.

Fowler, James H., II. "Constitutions and Conditions Contrasted:

Arizona and New Mexico, 1910." *Journal of the West* 13 (Oct. 1974): 51–58.

Fox, Stephen. *The Mirror Makers: A History of American Advertising and Its Founders*. New York: Morrow, 1984.

Foxcroft, Frank. "Constitution-mending and the Initiative." *The Atlantic Monthly* 97 (June 1906): 792–96.

Francisco, Don. "Advertising: An Essential Ingredient of Democracy." *California — Journal of the Pacific* 29 (Nov. 1939): 4–5.

———. "How Business Can Make Friends." *California — Magazine of the Pacific* 28 (Jan. 1938): 9, 39–40.

———. "Inside Story of California Chain Tax War." *Advertising and Selling* 28 (Feb. 11, 1937): 27, 53–54.

———. "Keying Advertising Strategy to 1933 Conditions." *California Journal of Development* 23 (May 1933): 8–9, 26.

French, Willard. "When History Repeats." *Lippincott's Monthly Magazine* 92 (Aug. 1913): 90–97.

Freyer, Tony A. *Producers versus Capitalists: Constitutional Conflict in Antebellum America*. Charlottesville: University of Virginia Press, 1994.

Fritz, Christian G. "The American Constitutional Tradition Revisited: Preliminary Observations on State Constitution-making in the Nineteenth-Century West." *Rutgers Law Journal* 25 (Summer 1994): 945–98.

———. "Popular Sovereignty, Vigilantism, and the Constitutional Right of Revolution." *Pacific Historical Review* 63 (Feb. 1994): 39–66.

———. "Rethinking the American Constitutional Tradition: National Dimensions in the Formation of State Constitutions." *Rutgers Law Journal* 26 (Summer 1995): 969–92.

Furner, Mary O. "Social Scientists and the State: Constructing the Knowledge Base for Public Policy, 1880–1920." In *Intellectuals and Public Life: Between Radicalism and Reform*, edited by Leon Fink, Stephen T. Leonard, and Donald M. Reid, 145–81. Ithaca: Cornell University Press, 1996.

Gable, John A. *The Bull Moose Years: Theodore Roosevelt and the Progressive Party*. Port Washington, N.Y.: Kennikat Press, 1979.

Galambos, Louis. "The Emerging Organizational Synthesis in American History." In *Men and Organizations: The American Economy in the Twentieth Century*, edited by Edwin J. Perkins, 3–15. New York: G. P. Putnam's Sons, 1977.

Galbreath, C. B. "Provisions for State-Wide Initiative and Referendum." *Annals* 43 (Sept. 1912): 83–84.

Garber, J. Otis. "The Use of the Recall in American Cities." *National Municipal Review* 15 (May 1926): 259–61.

Gardner, Charles O. "The Initiative and Referendum in Commission Cities." *Annals of the American Academy of Political and Social Science* 38 (Nov. 1911): 153–62.

Gardner, Clarence O. *The Referendum in Chicago*. Philadelphia: University of Pennsylvania Press, 1920.

Garner, James W. "Amendments of State Constitutions." *American Political Science Review* 1 (Feb. 1907): 213–47.

———. "Primary vs. Representative Government." *Proceedings of the APSA* 4 (1907): 164–74.

Gaston, Herbert E. *The Nonpartisan League*. New York: Harcourt Brace, 1920.

Geiges, Carl J. "Wildwood's Recall Election: A Clean Sweep for Clean Government." *National Municipal Review* 10 (Oct. 1921): 491–92.

Gerber, Elizabeth R. *The Populist Paradox: Interest Group Influence and the Promise of Direct Legislation*. Princeton: Princeton University Press, 1999.

Gilbert, James H. "Single-Tax Movement in Oregon," *Political Science Quarterly* 31 (Mar. 1916): 25–52.

Goldman, Eric F. "J. Allen Smith: The Reformer and His Dilemma," *Pacific Northwest Quarterly* 35 (July 1944): 195–214.

Gompers, Samuel. "Initiative, Referendum, and Recall." *American Federationist* 19 (Aug.–Dec. 1912): 618–1026.

———. "Organized Labor in the Campaign." *North American Review* 155 (July 1892).

Goodman, Paul. "The Emergence of Homestead Exemption in the United States: Accommodation and Resistance to the Market Economy." *Journal of American History* 80 (Sept. 1993): 470–98.

Goodwyn, Lawrence. *Democratic Promise: The Populist Moment in America*. New York: Oxford University Press, 1976.

Gosnell, Cullen B., and Lynwood M. Holland. *State and Local Government in the United States*. New York: Prentice-Hall, 1951.

Gosnell, Harold F. "The Polls and Other Mechanisms of Democracy." *Public Opinion Quarterly* 4 (June 1940): 224–28.

Gosnell, Harold G., and Margaret J. Schmidt. *Popular Law Making in the United States, 1924–1936*. New York State Constitutional Convention Committee, Problems Relating to Legislative Organization and Powers, 313–35. Albany, 1938.

Gould, Lewis L. *Progressives and Prohibitionists: Texas Democrats in the Wilson Era*. Austin: University of Texas Press, 1973.

Graham, Virginia. *A Compilation of Statewide Initiative Proposals Appearing on Ballots through 1976*. Washington, D.C.: American University, 1976.

Grant, H. Roger. "Origins of a Progressive Reform: The Initiative and Referendum Movement in South Dakota." *South Dakota History* 3 (Fall 1973): 390–407.

Grantham, Dewey W. *Southern Progressivism: The Reconciliation of Progress and Tradition*. Knoxville: University of Tennessee Press, 1983.

Graves, W. Brooke. *American State Government*. Boston: Heath, 1936.

Gray, Virginia. "Anti-Evolution Sentiment and Behavior: The Case of Arkansas." *Journal of American History* 57 (Sept. 1970): 352–66.

Greater California League. *The ABC of the Water and Power Act*. San Francisco, 1922.

——. *Haven't We Got Taxes Enough?* San Francisco, 1922.

——. *Shall California Be Sovietized?* San Francisco, 1922.

——. *Text Book of California Water and Power Act*. San Francisco, 1922.

Griffiths, David. "Anti-Monopoly Movements in California, 1873–1898." *Southern California Quarterly* 53 (June 1972): 93–121.

——. *Populism in the Western United States, 1890–1900*. Lewiston, N.Y.: Edwin Mellen, 1992.

Grosscup, Peter S. "How to Save the Corporation." *McClure's Magazine* 24 (Feb. 1905): 443–48.

——. "Is There Common Ground on Which Thoughtful Men Can Meet on the Trust Question?" *North American Review* 195 (Mar. 1912): 293–309.

Grossman, Lawrence K. *The Electronic Republic: Reshaping Democracy in the Information Age*. New York: Viking, 1995.

Guthrie, George W. "The Initiative, Referendum, and Recall." *Annals of the American Academy of Political and Social Science* 43 (Sept. 1912): 17–31.

Hague, John A. "The Massachusetts Constitutional Convention, 1917–1919." *New England Quarterly* 27 (June 1954): 147–67.

Hahn, Harlan. "Correlates of Public Sentiments about War: Local Referenda on the Vietnam War." *American Political Science Review* 64 (Dec. 1970) 1186–98.

——. "Northern Referenda on Fair Housing: The Response of White Voters." *American Political Science Review* 21 (Sept. 1969): 483–95.

Hahn, Steven. *The Roots of Southern Populism: Yeoman Farmers and the Transformation of the Georgia Upcountry, 1850–1890*. New York: Oxford University Press, 1983.

Hall, Arnold B. *Popular Government: An Inquiry into the Nature and Methods of Representative Government*. New York: Macmillan, 1921.

Hallett, George H., Jr. *The Constitutional Initiative: A Report Prepared for the Subcommittee on the Legislature of the New York State Constitutional Convention Committee, Feb. 1, 1938*. Albany, 1938.

———. "The Constitutional Initiative Starts a New Advance." *National Municipal Review* 24 (May 1935): 254–57.

"Ham and Eggs." *Tax Digest* 16 (Nov. 1938): 365–66.

Ham and Eggs for Californians. Life Begins at Fifty. $30 a Week for Life. Questions and Answers. California State Retirement Life Payments Act. Hollywood, 1938.

Hamill, Charles H. "Constitutional Chaos." *Forum* 48 (July 1912): 45–60.

Hamilton, Howard B. "Direct Legislation: Some Implications of Open Housing Referenda." *American Political Science Review* 64 (Mar. 1970): 124–37.

Hamilton, Phil. "$30 a Week for Life." *California—Magazine of the Pacific* 28 (Aug. 1938): 12–13, 26.

Hammack, David. *Power and Society: Greater New York at the Turn of the Century*. New York: Columbia University Press, 1982.

Hammer, Urs. *Vom Alpenidyll zum modernen Musterstaat: Der Mythos der Schweiz als "Alpine Sister Republic" in den USA des 19. Jahrhunderts*. Basel: Helbing and Lichtenhahn, 1995.

———. "William Denison McCrackan (1864–1923): A Progressive's View of Swiss History and Politics." *Yearbook of German-American Studies* 25 (1990): 77–92.

Handlin, Oscar, and Mary Flugg Handlin. *Commonwealth: A Study of the Role of Government in the American Economy. Massachusetts, 1774–1861*. New York: New York University Press, 1947.

———. "The Origins of the American Business Corporation." *Journal of Economic History* 5 (May 1945): 1–23.

Hands, Willis L. "Is the Initiative and Referendum Repugnant to the Constitution of the United States?" *Central Law Journal* 58 (Mar. 25, 1904): 244–48.

Hanson, Russell L. "'Commons' and 'Commonwealth' at the American Founding: Democratic Republicanism as the New American Hybrid." In *Conceptual Change and the Constitution*, edited by Terence Ball and J. G. A. Pocock, 165–93. Lawrence: University of Kansas Press, 1988.

———. "Democracy." In *Political Innovation and Conceptual Change*,

edited by Terence Ball, J. Farr, and R. L. Hanson, 68–89.
Cambridge: Cambridge University Press, 1989.

Harbaugh, William H. *The Life and Times of Theodore Roosevelt*. Rev. ed.
London: Oxford University Press, 1975.

Hart, Albert B. "Growth of American Theories of Popular Government."
American Political Science Review 1 (Aug. 1907): 531–60.

———. "Vox Populi in Switzerland." *The Nation* 59 (Sept. 13, 1894):
193–94.

Hart, Mervin K. "The People vs. the Representative." *The Outlook* (Nov.
30, 1907): 730–33.

Hart, Roger L. *Redeemers, Bourbons, and Populists: Tennessee, 1870–1896*.
Baton Rouge: Louisiana State University Press, 1975.

Hartog, Hendrick. *Public Property and Private Power: The Corporation of
the City of New York in American Law, 1730–1870*. Chapel Hill:
University of North Carolina Press, 1983.

Hartwell, Edward M. "Referenda in Massachusetts, 1776–1907."
Proceedings of the National Municipal League (1909): 334–53.

Hartz, Louis. *Economic Policy and Democratic Thought: Pennsylvania,
1776–1860*. Cambridge: Harvard University Press, 1948.

Hattam, Victoria. "Economic Visions and Political Strategies:
American Labor and the State, 1865–1896." *Studies in American
Political Development* 4 (1990): 82–129.

———. *Labor Visions and State Power: The Origins of Business Unionism in
the United States*. Princeton: Princeton University Press, 1993.

Haynes, C. H. "How Massachusetts Adopted the Initiative and
Referendum." *Political Science Quarterly* 34 (Sept. 1919): 454–75.

Haynes, George H. "Educational Qualifications for the Suffrage in the
United States." *Political Science Quarterly* 13 (Sept. 1898): 495–513.

———. "The Education of Voters." *Political Science Quarterly* 22 (Sept.
1907): 484–97.

———. "Massachusetts Public Opinion Bills." *Proceedings of the American
Political Science Association* 4 (1908): 152–63.

———. " 'People's Rule on Trial." *Political Science Quarterly* 28 (Mar.
1913): 18–33.

Haynes, John R. "The Actual Workings of the Initiative, Referendum,
and Recall." *National Municipal Review* 4 (Oct. 1912): 586–602.

———. "The Adoption of the Initiative, Referendum, and Recall by the
State of California." *West Coast Magazine* 11 (Jan. 1912): 294–96.

———. "California Sticks to the I. and R." *National Municipal Review* 12
(Mar. 1923): 116–18.

———. *Direct Government in California*, U.S. 64th Cong., 2d Sess., 1917. S. Doc. 738.

Hays, Samuel P. "The Changing Political Structure of the City in Industrial America." *Journal of Urban History* 1 (Nov. 1974): 6–38.

———. "The Politics of Reform in Municipal Government in the Progressive Era." *Pacific Historical Quarterly* 55 (Oct. 1964): 157–69.

Hazeltine, M. W. "The Referendum and Initiative in Switzerland," *North American Review* 185 (May 1907): 202–13.

Heckscher, August. *Woodrow Wilson*. New York: Charles Scribner's Sons, 1991.

Hendrick, Burton J. "Governor Hughes and the Albany Gang: A Study of the Degradation of the Republican Party in New York State." *McClure's Magazine* 35 (Sept. 1910): 495–512.

———. "The Initiative and Referendum and How Oregon Got It." *McClure's Magazine* 37 (July 1911): 234–48.

———. "Law-Making by the Voters." *McClure's Magazine* 37 (Aug. 1911): 435–50.

———. "The 'Recall' in Seattle." *McClure's Magazine* 37 (Oct. 1911): 647–63.

———. "Statement No. 1: How the Oregon Democracy, Working under the Direct Primary, Has Destroyed the Political Machine." *McClure's Magazine* 37 (Sept. 1911): 505–19.

Henry, Sarah M. "Democracy and Disfranchisement: The Southern Direct Legislation Movement in the Progressive Era." Paper presented at the convention of the American Historical Association, Washington, D.C., Jan. 1999.

———. "Progressivism and Democracy: Electoral Reform in the United States, 1888–1919." Ph.D. diss., Columbia University, 1995.

Hichborn, Franklin. "Political Activities of the Power Trust in California." *Public Ownership* 14 (Jan. 1932): 3–16.

———. *Story of the California Legislature of 1915*. San Francisco: Barry, 1915.

———. *Story of the Session of the California Legislature of 1911*. San Francisco: Barry, 1911.

Hicks, John D. *The Populist Revolt: A History of the Farmers' Alliance and the People's Party*. Minneapolis: University of Minnesota Press, 1931.

Hiebert, Ray G. *Courtier to the Crowd: The Story of Ivy Lee and the Development of Public Relations*. Ames: Iowa State University Press, 1966.

"High Court Rejects Curbs on Ballot Initiatives." *Washington Post*, Jan. 13, 1999.

Hill, Gladwin. *Dancing Bear: An Inside Look at California Politics*. New York: World, 1968.

Hoffman, Abraham. *Vision or Villainy: Origins of the Owens Valley–Los Angeles Water Controversy*. College Station: Texas A&M University Press, 1981.

Hofstadter, Richard. *The Age of Reform: From Bryan to F. D. R*. New York: Vintage, 1955.

——. "What Happened to the Antitrust Movement?" In *The Paranoid Style in American Politics and Other Essays*, edited by Richard Hofstadter, 188–237. New York: Knopf, 1965.

Holcombe, Arthur M. *State Government in the United States*. New York: Macmillan, 1931.

Hollingsworth, Charles M. "The So-Called Progressive Movement: Its Real Nature, Causes and Significance." *Annals* 43 (Sept. 1912): 32–48.

Holman, Frederick V. "Some Instances of Unsatisfactory Results under Initiative Amendments to the Oregon Constitution." Address to the Oregon Bar Association, Portland, Ore., Nov. 15, 1910.

Horowitz, David A. "The Crusade against Chain Stores: Portland's Independent Merchants, 1928–1935." *Oregon Historical Quarterly* 89 (Winter 1988–89): 341–68.

Horwill, Herbert W. "The Referendum in Great Britain." *Political Science Quarterly* 26 (Sept. 1911): 415–31.

Horwitz, Morton J. *The Transformation of American Law, 1780–1860*. Cambridge: Harvard University Press, 1977.

Houghton, Neal D. "Arizona's Experience with the Initiative and Referendum." *New Mexico Historical Review* 29 (July 1954): 183–209.

——. "The Initiative and Referendum in Missouri." *Missouri Historical Review* 19 (Jan. 1925): 268–99.

"How the Fight Was Won." *California — Magazine of the Pacific* 28 (Dec. 1938): 5, 30.

"How the Referendum Would Work." *The Nation* 5 (Aug. 30, 1894): 152–53.

Hubbard, H. A. "The Arizona Enabling Act and President Taft's Veto." *Pacific Historical Review* 3 (Fall 1934): 307–22.

Huckshorn, Robert J. *Party Leadership in the States*. Amherst: University of Massachusetts Press, 1976.

Hugins, Walter. *Jacksonian Democracy and the Working Class: A Study of the New York Workingmen's Movement*. Stanford: Stanford University Press, 1960.

Hunt, James L. "Populism, Law, and the Corporation: The 1897 Kansas Supreme Court." *Agricultural History* 66 (Fall 1992): 28–54.

Hunter, George S. "The Bull Moose Movement in Arizona." *Arizona and the West* 10 (Winter 1968–69): 343–62.

Hurst, James W. *The Legitimacy of the Business Corporation in the Law of the United States, 1780–1970*. Charlottesville: University of Virginia Press, 1970.

Hurt, R. Douglas. "The Farmers' Alliance and People's Party in Ohio." *Old Northwest* 10 (Winter 1984–85): 439–62.

Huston, James L. "The American Revolutionaries, the Political Economy of Aristocracy, and the American Concept of the Distribution of Wealth, 1765–1900." *American History Review* 98 (Oct. 1993): 1079–105.

Hutchinson, William H. *Oil, Land, and Politics: The California Career of Thomas Robert Bard*. Vol. 2. Norman: University of Oklahoma Press, 1965.

Hutson, James H. *Die Schweiz und die Vereinigten Staaten von 1776 bis Heute*. Bern: Stämpfli & Cie., 1992.

Hynes, Terry. "Media Manipulation and Political Campaigns: Bruce Barton and the Presidential Elections of the Jazz Age." *Journalism History* 4 (Autumn 1977): 93–98.

Illinois Legislative Reference Bureau. *The Initiative, Referendum, and Recall*. Constitutional Convention Bulletins, Bulletin no. 3. Springfield, 1920.

"The Initiative and Referendum." In *Bulletins of the Massachusetts Constitutional Convention, 1917–1918*, 1:179–286. Boston, 1918.

"Initiative and Referendum." *National Municipal Review* 1 (June 1912): 308–9.

Initiative Defense League. *Amend the Initiative*. Los Angeles, 1940.

"Initiatives." *California Outlook* 16 (June 27, 1914): 2–3.

"Insult Themselves." *California Outlook* 17 (Sept. 9, 1914): 4–5.

"The Insurgent League." *The Outlook* (Feb. 4, 1911): 256–57.

Issel, William, and Robert W. Cherny. *San Francisco, 1865–1932: Politics, Power, and Urban Development*. Berkeley: University of California Press, 1986.

Jackson, C. A. G. "The Ideal Government of the Capital of Vermont under Direct Legislation." *The American Federationist* 40 (Oct. 1908): 333–34.

Jamieson, Kathleen H. *Packaging the Presidency: A History and Criticism of Presidential Campaign Advertising*. 2d ed. New York: Oxford University Press, 1992.

Jenks, Jeremiah W. "Capitalist Monopolies and Their Relation to the State." *Political Science Quarterly* 9 (Sept. 1894): 486–509.

Jensen, Richard. "Armies, Admen, and Crusaders: Types of Presidential Election Campaigns." *History Teacher* 2 (Jan. 1969): 33–50.

Johnson, Arthur M. "Antitrust Policy in Transition, 1908: Ideal and Reality." *Mississippi Valley Historical Review* 48 (Dec. 1961): 415–34.

Johnson, Claudius O. "The Adoption of the Initiative and Referendum in Washington." *Pacific Northwest Quarterly* 35 (Oct. 1944): 291–303.

———. "The Initiative and Referendum in Washington." *Pacific Northwest Quarterly* 36 (Jan. 1945): 29–63.

Johnson, David A. *Founding the Far West: California, Oregon, and Nevada, 1840–1890*. Berkeley: University of California Press, 1992.

Johnson, Warren B. "Muckraking in the Northwest: Joe Smith and Seattle Reform." *Pacific Historical Review* 40 (Nov. 1971): 478–500.

Jones, Richard J. "Organized Labor and the Initiative and Referendum: 1885–1920." Master's thesis, University of Washington, 1963.

Jones, Ruth S. "Financing State Elections." In *Money and Politics in the United States: Financing Elections in the 1980s*, edited by Michael J. Malbin, 172–213. Washington, D.C.: AEI, 1984.

Judson, F. N. "The Future of Representative Government." *American Political Science Review* 2 (Feb. 1908): 185–203.

Junkin, Francis T. A. *Is Our Representative Government Imperiled?*, 62d Cong., 3rd Sess., 1912. S. Doc. 983.

Kahrl, William L. *Water and Power: The Conflict over Los Angeles' Water Supply in the Owens Valley*. Berkeley: University of California Press, 1982.

Kales, Albert M. *Unpopular Government in the United States*. Chicago: University of Chicago Press, 1914.

Kammen, Michael. *A Machine That Would Go of Itself: The Constitution in American Culture*. New York: Knopf, 1986.

———. *Sovereignty and Liberty: Constitutional Discourse in American Culture*. Madison: University of Wisconsin Press, 1988.

Kazin, Michael. *Barons of Labor: The San Francisco Building Trades and Union Power in the Progressive Era*. Urbana: University of Illinois Press, 1987.

———. "The Great Exception Revisited: Organized Labor and Politics in San Francisco and Los Angeles, 1870–1940." *Pacific Historical Review* 55 (Aug. 1986): 371–402.

Keller, Morton. "The Politics of State Constitutional Revision, 1920–1930." In *The Constitutional Convention as an Amending Device*,

edited by Kermit Hall et al., 67–86. Washington, D.C.: American
Historical Association, 1981.

——. "Public Policy and Large Enterprise: Comparative Historical
Perspectives." In *Law and the Formation of the Big Enterprises in the
Nineteenth and Early Twentieth Centuries*, edited by Norbert Horn
and Jürgen Kocka, 515–31. Göttingen: Vandenhoeck & Ruprecht,
1979.

——. *Regulating a New Economy: Public Policy and Economic Change in
America, 1900–1933*. Cambridge: Harvard University Press, 1990.

Kelley, Stanley. *Professional Public Relations and Political Power*.
Baltimore: Johns Hopkins University Press, 1956.

Kenny, John T. "The Legislature That Elected Mr. Hanna." *The Arena*
21 (Mar. 1899): 311–26.

Kerber, Stephen. "The Initiative and Referendum in Florida." *Florida
Historical Quarterly* 72 (Jan. 1994): 302–15.

Kerr, K. Austin. *Organized for Prohibition: A New History of the Anti-
Saloon League*. New Haven: Yale University Press, 1985.

——. "Organizing for Reform: The Anti-Saloon League and
Innovation in Politics." *American Quarterly* 32 (Spring 1980):
37–53.

Kerr, William T., Jr. "The Progressives in Washington, 1910–1912."
Pacific Northwest Quarterly 55 (Jan. 1964): 16–27.

Key, V. O., Jr. *American State Politics: An Introduction*. New York:
Knopf, 1956.

——. *Politics, Parties, and Pressure Groups*. 2d ed. New York: Crowell,
1948.

——. "Publicity of Campaign Expenditures on Issues in California."
American Political Science Review 30 (Aug. 1936): 713–23.

——. *Public Opinion and American Democracy*. New York: Knopf,
1964.

Key, V. O., Jr., and Winston W. Crouch. *The Initiative and Referendum
in California*. Berkeley: University of California Press, 1939.

Kimball, Everett. *State and Municipal Government in the United States*.
Boston: Ginn and Co., 1922.

King, Judson. "Demand a Workable Initiative and Referendum."
American Federationist 10 (Oct. 1912): 824–27.

——. *The First Year and a Look Ahead: What the National Popular
Government League Did in 1914. What Should Be Done in 1915*.
Washington, D.C.: National Popular Government League, 1915.

——. "How Oregon 'Stood Pat.'" *Twentieth Century Magazine* 4 (May
1911): 116–19.

———. *The State-Wide Initiative and Referendum*. 64th Cong., 2d Sess., 1917. S. Doc. 736.

King, Peter H. "Political TV: The Marketing of a Proposition." *Los Angeles Times*, November 9–15, 1986.

Kleberg, Rudolph. "State Control of Trusts." *The Arena* 22 (Aug. 1899): 191–200.

Kleppner, Paul. "Politics without Parties: The Western States, 1900–1984." In *The Twentieth Century West: Historical Interpretations*, edited by Gerald Nash and Richard Etulain, 295–338. Albuquerque: University of New Mexico Press, 1989.

———. "Voters and Parties in the Western States, 1876–1900." *Western Historical Quarterly* 14 (Jan. 1983): 49–68.

Knauth, Oswald W. *The Policy of the United States toward Industrial Monopoly*. New York: Columbia University Press, 1914.

Kohl, Lawrence F. *The Politics of Individualism: Parties and American Character in the Jacksonian Era*. New York: Oxford University Press, 1989.

Kolko, Gabriel. *Railroads and Regulation 1877–1916*. Princeton: Princeton University Press, 1965.

Kousser, J. Morgan. *The Shaping of Southern Politics: Suffrage Restriction and the Establishment of the One-Party South*. New Haven: Yale University Press, 1974.

La Follette, Robert M. *La Follette's Autobiography: A Personal Narrative of Political Experiences*. Madison: University of Wisconsin Press, 1960.

LaPalombara, Joseph G. *The Initiative and Referendum in Oregon, 1938–1948*. Corvallis: Oregon State College Press, 1950.

LaPalombara, Joseph G., and Charles B. Hagan. "Direct Legislation: An Appraisal and a Suggestion." *American Political Science Review* 45 (June 1951): 400–21.

Larson, Robert W. *Populism in the Mountain West*. Albuquerque: University of New Mexico Press, 1986.

Laurie, Bruce. *Artisans into Workers: Labor in Nineteenth-Century America*. New York: Hill and Wang, 1989.

———. *Working People of Philadelphia, 1800–1850*. Philadelphia: Temple University Press, 1980.

League to Protect the Initiative. *Vote "No" on Proposition 27! The Initiative and Referendum in Danger. Enemies of Popular Government Renew Effort to Crush Democracy in California*. Los Angeles, 1922.

Lears, Jackson. *Fables of Abundance: A Cultural History of Advertising in America*. New York: Basic Books, 1994.

Ledbetter, Calvin R., Jr. "Adoption of Initiative and Referendum in Arkansas: The Roles of George W. Donaghey and William Jennings Bryan." *Arkansas Historical Quarterly* 51 (Autumn 1992): 199–223.

———. "The Constitutional Convention of 1917–1918." *Arkansas Historical Quarterly* 34 (Spring 1975): 3–40.

Lee, Eugene C. "California." In *Referendums: A Comparative Study of Practice and Theory*, edited by David Butler and Austin Ranney, 227–56. Washington, D.C.: AEI, 1978.

———. "The Initiative and Referendum: How California Has Fared." *National Civic Review* 68 (Feb. 1979): 69–76, 84.

———. "Representative Government and the Initiative Process." In *California Policy Choices*, edited by John Kirlin and Donald Winkler. 6:225–53. Los Angeles, 1990.

"Legislative Information and the Public." *Transactions of the Commonwealth Club of California* 29 (June 26, 1934): 75–110.

"Letter from A. F. Hockenbeamer." *Journal of the Senate during the Fifty-second Session of the Legislature of the State of California*, 663–65. Sacramento, 1938.

Leubuscher, Frederic C. "The Proposed Direct-Legislation Constitutional Amendment for New York." *The Arena* 39 (June 1908): 661–65.

Lewallen, Robert D. " 'Let the People Rule': William Jennings Bryan and the Oklahoma Constitution." *Chronicles of Oklahoma* 73 (Fall 1995): 278–307.

Lewis, Austin. "San Francisco's New Charter." *The Arena* 22 (Sept. 1899): 368–75.

Lewis, D. C. "Arizona's Constitution: The Initiative, The Referendum, The Recall — Is the Constitution Republican in Form?" *Central Law Journal* 72 (Mar. 10, 1911): 169–77.

Lewis, William D. "A New Method of Constitutional Amendment by Popular Vote." *Annals of the American Academy of Political and Social Science* 43 (Sept. 1912): 311–25.

———. "The Recall of Judicial Decisions." *Proceedings of the Academy of Political Science* 2 (Jan. 1913): 37–47.

Lillard, Richard G. "Agricultural Statesman: Charles C. Teague of Santa Paula." *California History* 65 (Mar. 1986): 2–16.

Link, Arthur S. *Wilson: The Road to the White House*. Princeton: Princeton University Press, 1947.

Lippmann, Walter. *The Phantom Public*. Boston: Harcourt Brace, 1925.

———. *Public Opinion*. New York: Macmillan, 1922.

Lo, Clarence Y. H. *Small Property versus Big Government: Social Origins of the Property Tax Revolt*. Berkeley: University of California Press, 1990.

Lobingier, Charles S. "Direct Legislation in the United States: Development of the System." *Political Science Quarterly* 23 (Dec. 1908): 577–86.

———. "Direct Popular Legislation: The Chief Objections Examined." *The Arena* 35 (Sept. 1905): 235–37.

———. *The People's Law; or, Popular Participation in Law-Making*. New York: Macmillan, 1909.

Lodge, Henry C. *Speech of Hon. H. C. Lodge before the Central Labor Union of Boston, Sept. 15th, 1907*. Boston, 1907.

Long, Chester I. *The Return of Representative Government. Address Delivered before the Pennsylvania Bar Association, June 23, 1927*. Philadelphia, 1927.

Loring, Augustus P. "A Short Account of the Massachusetts Constitutional Convention, 1917–1919." *New England Quarterly* 6 (1933): 9–56.

Lowell, Abbott L. *Public Opinion and Popular Government*. New York: Longmans, 1913.

———. "Referendum in Switzerland and America." *Atlantic Monthly* 72 (Apr. 1894): 517–26.

Lowenstein, Daniel H. "California Initiative and the Single-Subject Rule." *UCLA Law Review* 30 (June 1983): 936–75.

———. "Campaign Spending and Ballot Propositions: Recent Experience, Public Choice Theory, and the First Amendment." *UCLA Law Review* 29 (Mar. 1982): 505–641.

Lower, Richard C. *A Bloc of One: The Political Career of Hiram W. Johnson*. Stanford: Stanford University Press, 1993.

Lowitt, Richard. *George W. Norris: The Making of a Progressive, 1861–1912*. Syracuse: Syracuse University Press, 1963.

Lowrie, S. Gale. "New Forms of the Initiative and Referendum." *American Political Science Review* 5 (Nov. 1911): 566–72.

Luce, Robert. *The Public Opinion Bill; Speech of Robert Luce before the Central Labor Union of Boston, October 20, 1907*. Boston, 1907.

Lundberg, Alfred J. "California Republic, 1940 Model." *California — Magazine of the Pacific* 29 (Oct. 1939): 4–5, 30, 32.

Luntz, Frank I. *Candidates, Consultants, and Campaigns: The Style and Substance of American Electioneering*. Oxford: Oxford University Press, 1988.

Lustig, R. Jeffrey. *Corporate Liberalism: The Origins of Modern American Political Theory, 1890–1920*. Berkeley: University of California Press, 1982.

Lutz, Donald S. *Popular Consent and Popular Control: Whig Political Theory in the Early State Constitutions*. Baton Rouge: Louisiana State University Press, 1980.

Lydenberg, Steven D. *Bankrolling Ballots Update 1980: The Role of Business in Financing Ballot Question Campaigns*. New York: Council on Economic Priorities, 1979.

Lyon, Henry S. "What Proportion of Voters Neglect to Go to the Polls?" *Yale Journal* 17 (May 1908): 85–92.

M. O'B. "Open-Air Parliaments in Switzerland." *The Nation* 80 (June 8, 1905): 456–57.

McAfee, Ward. *California's Railroad Era, 1850–1911*. San Marino: Golden West Books, 1973.

McCall, Samuel W. "Representative as against Direct Government." *Atlantic Monthly* 108 (Oct. 1911): 454–64.

McCarthy, Charles. *The Wisconsin Idea*. New York: Macmillan, 1912.

McCay, Bruce B. "Judicial Recall." *Century Magazine* 84 (May 1912): 15–21.

McClintock, Thomas C. "J. Allen Smith, a Pacific Northwest Progressive." *Pacific Northwest Quarterly* 53 (Apr. 1962): 49–59.

———. "Seth Lewelling, William S. U'Ren, and the Birth of the Oregon Progressive Movement." *Oregon Historical Quarterly* 68 (Sept. 1967): 197–220.

McCormick, Richard L. "The Discovery That Business Corrupts Politics: A Reappraisal of the Origins of Progressivism." In *The Party Period and Public Policy: American Politics from the Age of Jackson to the Progressive Era*, edited by Richard L. McCormick, 311–55. New York: Oxford University Press, 1986.

———. *From Realignment to Reform: Political Change in New York State, 1893–1910*. Ithaca: Cornell University Press, 1981.

———. "Introduction." In *The Party Period and Public Policy: American Politics from the Age of Jackson to the Progressive Era*, edited by Richard L. McCormick, 3–25. New York: Oxford University Press, 1986.

McCoy, Drew R. *The Elusive Republic: Political Economy in Jeffersonian America*. Chapel Hill: University of North Carolina Press, 1980.

McCrackan, W. D. *An American Abroad and at Home*. New York: Franklin, 1924.

———. "The Initiative in Switzerland." *The Arena*. 7 (Apr. 1893): 548–53.

———. "The Swiss and American Constitutions." *The Arena* 4 (July 1891): 172–79.

———. "The Swiss Referendum." *The Arena* 3 (Mar. 1891): 458–64.

———. *Swiss Solutions to American Problems*. New York: Concord Cooperative Printing, 1897.

McCraw, Thomas K. *Prophets of Regulation: Charles Francis Adams, Louis D. Brandeis, James M. Landis, Alfred E. Kahn*. Cambridge: Harvard University Press, 1984.

———. "Rethinking the Trust Question." In *Regulation in Perspective*, edited by Thomas K. McCraw, 1–55. Cambridge: Harvard University Press, 1981.

McCurdy, Charles W. "Justice Field and the Jurisprudence of Government-Business Relations: Some Parameters of Laissez-Faire Constitutionalism, 1863–1897." *Journal of American History* 61 (Mar. 1975): 970–1005.

McDonagh, Eileen. "The 'Welfare Rights State' and the 'Civil Rights State': Policy Paradox and State Building in the Progressive Era." *Studies in American Political Development* 7 (Fall 1993): 258–61.

McDonald, Terrence J. *The Parameters of Urban Fiscal Policy: Socioeconomic Change and Political Culture in San Francisco, 1860–1900*. Berkeley: University of California Press, 1986.

McDonald-Valesh, Eva. "The Strength and Weakness of the People's Movement." *The Arena* 5 (May 1892): 726–31.

McDonough, James B. "The Recall of Decisions: A Fallacy." *Central Law Journal* 75 (July 12, 1912): 35–40.

McGerr, Michael. *The Decline of Popular Politics: The American North, 1865–1928*. New York: Oxford University Press, 1986.

McGuigan, Patrick B. *The Politics of Direct Democracy in the 1980s: Case Studies in Popular Decision Making*. Washington, D.C.: Free Congress Foundation, 1985.

Mackaye, Susannah D. A. "California Proposition 63: Language Attitudes Reflected in the Public Debate." *Annals of the American Academy of Political and Social Science* 508 (Mar. 1990): 135–46.

McKee, Irving. "The Background and Early Career of Hiram Warren Johnson, 1866–1910." *Pacific Historical Review* 19 (Feb. 1950): 17–30.

McMath, Robert C., Jr. *American Populism: A Social History*. New York: Hill and Wang, 1993.

McNall, Scott G. *The Road to Rebellion: Class Formation and Kansas Populism, 1865–1900*. Chicago: University of Chicago Press, 1988.

McWilliams, Carey. "Government by Whitaker and Baxter." Parts 1–3.

The Nation (Apr. 14, Apr. 21, May 5, 1951): 346–48, 366–69, 418–21.

———. *Southern California Country: An Island on the Land*. New York: Duell, Sloan and Pearce, 1946.

Magleby, David B. *Direct Legislation: Voting on Ballot Propositions in the United States*. Baltimore: Johns Hopkins University Press, 1984.

———. "Taking the Initiative: Direct Legislation and Direct Democracy in the 1980s." *Political Science and Politics* 21 (Summer 1988): 600–611.

Manahan, James. *The Recall of Judges*. 62d Cong., 2d Sess., 1912. S. Doc. 941.

Margulies, Herbert F. *The Decline of the Progressive Movement in Wisconsin, 1890–1920*. Madison: University of Wisconsin Press, 1968.

Martin, Edward D. *History of the Grange; or, The Farmer's War against Monopolies*. Philadelphia: National Publishing Company, 1873.

Martin, Roscoe C. *The People's Party in Texas: A Study in Third Party Politics*. Austin: University of Texas Press, 1933.

Mathews, John M. *American State Government*. New York: Appleton, 1934.

Maxey, Edwin. "The Referendum in America." *The Arena* 24 (July 1900): 47–52.

May, James. "Antitrust in the Formative Era: Political and Economic Theory in Constitutional and Antitrust Analysis." *Ohio State Law Journal* 60 (1989): 258–395.

Maynard, David M. "The Operation of the Referendum in Chicago." Ph.D. diss., University of Chicago, 1930.

Meade, E. S. "The Fallacy of 'Big Business.'" *Annals* 42 (July 1912): 83–88.

Melcher, Daniel P. "The Challenge to Normalcy: The 1924 Election in California." *Southern California Quarterly* 60 (Summer 1978): 155–82.

Memorial of State Referendum League of Maine, Concerning Initiative and Referendum. 60th Cong., 1st Sess., 1908. S. Doc. 521.

Memorial Relative to a National Initiative and Referendum, 60th Cong., 1st Sess., 1908. S. Doc. 516.

Merwin, H. C. "The People in Government." *Atlantic Monthly* 63 (Apr. 1889): 433–41.

Meyers, Marvin. *The Jacksonian Persuasion: Politics and Belief*. Stanford: Stanford University Press, 1957.

Meyers, William. *The Image Makers: Power and Persuasion on Madison Avenue*. New York: Times Books, 1984.

Michelson, Charles. *The Ghost Talks*. New York: G. P. Putnam's Sons, 1944.

Milkis, Sidney M., and Daniel J. Tichenor. "'Direct Democracy' and Social Justice: The Progressive Party Campaign of 1912." *Studies in American Political Development* 8 (Fall 1994): 282–340.

Miller, George H. *Railroads and the Granger Laws*. Madison: University of Wisconsin Press, 1971.

Miller, Grace L. "The Origins of the San Diego Lincoln–Roosevelt League, 1905–1909." *Southern California Quarterly* 60 (Winter 1978–79): 421–43.

Minar, David W. "Voting Behavior on Recent Labor Measures in California." Master's thesis, University of California at Berkeley, 1951.

"Misuse of Referendum," *California Outlook* 12 (Feb. 3, 1912): 7–8.

Moffett, Samuel. "The Railroad Commission of California: A Study in Irresponsible Government." *Annals* 6 (1895): 469–77.

———. "The Referendum in California." *Political Science Quarterly* 13 (Mar. 1898): 1–18.

Monod, David. *Store Wars: Shopkeepers and the Culture of Mass Marketing, 1890–1930*. Toronto: University of Toronto Press, 1996.

Montgomery, David. *Beyond Equality: Labor and the Radical Republicans, 1862–1872*. New York: Knopf, 1967.

———. "William H. Sylvis and the Search for Working-Class Citizenship." In *Labor Leaders in America*, edited by Melvyn Dubofsky and Warren Van Tine, 3–29. Urbana: University of Illinois Press, 1987.

Montgomery, Mary, and Marion Clawson. *History of Legislation and Policy Formation of the Central Valley Project*. Berkeley: University of California Press, 1946.

Moore, Winston, and Marian Moore. *Out of the Frying Pan*. Los Angeles: De Voss, 1939.

Morris, John R. *Davis H. Waite: The Ideology of a Western Populist*. Washington, D.C.: University Press of America, 1982.

Morton, Richard A. "Edward F. Dunne: Illinois' Most Progressive Governor." *Illinois Historical Journal* 83 (Winter 1990–91): 218–34.

Mowry, George E. "The California Progressive and His Rationale: A Study in Middle Class Politics." *Mississippi Valley Historical Review* 36 (Sept. 1949): 239–50.

———. *The California Progressives*. Berkeley: University of California Press, 1951.

———. *Theodore Roosevelt and the Progressive Movement*. Madison: University of Wisconsin Press, 1946.

Munro, William B. *The Initiative, Referendum, and Recall*. New York: Appleton 1912.

———. "Initiative and Referendum." In *Encyclopedia of the Social Sciences*, edited by E. R. A. Seligman and Alvin Johnson, 8:50–52. New York: Macmillan, 1932.

Murrin, John M. "A Roof without Walls: The Dilemma of American National Identity." In *Beyond Confederation: Origins of the Constitution and American National Identity*, edited by Richard Beeman, Stephen Botein, and Edward C. Carter II, 333–48. Chapel Hill: University of North Carolina Press, 1987.

Myers, William A. *Iron Men and Copper Wires: A Centennial History of the Southern California Edison Company*. Glendale, Calif.: Trans-Anglo Books, 1983.

Myrick, O. H. "The Initiative and Referendum." *The Arena* 68 (May 21, 1909): 383–90.

Nash, Gerald D. "The California Railroad Commission, 1876–1911." *Southern California Quarterly* 44 (Dec. 1962): 287–305.

National Popular Government League. *The Initiative and Referendum Elections of 1924*. Bulletin No. 97. Washington D.C., 1925.

Nelson, William E. *Americanization of the Common Law: The Impact of Legal Change on Massachusetts, 1760–1830*. Cambridge: Harvard University Press, 1975.

Newlands, Francis G. "Review and Criticism of Anti-Trust Legislation." *Annals of the American Academy of Political and Social Science* 42 (July 1912): 289–95.

Nichols, Abner W. "Present Status of the Referendum Movement in Maine." *The Arena* 36 (Nov. 1906): 516–18.

Nisbet, Robert A. "The Dilemma of Conservatives in a Populist Society." *Policy Review* 4 (Spring 1978): 91–104.

———. "Public Opinion versus Popular Opinion." *Public Interest* 41 (Fall 1975): 166–92.

"Non-Partisan Ballot Acts." *Transactions of the Commonwealth Club of California* 10 (Oct. 1915): 459–86.

Nordin, D. Sven. *Rich Harvest: A History of the Grange, 1867–1900*. Jackson: University Press of Mississippi, 1974.

Nugent, Walter T. K. *Money and American Society 1865–1880*. New York: Free Press, 1968.

———. *The Tolerant Populists: Kansas Populism and Nativism*. Chicago: University of Chicago Press, 1963.

Oberholtzer, Ellis P. "Direct Legislation in America." *The Arena* 24 (Nov. 1900): 493–505.

——. "Law Making by Popular Vote; or, the American Referendum." *Annals* 2 (Nov. 1891): 324–44.

——. *The Referendum in America: A Discussion of Lawmaking by Popular Vote*. Philadelphia: University of Pennsylvania Press, 1893.

——. *The Referendum in America Together with Some Chapters on the Initiative and the Recall*. New York: Charles Scribner's Sons, 1912.

Odegard, Peter. *Pressure Politics: The Story of the Anti-Saloon League*. New York: Octagon, 1966.

Oestreicher, Richard. "Terence V. Powderly, the Knights of Labor, and Artisanal Republicanism." In *Labor Leaders in America*, edited by Melvyn Dubofsky and Warren Van Tine, 30–61. Urbana: University of Illinois Press, 1987.

——. "Urban Working-Class Political Behavior and Theories of American Electoral Politics, 1870–1940." *Journal of American History* 74 (Mar. 1988): 1257–86.

Official Report of the National Anti-Trust Conference. Chicago, 1900.

Ogburn, William F., and Delvin Peterson. "Political Thought of Social Classes." *Political Science Quarterly* 31 (June 1916): 300–317.

Olin, Spencer C., Jr. *California's Prodigal Sons: Hiram Johnson and the Progressives, 1911–1917*. Berkeley: University of California Press, 1968.

——. "Hiram Johnson, the Lincoln–Roosevelt League, and the Election of 1910." *California Historical Society Quarterly* 45 (Sept. 1966): 225–40.

O'Neal, Emmet. "Distrust of State Legislatures — The Cause; The Remedy." *North American Review* 199 (May 1914): 684–99.

——. *Representative Government and the Common Law: A Study of the Initiative and Referendum*, 62d Cong., 2d Sess., 1912. S. Doc. 240.

Ormsby, Herbert. "Our Neighbors 'The Ham and Eggers.'" *California — Magazine of the Pacific* 29 (July 1939): 14, 30–31.

Ostler, Jeffrey. *Prairie Populism: The Fate of Agrarian Radicalism in Kansas, Nebraska, and Iowa, 1880–1892*. Lawrence: University of Kansas Press, 1993.

Ostrander, Gilman M. *The Prohibition Movement in California, 1848–1933*. Berkeley: University of California Press, 1957.

Ostrogorski, Moisei. *Democracy and the Organization of Political Parties, Vol. II: The United States*. Edited and abridged by S. M. Lipset. Garden City, N.Y.: Anchor Books, 1964.

Ostrom, Vincent. *Water and Politics: A Study of Water Policies and*

Administration in the Development of Los Angeles. Los Angeles: Haynes Foundation, 1953.

Overton, Gwendolyn. "Democracy and the Recall." *Forum* 47 (Feb. 1912): 157–68.

Owen, Robert L. "The Initiative and Referendum in its Relation to the Political and Physical Health of a Nation." *Twentieth Century Magazine* 2 (June 1910): 195–98.

——. *Judicial Recall*, 62d Cong., 2d Sess., 1912. S. Doc. 249.

——. "The Restoration of Popular Rule: The Greatest of All Non-Partisan Issues." *The Arena* 39 (June 1908): 643–50.

Owens, John R., and Edward C. Olson. "Campaign Spending and the Electoral Process in California, 1966–1974." *Western Political Quarterly* 30 (Dec. 1977): 493–512.

Owens, John R., and Larry L. Wade. "Campaign Spending on California Propositions, 1924–1984: Trends and Voting Effects." *Western Political Quarterly* 39 (Dec. 1987): 675–89.

Owens, Kenneth. "Government and Politics in the Nineteenth-Century West." In *Historians and the American West*, edited by Michael P. Malone, 148–176. Lawrence: University of Kansas Press, 1983.

——. "Pattern and Structure in Western Territorial Politics." *Western Historical Quarterly* 1 (Oct. 1970): 373–92.

Paine, Robert T., Jr. "Direct Legislation in Massachusetts." *Twentieth Century Magazine* 2 (July 1910): 334–37.

——. "The Initiative, the Referendum, and the Recall in American Cities." *Proceedings of the National Municipal League* (1908): 223–46.

——. "Lincoln's Ideal Carried Out in Oregon." *The Arena* 40 (Oct. 1908): 283–86.

——. "The Referendum and Initiative in American Cities." *Equity* 12 (Jan. 1910): 223–46.

Palmer, Bruce. *"Man Over Money": The Southern Populist Critique of American Capitalism*. Chapel Hill: University of North Carolina Press, 1980.

"The Paramount Issue." *The Outlook* (May 28, 1910): 134.

Parsons, Frank. *The City for the People*. Philadelphia: C. F. Taylor, 1900.

——. *Direct Legislation; or, The Veto Power in the Hands of the People*. Philadelphia: C. F. Taylor, 1900.

Parsons, Stanley B., Karen T. Parsons, Walter Killilae, and Beverly Borgers. "The Role of Cooperatives in the Development of the Movement Culture of Populism." *Journal of American History* 69 (Mar. 1983): 885.

Peffer, William A. *The Farmer's Side: His Troubles and Their Remedies*.
New York: Appleton, 1891.

———. *Populism: Its Rise and Fall*, edited by Peter H. Argersinger.
Lawrence: University of Kansas Press, 1992.

Pegram, Thomas R. "The Dry Machine: The Formation of the Anti-
Saloon League of Illinois." *Illinois Historical Journal* 83 (Fall 1990):
173–86.

———. *Partisans and Progressives: Private Interest and Public Policy in
Illinois, 1870–1920*. Urbana: University of Illinois Press, 1992.

———. "Temperance Politics and Regional Political Culture: The Anti-
Saloon League in Maryland and the South, 1907–1915." *Journal of
Southern History* 63 (Feb. 1997): 57–90.

Pelletier, Laurence L. *The Initiative and Referendum in Maine*.
Brunswick, Maine: Bowdoin College, 1951.

People's Economy League. *"Power at Cost." But, Oh, the Cost!!! Vote No
on Water and Power Act November 7*. Los Angeles, 1922.

Perkins, George W. "Corporations in Modern Business." *North
American Review* 187 (Mar. 1908): 388–98.

———. "Initiative and Referendum and the A. F.of L." *American
Federationist* 18 (Mar. 1911): 198–202.

Perry, Louis B., and Richard S. Perry. *A History of the Los Angeles Labor
Movement, 1911–1941*. Berkeley: University of California Press, 1963.

Pessen, Edward. *Most Uncommon Jacksonians: The Radical Leaders of the
Early Labor Movement*. Albany: SUNY Press, 1967.

Petersen, Eric F. "The Struggle for the Australian Ballot in California."
California Historical Quarterly 51 (Fall 1972): 227–43.

Philipps, David G. "The Treason of the Senate." *Cosmopolitan Magazine*
40 (Mar. 1906): 487–502.

Pillsbury, A. J. "A Study of Direct Legislation in All of its Forms as
Exemplified in the Government of the State of California in State
Affairs from the Adoption of the Constitution to the Presidential
Election of 1928" (1929). Typescript, Library of the Institute of
Governmental Affairs, University of California at Berkeley, Berkeley,
California.

Pillsbury, E. S., and Oscar Sutro. *Initiative Legislation in the Supreme
Court of the United States* (October Term, 1908, No. 822). Pacific
States Telephone and Telegraph Company v. State of Oregon; Brief
for Plaintiff in Error. Washington, D.C., 1908.

Piott, Steven L. *The Anti-Monopoly Persuasion: Popular Resistance to the
Rise of Big Business in the Midwest*. Westport, Conn.: Greenwood
Press, 1985.

———. "Giving Voters a Voice: The Struggle for Initiative and Referendum in Missouri." *Gateway Heritage* 14 (Spring 1994): 20–35.

———. "The Origins of the Initiative and Referendum in America." *Hayes Historical Journal* 11 (Spring 1992): 5–17.

———. "The Origins of the Initiative and Referendum in South Dakota: The Political Context." *Great Plains Quarterly* 12 (Summer 1992): 181–93.

Piper, Kingsbury B. "The Victorious Campaign for Direct Legislation in Maine." *The Arena* 40 Dec. 1908): 546–61.

Pisani, Donald J. "Promotion and Regulation: Constitutionalism and the American Economy." *Journal of American History* 74 (Dec. 1987): 740–68.

Pitchell, Robert J. "The Electoral System and Voting Behavior: The Case of California's Cross-Filing." *Western Political Quarterly* 12 (June 1959): 459–84.

———. "The Influence of Professional Campaign Management Firms in Partisan Elections in California." *Western Political Quarterly* 11 (June 1958): 278–300.

Poindexter, Miles. *The Recall of Judges*. 62d Cong., 2d Sess., 1912. S. Doc. 472.

Pollack, Norman. *The Just Polity: Populism, Law, and Human Welfare*. Urbana: University of Illinois Press, 1987.

Pollock, James K. *The Initiative and Referendum in Michigan*. Ann Arbor: University of Michigan Press, 1940.

Pomeroy, Earl. *The Pacific Slope: A History of California, Oregon, Washington, Idaho, Utah, and Nevada*. New York: Knopf, 1965.

Pomeroy, Eltweed. "A Conversation with Eltweed Pomeroy, A.M., on Direct Legislation and Social Progress." *The Arena* 25 (Mar. 1901): 317–23.

———. "Democratic vs. Aristocratic Government." *The Arena* 28 (Aug. 1902): 119–24.

———. "Direct Legislation." In *The New Encyclopedia of Social Reform*, edited by W. D. P. Bliss, 384–87. New York: Funk & Wagnalls, 1908.

———. "Direct Legislation: Objections Answered." *The Arena* 22 (July 1899): 101–10.

———. "The Doorway of Reforms." *The Arena* 17 (Apr. 1897): 711–28.

———. "The Failure of Representative Government." *The Arena* 30 (Dec. 1903): 606–13.

———. "The First Discharge of a Public Servant." *Independent* 58 (Jan. 12, 1905): 69–71.

——. "How the Trusts Stifle Initiative." *The Independent* 54 (Sept. 4, 1902): 2132.

——. "Is Direct Legislation Un-American?" *The Outlook* (Feb. 16, 1895): 267–69.

——. "Needed Political Reforms." *The Arena* 28 (Nov. 1902): 464–70.

——. "The Nevada Referendum Victory as an Illustration of Democratic Progress." *The Arena* 33 (Mar. 1905): 267–69.

——. *Papers on Direct Legislation.* 55th Cong., 2d Sess., 1898. S. Doc. 340.

——. "Two Arguments against Direct Legislation." *The Arena* 31 (Feb. 1904): 153–57.

"Popular Government in Oregon." *American Federationist* 7 (July 1910): 601–2.

Posner, Russell M. "The Progressive Voters League, 1923–1926." *California Historical Society Quarterly* 36 (Sept. 1957): 251–61.

Post, Louis F. "The Initiative and Referendum." *Proceedings of the National Municipal League* (1906): 363–81.

Powers, James H. *"I & R" Ballot Questions, 1919–1986: Measures, Approvals, Rejections.* Boston: Massachusetts Legislative Research Bureau, 1987.

Price, Charles M. "Experts Explain the Business of Buying Signatures." *California Journal* 7 (July 1985): 283–86.

——. "The Initiative: A Comparative State Analysis and Reassessment of a Western Phenomenon." *Western Historical Quarterly* 28 (June 1975): 243–62.

——. "Initiative Campaigns: Afloat on a Sea of Cash." *California Journal* 19 (Nov. 1988): 180–86.

——. "The Mercenaries Who Gather Signatures for Ballot Measures." *California Journal* 12 (Oct. 1981): 357–58.

Price, Charles M., and Robert Waste. "Initiatives: Too Much of a Good Thing?" *California Journal* 22 (Mar. 1991): 116–20.

"A Primer of Direct-Legislation." *The Arena* 35 (May 1906): 507–11.

"The Progressive League Platform." *The Outlook* (Feb. 18, 1911): 346–48.

"Progressive Principles." *The Outlook* (Feb. 10, 1912): 301–2.

Proposed Amendments to Constitution, Propositions and Proposed Laws to be Submitted to the Electors of the State of California to be Held Tuesday, November 8, 1938, together with Arguments Respecting the Same. Sacramento, 1938.

Proposed Amendments to Constitution, Propositions and Proposed Laws to be Submitted to the Electors of the State of California to be Held Tuesday,

November 7, 1939, together with Arguments Respecting the Same. Sacramento, 1939.

"The Public Opinion Law of Massachusetts." *Bulletins of the Massachusetts Constitutional Convention*, 1917–1918. Vol. 1, Bulletin No. 7, 287–98. Boston, 1918.

Purcell, Edward A., Jr. *The Crisis of Democratic Theory: Scientific Naturalism and the Problem of Value.* Lexington: University of Kentucky Press, 1973.

Putnam, Jackson K. *Old-Age Politics in California: From Richardson to Reagan.* Stanford: Stanford University Press, 1970.

———. "The Persistence of Progressivism in the 1920s: The Case of California." *Pacific Historical Review* 35 (Nov. 1966): 395–411.

"Race Segregation in St. Louis." *National Municipal Review* 5 (Apr. 1916): 315.

Radabaugh, John S. "Tendencies of California Direct Legislation." *Southwestern Social Science Quarterly* 42 (June 1962): 66–78.

Radin, Max. "Popular Legislation in California." *Minnesota Law Review* 23 (Apr. 1939): 559–84.

———. "Popular Legislation in California: 1936–1946." *California Law Review* 35 (June 1947): 171–90.

Ramage, B. J. "Municipal Referendum." *The Nation* 74 (May 8, 1902): 364–65.

Ramsey, Russell. "Initiative, Referendum, and Recall Votes of 1919." *National Municipal Review* 9 (Mar. 1920): 146–50.

Ranney, Austin. *Curing the Mischiefs of Faction: Party Reform in America.* Berkeley: University of California Press, 1975.

———, ed. *The Referendum Device.* Washington, D.C.: AEI, 1981.

Ranson, William L. *Majority Rule and the Judiciary: An Examination of Current Proposals for Constitutional Change Affecting the Relation of Courts to Legislation.* New York: Scribner, 1912.

Rappard, William E. "The Initiative, Referendum, and Recall in Switzerland." *Annals of the American Academy of Political and Social Science* 43 (Sept. 1912).

Raucher, Alan R. *Public Relations and Business, 1900–1929.* Baltimore: Johns Hopkins University Press, 1968.

Raymond, Valerie. *Surviving Proposition Thirteen: Fiscal Crisis in California Counties.* Berkeley: University of California Press, 1988.

"'Real' Popular Government." *The Nation* 95 (Oct. 10, 1912): 324–25.

"The Recall of Officers." *Bulletins of the Massachusetts Constitutional Convention.* Vol. 2, Bulletin No. 26, 283–301. Boston, 1919.

Reed, Henry. "Some Late Efforts at Constitutional Reform." *North American Review* 121 (July 1875): 1–36.

Reed, Thomas H. *Government for the People.* New York: B. W. Huebsch, 1919.

"The Referendum." *The Nation* 58 (Mar. 22, 1894): 206–7.

"The Referendum in Maine." *The Nation* 93 (Sept. 21, 1911): 256.

Reinsch, Paul S. "The Initiative and Referendum." *Proceedings of the Academy of Political Science* 3 (Jan. 1913): 155–61.

Reiter, Howard L. "The Bases of Progressivism within the Major Parties: Evidence from the National Conventions." *Social Science History* 22 (Spring 1998): 83–116.

"Report of the Special Committee on Election Expenditures." *Journal of the Senate during the 45th Session of the Legislature of the State of California.* Sacramento, 1923.

Report of the Special Committee on Initiative, Referendum, and Recall of the Pennsylvania Bar Association. Cape May, 1912.

Report to the Department of State by the American Vice-Consul at Berne, Switzerland, Concerning the Practical Workings of the "Popular Initiative" in Switzerland. 61st Cong., 1st Sess., 1908. S. Doc. 126.

"Restriction of Initiative on Taxation." *Transactions of the Commonwealth Club of California* 15 (Sept. 1920): 250–55.

Ricci, David M. *The Tragedy of Political Science: Politics, Scholarship, and Democracy.* New Haven: Yale University Press, 1984.

Rice, Bradley R. *Progressive Cities: The Commission Government Movement in America, 1901–1920.* Austin: University of Texas Press, 1977.

Rice, Stuart A. *Quantitative Methods in Politics.* New York: Russell & Russell, 1928.

Riesman, Janet A. "Money, Credit, and Federalist Political Economy." In *Beyond Confederation: Origins of the Constitution and American National Identity,* edited by Richard Beeman, Stephen Botein, and Edward C. Carter II, 128–61. Chapel Hill: University of North Carolina Press, 1987.

Robinson, Claude E. "Recent Developments in the Straw-Poll Field." *Public Opinion Quarterly* 1 (July 1937): 45–57.

Rodgers, Daniel T. *Atlantic Crossings: Social Politics in a Progressive Age.* Cambridge: Harvard University Press, 1998.

———. *Contested Truths: Keywords in American Politics since Independence.* New York: Basic Books, 1987.

———. "In Search of Progressivism." *Reviews in American History* 10 (Dec. 1982): 113–32.

———. "Republicanism: The Career of a Concept." *Journal of American History* 79 (June 1992): 11–38.

Roe, Gilbert E. *Our Judicial Oligarchy*. New York: B. W. Huebsch, 1912.

Rogers, Lindsay. *The Pollsters: Public Opinion, Politics, and Democratic Leadership*. New York: Knopf, 1949.

Roosevelt, Theodore. "Arizona and the Recall of the Judiciary." *The Outlook* (June 24, 1911): 378–79.

———. "A Charter of Democracy: Address before the Ohio Constitutional Convention." *The Outlook* 100 (Feb. 24, 1912): 390–402.

———. "Nationalism and Democracy." *The Outlook* (Mar. 25, 1911): 622–25.

———. "Nationalism and Special Privilege." *The Outlook* (Jan. 28, 1911): 145–48.

———. "Progressive Democracy: The People and the Courts." *The Outlook* (Aug. 17, 1912): 855–57.

———. "The Progressives, Past and Present." *The Outlook* (Sept. 3, 1910): 19–30.

———. "The Right of the People to Review Judge-Made Law." *The Outlook* (Aug. 8, 1914): 843–44, 855–56.

Root, Elihu. "Experiments in Government and the Essentials of the Constitution." *North American Review* 198 (July 1913): 1–17.

Rosenbloom, David L. *The Election Men: Professional Campaign Managers and American Democracy*. New York: Quadrangle, 1973.

Ross, Dorothy. "The Liberal Tradition Revisited and the Republican Tradition Addressed." In *New Directions in American Intellectual History*, edited by John Higham and Paul K. Conklin, 116–31. Baltimore: Johns Hopkins University Press, 1979.

Ross, Irwin. "The Supersalesmen of California Politics: Whitaker and Baxter." *Harper's Magazine* 219 (July 1959): 55–61.

Ross, Steven J. "The Culture of Political Economy: Henry George and the American Working Class." *Southern California Quarterly* 65 (Summer 1983): 145–66.

———. *Workers on the Edge: Work, Leisure, and Politics in Industrializing Cincinnati, 1788–1890*. New York: Columbia University Press, 1985.

Ross, William G. *A Muted Fury: Populists, Progressives, and Labor Unions Confront the Courts, 1890–1937*. Princeton: Princeton University Press, 1994.

Rowell, Chester H. "The Measures on the Ballot." *California Outlook* 20 (Nov. 1916): 181.

———. "Non-Partisanship." *California Outlook* 18 (Mar. 27, 1915): 3.

———. "The Referendum on Non-Partisanship." *California Outlook* 18 (May 15, 1915): 3.

———. "Remarks on Mr. Herbert Croly's Paper on 'State Political Reorganization,'" *Proceedings of the APSA* 8 (1911): 140–51.

———. "The State." *California Outlook* 12 (Jan. 20, 1912): 13–14.

Rowley, William D. "The West as Laboratory and Mirror of Reform." In *The Twentieth Century West: Historical Interpretations*, edited by Gerald Nash and Richard Etulain, 339–57. Albuquerque: University of New Mexeco Press, 1989.

Rubens, William C. "The Labor Initiative of 1938: The Development of a New Orientation of Restrictive Labor Legislation in California." Master's thesis, University of California at Berkeley, 1950.

Ruppenthal, J. C. "Election Reforms: The Trend Toward Democracy." *Annals of the American Academy of Political and Social Science* 28 (Dec. 1906): 411–41.

Russell, Charles E. *The Story of the Nonpartisan League: A Chapter in American Revolution*. New York: Harper & Brothers, 1922.

Ryan, Daniel J. "The Influence of Socialism on the Ohio Constitution." *North American Review* 196 (Nov. 1912): 665–72.

Ryan, Oswald. "The Commission Plan of City Government." *American Political Science Review* 5 (Feb. 1911): 38–56.

———. *Municipal Freedom: A Study of the Commission Government*. Garden City, N.Y.: Doubleday, 1915.

Ryan, Thomas G. "Male Opponents and Supporters of Woman Suffrage: Iowa in 1916." *Annals of Iowa* 45 (Winter 1981–82): 540–42.

Ryant, Carl G. "The South and the Movement against Chain Stores." *Journal of Southern History* 39 (May 1973): 207–22.

Sabato, Larry, Jr. *The Rise of Political Consultants: New Ways of Winning Elections*. New York: Basic Books, 1981.

Saloutos, Theodore, and John D. Hicks. *Twentieth Century Populism: Agricultural Discontent in the Middle West, 1900–1939*. Lincoln: University of Nebraska Press, 1951.

Sanborn, J. B. "Popular Legislation in the United States: Value of the System." *Political Science Quarterly* 23 (Dec. 1908): 587–603.

Sanders, Elizabeth. "Farmers and the State in the Progressive Era." In *Changes in the State: Causes and Consequences*, edited by E. S. Greenberg and T. E. Mayer, 183–205. Newbury Park, Calif.: Sage, 1990.

———. "Industrial Concentration, Sectional Competition, and

Antitrust Politics in America, 1880–1980." *Studies in American Political Development* 1 (1986) 142–214.

"San Francisco Disgraced Itself." *California Outlook* 17 (Oct. 17, 1914): 4.

Schaffner, Margaret A. "The Initiative, The Referendum, and The Recall: Recent Legislation in the United States." *American Political Science Review* 2 (Nov. 1907): 32–42.

Scheiber, Harry N. "Government and the Economy: Studies of the 'Commonwealth' Policy in Nineteenth-Century America." *Journal of Interdisciplinary History* 3 (Summer 1972): 135–51.

Schiesl, Martin J. "Politicians in Disguise: The Changing Roles of Public Administrators in Los Angeles, 1900–1920." In *The Age of Urban Reform: New Perspectives on the Progressive Era*, edited by Michael H. Ebner and Eugene M. Tobin, 102–116. Port Washington, N.Y.: Kennikat, 1977.

———. *The Politics of Efficiency: Municipal Administration and Reform in America, 1880–1920*. Berkeley: University of California Press, 1977.

———. "Progressive Reform in Los Angeles under Mayor Alexander, 1909–1913." *California Historical Quarterly* 51 (Spring 1975): 37–56.

Schlup, Leonard. "Republican Insurgent: Jonathan Bourne and the Politics of Progressivism, 1908–1912." *Oregon Historical Quarterly* 87 (Fall 1986): 229–43.

Schmidt, David D. *Citizen Lawmakers: The Ballot Initiative Revolution*. Philadelphia: Temple University Press, 1989.

Schnader, W. A. "Proper Safeguards for the Initiative and Referendum." *American Political Science Review* 10 (Aug. 1916): 515–31.

Schumacher, Waldo. "Thirty Years of the People's Rule in Oregon: An Analysis." *Political Science Quarterly* 47 (June 1932): 242–58.

Schwartz, Arthur A. "Initiative Held in Reserve: Although Its Use in Ohio Has Diminished, It Has Proved Value, Enabling Aroused Public to Override Legislature." *National Municipal Review* 41 (Mar. 1952): 142–45, 174.

"The Seattle Recall." *The Outlook* (Feb. 11, 1911): 295.

Seavey, Clyde L. "The Single-Tax Amendment." *California Outlook* 20 (Nov. 1916): 182.

Segal, Morley. "James Rolph, Jr., and the Early Days of the San Francisco Municipal Railway." *California Historical Society Quarterly* 43 (Mar. 1964): 3–18.

Seidelman, Raymond. *Disenchanted Realists: Political Science and the American Crisis, 1884–1984*. Albany: SUNY Press, 1985.

Selig, John M. "San Francisco Upholds Mayor." *National Municipal Review* 35 (Oct. 1946): 467–69.

Seymour, Charles, and Donald P. Frary. *How the World Votes: The Story of Democratic Development in Elections.* Vol. I. Springfield, Mass.: C. A. Nichols, 1918.

Shade, William G. *Banks or No Banks: The Money Issue in Western Politics, 1832–1865.* Detroit: Wayne State University Press, 1972.

Shalhope, Robert E. *John Taylor of Caroline: Pastoral Republican.* Columbia: University of South Carolina Press, 1980.

———. "Towards a Republican Synthesis: The Emergence of an Understanding of Republicanism in American Historiography." *William and Mary Quarterly* 29 (Jan. 1972): 49–80.

Sharp, James R. *The Jacksonians versus the Banks: Politics in the States after the Panic of 1837.* New York: Columbia University Press, 1970.

Shefter, Martin. "Regional Receptivity to Reform: The Legacy of the Progressive Era." *Political Science Quarterly* 98 (Fall 1983): 459–83.

Sheppard, John S., Jr. "Concerning the Decline of the Principle of Representation in Popular Government." *Forum* 43 (June 1910): 642–50.

Sherman, Roger. *A Brief Review of the Legislation against Corrupt Practices at Elections.* Chicago: Hamilton Club of Chicago, 1899.

Sherwood, T. A. "The Initiative and Referendum under the United States Constitution." *Central Law Journal* 13 (Mar. 27, 1903): 247–51.

Shibley, George H. *A Brief Review of Organized Labor's Non-Partisan Campaign for Majority Rule.* Washington, D.C., 1902.

———. "Guarded Representative Government — The Vital Demand of Democracy." *The Arena* 35 (Nov. 1905): 462–64.

———. "The Initiative and Referendum in 1909." *American Federationist* 17 (Feb. 1910): 122–23.

———. "Initiative and Referendum in Practical Operation." *The Arena* 40 (Aug.–Sept. 1908): 142–50.

———. "Judges Attack Oregon Amendment for Majority Rule." *The Arena* 30 (Dec. 1903): 613–16.

———. *The Money Question.* Chicago: Stable Money Publishing Company, 1896.

———. *The People's Sovereignty versus Trustocracy.* Special issue of the *Pennsylvania Grange News.* Chambersburg, 1904.

———. "The Possibilities in Recent Electoral Reforms." *American Federationist* 17 (Mar. 1910): 214–16.

———. "Referendum and Initiative in Relation to Municipal Ownership." *Municipal Affairs* 6 (Winter 1902–3): 781–86.

———. "The Victorious March of Majority Rule." *The Arena* 29 (Feb. 1903): 173–85.

Shippee, Lester B. "Washington's First Experiment in Direct Legislation." *Political Science Quarterly* 30 (June 1915): 235–53.

Shockley, John S. *The Initiative Process in Colorado Politics: An Assessment.* Boulder: University of Colorado Press, 1980.

A Short Form of State Constitution Submitted to the New York State Constitutional Convention and the People of the State for Consideration, by the Referendum League of Erie County. Buffalo, 1914.

Shumsky, Neil. *The Evolution of Political Protest and the Workingmen's Party in California.* Columbus: Ohio State University Press, 1991.

Single Tax League of California. *Program of the Single Tax League.* Los Angeles, 1922.

Sinsheimer, Paul. "Commission Government: Public Utility Regulation in California." *The Outlook* (Sept. 6, 1916): 31–34.

Sitton, Tom. "Another Generation of Urban Reformers: Los Angeles in the 1930s." *Western Historical Quarterly* 18 (July 1987) 315–32.

——. "California's Practical Idealist: John Randolph Haynes." *California History* 67 (Mar. 1988): 2–17.

——. *John Randolph Haynes: California Progressive.* Stanford: Stanford University Press, 1992.

——. "John Randolph Haynes and the Left Wing of California Progressivism." In *California Progressivism Revisited*, edited by William Deverell and Tom Sitton, 15–33. Berkeley: University of California Press, 1994.

Sklar, Martin J. *The Corporate Reconstruction of American Capitalism, 1890–1916: The Market, the Law, and Politics.* New York: Cambridge University Press, 1988.

Skowronek, Stephen. *Building a New American State: The Expansion of National Administrative Capacities, 1877–1920.* Cambridge: Cambridge University Press, 1982.

Smith, Alford F. "Can We Afford the Initiative?" *National Municipal Review* 38 (Oct. 1949): 437–42.

Smith, Charles W. *Public Opinion in a Democracy: A Study in American Politics.* New York: Prentice-Hall, 1939.

Smith, Herbert K. "Corporate Regulation — An Administrative Office." *Annals of the American Academy of Political and Social Science* 42 (July 1912): 284–88.

Smith, J. Allen. "Effect of State Regulation of Public Utilities upon Municipal Home Rule." *Annals of the American Academy of Political and Social Science* 53 (May 1914): 85–93.

——. "Recent Institutional Legislation." *Proceedings of the American Political Science Association* 4 (1907): 141–51.

——. *The Spirit of American Government: A Study of the Constitution; Its Origin, Influence, and Relation to Democracy*. New York: Macmillan, 1907.

Smith, T. V. "The Voice of the People." *Annals* 169 (Sept. 1933): 109.

Sponholtz, Lloyd L. "The Initiative and Referendum: Direct Democracy in Perspective, 1898–1920." *American Studies* 14 (Fall 1973): 43–64.

——. "The Politics of Temperance in Ohio, 1880–1912." *Ohio History* 85 (Winter 1976–77): 4–27.

Stagner, Stephen. "The Recall of Judicial Decisions and the Due Process Debate." *American Journal of Legal History* 24 (July 1980): 257–72.

Starr, Kevin. *Inventing the Dream: California through the Progressive Era*. New York: Oxford University Press, 1985.

"The Statehood Veto." *The Outlook* (Aug. 26, 1911): 912.

Statewide Council against Single Tax. *Research Reference Manual*. San Francisco, 1938.

Steffens, Lincoln. "Sending a State to School." *American Magazine* 68 (Feb. 1909): 349–64.

——. "U'Ren, The Law Giver: The Legislative Blacksmith of Oregon and the Tools He Has Fashioned for Democracy." *American Magazine* 65 (Mar. 1908): 527–40.

Sterne, Simon. "Crude Methods of Legislation." *North American Review* 137 (June 1883): 158–71.

Stettner, Edward A. *Shaping Modern Liberalism: Herbert Croly and Progressive Thought*. Lawrence: University of Kansas Press, 1993.

Stimson, Grace. *Rise of the Labor Movement in Los Angeles*. Berkeley: University of California Press, 1955.

Stockbridge, Frank P. "The Single Taxers: Who They Are, and What They Are Doing." *Everybody's Magazine* 26 (Apr. 1912): 507–22.

Strum, Philippa. *Louis D. Brandeis: Justice for the People*. Cambridge: Harvard University Press, 1984.

——. *The Supreme Court and "Political Questions": A Study in Judicial Evasion*. Tuscaloosa: University of Alabama Press, 1974.

Sullivan, James W. *Direct Legislation by the Citizenship through the Initiative and Referendum*. New York: Twentieth Century Publisher, 1892.

——. "Direct Legislation in Massachusetts." *American Federationist* 1 (Mar. 1894): 9, 14.

——. "The Referendum in Switzerland." *The Chautauquan* 13 (Apr. 1891): 29–34.

Summers, Mark W. *The Era of Good Stealings*. New York: Oxford
    University Press, 1993.
——. *The Plundering Generation: Corruption and the Crisis of the Union,
    1849–1861*. New York: Oxford University Press, 1987.
*Supplemental Memorial of Initiative and Referendum League relative to
    National Initiative and Referendum*. 60th Cong., 1st Sess., 1908.
    S. Doc. 529.
Swanson, David L., and Paolo Mancini, eds. *Politics, Media, and Modern
    Democracy: An International Study of Innovations in Electoral
    Campaigning and Their Consequences*. Westport, Conn.: Praeger,
    1996.
Taft, Philip. *Labor Politics, American Style: The California State Federation
    of Labor*. Cambridge: Harvard University Press, 1968.
Taft, William H. *Popular Government: Its Essence, Its Permanence, and Its
    Perils*. New Haven: Yale University Press, 1913.
——. *Special Message of the President of the United States, Returning
    without Approval House Joint Resolution No. 14*. 62d Cong., 1st Sess.,
    1911. H. Doc. 106.
Tatalovich, Raymond. *Nativism Reborn? The Official English Language
    Movement and the American States*. Lexington: University of
    Kentucky Press, 1995.
Taylor, Charles F. "The March of Democracy in Municipalities."
    National Municipal Review 2 (Apr. 1913): 194–99.
——. "Municipal Initiative, Referendum, and Recall in Practice."
    National Municipal Review (Oct. 1914): 693–701.
Taylor, Frank J. "Advertising Man." *California — Magazine for Pacific
    Business* 27 (July 1937): 20–21, 30.
Taylor, George Rogers. *The Transportation Revolution, 1815–1860*. New
    York: Rinehart & Co., 1951.
Teaford, Jon C. "Finis for Tweed and Stevens: Rewriting the History of
    Urban Rule." *Reviews in American History* 10 (1982): 133–49.
——. *The Unheralded Triumph: City Government in America, 1870–1900*.
    Baltimore: Johns Hopkins University Press, 1984.
Teague, Charles C. *Fifty Years a Rancher*. Los Angeles: Ward Ritchie,
    1944.
Teal, Joseph N. "The Practical Workings of the Initiative and
    Referendum in Oregon." *Proceedings of the National Municipal League*
    (1909): 309–25.
Tedlow, Richard S. *Keeping the Corporate Image: Public Relations and
    Business, 1900–1950*. Greenwich, Conn.: JAI Press, 1979.
Thatcher, George A. "The Initiative, Referendum and Popular Election

of Senators in Oregon." *American Political Science Review* 2 (Nov. 1908): 601–5.

———. "The Initiative and Referendum in Oregon." *Proceedings of the American Political Science Association* 4 (1907): 198–221.

Thayer, Ezra R. *Recall of Judicial Decisions.* 63d Cong., 1st Sess., 1913. S. Doc. 124.

Thelen, David P. *The New Citizenship: Origins of Progressivism in Wisconsin, 1885–1900.* Columbia: University of Missouri Press, 1972.

"$30 a Week for Life." *Tax Digest* 16 (Oct. 1938): 340–41, 353–57.

"$30 Every Thursday: Analysis of Proposed Life Payments Initiative." *Tax Digest* 16 (Sept. 1938): 300–301, 311.

Thomas, David Y. "Direct Legislation in Arkansas." *Political Science Quarterly* 29 (Mar. 1914): 84–110.

———. "The Initiative and Referendum in Arkansas Come of Age." *American Political Science Review* 27 (Feb. 1933): 66–75.

Thomas, Tom E. "Corporate Political Strategy and Influence in the California Initiative Process." Ph.D. diss., University of California at Berkeley, 1989.

———. "Has Business 'Captured the California Initiative Agenda?'" *California Management Review* 33 (Fall 1990): 131–47.

Throne, Mildred. "The Anti-Monopoly Party in Iowa, 1873–1874." *Iowa Journal of History* 52 (Oct. 1954): 289–326.

Timberlake, James H. *Prohibition and the Progressive Movement, 1900–1920.* Cambridge: Harvard University Press, 1965.

Tobin, Eugene M. *Organize or Perish: America's Independent Progressives, 1913–1933.* Westport, Conn.: Greenwood Press, 1986.

Treleven, Dale E. "Railroads, Elevators, and Grain Dealers: The Genesis of Antimonopolism in Milwaukee." *Wisconsin Magazine of History* 52 (Spring 1979): 205–22.

Troy, Gil. *See How They Ran: The Changing Role of the Presidential Candidate.* New York: Free Press, 1991.

Turner, James. "Understanding the Populists." *Journal of American History* 67 (Sept. 1980): 354–73.

Unger, Irwin. *The Greenback Era: A Social and Political History of American Finance, 1865–1879.* Princeton: Princeton University Press, 1964.

U'Ren, William S. "The Initiative and Referendum in Oregon." *The Arena* 29 (Mar. 1903): 270–75.

———. "Remarks on Mr. Herbert Croly's Paper on 'State Political Reorganization.'" *Proceedings of the American Political Science Association* 9 (1911): 136–39.

———. "Single Tax." *Annals of the American Academy of Political and Social Science* 58 (Mar. 1915): 222–27.

———. "State and County Government in Oregon and Proposed Changes." *Annals of the American Academy of Political and Social Science* 47 (Mar. 1913): 271–73.

Urofsky, Melvin I. *A Mind of One Piece: Brandeis and American Reform.* New York: Charles Scribner's Sons, 1971.

———. "Proposed Federal Incorporation in the Progressive Era." *American Journal of Legal History* 26 (Apr. 1982): 160–83.

———. "Wilson, Brandeis, and the Trust Issue, 1912–1914." *Mid-America* 49 (Jan. 1967): 3–28.

U.S. Senate. *Hearings before a Subcommittee of the Committee on Education and Labor, Pursuant to S. R. 266, A Resolution to Investigate Violations of the Right of Free Speech and Assembly and Interference with the Right of Labor to Organize and Bargain Collectively, Part 75. 76th Cong., 3rd sess., 1940.*

U.S. Senate. *Violation of Free Speech and the Rights of Labor. Report of the Committee on Education and Labor, Pursuant to Senate Resolution 266, Employers' Associations and Collective Bargaining in California.* 78th Cong., 2d sess., 1942.

Utility Corporations, Letter from the Chairman of the Federal Trade Commission in Response to Senate Resolutions Nos. 83 and 112, Exhibits 4048–4489. 70th Cong., 1st Sess., 1930. S. Doc. 92, Parts 10–16.

Valelly, Richard M. *Radicalism in the States: The Minnesota Farmer–Labor Party and the American Political Economy.* Chicago: University of Chicago Press, 1989.

Viehe, Fred W. "The Recall of Mayor Frank L. Shaw: A Revision." *California History* 50 (Winter 1980–81): 290–305.

Voss, Kim. *The Making of American Exceptionalism: The Knights of Labor and Class Formation in the Nineteenth Century.* Ithaca: Cornell University Press, 1993.

Vrooman, Carl. *Initiative and Referendum in Switzerland.* Washington, D.C.: Government Printing Office, 1913.

———. "Twentieth Century Democracy." *The Arena* 22 (Nov. 1899): 584–97.

Wachtel, Ted. *The Electronic Congress: A Blueprint for Participatory Democracy.* Pipersville, Pa.: Piper's Press, 1992.

Wagoner, Jay J. *Arizona Territory, 1863–1912: A Political History.* Tucson: University of Arizona Press, 1970.

Walcott, E. A. "The Initiative, Referendum, and Recall in San Francisco." *National Municipal Review* 2 (July 1913): 468–69.

Walker, S. H., and Paul Sklar. "Business Finds Its Voice." *Harper's Magazine* 176 (Mar. 1938): 428–40.

Wallace, Schuyler. "The Initiative and Referendum and the Elections of 1922." *National Municipal Review* 12 (April 1923): 192–204.

Walworth, Arthur C. *Woodrow Wilson*, 3rd ed. New York: W. W. Norton, 1978.

Ward, John W. *Andrew Jackson: Symbol for an Age*. New York: Oxford University Press, 1955.

Warner, Hoyt L. *Progressivism in Ohio, 1897–1917*. Columbus: Ohio State University Press, 1964.

Wasserman, Ira M. "Status Politics and Economic Class Interests: The 1918 Prohibition Referendum in California." *Sociological Quarterly* 31 (Summer 1990): 475–84.

Watkins, Marilyn P. *Rural Democracy: Family Farmers and Politics in Western Washington, 1890–1925*. Ithaca: Cornell University Press, 1995.

Watson, Harry L. *Jacksonian Politics and Community Conflict: The Emergence of the Second American Party System in Cumberland County, North Carolina*. Baton Rouge: Louisiana State University Press, 1981.

Watson, Thomas E. "Why the People's Party Should Elect the Next President." *The Arena* 6 (July 1892): 201–4.

Weaver, James B. *A Call to Action: An Interpretation of the Great Uprising: Its Source and Causes*. Des Moines: Iowa Printing Company, 1892.

Weinstein, Allen. *Prelude to Populism: Origins of the Silver Issue, 1867–1878*. New Haven: Yale University Press, 1970.

Weinstein, James. *The Corporate Ideal in the Liberal State, 1900–1910*. Boston: Beacon Press, 1968.

———. "Organized Business and the City Commission and Manager Movements." *Journal of Southern History* 28 (May 1962): 166–82.

Wellman, Walter. "The Management of the Taft Campaign." *American Review of Reviews* 38 (Oct. 1908): 342–48.

Wesser, Robert F. *A Response to Progressivism: The Democratic Party and New York Politics, 1902–1918*. New York: New York University Press, 1986.

Westbrook, Robert D. "Politics as Consumption: Marketing the Modern American Election." In *The Culture of Consumption*, edited by Richard W. Fox and T. J. Jackson Lears, 143–73. New York: Pantheon, 1983.

Westin, Alan F. "Populism and the Supreme Court." *Supreme Court Historical Society Yearbook*, 1980, 62–77.

Weyl, Walter E. *The New Democracy: An Essay on Certain Political and Economic Tendencies in the United States*. New York: Macmillan, 1912.

Whitaker, Clem. "The Public Relations of Election Campaigns." *Public Relations Journal* 2 (July 1946): 7–10, 35.

White, William A. "The Insurgence of Insurgency." *American Magazine* 71 (Dec. 1910): 170–74.

Wiebe, Robert H. *The Search for Order, 1877–1920*. New York: Hill and Wang, 1967.

———. *Self-Rule: A Cultural History of American Democracy*. Chicago: University of Chicago Press, 1995.

Wilcox, Delos F. *Government by All the People*. New York: Macmillan, 1912.

Wilentz, Sean. "Artisan Republican Festivals and the Rise of Class Conflict in New York City, 1788–1837." In *Working-Class America: Essays on Labor, Community, and American Society*, edited by Michael H. Frisch and Daniel J. Walkowitz, 37–77. Urbana: University of Illinois Press, 1983.

———. *Chants Democratic: New York City and The Rise of the American Working Class, 1788–1850*. New York: Oxford University Press, 1984.

Willard, Charles D. "A Political Experiment." *The Outlook* (Oct. 22, 1904): 472–75.

Wilson, Woodrow. *Constitutional Government in the United States*. New York: Columbia University Press, 1908.

———. *The New Freedom: A Call for the Emancipation of the Generous Energies of a People*. New York: Doubleday, 1913.

———. *The Papers of Woodrow Wilson*. Edited by Arthur S. Link. Princeton: Princeton University Press, 1976.

———. *The State: Elements of Historical and Practical Politics*. Boston: D. C. Heath, 1898.

Winslow, C. I. "The Referendum in Maryland." *American Political Science Review* 27 (Feb. 1933): 75–79.

Wood, Gordon S. *The Creation of the American Republic, 1776–1787*. Chapel Hill: University of North Carolina Press, 1969.

Woodman, Harold D. "Chicago Businessmen and the 'Granger' Laws." *Agricultural History* 36 (Jan. 1962): 16–24.

Woods, D. W. *Proposals for Changes in the Initiative Procedure*. Los Angeles, 1940.

Woods, Thomas A. *Knights of the Plow: Oliver H. Kelley and the Origins of the Grange in Republican Ideology*. Ames: Iowa State University Press, 1991.

Woodward, C. Vann. *Origins of the New South, 1877–1913*. Baton Rouge: Louisiana State University Press, 1951.

Woodward, Robert C. "William S. U'Ren: A Progressive Era Personality." *Idaho Yesterdays* 4 (Summer 1960): 4–10.

———. "W. S. U'Ren and the Single Tax in Oregon." *Oregon Historical Quarterly* 61 (Mar. 1960): 46–63.

Works, John D. "A City's Struggle for Political and Moral Freedom." *The Arena* 41 (Jan. 1909): 353–57.

Wright, James. *The Progressive Yankees: Republican Reformers in New Hampshire, 1906–1916*. Hanover: University Press of New England, 1987.

Wuarin, Louis. "Recent Political Experiments in the Swiss Democracy." *Annals of the American Academy of Political and Social Science* 6 (Nov. 1895): 361–80.

Wyman, Bruce. "Unfair Competition by Monopolistic Corporations." *Annals of the American Academy of Political and Social Science* 42 (July 1912): 67–73.

Wyman, Roger E. "Middle-Class Voters and Progressive Reform: The Conflict of Class and Culture." *American Political Science Review* 68 (June 1974): 488–504.

Yellowitz, Irwin. *Labor and the Progressive Movement in New York State, 1897–1916*. Ithaca: Cornell University Press, 1965.

Young, Arthur N. *The Single Tax Movement in the United States*. Princeton: Princeton University Press, 1916.

Zahler, Helene S. *Eastern Workingmen and National Land Policy, 1829–1862*. New York: Columbia University Press, 1941.

Zanden, James W. Vander. "Votes on Segregationist Referenda." *Public Opinion Quarterly* 25 (Spring 1961): 92–105.

Zimmermann, Joseph F. *The Initiative: Citizen Law-Making*. Westport, Conn.: Greenwood Press, 1999.

———. *Participatory Democracy: Populism Revisited*. New York: Praeger, 1986.

Zimmerman, Tom. "'Ham and Eggs' Everybody!" *Southern California Quarterly* 52 (Spring 1980): 77–96.

Zisk, Betty H. *Money, Media, and the Grass Roots: State Ballot Issues and the Electoral Process*. Newbury Park, Calif.: Sage, 1987.

INDEX